Y0-BXG-280

BRIDGING THE GAP

BENJAMINS TRANSLATION LIBARY

The Benjamins Translation Library aims to stimulate academic research and training in translation studies, lexicography and terminology. The Library provides a forum for a variety of approaches (which may sometimes be conflicting) in a historical, theoretical, applied and pedagogical context. The Library includes scholarly works, reference books and post-graduate text books and readers in the English language.

Volume 3

Sylvie Lambert and Barbara Moser-Mercer (eds)

Bridging the Gap: Empirical research in simultaneous interpretation

BRIDGING THE GAP

EMPIRICAL RESEARCH IN SIMULTANEOUS INTERPRETATION

Edited by

SYLVIE LAMBERT
University of Ottawa

BARBARA MOSER-MERCER
Université de Genève

JOHN BENJAMINS PUBLISHING COMPANY
AMSTERDAM/PHILADELPHIA

The paper used in this publication meets the minimum requirements of American National Standard for Information Sciences — Permanence of Paper for Printed Library Materials, ANSI Z39.48-1984.

Library of Congress Cataloging-in-Publication Data

Bridging the gap : empirical research in simultaneous interpretation / edited by Sylvie Lambert and Barbara Moser-Mercer.
p. cm. -- (Benjamins translation library, ISSN 0929-7316 ; v. 3)
1. Translating and interpreting. 2. Neuropsychology.
I. Lambert, Sylvie. II. Moser-Mercer, Barbara. III. Series.
P306.2.B75 1994
418'.02--dc20 94-9728
ISBN 90 272 2144 8 (Eur.)/1-55619-481-1 (US) (alk. paper) CIP

John Benjamins Publishing Co. · P.O. Box 75577 · 1070 AN Amsterdam · The Netherlands
John Benjamins North America · 821 Bethlehem Pike · Philadelphia, PA 19118 · USA

FOREWORD

Nearly twenty years have passed since David Gerver wrote the first comprehensive review of empirical studies on simultaneous interpretation carried out until then (Gerver, 1976). Surprisingly few collections on simultaneous or conference interpreting have been published since then. Noteworthy exceptions are Gran and Taylor's *Aspects of Applied and Experimental Research on Conference Interpretation* (1990) and *The Interpreters' Newsletter* from the University of Trieste, Italy.

Not only have there been few reviews, but there has also been relatively little research on the topic to review, or at least little that was being brought to light in published form. Gerver discussed some of the reasons for this apparent lack of research. First, simultaneous interpretation is a comparatively recent phenomenon. Furthermore, the process is extremely complex: although simultaneous listening and speaking rarely occurs in everyday verbal behaviour, simultaneous interpreters manage not only to listen and speak simultaneously for reasonable lengths of time, but also carry out complex transformations on the source-language message while delivering their translation of the target language.

Such complexity has no doubt daunted many who might otherwise have been seriously interested in probing the subject, the problem being one of defining and isolating both independent and dependent variables and then finding experimental designs capable of handling the multiplicity of factors involved, especially the relatively small number of sufficiently skilled interpreters available as subject-collaborators who are in one place, who have a specific language combination, and who are willing to become involved in research.

Another discouraging factor is that some interpreters tend to be overly critical of the precious little research carried out so far on the grounds that too few subjects were used in the experiments, or that bilinguals were compared to professional interpreters, or that the texts used for interpretation material were artificially created (see Gile, in this volume).

In my own experiment on the advantages of interpreting with one ear as opposed to two for instance (Lambert, in this volume), the professional interpreters who served as subjects, complained that the message they had to interpret had been transmitted to them via tape-recorder and not from a live speaker in a real-life interpretation situation, and that this factor had undoubtedly negatively affected their performance. What did not occur to them was that in order for an experiment of this nature to be published in a respectable journal, let alone be taken seriously, stringently controlled experimental conditions had to be adhered to. In other words, a minimum of twenty other subjects had to participate in the same experiment, interpret the very same passage, have either French or English as an A or B language, be dominantly right-handed, suffer from no hearing defects, and have a minimum of five years' experience as an interpreter.

The purpose of preparing this collection of reports on empirical and experimental research in simultaneous interpretation, designed to bridge the gap between the vocational and scientific facets of this truly fascinating skill, is to attempt to show that the empirical study of simultaneous interpretation, as tedious and speculative as it may sometimes appear, is bound to contribute greatly to general knowledge, not only in a developing field, but also in related psycholinguistic disciplines. Moreover, this type of empirical scholarship may have tangible and practical repercussions. As put forth by Gran and Fabbro (in this volume), knowledge achieved through experimental research, as conceived by Galileo, derives from continuous contact with and interest in the surrounding empirical world, coupled with an exploratory attitude towards it, not to mention an open, never-ending discussion and critique of methods and results among researchers and scientists. Furthermore, the experimental approach offers a powerful opportunity to question and argue with established authorities.

In other words, being a professional interpreter may not be sufficient to explain what interpretation is all about or how it should be practised and taught. Apart from reports on personal experiences and discussions on the already-known aspects of simultaneous interpretation, inquiries motivated by a desire to broaden existing knowledge could profitably be generated for the benefit of all those with a genuine desire to explore and analyze the full depths and mysteries of the interpretation process.

Barbara Moser-Mercer introduces the first set of research reports grouped under the heading "Pedagogical Issues", by describing the nature of the gap between the natural science and the liberal arts communities. The set includes papers by Janet Altman, Daniel Gile, Barbara Moser-Mercer, Etilvia Arjona-Tseng and Andrzej Kopczynski.

In order to predict, and eventually forestall the production of errors by student-interpreters, and thereby contribute to the improvement in teaching methods, **Janet Altman**, formerly affiliated with Heriot-Watt University in Edinburgh, Scotland, and now working free-lance, examines the most frequently recurring types of errors in simultaneous interpretation. The seriousness of errors/mistakes was judged according to how adversely they affected the communication of the speaker's message: omissions, additions, inaccurate renditions of individual test items, distortions of longer phrases through errors, lack of fluency and loss of rhetorical effect for mistakes. Altman establishes a hierarchy in which errors are classified in terms of both type and seriousness.

Daniel Gile (Director of the Centre d'Etudes sur l'Enseignement de l'Interprétation at the Institut Supérieur d'Interprétation et de Traduction, or ISIT, in Paris), examines the major methodological issues and problems in research on translation and interpretation, ranging from materials, experimental conditions and tasks, quantification and quality assessment. He also proposes invaluable strategies for future directions translation and interpretation research should take, including institutional strategies, research programs, interdisciplinary contacts, dissemination of information in Translation and Interpretation research circles. Gile is the author of the Paris-based *International Interpretation Research and Theory Information Network*, or **IRTIN**, which publishes a bulletin twice a year.

Barbara Moser-Mercer received her diploma in Translation, her M.A. in Conference Interpretation, her Ph.D. in Linguistics from the University of Innsbruck, and was a Fulbright research scholar at the University of Rochester. She has been a freelance conference interpreter since 1975 and is a member of the International Association of Conference Interpreters, or AIIC, its research committee and its committee on relations with Central and Eastern Europe. She has taught translation and interpretation at the Monterey Institute of International Studies and at the Ecole de Traduction et d'Interprétation of the University of Geneva, and still divides her time between these two schools. Her research interests include the modelling of the interpreting process and aptitude testing for interpreting. More recently, she has taken a leading role in the training of interpreter trainers, both in Western and Eastern Europe. Her contribution in this collection provides a survey of different types of aptitude tests for conference interpreting candidates. Ten different testing parameters are covered in three categories, i.e., knowledge, skills, and personality traits. Methodological issues for seven different types of tests are described, together with a brief discussion on subjective vs. objective testing in interpreting. The article closes with a research agenda.

In her paper, **Dr. Etilvia Arjona-Tseng** describes the development of numerous empirical tests for the selection of translation and interpreting students at Fu Jen Catholic University in Taiwan. In keeping with Chinese educational traditions, students in Taiwan must be assured of passing the final examination once they have been accepted for graduate studies. The procedures in place have been highly successful in meeting this goal. This chapter includes a discussion of the usefulness of a rigid entrance examination, allowing nearly one hundred per cent guarantee that students eventually graduate as interpreters, as opposed to traditional selection methods where student attrition is much higher. Dr. Arjona-Tseng has headed several translation and interpretation departments, namely at the Monterey Institute of International Studies, the Graduate Institute of Translation and Interpretation Studies at Fu Jen Catholic University in Taiwan, and more recently, the Center for Interpretation and Translation at the University of Hawai'i at Manoa.

Dr. Andrzej Kopczynski contributes a chapter dealing with the notion of quality in conference interpreting. Kopczynski received his M.A. from the University of Warsaw; his Ph.D. degree and his post-doctoral work were conducted at the University of Poznan. Currently active as both a simultaneous and conference interpreter, he is the author of *Conference Interpreting: Some Linguistic and Communicative Problems* (Poznan, 1980), and served as president of the Association of Polish Translators and Interpreters between 1981 and 1985. Presently, Kopczynski is an associate professor at the Institute of Applied Linguistics, University of Warsaw.

In the section entitled "Simultaneous Interpretation", contributions were made by Linda Anderson, Henri C. Barik, Ghelly V. Chernov, Mike Dillinger, William P. Isham, Tatiana Klonowicz and Miriam Shlesinger.

Following Master's studies in Linguistics and Translation at the Université de Montréal, **Linda Anderson** began her career as a free-lance conference interpreter in 1969, at the same time as she taught technical translation and conference interpretation at the Université de Montréal. A subsequent Master's degree in Experimental Psychology (specifically Cognitive Psychology and Psycholinguistics) obtained from Concordia University in 1979 yielded the experimental investigation of which this article is a summary report. Anderson is currently finishing a book on the psychology of cultural adaptation. Her chapter in this volume includes three experiments investigating the mysteries of the interpreter's "black box": the first two experiments examine the impact of two aspects of interpreter working conditions which are widely assumed to be paramount, namely prior linguistic and present visual context surrounding presentation of a speech. The third experiment focusses on the language-switch factor, hypothesizing that the "translation" operation is incidental to the central task of simultaneous interpretation.

Dr. **Henri C. Barik** is one of the pioneers in research on the types and forms of errors occurring in simultaneous interpretation. His contribution is based on chapters of an unpublished doctoral dissertation submitted to the Department of Psychology of the University of North Carolina, at Chapel Hill. Another summary of his dissertation appears in *Babel*, entitled "Interpreters Talk a Lot, Among Other Things" (Barik, 1972). One of the main reasons for including such a ground-breaking article in this collection is that, to date, other than for Janet Altman (in this volume), no other research has ever dared grapple with such a controversial subject. Errors provide researchers with concrete and palpable signs of how the translation/interpretation process works. To this effect, Barik offers the most comprehensive coding scheme for omissions, additions, not to mention substitutions and errors committed by interpreters, mild semantic errors, gross semantic errors, errors stemming from assumed misunderstanding, errors of false reference, errors of meaning, mild phrasing changes, substantial phrasing changes, errors of mistranslation, and finally, errors due to misundertanding.

Ghelly V. Chernov, President of the Moscow International School of Translating and Interpreting (MISTI), and former head Russian interpreter at the United Nations in New York, provides a probability prediction model for simultaneous interpretation. Chernov regards the probability prediction of the verbal and semantic structure of the oral message in progress as the most essential psycholinguistic factor explaining the phenomenon of simultaneity in simultaneous interpretation. Furthermore, his model presupposes concurrent operation of the probability prediction machinery at several levels at each given moment in time, namely, multichannel information processing, heuristic interplay of levels from bottom to top and from the top down as the message is scanned for information density peaks.

After working as a freelance translator and interpreter in Brazil, **Mike Dillinger** received his M.A. and Ph.D. from McGill University in Linguistics and at the Laboratory of Applied Cognitive Science, in Montreal, Canada, respectively. He is currently Professor of Linguistics at the Federal University of Minas Gerais (Belo Horizonte, Brazil) where his research centres on the development of processing models of language skill. According to Dillinger, the most important issue in understanding how interpretation is carried out is identifying and characterizing the subprocesses which underlie the interpreting skill. The chapter included in this volume focusses on the comprehension phase of interpreting, permitting him to identify the similarities and differences between experienced and inexperienced interpreters with respect to a variety of processes widely assumed to underlie skill in comprehension. The pattern of his results show that experience with interpreting does not result in qualitative differences in processing but rather in an overall increase in quantity of processing.

William P. Isham obtained his doctorate at Northeastern University in the Department of Psychology, under the tutelage of Dr. Harlan Lane. He is a nationally certified interpreter, holding the Comprehensive Skills Certificate from the Registry of Interpreters for the Deaf. He also holds a Master's Degree from Gallaudet University, where he was also a staff interpreter, as well as the coordinator of their interpreting services department. Isham took his post-doctorate at the University of Paris V. He currently teaches interpretation at the Signed Language Interpreter Education Program in the Department of Linguistics at the University of New Mexico. In this volume, Isham investigated the memory for the form of English sentences after they had been interpreted into French. French/English bilinguals who listened to English passages were compared to professional interpreters. Results indicated that interpreters differed from English/French bilinguals in their strategy for processing incoming sentences. This difference is discussed in terms of "form-based" and "meaning-based" approaches to the simultaneous interpretation task.

Tatiana Klonowicz is a professor of Psychology, specializing in stress and in the psychology of personality at the Faculty of Psychology, University of Warsaw. She is also a simultaneous interpreter in Russian and English. The chapter in this volume, which is part of a larger research project, is an attempt to link these two professions. She investigated patterns of cardiovascular activity associated with simultaneous interpretation. Blood pressure and heart rate were measured before and after each work shift (or turn) throughout a morning conference session. The results, which replicate and extend those reported in previous studies, indicate that cardiovascular activity increases systematically with the beginning of a turn (the mobilization wave). After completion of the turn and during the early hours of work, cardiovascular activity drops back to normal (the normalization wave). Later in the day however, normalization gradually fades, indicating that the initial good adjustment of resources to task demands is upset by prolonged mental effort.

Miriam Shlesinger, a senior lecturer in Translation and Interpretation at Bar-Ilan University in Israel, immigrated from the United States to Israel in 1964. In addition to being an active interpreter, she has also conducted research on simultaneous interpretation, including such topics as stylistics shifts in interpretation, interpreter latitude vs. due process: simultaneous and consecutive interpretation in multilingual trials, and monitoring the courtroom interpreter. She is currently researching shifts in cohesion in interpreted texts. Shlesinger is also style editor of *TARGET: International Journal of Translation Studies*. In this volume, Shlesinger examined three distinct intonational features of interpretation and how these affected listeners' perception. To this effect, analysis of recordings made by eight professional interpreters in real (conference) settings allowed for a description of features which included pauses within constituents, tentative pauses in final position, stress incompatible with the given-new contrast, non-standard matching of pitch movement and discourse pattern, and nonstandard prosody (duration and speed).

The third and final set of articles regroups some of the very latest neuropsychological research carried out on simultaneous interpretation by authors such as David Corina, Jyotsna Vaid, Valeria Daró, Franco Fabbro, Laura Gran, Sylvie Lambert, Adele Green, Nancy Schweda-Nicholson, Nancy White and Richard Steiner.

David Corina obtained his M.A. in Linguistics from Gallaudet and his Ph.D. in Psychology and Cognitive Science from the University of California, San Diego. He is currently an assistant professor in Psychology at the University of Washington, Seattle. A fluent signer of American Sign Language, Corina's research involves the study of the cognitive representation of language as an avenue to understanding biological constraints on language. His research approach combines psycholinguistic experimentation, neuropsychological studies, theoretical linguistics and computer modelling.

Jyotsna Vaid received her M.A. and Ph.D. in Psychology at McGill University (under the supervision of Wallace E. Lambert). She carried out her post-doctoral research at the Center for Research in Language at the University of California San Diego and at the Salk Institute for Biological Studies. She has published widely on cognitive and neuropsychological aspects of bilingualism, including an edited volume, entitled *Language Processing in Bilinguals* (Erlbaum: 1986). She is currently working on a volume entitled *Language and Number Use: A Cross-linguistic Perspective*. Her research in this volume used a concurrent activities paradigm to compare patterns of brain lateralization in right-handed hearing interpreters for the deaf for American Sign Language and English. The interpreters had learned ASL either in infancy or in adolescence. Subjects were asked to shadow spoken or signed lexical items while concurrently tapping as rapidly as possible with their right or left index finger. Tapping interference was greatest for pseudo-signs; moderate interference was found for ASL signs, and the smallest amount of interference was obtained for English words. In addition, greater right than left hand tapping interference was obtained for each condition, but only when the particular condition was presented first. There were no bilingual subgroup differences. These findings are discussed with reference to previous dual-task studies of bilinguals and are interpreted in terms of the "cerebral functional distance" principle.

Valeria Darò graduated in Conference Interpretation from the School for Interpreters and Translators at the University of Trieste, where she has now been appointed on a contract basis as Professor of consecutive interpretation from German into Italian. She has been carrying out experimental research in Neurolinguistics, with particular emphasis on the problems related to simultaneous and consecutive interpretation. Darò's chapter describes some experimental works carried out over the last few years aimed at investigating the non-linguistic aspects which influence simultaneous interpreters' performance, namely certain neuropsychological aspects, such as memory and attention during the complex task of simultaneous interpretation, non-linguistic aspects of verbal communication, such as speaking speed and its effects on the performance of interpreters, and finally emotional, suprasegmental aspects of speech in polyglot subjects. On the basis of certain experimental results, the author proposes some practical implications for teaching and acquiring simultaneous interpretation techniques.

Franco Fabbro has a degree in Medicine and a Ph.D. in Neurology. At present, he is Assistant Professor of Human Neurophysiology at the Faculty of Medicine at the University of Trieste, Italy. Fabbro has been devoting himself to clinical and experimental research in the field of neurolinguistics of bilingualism and polyglossia.

Laura Gran obtained her diploma in Conference Interpretation and works as an associate professor of consecutive and simultaneous interpretation from English into Italian at the School for Interpreters and Translators at the University of Trieste. She has also worked as a free-lance interpreter predominantly for the European Parliament and is a member of the Association Internationale des Interprètes de Conférence, or AIIC. Since 1988, she has been the editor of *The Interpreters' Newsletter*. Moreover, she has been carrying out experimental research on the neurology of simultaneous and consecutive interpretation.

The chapter submitted by **Franco Fabbro** and **Laura Gran** is a review of the clinical and experimental research on the cerebral organization of bilinguals and polyglots. Actually, the neuropsychology and the neurolinguistics of multilingualism represent one possible scientific paradigm for experimental studies on simultaneous interpretation. Moreover, the results of some neuropsychological experiments on interpretation, which the authors have carried out over the last few years, and their practical repercussions, are presented in detail.

Sylvie Lambert is currently an assistant professor at the University of Ottawa's School of Translators and Interpreters, where she has been teaching since 1984. Formerly a lecturer at the Monterey Institute of International Studies in Monterey, California, and a research assistant for Patricia E. Longley at the Polytechnic of Central London, Lambert obtained her Ph.D. in Cognitive Psychology under the supervision of the late David Gerver, Department of Psychology, University of Stirling, Scotland. In an attempt to bring together information about simultaneous interpretation, on the one hand, and cerebral dominance, on the other, her study in this volume examines the relative proficiency of interpreters when processing information received through one ear or the other as opposed to two ears. The subjects were both professional and student interpreters, who were asked to simultaneously interpret spoken passages from L2 to L1: one passage was presented to the subject-interpreters' **left ear**, one to their **right ear**, and one to **both ears**

Adele Green is a staff psychologist, Department of Clinical Psychology, Kennedy Krieger Institute of the Johns Hopkins Medical Center. She holds a part time faculty appointment in the Department of Neurology at the Johns-Hopkins Medical School. Prior professional experience, including university teaching and research responsibilities, enabled her to publish several studies on the dual task paradigm, and on how to teach and develop curriculum materials for English-as-a-Second Language. Green is coauthor of two textbooks, one in ESL, and the other in cross-cultural awareness. Her research reported in this volume made use of a verbal/manual interference procedure to study hemispheric specialization for two linguistic tasks -- shadowing and paraphrasing/interpreting spoken text--. Two of the groups consisted of professional Spanish-English interpreters, classified according to the age of second language acquisition. Subjects in the third groups were unilingual

English controls who had been individually matched with the interpreters in age, sex, handedness and educational experience. The study revealed an overall right-hand interference effect and an interesting interaction, namely that greater right than left hand tapping interference characterized the unilinguals but not the bilinguals who showed no hand asymmetries. The results are discussed in terms of previous studies of lateralization in bilinguals.

ACKNOWLEDGEMENTS

I am most grateful to my husband, **Rafael Tierrafría**, without whose help, patience and computer skills, none of this would have been possible. I would also like to thank those who, unknowingly, encouraged me to persevere with this idea, namely my co-editor, **Barbara Moser-Mercer**. I also wish to thank three graduate students from the School of Translators and Interpreters who helped with the tedious and thankless task of word-processing and formatting: **Lynne Bowker**, **Karen Eck** and **Sarah Lott**.

In closing, I would like to dedicate this book to the memory of my thesis advisor, the late **David Gerver**.

Sylvie Lambert
School of Translation and Interpretation
University of Ottawa

CONTENTS

Foreword 5

INTRODUCTION

Barbara Moser-Mercer
Paradigms gained or the art of productive disagreement 17

PEDAGOGICAL ISSUES

Janet Altman
Error analysis in the teaching of simultaneous interpretation: A pilot study 25
Daniel Gile
Methodological aspects of interpretation and translation research 39
Barbara Moser-Mercer
Aptitude testing for conference interpreting: Why, when and how 57
Etilvia Arjona-Tseng
A psychometric approach to the selection of translation and interpreting students in Taiwan 69
Andrzej Kopczynski
Quality in conference interpreting: Some pragmatic problems 87

SIMULTANEOUS INTERPRETATION

Linda Anderson
Simultaneous interpretation: Contextual and translation aspects 101
Henri C. Barik
A description of various types of omissions, additions and errors of translation encountered in simultaneous interpretation 121
Ghelly Chernov
Message redundancy and message anticipation in simultaneous interpreting 139
Mike Dillinger
Comprehension during interpreting: What do interpreters know that bilinguals don't? 155
William P. Isham
Memory for sentence form after simultaneous interpretation: Evidence both for and against deverbalization 191
Tatiana Klonowicz
Putting one's heart into simultaneous interpretation 213
Miriam Shlesinger
Intonation in the production and perception of simultaneous interpretation 225

NEUROPSYCHOLOGICAL RESEARCH

David P. Corina and Jyotsna Vaid
Lateralization for shadowing words versus signs: A study of ASL-English interpreters 237
Valeria Darò
Non-linguistic factors influencing simultaneous interpretation 249
Franco Fabbro and Laura Gran
Neurological and neuropsychological aspects of polyglossia and simultaneous interpretation 273
Sylvie Lambert
Simultaneous interpretation: One ear may be better than two 319
A. Green, N. Schweda-Nicholson, J. Vaid, N. White & R. Steiner
Lateralization for shadowing vs. interpretation: A comparison of interpreters with bilingual and monolingual controls 331

INTRODUCTION

Paradigms Gained
or the Art of Productive Disagreement

Barbara Moser-Mercer
ETI, Université de Genève

Ever since interdisciplinarity made its debut in interpretation research in Venice some 14 years ago (NATO Symposium on Language, Interpretation and Communication, 1978), there has been a debate over which research community had adopted the more sophisticated and comprehensive theory of interpretation. To this day, members of one community may often not enter into a dialogue with representatives of the other, not because all the questions ever raised with regard to interpretation have already been answered, but because all too often an adamant defense of one's own theory might preclude the open-mindedness required for cross-fertilization to occur.

The interpretation research community can be broadly divided into two sub-communities, whereby affiliation is dictated by intellectual preference. The first group prefers explorations which require precision of logical processes, and where members are interested in the natural sciences and quantification; the second group prefers explorations which involve the intellect in a less logically rigorous manner, where members are interested more in a liberal arts approach and general theorizing. Since both groups are intelligent, it is not difficult for members of one group to understand what members of the other group are studying. Yet, there exists a notable communication gap between the two. Many times the natural science oriented group has attempted to propose certain concepts to the liberal arts group, only to discover with exasperation that their explanations probably sounded too abstract and abstruse, although the ideas involved usually were quite simple. Conversely, the liberal arts group has tried to convey its concepts in terms which seemed laudably lucid to them, but which to the exasperation of the natural science group seemed hopelessly vague and ambiguous.

Based on the definition that a research community consists of the practitioners of a scientific specialty, bound together by common elements in their education and apprenticeship, and who consider themselves as responsible for the pursuit of a set of shared goals, including the training of their successors, professional communication within the community should not be so arduous as to give rise to so many misunderstandings and elicit such significant disagreement (Kuhn 1977).

Perhaps, then, the issue concerns not sub-groups of one and the same scientific community, but rather two quite distinct communities sharing nothing more than the basic subject of inquiry - namely interpretation - with both communities operating within very distinct paradigms. A paradigm is what the members of a scientific community, and they alone, share. The term has been employed frequently to denote the specific intellectual preference, rules and research approach of a particular scientific community, chosen by it for their usefulness in developing a theory of the subject under study. The goal of each community is, after all, the construction of a theory that can best account for and explain the phenomenon under study. Both interpretation research communities would probably agree on that point. Where the two part is over the notion of what a good theory should be.

Among the criteria adopted for good scientific theories, collectively the following five would appear to indicate what is at stake. First of all, a theory should be accurate; consequences deduced from a theory should be in proven agreement with the results of existing experiments and observations. Secondly, a theory should be consistant: internally with regard to its logical argument and externally with other currently accepted theories applicable to related aspects of nature. Third, a theory should be broad in scope: its consequences should extend far beyond the particular observations it was initially designed to explain. Fourth, a theory should be simple, bringing order to phenomena that would otherwise be unstructured and confusing. Lastly, a theory should be *fruitful* of new research findings, and should disclose new phenomena or previously unnoted relationships among those already known. This is particularly relevant to theory choice: a researcher choosing between two theories usually knows that his decision will have a bearing on his subsequent research career. Of course he is especially attracted by a theory that promises the concrete successes for which researchers are ordinarily rewarded (Kuhn 1977).

Proceeding on my *a priori* assumption that both interpretation research communities strive to develop a solid theory of interpretation, it is interesting to examine which of the above criteria have been given priority by each community. Accuracy, which usually denotes quantitative agreement, is particularly decisive in theory formation, since it is necessary for a theory's predictive and explanatory powers. Within the liberal arts paradigm, accuracy is seldom considered, whereas it ranks high with the natural science community. Consistency and simplicity, in turn, are the hallmarks of the liberal arts approach. As a consequence, this approach has had a considerable influence on pedagogy: the natural science community seems to be still so overwhelmed by the complexity of the interpreting process that the idea of developing a simple model is rejected almost right away. With regard to scope, no one community has yet made any particular claims, for quite obvious reasons: both are still borrowing, sometimes heavily, from other related fields and cannot as yet foresee extending their own conclusions to neighboring fields. We should not confuse this definition of scope with some efforts in the late sixties and early seventies whereby psychologists and psycholinguists used interpretation as an experimental condition to explain certain phenomena of language comprehension in general (Treisman 1965a, Goldman-Eisler 1972, Oléron and Nanpon 1965, and more recently Dillinger 1989). Scientists chose not just on the basis of one but of several criteria; subjective factors and individual criteria play an important role as well, despite the fact that subjectivity is obviously not a *desideratum* in any scientific endeavor. But as Frey (1970) points out, science is never purely scientific in the narrow sense of the term, in that it would accept and rely only on verifiable and provable statements. "We can thus justifiably claim that each specialty has ... (also) metaphysical components" (Frey 1970 :113). Intuition, observation and discovery of relationships constitute acceptable procedures for developing hypotheses and theories. But these theses are scientifically tenable only if they are verifiable and when they are verified. Intuition and observation in themselves do not constitute methods of scientific justification.

With this overview of the areas of real and potential disagreement between the two interpretation research communities, it may be helpful to evaluate the stage of theory formation each one has reached. The liberal arts community which is best represented by the works of the Paris school (Seleskovitch 1975, Lederer 1981, Seleskovitch and Lederer 1989, *et al.*; a rather similar approach has recently been proposed by Vermeer 1984), considers itself as being at a rather well developed stage of theory formation. The theory's general consistency (although there do exist certain internal and external inconsistencies, see Gile 1990c) its comprehensiveness and simplicity, its intuitive explanatory value and consequent appeal to pedagogy have all combined to give it widespread acceptance. Thus, in many ways, this theory meets many of the demands placed on theories in general. There have been only a few attempts at verifying the theory, partly because it does not lend itself readily to verification. Returning to our notion of paradigm, this community has an accepted paradigm. Researchers working within it consider it sufficient to adopt the existing theory, whereas a logical consequence would be for those attracted to this paradigm to consider it as a lightly held tentative hypothesis, test their observational data against it and either accept or reject all or part of it. As yet there is no indication, however, that the liberal arts community is ready to accept such an approach.

The natural science community presents a somewhat more heterogeneous picture, but most members would agree that the approaches adopted by Barik (1969), Pinter (1969) and Gerver (1976) and continued by Moser (1978), Stenzl (1983), Lambert (1985), Mackintosh (1985), Gile (1985), Gran and Fabbro (1988) to name but a few, would all qualify under the same natural science paradigm. While some members of this community, in analogy to the liberal arts group, have attempted to develop models of the interpretation process that would later be encompassed by a more comprehensive theory, others have selected very specific aspects of interpretation and designed experimental studies around them. Common to all members of this community is the quest for an accurate and verifiable, albeit not necessarily simple theory of interpretation, one with a high degree of explanatory power which would objectively describe the act of interpretation while at the same time fulfill the stringent criteria of scientific inquiry. This community is much further removed from an all-embracing theory than the liberal arts group is; from a developmental perspective it is still at the beginning of the theory-construction stage, where hypotheses are being proposed, tested and often rejected. Such rigorous testing will eventually bring this community within reach of an accurate and verifiable theory (Dodds 1989). This theory will probably still have to rely for some of its components on intuitive assumptions, but will largely be the result of an abstraction from a large number of observations. The patterns thus obtained should then be encountered in similar form by other researchers engaged in experimentation. Thus the paradigm will have evolved into a verifiable theory of interpretation. This is not a result to be achieved in the lifetime of one researcher; from the very beginning the natural science community placed considerable emphasis on interdisciplinarity (the recent flourishing of research activity at the Trieste School is an excellent example of interdisciplinarity stimulating scientific inquiry). But despite the lack of an explicitly stated and consistent paradigm this community is actively engaged in theory construction. Considerable work is required, both theoretical and experimental, before any new theory can display sufficient accuracy and scope to generate widespread conviction. In short, it has to be tested over time, even by researchers working within a rival paradigm. Such a mode of development, however, requires a decision process which permits researchers to disagree. If all scientists were conforming in their views, all would make the same decisions at the same time (Kuhn 1977). It is doubtful whether science would survive. The blow for interpretation research would be devastating. After all, much of it feeds on the fundamental tension between the two research communities, a point often overlooked by advocates of either paradigm.

Thus, disagreement is essential and productive, but both communities should steer clear of the danger so aptly described by Chomsky (1977, p. 82): "There is no place for any *a priori doctrine* (emphasis is mine) concerning the complexity of the brain or its uniformity as far as the higher mental functions are concerned."

References

Alston, W.P. 1964. *Philosophy of Language.* Englewood Cliffs: Prentice Hall.

Barik, H.C. 1969. *A Study of Simultaneous Interpretation.* University of North Carolina, Chapel Hill. [Unpublished Doctoral Dissertation.]

Chernov, G. 1979. "Semantic Aspects of Psycholinguistic Research in Simultaneous Interpretation". *Language and Speech.* 22:3. 277-295.

Chomsky, N. 1979. *Language and Responsibility.* New York: Pantheon Books.

Dillinger, M. 1989. *Component Processes of Simultaneous Interpreting.* McGill University, Montreal, Canada. [Unpublished Doctoral Dissertation].

Dodds, J. 1989. "Linguistic Theory Construction as a Premise to a Methodology of Teaching Interpretation". L. Gran and J. Dodds, eds. *The Theoretical and Practical Aspects of Teaching Conference Interpretation.* Udine: Campanotto Editore. 28-41.

Frey, G. 1970. *Philosophie und Wissenschaft.* Stuttgart: Kohlhammer.

Gadenne, V. 1976. *Die Gültigkeit Psychologischer Untersuchungen.* Stuttgart: Kohlhammer.

Gerver, D. 1976. "Empirical Studies of Simultaneous Interpretation: A Review and a Model". R.W. Brislin, ed. *Translation: Applications and Research.* New York: Gardner. 165-207.

Gile, D. 1985. "Le Modèle d'Effort et d'Equilibre d'Interprétation en Interprétation Simultanée". *META* XXX:1. 44-48.

Gile, D. 1990c. "Scientific Research versus Personal Theories in the Investigation of Interpretation". L. Gran and C. Taylor, eds. *Aspects of Applied and Experimental Research in Conference Interpretation.* Udine: Campanotto Editore. 28-41.

Goldman-Eisler, F. 1972. "Segmentation of Input in Simultaneous Interpretation". *Journal of Psycholinguistic Research* 1. 127-140.

Gran, L. and Dodds, J. 1989. *The Theoretical and Practical Aspects of Teaching Conference Interpretation.* Udine: Campanotto Editore.

Gran, L. and Fabbro, F. 1988. "The Role of Neuroscience in the Teaching of Interpretation". *The Interpreter's Newsletter* 1. 23-41.

Gran, L. and Taylor, C. 1990. *Aspects of Applied and Experimental Research in Conference Interpretation.* Udine: Campanotto Editore.

Kuhn, T.S. 1977. *The Essential Tension: Selected Studies in Scientific Tradition and Change.* Chicago: University of Chicago Press.

Kutz, W. 1990. *Forschungsprojekt: Didaktik des Dolmetschens.* Leipzig, Karl-Marx Universität. [Unpublished Manuscript.]

Lambert, S. M. 1983. *Recall and Recognition in Conference Interpreters.* University of Stirling, Scotland. [Unpublished Doctoral Dissertation.]

Lederer, M. 1981. *La Traduction Simultanée: Expérience et Théorie.* Paris: Minard.

Mackintosh, J. 1985. "The Kintsch and Van Dijk Model of Discourse Comprehension and Production Applied to the Interpretation Process". *META* XXX:1. 37-43.

Moser, B. 1978. "Simultaneous Interpretation: A Hypothetical Model and its Practical Application". D.Gerver and W.H. Sinaiko, eds. *Language, Interpretation and Communication.* London: Plenum Press. 353-368.

Oléron, P. and Nanpon, H. 1965. "Recherches sur la Traduction Simultanée". *Journal de Psychologie Normale et Pathologique* 62. 73-94.

Pinter (Kurz), I. 1969. *Der Einfluss der Ubang und Konzentration auf simultanes Sprechen und Hören.* Universität Wien, Austria. [Unpublished Doctoral Dissertation.]

Seleskovitch, D. 1975. *Langage, Langues et Mémoire.* Paris: Minard.

Seleskovitch, D. and Lederer, M. 1989. *Pédagogie Raisonnée de l'Interprétation.* Paris, Didier.

Stenzl, C. 1983. *Simultaneous Interpretation - Groundwork towards a Comprehensive Model.* University of London, England. [Unpublished Doctoral Dissertation.]

Treisman, A. 1965a. "The Effects on Redundancy and Familiarity on Translating and Repeating back a Native and a Foreign Language". *British Journal of Psychology* 56. 369-379.

Vermeer, H.J. and Reiss, K. 1984. *Grundlegung einer allgemeinen Translationstheorie*. Tübingen: Niemeyer.

Zukov, G. 1979. *The Dancing Wu Li Masters: An Overview of the New Physics*. New York: William Morrow and Co.

PEDAGOGICAL ISSUES

Error Analysis in The Teaching of Simultaneous Interpreting: A Pilot Study

Janet Altman
Heriot-Watt University, Edinburgh, Scotland

1. Introduction

The field of simultaneous interpretation (SI), and more specifically that of the methodology of teaching SI, will always welcome new research. Hence, it is to be hoped that an analysis of the most frequently recurring types of error might make it possible to predict, and perhaps even forestall, the production of errors by student-interpreters, thereby contributing to improvements in teaching methods. The comments presented here are inevitably limited in scope, since they are based upon the observation of one investigator alone and on a restricted sample of empirical data. Perhaps they might serve to suggest a method whereby a more exhaustive study could be untertaken.

1.1. Error Analysis

Corder (1981) justifies the analysis of errors on pedagogical grounds:

> a good understanding of the nature of error is necessary before a systematic means of eradicating them (can) be found.

However, as pointed out by Gile (1985), it is more difficult to apply error analysis to interpreting than it is to language teaching. Such difficulty is attributable to a number of factors: heterogeneity of the subject matter, presentation and other features of the source text (ST), relevance to be assigned to intonation and other para-linguistic devices, the need to assess performance in the mother tongue as opposed to the foreign language (FL), etc. Subjectivity in evaluating results is a hazard highlighted by both Barik (1971) and Gile (1985): a certain amount is unavoidable in the case of the present study, but would hopefully be reduced to a minimum in a more thorough investigation.

1.2. What Constitutes an Error

Let us begin by defining what, for the purposes of this article, constitutes an error. Corder (1981) makes a useful distinction between mistakes, or errors of performance, and errors *per se*, or errors of competence. While maintaining that the latter are the ones to which error analysis should address itself, he accepts that to determine what constitutes an *error* as opposed to a *mistake* can be somewhat difficult. We shall come back to this question later.

Turning to the authors who have examined errors in SI, Barik (1971) is considered by some as over-restrictive. He reserves the word *error* for substitutions of material by the interpreter which are *at considerable variance with the original version*, a definition which (for the author) includes semantic inaccuracies and phrasing changes but excludes omissions and additions. Kopczynski (1983), on the other hand, proposes a definition which embraces both deviations from the linguistic norm of the target language (TL) and utterances which hamper the communication function of the speech act. Since the interpreter's prime task is to communicate a message between the original speaker and a listener (or group of listeners) under a given set of circumstances, the latter would appear to be the crucial criterion. All the inaccuracies listed below will therefore be evaluated in terms of the extent to which they constitute an obstacle to communication.

2. Procedure

For this purpose we must assume, somewhat unrealistically, that a "perfect" interpretation (i.e. one where communication is 100% successful) is hypothetically possible. Gile (1983) asserts that the standard of even professional performances varies considerably. Gile defines quality in interpreting as:

une somme pondérée de la fidélité informationnelle et de la qualité de la présentation du discours de l'interprète, dont les coefficients sont fonction de la nature du message et de la situation.

3. Materials

Gile's *coefficients* are of greater relevance in the professional context than they are in the classroom however: the speeches used in this research had been carefully selected and edited, and were all delivered under language laboratory conditions. It could be said, therefore, that although all the texts used had originally been presented in conference settings, the eventual source data remained relatively inauthentic. The present research focuses upon two main groups of inaccuracies, namely those relating to the information content of the message, and those affecting its presentation. Although those in the former group constitute errors as such, the latter may, perhaps, be better relabelled as mistakes. The findings presented here derive from an evaluation of empirical data collected in the following way.

4. Method

Five final-year undergraduate students simultaneously interpreted a series of five speeches from French into English, i.e. into the mother tongue. An excerpt lasting two-and-a-half minutes was selected from the central portion of each speech, and all the tape-recorded student versions of the same section were subsequently transcribed. A corpus of 25 different English passages was thus created. The subject matter of all five speeches derived from the field of economics. A certain familiarity with this subject matter can be assumed given that the subjects were students who, at the time, were following a background studies course in international economics.

In each of the examples provided below, a segment of ST is followed by its rendition by one or more student-interpreters, labelled A, B, C, etc., where necessary. The seriousness of the errors or mistakes committed was judged according to how adversely they affected the communication of the speaker's message. We shall attempt to determine the causes of the errors and mistakes identified.

5. Evaluation

This heading includes a) omissions, b) additions, c) inaccurate renditions of individual text items, and d) distortions of longer phrases.

5.1. Omissions

(1) ...des engagements "anti-protectionnistes" pris il y a quinze jours par les cinq principaux pays industrialisés.

Interpretation (INT):

...the commitment against... euhm... protectionist measures taken by the five...

The omission of *il y a quinze jours* impairs the speaker's message only minimally, since the context would presumably have made it clear to the target audience which *engagements* were meant. As to the reason for the omission, difficulty in processing the term coined by the speaker in the preceding phrase, as evidenced by the audible hesitation, seems to have distracted the student-interpreter's attention and caused him to skip over it.

(2) ...les gains de productivité...retrouvent leurs maxima historiques. L'investissement repart. Et pourtant...

INT. A: ...are regaining their historically just levels. However...

INT. B: ...are regaining their historical position. However...

The omission in both cases relates to a self-contained item of information which the listener could not have supplied on the basis of previous knowledge. The omission is therefore more serious than that in example 1. It is, however, not such that communication between the speaker and his audience would necessarily break down. The cause in both interpretations A and B seems to have been a failure to grasp the meaning of *leurs maxima historiques*, and to have dwelt on it for too long. All the other subjects dealt satisfactorily with this lexical item and had no difficulty in conveying the idea *l'investissement repart*.

The corpus did not present any omissions of material which would have left the listener completely unable to follow the proceedings: such crucial omissions would relate to utterances which lend structure to the meeting situation (e.g. *We shall now proceed to a vote*), or which communicate a particular message to a specific recipient (e.g. *I should like to thank you, Mr. X.*)

The causes of examples 1 and 2 were similar, namely difficulty/delay in processing a preceding text item, engendering a temporary loss of concentration on the ST input.

Another type of omission related to problematic lexical items *per se*.

(3) ...tous les prêteurs...
INT.: ...everyone...

Here, by omitting to render a word, the student-interpreter has given universal significance to, and therefore badly distorted, the ST message. (See also example 7).

5.2. Additions

One type of addition which is not necessarily detrimental to the conveying of information, is when the student-interpreter provides two versions of the same word:

(4) ...les mécanismes profonds de notre économie.
INT.: ...the...the...euhm...deep mechanisms or the underlying mechanism of our economy.

We can tell from the hesitant start that the student was struggling to find a TL term corresponding to *profonds*. She reluctantly used *deep*, but corrected herself when a more pertinent term came to mind. We shall come back to this tendency among student-interpreters to correct their own output in the simultaneous mode, when considering the issue of message presentation below.

(5) ...un processus fatal de détérioration dont tous les pays seront les victimes.
INT.: ...which would affect all countries in a very adverse and negative way.

In this case, the subject has obviously conveyed meaning rather than merely transposing words, which is of course the interpreter's task. For this, he can only be praised. In doing so, however, he has taken too much liberty and allowed himself to exaggerate. ...*affect in a very negative way* would have served speaker's purpose, but the addition of *adverse* causes him to over-emphasize the message.

(6) ...11,700 millions d'ECUs, soit 14%...
INT.: ...11,700 million ECUs, or to quote another figure, 14%

The subject has used an entire phrase where one word would have sufficed. In so doing, she has produced a statement which would probably mislead the listener into regarding *14%* as new information, as opposed to a reformulation of the previous figure. The cause would appear to be a desire to improve upon the style of the ST. Such an inclination to *embroider* should be discouraged by interpreter-trainers, since the danger of distorting meaning thereby is a very real one.

(7) ...tous les prêteurs ont un rôle important à jouer, qu'il s'agisse des institutions multilatérales, des gouvernements des pays créanciers ou de la communauté privée.
INT:. ...everyone has an important role to play, be they multilateral institutions or governments or debtor countries or creditor countries or...

In this context, namely that of providing financial assitance to the Third World, the addition of *debtor countries* constitutes an extremely serious error on the part of the subject, since debtor countries could not possibly be included with the other agencies mentioned. An addition of this nature might, at best, thoroughly confuse the listener. At worst, it could engender a loss of confidence in either the interpreter or the speaker, or both, or even provoke a protest which could eventually halt the proceedings. As to its cause, it appears that in addition to omitting *les prêteurs* (see example 3), the subject failed to internalize the word's significance, which, in turn, seems to have led him to wrongly anticipate, on the basis of his own knowledge, that such a list of actors would also include the debtor countries.

It therefore proves possible, in the case of both omissions and additions, to assess the seriousness of errors committed in terms of the extent to which they affect the communicative impact of the speaker's message. The errors listed above have been placed in order of increasing gravity (1, 2 and 3, under *Omissions* and 4, 5 6 and 7 under *Additions*).

5.3. Inaccurate Renditions of Individual Lexical Items

(8) ...une vingtaine de grands industriels européens...
INT.A.: ...around 20 large European companies...
INT.B.: ...around 20 European firms...

Not one of the subjects supplied the term *industrialists*. However, since the term *industrie* and *industriel* are so semantically similar, the error can be considered as minor. Interestingly, subjects claimed during subsequent discussion that the collocation of *industriels* with *grands* was what had confused them; perhaps a more viable explanation may be the comparative frequency of use of the two expressions and the resulting assumptions on the part of the student-interpreters.

(9) ...le point préoccupant, le point de plus en plus préoccupant...
INT.A.: ...the most important point, and one which is becoming more and more important...
INT.B.: ...a topic which is becoming all the more important...
INT.C.: ...the most...euhm...important point...

Despite the repetition of the adjective, over half of the subjects participating in the experiment substituted the inaccurate and bland word *important* for *préoccupant*. By replacing a specific term with a general one, the denotive meaning (the voicing of concern) borne by the original is lost. Furthermore, versions B and C fail to convey the rhetorical impact achieved by the repetition. This error is significant albeit unlikely to seriously impair a listener's comprehension of the message.

(10) (a) On peut, je crois, féliciter la Commission...
INT.: I believe we should welcome the fact that the Commission...

(10) (b) De nombreux orateurs se sont...félicités des engagements pris.
INT.: Many speakers...congratulated the...commitments made.

The errors here are serious, (b) more so than (a). The substitution of *se féliciter* for *féliciter* (and *vice versa*) in the subjects' minds greatly impairs the communicative force of both statements: a Commission representative dependent upon interpretation (a) would be unaware of the gratitude being expressed while nevertheless sensing the speaker's appreciation; interpretation (b) is nonsense. It would appear that in both cases, the student-interpreters were over-concentrating on the words used to convey the message, at the expense of the message itself.

Perhaps mention should be made at this stage of simultaneous interpreters' nemesis, namely digits. As might have been expected, the degree of accuracy regarding interpretation of digits in the present experiment varied from one subject to the next. Success appears to have been contingent upon such factors as clarity and speed of the speaker's enunciation of figures, density of ST presentation of figures, juxtaposition of figures and complex information content, and finally the amount of digits involved.

5.4. Inaccurate Rendition of Longer Phrases

(11) ...la Commission de l'énergie et des technologies nouvelles.
INT.A.: ...the Commission on Energy and Research and Development.
INT.B.: ...the Commission on Energy, Research and Technology.

The value of the above-mentioned examples is to illustrate how important it is to take into consideration situational and contextual factors when identifying interpreter errors. In fact, only if taken at face value does 11B constitute a mistake at all. As at the start of all classes, the group had been made fully aware of the circumstances under which the speech had originally been delivered: the speaker was reporting to the European Parliament on behalf of the Committee on Energy, Research and Technology. The students, upon hearing a reference to the Committee, drew upon their prior knowledge and attempted (B, successfully, and A less so) to reproduce its correct title. Every student re-introduced the word *research*.

(12) (On the subject of unemployment)...les phénomènes d'économie submergée et de travail au noir...
INT.A.: ...the hidden factors within the economy and the black market...
INT.B.: ...black market labour...
INT.C.: ...the submerged economies and black workers...
INT.D.: ...moonlighting and other such difficulties...
INT.E.: ...moonlighting and the black economy...

Only interpreter E produced an entirely satisfactory interpretation. And yet the speaker's idea had obviously been grasped by A, B and D, who drew upon their world knowledge and, with varying amounts of success, conveyed the message. The problem here is perhaps that although the concept is common to both the SL and TL, the form of reference is not fixed in English. Interpreter C, on the other hand, seems to have applied her world knowledge incorrectly and to have assumed that the speaker was alluding to the customarily higher rates of unemployment among black people.

(13) ...nos interlocuteurs, tant espagnols que portugais, sont très désireux d'être associés aux travaux communautaires et mesurent parfaitement certaines de leurs faiblesses...

INT.: ...are anxious to see a Community investigation into their weaker areas...

By merging two phrases, i.e. two ideas, into one and inventing the notion of *investigation* as a means of linking the two together, the interpreter has produced a statement which is grammatically acceptable but logically dubious. Such an assertion could be expected at the very least to startle a listener. The error was most likely caused because the interpreter felt that she was falling behind the speaker. Her attempt to compress the content in order to reduce her excessive lag or *décalage* failed.

(14) L'Espagne...a beaucoup progressé...C'est, à un moindre titre, le cas du Portugal.

INT.: ...this is the case particularly for Portugal.

The effect of this error is called a *contresens*. Such an utter misrepresentation can only be attributed to the student's inadequate mastery of the FL, i.e. her failure to understand the significance of the expression *à un moindre titre*. A certain number of comprehension errors must be expected in the case of student interpreters however carefully speech materials are selected and edited.

6. Hierarchy of Errors

Having classified the errors committed in terms of both type and seriousness, let us attempt to analyze their causes. In doing so, we are compelled to remain at the level of conjecture: as pointed out by Mason (1989), we have no access to the psychological mechanisms at work in the interpreter's mind during the listening process. This makes it exceedingly difficult to distinguish between the interpreter as listener and as text producer, and hence to determine the exact cause of error. However, we could tentatively establish the following hierarchy, proceeding as before, from the least to the most significant error:

(i) excessive concentration on a preceding item due to processing problems, resulting in a lack of attention and hence omission (examples 1 and 2);
(ii) attempt to improve TL style, leading to a tendency to overstate the case or to embroider the text unnecessarily (examples 5 and 6);
(iii) difficulty in finding the correct contextual equivalent for a given lexical item (examples 3, 4, 8, and possibly 9);
(iv) drawing erroneously upon one's store of background/general knowledge (examples 7 and 12C);
(v) compression of two information items into one, thereby producing a third, incorrect item (example 13);
(vi) shortcomings in mastery of the FL, leading to misunderstandings and therefore misinterpretations of the original speech (examples 10 and 14).

The further down this list an error type occurs, the more likely it seems to be to have a detrimental effect on the interpreter's communication of the message information content. Sager (1983) would probably agree that the causes referred to under (vi) are the most serious. On the subject of written translation, Sager states that errors *resulting from misinterpretation of the text* are one of the two major concerns of quality assessment, the other being those errors attributable to *inadequate expression* (see below).

The nature of the link between the cause of an error and its effect on communication is a complex one, as can be seen by a comparison of errors identified above under (vi): whereas the apparent cause of both examples 10 (a) and 10 (b) was equally serious, in the former case, the effect is minimal since the message is conveyed at least in part, whereas in the latter, communication breaks down. Conversely, the addition in 6, whose cause is seemingly trivial (stylistic embellishment), might distort the message received by the listener.

7. Presentation of the Message

Since we are dealing with adult native speakers of English, it could be argued at this point that the infelicities described below constitute, in Corder's terms

(1981), *mistakes* as opposed to *errors* as such. Those which affect the quality of presentation can be divided into two groups: e) lack of TL fluency and f) loss of rhetorical effect.

7.1. Lack of TL Fluency

(15)
INT.: ...increases in productivity, despite mediocre growth rates, is a record...

This is one of several examples provided by the corpus of a plural subject followed by a singular verb. Other grammatical slips relate to tense: most commonly misused are the English simple past and perfect tenses. Such utterances are unlikely to disturb a listener, and may even slip by unnoticed, thus making them irrelevant as long as they do not exceed a certain frequency threshold. All native speakers make grammatical mistakes from time to time: the fact that these occur more commonly in SI can be attributed to the peculiar degree of attention-splitting which the activity requires.

(16) C'est ce qui me permettra de traiter la deuxième solution.
INT.: This is what will allow me to look at the second solution.

Unlike the case illustrated in example 15, the above statement is one which a native speaker is highly unlikely to produce spontaneously. With the exception of *traiter: to look at*, the sentence is a word-for-word calque of the French, and not an interpretation at all. Happily, the corpus contains few such awkward passages. The message is nevertheless conveyed, since a transition from point one to point two would be perceived by the receiver. The mistake is therefore not too serious. But the subject has failed to analyze the content before re-expressing it, and the result sounds highly unidiomatic. A proliferation of similarly garbled utterances would require so much additional concentration on the part of the listener that ultimately, he would probably "switch off", i.e. the communication might cease altogether.

(17) Les politiques économiques qui s'imposent, doivent...
INT.: The econo -- the necessary economic policies...

In this case, the subject's delivery is both jerky and halting. False-starts such as the one illustrated here can become highly irritating for the listener and deflect his or her concentration from the speaker's message. The beginnings of sentences are particularly vulnerable to this type of slip, since speakers normally pause briefly between one idea and the next, which allows the student-interpreter to catch up and be ready for the next point. S/he fails to resume the necessary lag and embarks on an English phrase before ensuring that s/he has heard all possible qualifiers of the French noun.

(18)
INT.: ...efforts undertaken...which might be outside our--which would fall within clearly defined programmes...

The subject realises that she at first misunderstood the original text and makes a hasty adjustment to her own statement. The fact that she corrects her own error demonstrates that she is monitoring her output, which is a positive indication. Yet, once again, the break in TL flow would probably disorient the listener, and could cause him to lose confidence in the interpreter. Arguably, this mistake, including that of example 17, could have been avoided if sufficient lag had occurred.

Fluency in the TL is the one single aspect of an interpretation which most palpably distinguishes a professional performance from that of a trainee. It takes a good deal of experience to minimize the sorts of mistakes illustrated in examples 15 to 18 which are caused mostly by a tendency to focus too much on the input channel at the expense of the output. In addition to increased self-monitoring, students need to fine tune aspects of interpreting techniques such as lagging, before they can attain the desirable smoothness of delivery.

7.2. Loss of Rhetorical Effect

(19) Ne serait-il pas temps que...?
INT.: It is high time that...

Only one subject involved in the study failed to phrase the above as a rhetorical question. Her version lacks the immediacy of the others, an immediacy which is achieved not only through the use of the interrogative form itself, but also by means of the consequent change in intonation pattern.

(20) Les idées cheminent. Concrétisons-les.
INT.A.: These ideas must be made more concrete.
INT.B.: We must reinforce them.

Neither student has experienced difficulty in understanding both the linguistic and semantic meanings of the above-statement, but they have omitted to convey its rhetorical impact. The speaker's appeal to his audience is thereby sacrificed, and from the communicative point of view, the interpreters have done him an injustice.

It is my experience that student-interpreters prove to be singularly insensitive to rhetorical usage. Even in their mother-tongue, many do not spontaneously appreciate the difference, for example, between *we must...* and *let us...* . Rhetorical statements cause greater difficulty than do rhetorical questions, presumably because intonation varies to a lesser extent. Nevertheless, the interpreter-trainer is rewarded particularly quickly in this domain for devoting a certain amount of class time to the problem: a feeling for, and an ability to use rhetorical devices soon develops, and mistakes in this category begin to disappear rapidly.

7. Conclusion

The above-mentioned examples constitute some of the findings of an experimental investigation of student errors in simultaneous interpreting. Because of the small scale of the project, no definitive conclusions can be reached, nor can the categories established be considered exhaustive. Although successful communication of the speaker's message has been used here as a yardstick, it is not necessarily the only valid criterion against which to analyze error production.

Nevertheless, these data have enabled us to identify certain types of recurring errors. Many of the problems highlighted here derive from the French-English language pair, whereas others reside in the nature of the interpreting process as such. It would be interesting to conduct similar studies using different language combinations and to compare the findings. It is hoped that the results of a more systematic, multi-lingual investigation might one day corroborate those of this small-scale pilot study. The next stage would then be for interpreter-trainers to adapt their pedagogical approach accordingly: by anticipating, and, wherever possible, forestalling the errors made by beginner-interpreters.

References

Barik, H. 1971. "A Description of Various Types of Omissions, Additions and Errors of Translation Encountered in Simultaneous Interpretation". *META* 16:4. 199-210.

Corder, S.P. 1981. *Error Analysis and Interlanguage*. Oxford University Press.

Gile, D. 1983. "Aspects Méthodologiques de l'Evaluation de Qualité du Travail en Interprétation Simultanée". *META* 28:3. 236-243.

Gile, D. 1985. "La Sensibilité aux Ecarts de Langue et la Sélection d'Informateurs dans l'Analyse d'Erreurs: une Expérience". *Incorporated Linguist* 24:1. 29-32.

Kopczynski, A. 1983. "Deviance in Conference Interpreting". A. Kopczynski, ed. *The Mission of the Translator Today and Tomorrow.* Polska Agencja Interpress. 401.

Mason, I. 1989. "The Interpreter as Listener: An Observation of Response in the Oral Mode of Translating". G. McGregor and R. White, eds. *Reception and Response.* Croom Helm.

Sager, J.C. 1983. "Quality and Standards - The Evaluation of Translations". C. Picken, ed. *The Translator's Handbook.* London: Aslib.

Methodological Aspects of Interpretation and Translation Research

Daniel Gile
INALCO and CEEI (ISIT)

1. Introduction

Because of their importance in the development of culture and because they involve language, interpretation and translation have been the focus of much reflection and have generated a large body of literature, from St. Jerome and Calvin to Catford, Nida, Mounin, Steiner, not to mention countless other less well-known authors. However, most of the writings on I/T are normative or philosophical, and scientific research in the field is very recent, only several decades old. One of the driving forces behind the development of I/T research were efforts in the field of machine translation, which started in the fifties, dwindled temporarily and later regained momentum. Other vectors of translation research include the increasing use of mathematical methods and statistics in behavioural and linguistic sciences and the interest psychologists and psycholinguists have taken in I/T.

Many practitioners reject the idea of scientific research on translation and interpretation: some fear these disciplines may lose the aura of mystery surrounding their profession if dissected under a microscope; others do not believe science can shed much light on the processes and interactions involved; whereas others appear to fear that their intuitive theories and position in academia, or even that their social status may be threatened by scientific studies of I/T. As put very lucidly by Shlesinger (1989):

> ...those describing interpretation from the practitioner's standpoint are sometimes prone to a certain lack of detachment which surfaces in these writings in the form of a sense of awe at an impossible job incredibly done.

and by Stenzl (1983):

> We are quite pleased when psychologists confirm that ours is a complex job which requires a number of highly developed skills, but we are perhaps less inclined to document the limits of our skills and to face the occasions when we did not properly understand a speaker or were unable to adequately render a message even if we had understood it.

However, other practitioners and many I/T teachers have been fostering 'real research' so as to be able to test intuitions and go beyond them through observation and experimentation (in the field of interpretation, see for example Stenzl 1983, Arjona-Tseng 1989, as well as Gran and Taylor 1990).

Interpretation and translation can be studied under a wide variety of angles: the economics of I/T, market development of I/T, the psychology of translators and interpreters, their sociology, their health, etc. This paper deals with research on and around I/T *processes*, which raises more *I/T specific* methodological issues. The subject has been discussed by Toury (1991) in an article with a rather theoretical view of the issues and focusing on translation. The present paper tackles more practical issues in research methodology and leans essentially towards interpreting, though most comments also apply to translation.

2. Basic I/T Characteristics and Their Implications on Research

If translation and interpretation are represented as a process P acting on an input I and producing an output O (Figure 1), the following comments become evident:

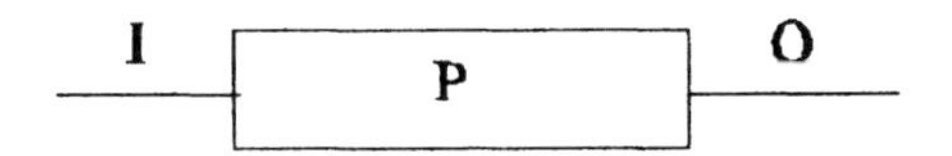

Figure 1. *Translation/Interpretation process*

2.1. In I/T, Input and Output can be Observed and Recorded Under Particularly Favourable Conditions

In translation, both input and output are *entirely* contained in written documents, providing an extraordinarily favourable observation and recording condition from the research angle. In simultaneous interpretation, input comes essentially through the interpreters' earphones and can therefore be observed and recorded. However, some interpreters stress that visual input is important to them, but as yet, this claim is still unsupported experimentally (Anderson 1979). The need for such visual input could be observed and recorded by way of video cameras placed in the interpretation booth, for example. With regard to the interpretation output as it reaches the audience, it is entirely contained in the message sent to the listeners' earphones, and is therefore easy to observe and to record. In consecutive interpretation, the visual components of both input and output are more important and more difficult to record because the relevant visual field is larger, but it could nonetheless still be captured to a certain extent.

2.2. Processes are NOT Easy to Observe and Record

In written translation, it is possible to observe some parts of the processes involved, such as the reading and writing as well as the documentary and terminological 'research'. In some cases, intermediary target language texts may be observed as well. But the actual *mental* process of translation remains invisible. Even the *Thinking Aloud Protocols* used in research on translation are only a *reflection* of the mental processes involved (Krings 1986). Similarly, in consecutive interpretation, it is possible to observe and record the note-taking part of the process and to monitor interpreters listening and providing their oral rendition, but the mental interpretation process itself is invisible.

2.3. Although Many Rules on Output, Including Relations between Output and Input Have Been Described, Much of the Process Leading from Input to Output Remains Unknown

This third principle is a corollary of the second. Given the invisible nature of the processes, they can be explored only by inference. There is a large consensus on the general directions, if not on the precise quantitative assessment, of I/T quality parameters, such as fidelity, linguistic correctness, stylistic and terminological acceptability (see discussion below). There are also certain widely-accepted operational rules regarding I/T preparation strategies, documentary and terminological 'research', problem-solving tactics, etc. However, most of the I/T processing which does not involve conscious decision-making, i.e. the reading and speech recognition operations, the unconscious inferencing during comprehension of source language speech or text, the meaning-to-language or language-to-language retrieval of target language terms and structures, remains largely unknown. Research in speech production and comprehension in psycholinguistics, studies on reading and experiments and models on attention in cognitive psychology as well as some artificial intelligence research, particularly as applied to machine translation, certainly do contribute their share of ideas. However, at this time, no single paradigm is fully accepted nor accounts for all phenomena observed in I/T processes. This comes as no surprise, given that the study of language comprehension and production, both in the oral and the written mode, is still in a developmental phase. Furthermore, I/T processes also involve language-switching, processing capacity constraints and linguistic interference between the source and target languages.

2.4. I/T Situations and Operations are Highly Variable

Variability in I/T is striking, even to the casual observer. Variability is a salient feature of I/T in communication situations with respect to subject matter, source language material and speeches, content density and logic, linguistic quality, the range of working conditions, differences between individual translators and interpreters in terms of talent, training, experience, working methods and motivation. This variability can also be observed in the same individual who does the same translation or interpretation twice, during training in I/T schools for example, as well as in the rare case when professionals are required to interpret or translate the same source language speech or text twice.

2.5. I/T Operational Environments are Fairly Simple

Technically speaking, in the case of translation, 'physical' I/T environments are easily described as consisting of a chair, a desk, paper and pencil, a typewriter or a computer, and sometimes a dictating machine. For consecutive interpretation, they include any room or space where two persons meet and hold a discussion. For simultaneous interpretation, a booth with electronic equipment as well as an electronically equipped meeting room are required (except when a TV monitor is used, as is often the case in satellite conferences and for TV interpretation).

* * *

With respect to scientific research on I/T, these basic characteristics suggest the following methodological principles:

a) The most logical way to undertake any study of I/T mental processes would be through the study of correlations between input and output or input and process *product*. As Hoffstaedter puts it, "A critical point in the investigation of mental processes is...that the processes themselves can never be observed directly...their investigation is always based on the PRODUCTS of such processes" (Hoffstaedter 1987, quoted in Toury 1991).

b) Because of variability, general conclusions regarding I/T mental processes can only be drawn on the basis of observations covering a wide range of variables and parametric values. This means that empirical studies, both observational and experimental, need to be plentiful before data can be considered as being representative of more than a limited population of practitioners and of more than a limited range of environmental I/T conditions and tasks.

Until now, not only have there been few scientific studies of I/T, but, as noted by Toury (1991) regarding translation, and by Gile (1990a) and others, with respect to interpretation, most studies were limited to very small samples of subjects, languages and text or speech types. Generalizations are therefore still premature.

c) Observational studies are the logical starting point. They are methodologically simple, as input and output can be easily observed and recorded without influencing translators' and interpreters' behaviour, whereas experimental studies may produce data unrepresentative of I/T if not conducted with proper methodological care and sufficient know-how. Moreover, observational studies are inexpensive, because material requirements are generally limited to photocopies of documents and cassette tapes. In some cases, video cameras and video-players may also be necessary, but no complex, expensive and sensitive equipment and no carefully prepared settings are required.

d) Experimental studies are technically easier to carry out in I/T than in most other fields of human behaviour. In translation, the fact is obvious, since material requirements for experiments are limited to 'source texts' which can be controlled at will. In consecutive interpretation, material requirements involve space and at least one 'speaker' and one 'client'. In the case of simultaneous interpretation, a meeting room, an electronically-equipped booth, at least one 'speaker' and an audience are required. But in all these cases, it is technically easy to create an experimental environment that is quasi-identical to actual field conditions. As pointed out by cognitive psychologist Flores d'Arcais (1978): "...after all, there are probably very few "real life" situations which are more similar to a laboratory psychological experimentation than the situation of an interpreter in a conference booth...".

In spite of these rather favourable conditions for its scientific study, I/T was not scientifically researched until approximately three decades ago. Since then, several theses and dissertations, as well as a number of studies and papers have been devoted to the subject. A significant proportion of these suffer from methodological weaknesses. The following is an attempt to present those which occur most frequently.

3. Major Methodological Issues and Problems in I/T Research

3.1. Subjects in I/T Experimentation

Access to translators and interpreters for research purposes may be difficult for geographic reasons, because of a lack of physical availability of practitioners, for professional reasons (confidentiality of translated material), and for personal reasons: many translators and interpreters do not appreciate having their work carefully scrutinized by anyone but their clients. Researchers therefore tend to take as subjects either I/T students or 'bilinguals', that is, non-practitioners having knowledge of languages.

This strategy is widely challenged by practitioners, especially in the field of conference interpretation (see for example Gile 1990a). A professional's approach and appropriate working methods in I/T are the result of training, experience and selection: not only do they have to be acquired and fine-tuned, but some students may never become professional translators or interpreters because they prove incapable of mastering and/or applying them. There may be very significant differences in the way professionals on the one hand, and students or amateur translators/interpreters on the other, perform I/T tasks, and experiments conducted with the latter subjects may not be representative of the activity to be examined.

This does not mean that no I/T studies using students or amateurs as subjects should be undertaken. Students, who are readily available, numerous and motivated, represent an especially valuable human resource. Moreover, they can gain a lot from the exercise and the careful scrutiny of their work, which is part of the process, provided ethical rules and respect for them are observed. However, caution is called for when using them in experiments or observational studies of *professional* translation or interpretation. They can be used when sufficient evidence is available to indicate that they are comparable to professionals in the type of behaviour under study. When no such evidence exists, one possible suggestion might be to combine samples of professionals *and* students, enabling comparisons between the two, and possibly accumulating data on comparability or non-comparability. This has indeed been done, though not with this aim in mind, in Dillinger's (1989) and Viezzi's (1989) recent studies, not to mention studies having the specific objective of comparing students' and experienced professionals' performance (see for example Pinter, 1969).

3.2. Materials

Similarly, investigators have conducted experiments using input materials which were very different from materials found in the field. This problem is more tangible in interpretation than in translation, since written translation is performed on a wide sample of texts, whereas interpretation is performed on speech types occurring in a smaller number of communication situations. Therefore, although interpreting sentences read out of context or written material not intended for oral communication may deepen insight on aspects of language comprehension and production or on other aspects of language-related skills, both processes and results may be quite different from those that occur in actual interpretation. For example, in a recent paper (1990), Dillinger defended the texts he used for an earlier experimental study of comprehension in simultaneous interpretation (1989) against a critic who challenged the validity of these texts, written especially for the experiment rather than taken from an authentic conference. Dillinger's reaction was:

> One might ask...*why* this would make a difference. No one knows what the differences are (if there are any) between the texts used here and the sorts of texts found in actual conference situations. The hypothesis that the texts are different and the processes involved in comprehending and interpreting them are qualitatively different because one text was presented to an audience and the other was not is not only unsupported by any evidence, but also seems entirely implausible (p.43).

No scientific evidence indicated the existence of such a difference, but interpreters report reacting to factors that have not yet been quantified or even specifically identified. Those who engage in research themselves have stressed time and time again the need to use experimental materials and conditions as close as possible to field conditions because of this. In Dillinger's case, since the whole validity of the experiment relies on the speeches, we feel that starting out with the assumption that *there is no difference* constitutes a methodological error.

3.3. Experimental Conditions and Tasks

Along the same lines, one might note that experimental studies have been conducted under conditions or with tasks somewhat far removed from field conditions, including translation into and from languages which are not the practitioners' usual active or passive languages or 'translation' of random sequences of words (Treisman 1965).

Again, experimenters may argue that no evidence points to a significant difference between such tasks and authentic translation or interpretation. Again, when no evidence or rationale in favour or against is available, the best policy seems to take as a starting point the hypothesis that the general feeling of I/T practitioners may be right. One should not forget that many research decisions are partly made on the basis of intuitive, scientifically unsubstantiated knowledge of the subject or phenomenon under study.

3.4. Quantification and Quality Assessment

Scientific researchers in I/T still hear practitioners say that translation and interpretation cannot be measured because they are "akin to the arts" or very complex and "cannot be reduced to formulas". A thorough discussion of this issue is beyond the scope of this paper. However, it may be appropriate to stress that quantification in the behavioural sciences is not tantamount to attempting to equate a behaviour with a set of equations or figures. The idea is to find indicators that can be 'measured', if only approximately, and yield data that will contribute to a better knowledge of the phenomenon. In this respect, many indicators seem to be relevant to I/T, depending on the aspect of interpretation or translation under study: translation speed, translation costs, source text length to target text length ratio, etc. In quality assessment, one common indicator is the number of language errors in a target language text or speech; another is the number of 'translation errors'.

Error counts have been used to evaluate quality in general, and fidelity in particular. However, researchers have had difficulties in such endeavours. One specific example is that of Henri Barik (1969), whose definition of errors includes linguistic transformations not necessarily considered as errors in an interpreter's mind (see Gile 1989). It would seem that Barik did not consult interpreters when defining errors. The question is not so much whether his definition is better than that of the practitioners'; the point is that the latter aim to reduce the number of errors as *they* see them and may do nothing to try to reduce the number of errors as defined by Barik, in which case his error count may be uncorrelated with the difficulty of the task.

Barik's definition of errors has also been challenged by Gerver (1976) as being "purely subjective" (Gerver applied this qualifier to his own definition as well), and by Stenzl (1983) as too vague. Stenzl reports that when she tried to replicate Barik's results and to identify errors in his transcripts according to his own definitions, she found that her data did not agree with his.

Another quality assessment problem resides in language acceptability evaluations. Not only are both the sensitivity and standards of native speakers highly variable, as illustrated in Gile (1985), but no evidence is available regarding the sensitivity and standards of delegates in international conferences or the quality standards aimed for by practitioners while interpreting.

The very basic question of quality definition in interpretation has only been dealt with intuitively and prescriptively until very recently. The International Association of Conference Interpreters (AIIC) tried to organize meetings with interpretation users in order to elicit some kind of feedback, but these attempts were never very successful. The most straightforward scientific way of collecting data on actual quality perception delegates would clearly be by way of questionnaires or interviews (Gile, 1983). The first study along such lines was conducted in Trieste by Meak (1983). Another was carried out by Buehler (1986), a third by Kurz (1989), and a fourth by Gile (1990c). But in view of the variability mentioned earlier, these studies constitute only a beginning and much replication and further studies are definitely required before quality of interpretation can be said to be understood. Methodologically, quality assessment of translation seems less daunting, at least as regards non-literary translation, because language standards relating to formal written texts are easier to identify and because variables and parameters of reception conditions are less complex in translation than in interpretation. However, as pointed out by Stenzl (1983), Gerver's method of having interpretation assessed by 2 judges who "...had experience of marking translation from the French, up to a first year University standard..." and who then corrected interpretation transcripts

(1976), is likely to be a poor reflection of the reactions of delegates sitting in the conference room.

3.5. Drawing Conclusions

Experimental design and conclusion-drawing issues are not much different in I/T from what they are in other disciplines of the behavioural sciences. Most specific methodological difficulties and flaws seem to occur because of the researchers' background. The examples discussed below illustrate this fact, but do not point at difficulties inherent to I/T research as such.

The most basic difficulties in I/T conclusion drawing are related to the validity of experiments with respect to professional I/T, as explained above regarding subjects, materials, environmental conditions, tasks and evaluations. Methodological weaknesses associated with this type of validity are found mostly in research undertaken by non-practitioners of I/T, because they may not be aware of specific I/T rules and effects in speech or text production standards, strategies and tactics.

For instance, some non-interpreting researchers engaged in interpretation research may be unaware that interpreters may deliberately opt to change the surface structure of a sentence or select words which are morphologically remote from the source language so as to avoid linguistic interference. In other words, a deviation from the source language structure may mean the interpreter is controlling the situation, whereas the selection of target language structures similar to source language structures indicates that the interpreter may be short of processing capacity. Similarly, the use of one word as opposed to another which resembles the corresponding source language word, could be an indication that the interpreter has sufficient processing capacity left to consciously resist linguistic interference, a fact which should not be mistaken for an indication of failure to find the 'right' word. One can point out in this context that the interpreters' view of fidelity may be quite different from that of the translators', since thcy deal with externally-paced message reception, as opposed to internally-paced visual reception. This may lead to errors both in quality assessments and in evaluations of difficulty. Barik's approach to errors is a good case in point, as mentioned above.

A second major weakness in I/T research involves extrapolation. The flaws referred to here are not the technical problems caused by 'convenience sampling' in statistical inference ('convenience sampling' is the selection of subjects *because* they are available, as opposed to random sampling-based methods which make inferential mathematics and hypothesis rejection or non-rejection applicable - see for instance Hansen, Hurwitz and Madow 1953 and Snedecor and Cochran 1967); neither are we referring to cases in which non-professionals are selected for experiments on professional practice. The problem is that even when professionals are given tasks that can be considered valid as I/T tasks, even in observational studies, which deal by definition with real I/T tasks, researchers tend to extrapolate somewhat uncautiously.

One such example can be found in Dillinger's (1989) general conclusions on interpretation based only on a single set of experiments with a total of 24 subjects, working on two speeches in only two languages. Another example involves Seleskovitch (1975) making general statements on interpretation on the basis of a single experiment with a total of 12 subjects working in the consecutive mode on two English speeches. *Inter alia,* she considers that deverbalization is an established fact because in her experiment, with the exception of some specific types of words, notes taken by interpreters do not list "word-equivalents" in the target language. Other possible explanations are not considered. This weakness is not linked to sophisticated methodology or highly specialized knowledge and can be spotted by analysis of the logic of her conclusions.

Toury (1991) mentions other weaknesses in the rationale of I/T researchers. The most striking example he refers to is a study by Sandrock (1982) on the use of the *Thinking Aloud Process (TAP)* in translation research: a comparison was made between two translations of the same text, one traditional and the other resulting from a verbalization and TAP process. The problem, as pointed out by Toury, is that one translation was produced by a learner of English, and the other was given as a "Model translation" in a manual. It is therefore possible, and even plausible, that differences resulted not only from differences in the processes, but also from differences in the translation expertise of the authors of the two target language texts.

4. Strategies for I/T Research

I/T research has been making some headway over the past decade or so, mostly because of importation of experimental methods from other disciplines (Toury 1991). As Toury also points out, the implementation of such methods as well as observational methods in I/T is still suffering from weaknesses. We believe that proper scientific research is required, because too many widely accepted ideas are based solely on intuitive personal speculation and have resulted in some stagnation in I/T, as also noted by Toury (1991 - see also a discussion of the problem in Gile 1990a).

However, we do not share Toury's view that empirical methods require "translational hypotheses" to be tested. Scientific investigation in most fields starts with exploration of reality in the field, that is with observational studies. Systematic observation of reality is a valuable scientific act *per se* (see Fourastié 1966), which should not be snubbed by more fashionable experimentation, which practically "haunts" the scientific scene (Toury 1991). Another type of experimenting, known as *open experimenting*, consists in generating controlled conditions not in order to test a specific hypothesis, but for the purpose of examining the resulting situation as a whole and trying to make inferences on that basis. Open experimenting is also very valuable (see Gile 1990b). In our view, the most fundamental reasons for methodological weaknesses, as discussed above, lie in what can be summarized as insufficient expertise in scientific research on the part of I/T practitioners engaged in research (were they better trained, I/T researchers outside I/T could avoid most of their own errors by reading their work and cooperating with them).

We believe that improvement of the situation can be accelerated by appropriate strategies. Some suggestions are formulated below with this goal in mind. "Institutional strategies" aim at creating a favorable I/T research environment by the action of I/T schools, associations and governmental agencies entrusted with I/T responsibilities. "Personal strategies" are proposed to individual researchers who wish to engage in I/T research.

4.1. Institutional Strategies

Highest priority should clearly be given to research training. The logical forum for such training would be the postgraduate I/T schools attached to universities.

Clearly, interdisciplinary cooperation is required at least in the early stages of methodological training of I/T students and practitioners for research. We believe the programme should include some concepts from the philosophy of science, training in statistics for the social sciences and the presentation of research methods used in behavioural sciences. At a later stage, the I/T teaching staff could adapt the concepts and methods to I/T research.

Since there are I/T instructors with a scientific background who teach at various locations, pooling together I/T research expertise through "international I/T research advisory boards", possibly specialized in translation or interpretation, may provide institutions and individuals with better consultative services and research guidance. The activity of such boards could be informal, but a formal agreement between institutions offering I/T research training at the graduate or doctoral level, which would allow their students to choose board members as M.A. or Ph.D. supervisors outside their school, could have distinct advantages.

4.2. Research Programs

Besides training, actual research programs would be helpful in improving the overall situation, and I/T schools seem once again to be in the best position to foster such programs. One obvious possibility is to involve research trainees in programs as described above in actual research. Another approach is the "thesis" required at the end of basic I/T training in some schools, such as the Scuola Superiore di Lingue Moderne per Interpreti e Traduttori in Trieste. Such "theses" are a good opportunity for students to carry out actual research, as demonstrated by several theses published in Gran and Taylor (1990) and in *The Interpreter's Newsletter*.

In research programs of this type, schools have an opportunity to *replicate* observations and experiments, which is a good way to corroborate results and to enlarge samples.

4.3. Interdisciplinary Contacts

Another role of institutions with respect to I/T research is to establish and improve interdisciplinary contacts. This can be done by inviting scientists from other disciplines such as linguistics, philosophy of science, and psychology, to lecture to students or to participate in I/T research projects. This can also be done by actively fostering information exchanges, for instance by sending such scientists information about I/T studies and projects which could be of interest to them.

4.4. Dissemination of Information in I/T Research Circles

The situation of translation and interpretation research differs greatly with respect to dissemination of information. The translation research community is much older, larger, wealthier, and better organized. There are numerous translation journals and an increasing number of conferences dealing with translation studies. Furthermore, translator researchers have traditionally kept in touch with the academic communities of linguists, philosophers, literature scholars, and more recently, have been drawing the attention of the artificial intelligence community.

Interpretation researchers are still to a large extent isolated and unaware of each other's work, though much headway has been made in the past few years with the Trieste school's initiatives, in particular its seminar on interpretation training (Gran and Dodds 1989) and the launching of an interpretation journal, *The Interpreter's Newsletter*. Another effort is underway through the creation, in 1990, of the Paris-based *IRTIN*, or *International Interpretation Research and Theory Information Network*, which publishes a bulletin twice a year. The International Association of Conference Interpreter's Research Committee also endeavours to foster dissemination of information on interpretation research and is due to publish a rather extensive interpretation bibliography soon.

Multi-centre contacts have been a reality in I/T for many years, but multi-centre research is still to come. This, along with replication, is a good way of overcoming sample size and sample diversity (in particular as regards languages) limitations. Because so little empirical research has been carried out to date, simple projects which cost little and which are easy to coordinate are still very valuable.

5. Strategies for Individuals

5.1. Strategies for I/T Practitioners

I/T practitioners with no research training or background, wishing to engage in I/T research can do so because much can still be done with very simple methods. The following guidelines may be useful in such an endeavour:

- *The selection of research projects:* Research topics should be well defined and not overly ambitious. A completed project can be extended or followed up, but many initial projects are never completed because sights are set too high. The methods, potential difficulties and ways around them as well as a timetable should be clear from the start. The advice of more experienced I/T researchers should be very useful in this respect.
- *Research advisors:* Pending the arrival of a generation of well-trained I/T researchers, it seems advisable to have two advisors, one from I/T and the other from science, preferably from psychology or linguistics, even if only one of them is the official advisor. Of course, each advisor must be open-minded enough to welcome the contribution of the other. Institutional action along the lines advocated above may be of help in this respect.

- *Research design and methods:* Unless they are sure to be able to rely on their advisors for close monitoring and methodological help, budding I/T researchers should aim at very simple design and methods. Observational studies and "open experimenting" (in which a situation is generated and observed but no statistical inferencing for hypothesis-testing purposes is done) are methodologically simpler that the more traditional hypothesis-testing. Inferential statistics are often challenging, even for experienced researchers: see for example Gore and Altman (1982) for a wide discussion of the issues. It is interesting to note that in a study of 149 medical papers published in several journals, only 28% were judged of acceptable statistical quality (Schor and Karten 1966). It is therefore easier and at least as valid to use descriptive statistics rather than inferential statistics, though analyses cannot be as fine as with inferential statistics (see a discussion of the issue in Gile 1989 and 1990c).
- *Drawing conclusions:* Bearing in mind the weaknesses discussed earlier in this paper, I/T practitioners should be very careful in drawing conclusions and extrapolating. Unlike researchers in most other disciplines, when they engage in I/T research, they are required to deal objectively and without bias with an activity in which they are intimately involved in their daily life and regarding which they have developed their own intuitive ideas. Again, the presence of non-I/T scientists as advisors can be very valuable, as their views are more objective and their thinking more in line with the Cartesian discipline of scientific reasoning.

6. Strategies for Non-Practitioners

Non-practitioner I/T researchers do not have to overcome personal involvement and are already familiar with and experienced in scientific thinking. This does not prevent them from having preconceived ideas about I/T, but scientific discipline probably makes it easier to examine them more objectively on the basis of scientific data. On the other hand, like the public at large, they often consider they are familiar with I/T because of their experience with school 'translation' as part of foreign language learning or because they have had some occasional experience in translating and interpreting. Such experience is often fallacious, as school translation and amateur translating and interpreting may be quite different from professional practice as regards strategies, tactics, user expectations etc. This deceptive sense of familiarity may explain partly the fact that many non-I/T practitioners who engaged in I/T research did not consult practitioners before and during their study on methodological questions, which resulted in errors as discussed in Toury (1991) and in this paper.

For all these reasons, we believe it is essential for investigators coming into I/T to consult with practitioners. Special attention should be given to the first three items mentioned in the section on methodological issues and problems in an earlier part of this paper, namely subjects, materials, experimental conditions and tasks, as this is where critical comments from practitioners may prove to be most useful.

References

Anderson, L. 1979. *Simultaneous Interpretation: Contextual and Translation Aspects.* Concordia University, Montreal, Canada. [Unpublished Masters' Thesis.]

Arjona-Tseng, E. 1989. "Preparing for the XXIth Century" (Keynote speech). *Proceedings of the Twentieth Anniversary Symposium on the Training of Teachers of Translation and Interpretation*, Monterey Institute of International Studies, Monterey, California.

Barik, H.C. 1969. *A Study in Simultaneous Interpretation.* University of North Carolina, Chapel Hill. [Unpublished Doctoral Dissertation.]

Buehler, H. 1986. "Linguistic (Semantic) and Extra-linguistic (Pragmatic) Criteria for the Evaluation of Conference Interpretation and Interpreters". *Multilingua* 5. 231-235.

Dillinger, M. 1989. *Component Processes of Simultaneous Interpreting.* McGill University, Montreal, Canada. [Unpublished Doctoral Dissertation.]

Dillinger, M. 1990. "Comprehension During Interpreting: What Do Interpreters Know that Bilinguals Don't?". *The Interpreter's Newsletter* 3. 41-58.

Flores d'Arcais, G.B. 1978. "The Contribution of Cognitive Psychology to the Study of Interpretation". D. Gerver and W. H. Sinaiko, eds. *Language Interpretation and Communication.* New York and London: Plenum Press, Nato Conference Series. 385-402.

Fourastié, J. 1966. *Les Conditions de l'Esprit Scientifique.* Paris: Gallimard.

Gerver, D. 1976. "Empirical Studies of Simultaneous Interpretation: A Review and a Model". R. Brislin, ed. *Translation.* New York: Gardner Press. 165-207.

Gile, D. 1983. "Aspects Méthodologiques de l'Evaluation de la Qualité du Travail en Interprétation Simultanée". *META* 28:3. 236-243.

Gile, D. 1985. "La Sensibilité aux Ecarts de Langue et la Sélection d'Informateurs dans l'Analyse d'Erreurs". *The Incorporated Linguist* 24:1. 29-32.

Gile, D. 1989. *La Communication Linguistique en Réunion Multilingue - Les Difficultés de la Transmission Informationelle en Interprétation Simultanée.* Université de Paris III. [Unpublished Doctoral Dissertation.]

Gile, D. 1990a. "Scientific Research vs. Personal Theories in the Investigation of Interpretation". L. Gran and C. Taylor, eds. *Aspects of Applied and Experimental Research on Conference Interpretation*. Udine: Campanotto Editore. 28-41.

Gile, D. 1990b. "Observational Studies and Experimental Studies in the Investigation of Interpretation". Paper presented at the Scuola Superiore di Lingue Moderne per Interpreti e Traduttori, Universita degli Studi di Trieste, March 19, 1990. (Mimeo.).

Gile, D. 1990c. "L'Evaluation de la Qualité de l'Interprétation par les Délégués: Une Etude de Cas". *The Interpreter's Newsletter* 3. 66-71.

Gile, D. 1990d. "Research Proposals for Interpreters". L. Gran and C. Taylor, eds. *Aspects of Applied and Experimental Research on Conference Interpretation*. Udine: Campanotto Editore. 226-236.

Gore, S.M. and Altman, D.G. 1982. *Statistics in Practice*. London: British Medical Association.

Gran, L. and Dodds, J. 1989. *The Theoretical and Practical Aspects of Teaching Conference Interpretation*. Proceedings of the First International Symposium on Conference Interpreting at the University of Trieste. Udine: Campanotto Editore.

Gran, L. and Taylor, C. 1990. *Aspects of Applied and Experimental Research on Conference Interpretation*. Udine: Campanotto Editore.

Hansen, M., Hurwitz, W. and Madow, W. 1953. *Sample Surveys Methods and Theory*. New York, London and Sydney: John Wiley & Sons, Inc.

Hoffstaedter, P. 1987. "Poetic Text Processing and its Empirical Investigation". *Poetics* 16. 75-91.

Kurz, I. 1989. "Conference Interpreting: User Expectations". *ATA - Proceedings of the 30th Annual Conference*. Medford, NJ: Learned Information Inc. 143-148.

Krings, H.P. 1986. *Was in den Koplen der Ubersetzer vergeht*. Tübingen: Narr.

Meak, L. 1983. *La Selezione dell'Informazione per l'Interpretazione Simultanea della Literatura Medica*. Trieste, Universita degli Studi di Trieste, Scuola Superiore di Lingue Moderne per Interpreti e Traduttori. [Unpublished monograph].

Pinter, I. 1969. *Der Einfluss der Uebung und Konzentration auf Simultanes Sprechen und Hören*. University of Vienna. [Unpublished Doctoral Dissertation].

Sandrock, U. 1982. *Thinking-Aloud Protocols (TAPs - Ein Instrument zur Dekomposition des Komplexen Prozesses 'Ubersetzen')*. Kassel: Gesamthochschule Kassel. (Mimeo.).

Seleskovitch, D. 1975. *Langage, Langues et Mémoire*. Paris: Minard.

Shlesinger, Miriam. 1989. *Simultaneous Interpretation as a Factor in Effecting Shifts in the Position of Texts on the Oral-Literate Continuum*. Tel-Aviv University. [Unpublished Masters' Thesis.]

Schor, S. and Karten, I. 1966. "Statistical Evaluation of Medical Journal Manuscripts". *JAMA* 195. 1123-1128.

Snedecor, G.W. and Cochran, W.G. 1967. *Statistical Methods*, 6th Edition. Ames, Iowa: The Iowa State University Press.

Stenzl, C. 1983. *Simultaneous Interpretation - Groundwork Towards a Comprehensive Model*. University of London. [Unpublished Masters' Thesis.]

Toury, G. 1991. "Experimentation in Translation Studies: Achievements, Prospects and some Pitfalls". Sonja Tirkonnen-Condit. ed. *Empirical Research in Translation and Intercultural Studies: Selected Papers of the TRANSIF Seminar, Savonlinna 1988*. Tübingen: Gunter Narr. 45-66.

Treisman, A. 1965. "The Effects of Redundancy and Familiarity on Translation and Repeating Back a Native and Foreign Language". *British Journal of Psychology* 56. 369-379.

Viezzi, M. "Information Retention as a Parameter for the Comparison of Sight Translation and Simultaneous Interpretation: An Experimental Study". *The Interpreters' Newsletter* 2.

Aptitude Testing for Conference Interpreting: Why, When and How

Barbara Moser-Mercer
Université de Genève

1. Introduction

With international communication assuming ever-increasing importance and more highly qualified conference interpreters needed to meet the growing demand, the world can no longer rely on natural talent alone as it did for its first generation of conference interpreters. Today, most every aspiring interpreter undergoes more or less extensive training to prepare for a demanding professional career. Usually, the first hurdle to be taken is an aptitude test.

Over the years it has become apparent that knowing several languages is but one prerequisite for succeeding as an interpreter and that certain other qualities must be present before training even begins. This article will review the different types of aptitude tests employed, systematic research carried out on aptitude testing and will attempt to identify future areas of research on the subject.

2. Types of Aptitude Tests

Depending on the type of training program (intensive short-term program, four-year university program, etc.) aptitude tests are administered either 1) before students are admitted to an undergraduate training course in translation and interpretation, with no further screening carried out once the student has been enrolled in the program, or 2) before admitting students to an undergraduate training course in translation, but with additional aptitude testing required for students who wish to enter the interpreting section after having pursued translation courses (usually for two years), or 3) before admitting candidates to a postgraduate training course of longer duration (18 - 24 months) or 4) before admitting candidates to a postgraduate or in-house intensive short-term training course (6 - 8 months).

Depending on the legal situation and/or academic policy, aptitude tests are either 1) eliminatory, if one or more parts of the test have not been passed, whereby the candidate often has a chance to sit for the test again after a certain time (usually one year) has elapsed, or 2) the test serves as guidance for students and instructors. Candidates performing poorly on such a test are merely advised to change their course of study.

Lastly, we can distinguish between one-time tests of short duration, where the entire testing procedure is completed within 2 to 8 hours, and long-term testing over a period of several weeks or even months, where the candidates' progress along several clearly defined parameters is monitored and where the rate of progress, provided a certain baseline-level is present at the outset, emerges as the primary criterion for admission (Moser-Mercer, 1978).

3. What is Being Tested

To this broad spectrum of tests, each geared to the specific requirements of a given program, corresponds a similar variety of parameters tested.

3.1. Knowledge

3.1.1. Mother tongue(s) and foreign languages. These are tested either by way of written translation tests and/or oral interviews. In many institutions, mastery of translation is still seen as an important prerequisite for entering an interpreting program. Despite considerable advances in foreign language testing, little use seems to have been made of the insight and experience gained in that field. Most interpreter-trainers intuitively know what level and type of linguistic competence is needed at a given level of training, but with so many different types of programs, and new programs being developed, a clearer definition of linguistic competence ought to be developed to guide both potential students and trainers in their assessment. This is particularly true for distinguishing communicative competence (in a B-language) from passive competence (in a C language), and the mastery of a range of registers, styles and idioms in an A language. Recent interdisciplinary studies in neurophysiology and interpretation (e.g. Gran 1989, Fabbro and Gran in this volume, and Fabbro 1989) have shown the degree and type of bilinguality of students to be of importance for succeeding in their studies.

More detailed information is also needed on how much a student can be expected to progress in all of his languages during a given period of training. Here, one might expect more improvement to be made in two years' time than in 6 months. But this has not yet been investigated. Variables such as whether a candidate studies interpreting in the country of his A-, B- or C-language and continued exposure to those of his languages not spoken in that particular country may all play a significant role.

3.1.2. General education ("culture générale"). In spite of the fact that all trainers agree upon the need for a future interpreter to have a well rounded education and a keen interest in current affairs, the testing of this parameter usually proves to be extremely difficult and often a candidate fails for not having had enough factual bits at his or her fingertips. Here too, a number of tests have been developed for other fields of study (SAT - Scholastic Aptitude Test, GRE - Graduate Record exam), sections of which could be used successfully to screen potential interpreters.

3.2. Skills

3.2.1. Comprehension (analysis and synthesis). While intimately tied to linguistic competence and general background knowledge, comprehension of a message requires in addition analytical skills and an ability to go beyond the information at hand to establish the broader picture. This involves looking beyond the immediate message and evaluating the communicative setting as a whole.

Written comprehension tests are sometimes used to evaluate this skill. Although useful as early screening devices, they fail to assess the specific skills needed in oral communication such as speed of analysis, oral comprehension and memory capacity.

3.2.2. Speed of comprehension and production. This parameter can be tested as part of an aural comprehension test by increasing the speed and/or complexity of the incoming message. Even though any candidate should already be capable of comprehending general material at normal speaking speed (90-110 words/minute), the length of the training course will determine how much higher the acceptable baseline should be as there is room for improvement through training.

3.2.3. Memory capacity. Although testable in itself (psychological research has produced a number of memory tests), care should be taken in the selection of such tests. Standard recall and recognition tests for isolated items of information, albeit useful in interpretation research, do not appear to be the optimal tools for assessing interpreting candidates. Testing memory for complete ideas and logical relations should take precedence over testing memory for isolated facts, although it cannot be denied that interpreters have ample opportunity to process somewhat isolated facts such as numbers and enumerations.

3.2.4. Simultaneity of listening and speaking. This usually does not represent an unsurmountable hurdle for candidates and increased competence is achieved through practice; sometimes, however, it remains a stumbling block. Here, only long-term testing can provide a more definitive answer. Shadowing exercises (semantic rather than phonetic shadowing) have been used in a number of entrance exams to test candidates' ability to listen and speak simultaneously. Even though the shadowing task *per se* has been the subject of much controversy lately, it is important to point out that were we to develop a scale of progressive difficulty for interpreting, *semantic* shadowing would precede paraphrasing, which would then be followed by simultaneous interpreting. Perhaps we are throwing out the baby with the bathwater if we claim that shadowing had nothing to do with interpreting. For further and more detailed discussion see Kraushaar & Lambert (1987) Green *et al.* (in this volume), and Moser-Mercer (1984).

3.2.5. Voice and diction. Although these two parameters need not be tested separately, they should be evaluated very carefully during other oral performance tests, given that even the slightest problem in this area can rarely be corrected within a short period of time, if ever.

3.3. Personality Traits

3.3.1. Stress tolerance. Even though every conference interpreter will attest to interpreting often being a very stressful activity, a stress survey carried out among AIIC-interpreters failed to meet with sufficient interest among colleagues and no follow-up was ever conducted. Gerver *et al.* (1981) rightly pointed out that

> there can be no doubt that the speaker-paced nature of simultaneous interpreting involves speed-stress of the classic kind ... it may be that the particular stress experienced by simultaneous interpreters needs to be evaluated with linguistic materials rather than general purpose materials. (p. 21)

Although testing situations usually create stress for any given candidate, such one-time exposure to a type of stress that is perhaps not even typical of simultaneous interpreting may not be the best screening device. Performance under stress must be observed over time and candidates must be given a chance to adjust to the stresses involved in interpreting. These may have multiple origins: the speaker's speed of delivery and accent, the difficulty of the topic, poor working conditions (sound, lighting, view, ventilation, etc.), the interpreter's inadequate preparation, his or her physical condition on a particular day, his/her relation with booth- and team-mates, the number of consecutive meetings and the number of hours worked, etc. Obviously, experienced interpreters will have built up a certain baseline below which they will not drop. At the selection stage, the question to be asked is whether a candidate can build up to this level within the time-frame of the training course.

3.3.2. Resilience. Often considered an integral part of stress management, resilience is needed to manage long-term exposure to a strenuous working situation. Being able to perform as well at the beginning as at the end of a six-hour testing session, is a reflection of the candidate's resilience. But those who fail at first, due to lack of resilience, may be likened to sprinters who would not dream of running a marathon without appropriate training. Longer-term testing would be more advantageous here as well.

3.3.3. Learning curves. Learning encompasses the organization of sensory experiences, the acquisition of strategies in problem solving, the processes of abstraction: in short it is a change that occurs in a person at a particular time as a function of experience (Crowder 1976). Learning can be intentional or incidental; it can occur through rote memorization or through understanding;

it can occur quickly or slowly, gradually or all at once. Whereas interpreting involves both incidental and intentional learning as well as rote memorization and learning through understanding, all learning in a professional setting must occur relatively rapidly. Many interpreting programs, particularly those at the post-graduate level, emphasize this but do not test for learning speed at the outset. Differences in learning curves are best observed over a longer period of testing (several weeks), but given the importance of ongoing learning at the professional level and the fact that the speed with which an interpreter is able to acquire information co-determines the quality of his performance, it appears that the learning parameter deserves more careful treatment during entrance testing.

4. Methodology

Whereas in the previous section, an attempt was made to enumerate as many testing parameters as possible, the following section strives to inventory some of the methods currently used in a number of institutions to measure these parameters. Some schools have developed quite elaborate marking sheets for jurors to evaluate candidates along several parameters, but often one and the same test is used to measure two or more parameters at a time (e.g. a written translation test is used to measure competence in both native and foreign languages). Obviously, this does not facilitate objective testing and may often lead to false positive or false negative results, especially in borderline cases. Although it appears important to strike a balance between the number of parameters measured and the number of individual tests developed to measure them, most entrance aptitude tests for interpreters err in the direction of too few individual tests.

4.1. Written Translation Tests (B to A, C to A, and A to B)

These often serve as a first hurdle before the candidate is admitted to the oral part of the aptitude test. In most institutions these tests are designed to measure the following parameters: competence in language A, comprehension in languages B and C, accuracy, powers of analysis and synthesis.

4.2. *The Oral Interview or Oral Exposé*

Either in its unstructured or more structured (prepared) version, the oral interview often serves to measure any combination of the following parameters: communicative competence in the candidate's languages (usually A and B), knowledge of current affairs, "culture générale", voice, diction, projection, assertiveness, and stress-tolerance.

4.3. *Sight Translation*

This task is used to measure competence in language A, comprehension in languages B and C, speed of comprehension and production, accuracy, stress-tolerance, projection, and assertiveness.

4.4. *Paraphrasing*

Oral paraphrasing of a message received orally is commonly used to test for native language competence. Other parameters, however, such as accuracy, speed of comprehension and production, ability to listen and speak simultaneously, projection, stress tolerance and assertiveness, are often considered at the same time.

4.5. *Memory Tests*

In their long-term study, Gerver *et al.* (1981) tested memory for text and employed recall protocols and summaries that reflect the gist of the text rather than details. According to this study, such tests are a good indicator of "the abilities required for interpreting and, in particular, subsets of abilities particular to the two modes of interpretation." (p. 21) These test materials need to be constructed carefully. Gerver *et al.* used texts in the form of speeches, where each text (1000 words) was composed of rhetorical discourse containing setting, main issue, arguments for, secondary issue, arguments against, refutation, irrelevant issue, and a conclusion. No special demands should be made in terms of subject matter or vocabulary, and the material should be unfamiliar enough to prevent "guessing". (For an example of such a memory test, see Lambert 1983).

Should the construction and marking of such memory tests prove to be too time-consuming, Gerver *et al.* propose the use of "Logical Memory" tests from the Wechsler Memory Scale (Wechsler, 1938). Although more removed from the actual interpreting situation, these shorter memory tests are easy to administer and constitute a useful additional tool for the selection of interpreters.

In general, memory tests provide a better indication of aptitude for consecutive than for simultaneous interpretation.

4.6. The Cloze-Test

Oral cloze-tests have been used to evaluate candidates' ability to perform successfully when speed of decision-making is required. According to Stubbs and Tucker (1974), such tests measure lexical, syntactic and semantic aspects of language processing. To construct a cloze test, one selects a passage of prose, such as a speech, in the case of interpreter-candidates, and omits every tenth word, for example. The candidate then has to write down the missing words on hearing the passage (in his foreign language). To perform successfully, a candidate must perceive the structure and internal relationship of a text and be able to anticipate information, in other words, provide "closure". Thus, the cloze-test addresses a number of sub-skills in the interpreting process. (For a more detailed discussion of subskills, see Moser 1978)

4.7. Consecutive and Simultaneous Interpreting

Whereas the standards of performance applied at the aptitude test level must, by definition, be lower than those expected at the diploma level, the candidate is nevertheless asked to perform a complex skill for which s/he has not yet been trained. The only rationale for employing such a test ought to be that interpreters are still, to a large extent, "born" and not made. If memory is the parameter to be measured (in a consecutive test, for example) then other memory tests are available (see Lambert 1983), that would provide a "purer" measure without all the confounding variables introduced through consecutive or simultaneous interpreting.

5. Overall Evaluation

It is safe to say that standardized tests have hardly ever been used in the testing and selection of conference interpreters. The "standardized" translation tests referred to by Bowen (1989) in no way meet the criteria of true standardization. This makes for considerable variation in the evaluation of tests. Whereas some schools employ a straightforward pass/fail for every subtest of a testing session, whereby one negative grade entails an overall fail, other institutions allow negative grades in certain specified subtests, as long as the overall score is a pass. Most schools use a special roster or matrix to record grades or points so as to provide some measure of standardization. In some schools, the jury is composed exclusively of faculty members working at the schools; in others, outside members are solicited regularly. Sometimes jury members are briefed either orally or in writing as to what they should look for in candidates and it is not unusual for extraneous factors such as market demand for a particular language combination or minimum/maximum class size to enter into the final judgment.

On the whole, then, subjective evaluation prevails in tests for interpreting aptitude as objective tests are for the most part not available. The dearth of statistical information on aptitude testing, the almost total lack of data relating pass/fail results in aptitude tests to pass/fail results in final exams, leaves the evaluation of aptitude for interpreting wide open to criticism. Such a situation is not only uncomfortable for both teacher/trainers, administrators and candidates, but leaves the testers unprotected from legal challenge. Already, candidates failing their aptitude tests and recognizing the lack of objectivity of such tests are beginning to appeal negative decisions. The onus is definitely on the schools to develop a coherent set of tests that measure in the most objective way the largest possible number of identified subskills so as to offer every candidate a fair chance to succeed, as well as discriminate between adequate aptitude and lack thereof.

6. Research Agenda

Every school will have to develop its own testing procedure. However, this does not mean that the parameters to be measured ought to change from one school to another. The final goal of any program is to train professionals who will be able to work side by side with experienced interpreters once they have obtained their diploma.

Thus the first step should involve the development of as complete an inventory of parameters (subskills) as possible.

Second, the length of the training program is used to determine the acceptable baseline for each parameter and perhaps even their weighting within a carefully constructed set of tests. This will mean that for short intensive training programs, little or no margins are allowed for certain subskills, whereas in a two-year program considerably more room is given for learning to occur. The weighting of certain parameters will assume greater importance in short-term courses: is a particular candidate a fast enough learner to make up weaknesses in one or several parameters?

Third, the length of the testing period is chosen: short-term or longer-term testing. (For a complete discussion, see Moser-Mercer 1984).

The next step involves the selection of tests and the assignment of parameters to each test. Development of evaluation procedures, scoring sheets, jury composition, instruction, and statistical evaluation complete the preparatory phase.

For improvements in aptitude testing to occur, we need statistical analyses of results, follow-up of successful candidates through their final exams - a promising start is the compilation and comparison of exam data by Gingiani (1990) - and relating of time spent in training as well as final exam performance with performance in their aptitude tests.

Sufficient data gathered over a period of time will allow us to evaluate the predictive power of individual tests, i.e. to what extent each test is an indicator of successful performance in the final exam. Some might even wish to follow up graduates into their professional practice.

Collaboration on testing among two or more schools with similar programs would considerably shorten the time needed to evaluate certain tests and provide all involved in this task with more reliable tests much sooner. Given the enormous moral obligation of testers and the large number of candidates to be tested for new language combinations entering the international conference arena, time is of the essence.

References

Bowen, D. and M. 1989. "Aptitude for Interpreting". L. Gran and J. Dodds, eds. *The Theoretical and Practical Aspects of Teaching Conference Interpretation.* Campanotto: Udine. 109-125.

Crowder, R.G. 1976. *Principles of Learning and Memory.* Hillsdale: Lawrence Erlbaum Associates.

Dodds, J.M. 1990. "On the Aptitude of Aptitude Testing". *The Interpreters' Newsletter* 3. 17-22.

Fabbro, F. 1989. "Neurobiological Aspects of Bilingualism and Polyglossia." L. Gran and J. Dodds, eds. *The Theoretical Aspects of Teaching Conference Interpretation.* Campanotto: Udine. 71-82.

Fabbro, F. and Gran, L. 1994. "Neurological and Neuropsychological Aspects of Polyglossia and Simultaneous Interpretation". S. Lambert and B. Moser-Mercer, eds. *Bridging the Gap: Empirical Research on Conference Interpreting.* Benjamins: Amsterdam.

Gerver, D., Longley, P., Lambert, S. and Long, J. 1984. "Selecting Trainee Conference Interpreters: A Preliminary Study." *Journal of Occupational Psychology* 57. 17-31.

Gran, L. 1989. "Interdisciplinary Research on Cerebral Asymetries: Significance and Prospects for the Teaching of Interpretation". L. Gran and J. Dodds, eds. *The Theoretical Aspects of Teaching Conference Interpretation.* Campanotto: Udine. 93-100.

Gingiani, A. 1990. "Reliability of Aptitude Testing: A Preliminary Study". L. Gran and C. Taylor, eds. *Aspects of Applied and Experimental Research in Conference Interpretation.* Campanotto: Udine.

Keiser, W. 1978. "Selection and Training of Conference Interpreters." D. Gerver and W.H. Sinaiko, eds. *Language, Interpretation and Communication.* New York: Plenum. 11-24.

Kraushaar, B. and Lambert, S. 1987. "Shadowing Proficiency According to Ear of Input and Type of Bilinguality". *Bulletin of the Canadian Association of Applied Linguistics (CAAL)* 9:1. 17-31.

Lambert, S. 1983. *Recall and Recognition among Conference Interpreters.* University of Stirling, Scotland. [Unpublished Doctoral Dissertation.]

Longley, P. 1989. "The Use of Aptitude Testing in the Selection of Students for Conference Interpretation Training". L. Gran and J. Dodds, eds. *The Theoretical and Practical Aspects of Teaching Conference Interpretation.* Udine: Campanotto. 105-108.

Moser, B. 1978. "Simultaneous Interpreting: A Theoretical Model and its Practical Application". D. Gerver and W.H. Sinaiko, eds. *Language, Interpretation and Communication*. New York: Plenum. 353-368.

Moser-Mercer, B. 1984. "Testing Interpreting Aptitude". W. Wilss and G. Thome, eds. *Translation Theory and its Implementation in the Teaching of Translating and Interpreting*. Tübingen: Narr.

Stubbs, J.B. & Tucker, G.R. "The Cloze Test as a Measure of English Proficiency". *Modern Language Journal* 58. 239-241.

A Psychometric Approach to the Selection of Translation and Interpreting Students in Taiwan

Etilvia Arjona-Tseng
University of Hawaii at Manoa

1. Introduction

This chapter describes the process used to develop a battery of tests for selecting the first three incoming classes for the Graduate Institute of Translation and Interpretation Studies (GITIS) at Fu Jen Catholic University. It also describes the selection of students for the English, Japanese, Mandarin, and Spanish programs. However, this description focuses on the English test sections only, since these sections constituted the core testing framework[1] from which parallel test sections in the other languages were developed.

The GITIS is the first attempt to create, in the Republic of China on Taiwan (ROC), a graduate-level professional school for translation and interpretation studies focusing on training practitioners in Mandarin Chinese and languages important to the Asia-Pacific region. The literature on existing Translation and Interpreting screening examinations generally focuses on descriptions of test structures and the types of mistakes the examinees make. We need a literature that addresses rater-training issues, decision-making rules, reliability and validity issues, scaling, scoring, and test-equating procedures (Gerver, Longley, Long and Lambert 1984; Lambert and Meyer 1988; Stansfield, Scott and Kenyon 1991). This chapter, therefore, attempts to address this need by discussing a psychometrically-based approach used to develop the entrance examination at GITIS.

2. The Research Basis of GITIS Examinations

The test construction process described herein is guided by findings from the Gerver studies at the Polytechnic of Central London (Gerver *et al.* 1984) and the experience gained in the U.S. Federal Court Certification Project (Arjona 1984; 1985). It is guided, as well, by general psychometric principles for test construction, edumetric measurements, as well as aptitude testing (Allen 1979; Anastasi 1988; Cronbach 1984; Cronbach and Snow 1977; Ebel and Frisbie 1986; Osterlind 1989).

3. The Approach to Test Construction

A test construction framework was developed. From this blueprint, English-language and L_2-language[2] test section matrices were developed. Thus, the English-language blueprint served as the basis for obtaining parallel texts in the other languages. A number of rating and scoring guidelines were also developed. Resulting data were subsequently used for test data analysis, item analysis, and inter- and intra-rater reliability studies. Data analyses from the pilot tests of the written examinations were used to fine-tune the examinations and obtain final test versions. Raters for both the written and oral portions were put through training sessions to ensure that a structured and standardized method of evaluation was followed.

The systematic use of quantifiable subjective and objective scoring methods enabled us to obtain correlations about the reliability of our tests and examiners. One example is provided by the scale for scoring the written compositions (see Illustration 1a, b, c, d, pages 71, 72, 73). Using this scale meant that scores given by each rater could be quantified. We could obtain inter- and intra-rater correlations. This meant that during the training sessions, raters were trained to an acceptable level of inter-rater reliability. This approach also enabled us to pinpoint reasons for a rater's unreliable ratings.

4. Entry Requirements for ROC Graduate School

In the ROC, the Ministry of Education decides how many students a graduate school may accept each year. GITIS was allowed 14 places to be divided among all its language programs each year, as the need arises[3]. The first year, 6 places were assigned to the Mandarin/English program, and 4 places each to Mandarin/Spanish and to Mandarin/Japanese. This *numerus clausus* does not apply to non-ROC candidates, who fall into a special quota. Two scholastic criteria determine entrance to a graduate institute: one, having an undergraduate diploma recognized by the Ministry of Education, and, two, passing the entrance examination prescribed by the graduate school to which the candidate has registered as an option.

Contrary to the ministry-controlled rules for undergraduate admissions, graduate institutes are granted flexibility in the design and administration of their own entrance examinations. Proposed graduate examinations can only be approved, *grosso modo*, by the Ministry of Education. The university is, therefore, the party responsible for administering graduate entrance examinations which do not deviate from the prescribed ministerial format.

Scales for Rating Writing Sample:

Illustration 1a. *Holistic Grade: Evaluates your General Impression of the Writing Samples*

5 **outstanding**, message expressed in a clear and highly effective manner, story line flows easily and is expressed with clarity; use of vocabulary and tools of language denotes exceptional command of the language.

4 **very good**, message can be understood with no difficulty; story line can be followed with no difficulty; use of vocabulary and tools of language denotes good command of the language.

3 **good**, despite distortions, message can be understood with some difficulty; story line can be followed albeit with some difficulty; average use of vocabulary and tools of language.

2 **borderline**, message can be followed with significant difficulty; story line difficult to follow; deficient use of vocabulary and tools of language.

1 **deficient**, difficult to follow message; story line totally garbled; clearly lacks vocabulary and other tools of language.

Illustration 1b. *Comprehensibility (Message) Grade: Measures how Clearly you Understand the Message Expressed in the Writing Samples.*

5	**outstanding**, message expressed in a clear and highly effective manner.
4	**very good**, story line can be followed with no difficulty.
3	**good**, despite distortions, message can be understood with some difficulty.
2	**borderline**, message can be followed with significant difficulty.
1	**deficient**, difficult to follow message.

Illustration 1c. *Coherence and Clarity of Expression*

5	**outstanding**, story line flows easily and is expressed with clarity.
4	**very good**, story line can be followed with no difficulty.
3	**good**, despite distortions, story line can be followed albeit with some difficulty.
2	**borderline**, story line difficult to follow.
1	**deficient**, story line totally garbled.

Illustration 1d. *Use of Language*

---

5 **Outstanding**, use of vocabulary and tools of language denotes exceptional command of the language.

4 **very good,** use of vocabulary and tools of language denotes good command of the language.

3 **good,** average use of vocabulary and tools of language.

2 **borderline,** deficient use of vocabulary and tools of language.

1 **deficient,** clearly lacks vocabulary and other tools of language.

---

5. The Proposed GITIS Examinations

The GITIS entrance examinations required proposing a plan that matched both ministerial prescriptions and institutional regulations. It entailed convincing the University of the need for change. The approved standard pattern for entrance examinations in this section of Fu Jen University[4] allows for two days of testing, a 90-minute testing period for each test section, and examinations in three categories, namely university proficiency, professional examinations, and oral examinations. (see Illustration 2, pages 74-75). The first task was to determine where this pattern allowed for flexibility. This was found in the examination categories. The 'university' or 'core subjects' category justified testing Chinese proficiency, current events, and world culture. The 'professional subjects' or 'foreign language' categories justified L_2 and L_3 testing; the 'oral examination' category allowed for a separate series of individual and group tests to be administered as selection examinations.

Illustration 2. *GITIS Entrance Examination Matrix*

Category	Test Section	Test Session	Test Sessions	Sub-section
University	1	Mandarin	Session 1	Synonyms
			Session 2	Antonyms
			Session 3	Stylistics and Usage
			Session 4	Writing Sample
	2	Culture	Session 1	World Culture
			Session 2	Current Events
Foreign Language	1	FL2	Session 1	Synonyms
			Session 2	Antonyms
	2		Session 3	Stylistics and Usage
			Session 4	Writing Sample
	1	FL3	Session 1	Synonyms
			Session 2	Antonyms
	2		Session 3	Stylistics and Usage
			Session 4	Writing Sample
		Mandarin		Interview
				Sight Translation

Oral Examination		Group Test		Recall
				Aural Discrimination
		Individual Test: FL2		Interview
				Sight Translation
		Individual Test: FL3		Interview
				Sight Translation

For design purposes, Mandarin was the first or 'A' language for all candidates; English was designated as the 'B' language, and Spanish or Japanese became the 'C' language. For scoring purposes, however, candidates could choose which language counted as L_1 ('A'), L_2 ('B'), and L_3 ('C'). All candidates had Mandarin and English. Only candidates for the Spanish and Japanese programs had L_3 tests. The second task was to define the content of each test 'section' (see Illustration 2, pages 74-75). The 90-minute test period rule allowed for divisions into two 45-minute sessions. Therefore, a series of sub-divisions provided the final number of tests needed. Each test *category* was divided into test *sections*, divided into test *periods*, which, in turn, were divided into two test *sessions*.

The GITIS entrance examinations had several goals. The College Dean had told me on repeated occasions, that in the ROC, admission to graduate school implies successful graduation. Therefore, the attrition rate in ROC graduate schools is customarily very low. This is contrary to the traditionally high attrition rates in Translation and Interpreting schools. Making student selection highly predictive of success became a priority goal.

The final approved test matrix called for a two-part examination. Part I was a five-part written test[5] that served to screen only those candidates with an acceptable minimal proficiency in their 'A' and 'B' languages. These candidates took the subsequent oral examination. The series of written examinations tested breadth of vocabulary (synonyms test), analogical thinking (antonyms), grammar (stylistics and usage), use of language (writing sample), and current events/world culture. As mentioned above, parallel versions were developed in English, Japanese, Mandarin, and Spanish. Part II of the test consisted in a series of individual oral and group tests which served as the final selection mechanism.

6. The Group Tests

The second part of the GITIS entrance examinations consisted of a series of oral tests administered either as individual or group tests. The group tests chosen were based primarily on prior research carried out at the Polytechnic of Central London, in England, for the selection of candidates for interpretation (AIIC 1978; Gerver *et al.* 1984). Two group tests were administered in a language laboratory where candidates took a recall test in both their 'A' and 'B' languages. After listening to the recording of a short passage, candidates were asked to write down their recall of the text as verbatim as possible. This test was scored using a scoring graph developed for scoring a similar test during the U.S. Federal Court Interpreter Examinations (Arjona 1985. See Illustration 3, page 77, for scoring graph). An aural discrimination test (see Illustration 4, page 78, for sample text) tested the candidates' ability to discriminate three types of embedded errors (grammatical, phonological, lexical) in a recorded discourse. This test was administered in all languages.

Scores obtained in these group tests were not included in the computation of student ranking. These test results were used only to guide and inform, when necessary, the jury's final decision, and were especially valuable for borderline cases.

Illustration 3. *Scoring Graph for English Recall*

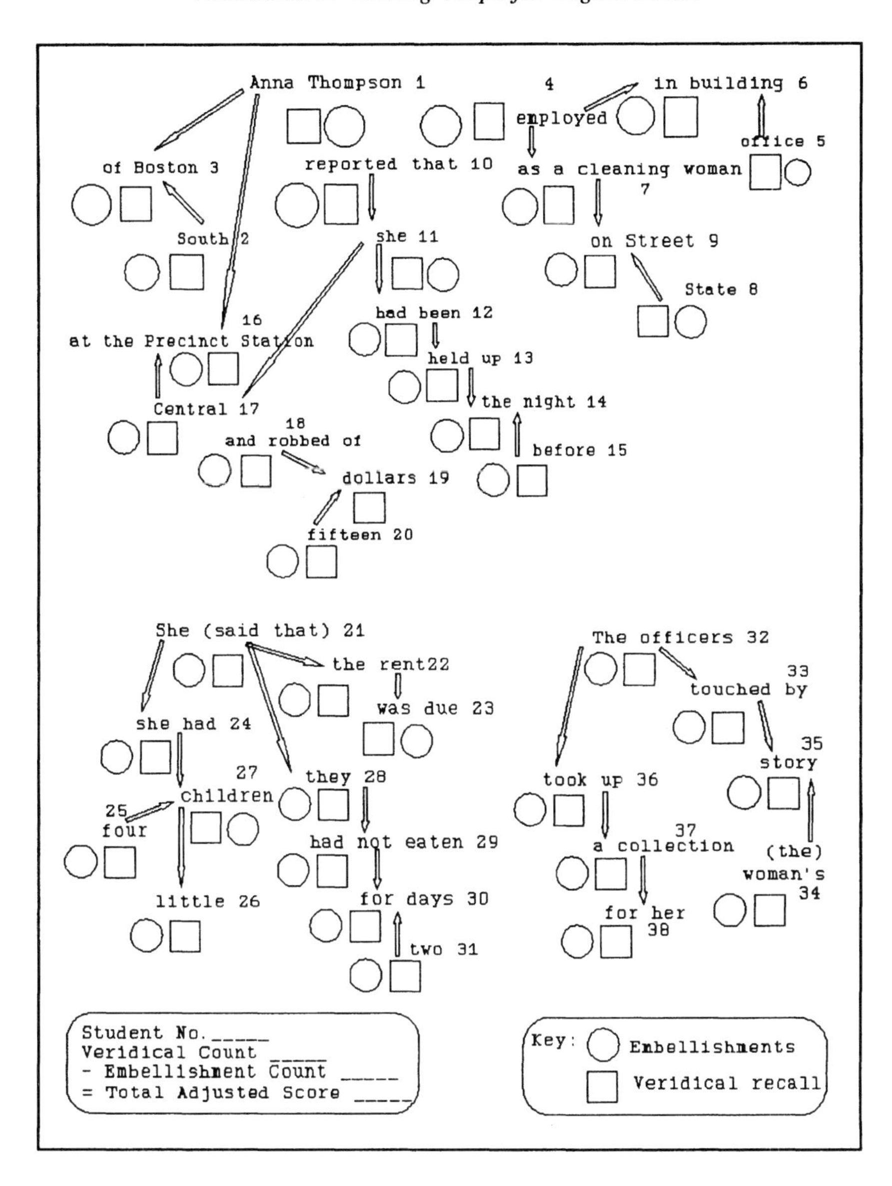

Illustration 4. *Aural Discrimination Test*

A friend who works for one of the city's biggest drug firms was telling me about the dress node in his office. It's all unwritten, of course, he explained, "but every desk in the office wears a suit and a time, even the guys who don't see anybody at all. You walk in wearing a cast and when you gone to your desk, you take your jacket off and hang it down on the hack of your chair. You never work in your macket. Then at lunch time, you put on your jacket before you go down to the asylum and when you get back, you take it on and hang it up on the back of your chair again. When it's time to leave at night, you put on your jacket and go home."

This office uniform, he went on, was necessary because one never know when one might be summoned to the boss's shadow or an important feeting - even though wearing a suit in crowded nubways and buses was a drag, particulary in heaven. There were no way he could come to work in shirtsleeves, he moaned - there were always that "important meeting" that might came up.

I proposed what I thought was a brilliant library. "Why not", I asked, "left a suit or a neutral jacket in your office all the time, so that it's there if you need it?"

"No good", he replied. "You has to be seen nalking in and out wearing a suit." End of discussion.

---

7. The Individual Tests

A six-member jury administered an oral interview and two sight translations to each candidate. This examining panel consisted of professional interpreters from the United States, Europe, and the Asia-Pacific region, who were invited to serve as external examiners. One day of training was provided prior to the examination date. The panel developed a series of questions for the oral interview. During the interview, examiners followed a pre-assigned questioning sequence to ensure standardization. Each examiner independently assessed the candidate's performance.

Candidates had to sight translate two texts (see Illustration 5, page 79), one each from their 'A' to their 'B' language, and *vice-versa*. Specific rating sheets were used to guide and focus the examiners' assessment of a candidate's performance (See Illustration 6, page 80). Depending on the number of languages tested, each individual test lasted from 50 to 75 minutes. Once all candidates were examined, the panel discussed each candidate individually and selected the successful ones.

Three types of results were possible: 'pass', 'conditional pass', and 'no pass'. A 'pass' meant that the candidate's command of all languages was judged satisfactory for admission into the Translation and Interpretation program. A 'conditional pass' meant that, in the panel's opinion, the candidate was trainable, but that one or both languages might require additional study abroad. The selection was very stringent. The first year, 225 candidates sat for the examinations; only 4 of the 197 applicants were successful in English and none of the 7 out of 21 applicants were successful in Spanish or Japanese. The second year, 189 candidates applied for English and 5 received 'conditional passes'. The third year, 179 applied for English, and two received 'conditional passes'; 21 applied for Japanese, and none was admitted. In total, during the first three years, only one candidate was given clear 'pass'.

Illustration 5. *Sight Translation Text*

The Comics Page, Values, and American Society

All of a sudden, America has discovered popular culture. It has always been there - but because it has been so ubiquitous and all-pervasive, we never have really noticed it. Perhaps our current concern with violence has led us to wonder if there is some connection between the mass media and everyday life. Whatever the case, we have lately become conscious of our general environment and there has been an explosion of interest in it - both in its physical manifestations (ecology) and its cultural ones (particularly popular culture).

Most of our attention (literally and figuratively) has been directed towards television, the dominant medium of our time, whose impact upon our phyches and the social fabric has yet to be fully understood. But not very far behind television, in terms of popularity, is the comic strip, a form of mass culture that has been around for many decades as an important ingredient of our daily newspapers.

Although comic strips do not have the psychological impact of television, numerous studies have demonstrated that comics do play an important role in the lives of the people who read them - as sources of diversion, escapism, and information about life. It is obvious, of course, that the terms "comic strips" or "funnies" are no longer appropriate. A large number of them have no humor, but crime, adventure, or love as their basic theme.

Relevance is everything to contemporary mass culture criticism. For something to be popular, it must deal with themes that are meaningful to large numbers of people. That is why conventions in the various popular art forms are important. If we accept the hypothesis that our popular arts mirror our culture, that somehow they are tied to our concerns and are based upon widespread assumptions, then the study of our popular culture becomes an important means of understanding our society.

Illustration 6. *Sight Translation Rating Scale*

Oral Entrance Examinations
Sight Translation Rating Scale: Chinese
Graduate Institute of Translation and Interpretation Studies
Fu Jen University
24205 Hsinchuang, ROC
903-1111 ext. 2415 or 2566
FAX 886-2-901-4733

Name: ________________ (Chinese)
Name: ________________ (English)

Student No.: ________
Chinese: ________
English: ________
Japanese: ________

Scale: 1=unsatisfactory 2=fair use or slightly objectionable 3=excellent/none

Language Use

Grammar	1 2 3	________
Register	1 2 3	________
Appropriateness	1 2 3	________

Translation

Appropriateness	1 2 3	________
Terminology	1 2 3	________

Fidelity

Over-translation	low med hi	________
Under-translation	low med hi	________

Resourcefulness 1 2 3 ________

Delivery 1 2 3 ________

Stage Presence 1 2 3 ________

________ Date ________ Examiner

8. The Traditional Test Scoring System

In China, scoring of examinations has followed a norm-references tradition since the time of the Imperial examinations. The traditional approach is believed to ensure a fair test to every candidate. This tradition requires that the following rules be adhered to:

- all candidates must be judged the same way - which was interpreted to mean that separate cut-off scores for 'A', 'B', and 'C' languages could not be made;
- rank ordering must be used to determine 'pass'/'no pass';
- a list of clear 'passes' must be made;
- a list of candidates falling within a second acceptable passing range must be made to fill any vacancies in the clear 'pass' list[6].
- the passing score must be linked to the number of places allotted by the Ministry for the incoming class;
- non-ROC candidates are customarily exempt from the regular examination process.

These rules severely constrained the testing process because the goal was to select only those candidates who were trainable in the opinion of an expert panel of professional translators and interpreters. The criterion-referenced[7] approach used for GITIS test construction meant that norm-referenced test[8] interpretations and rank ordering of candidates for selection purposes could not be acceptable selection methods.

9. The Written Scores

As mentioned, the written examinations were designed as preliminary screening mechanisms. Cut-off scores were established by an expert judgement procedure, or Angoff method. This procedure requires expert judges to state, in their opinion, which items of a given test a minimally competent person can answer correctly. Then, assuming blind guesses on the remaining items, a guessing score is computed, which serves, in turn, as the basis for computing expected chances and the passing score. The number of 'passes' and the cut-off scores can thus be established independently of any norm-referenced ranking, based on a group's level of linguistic proficiency. Once the cut-off score was established, a decision matrix was developed. Candidates who met the successful criterion level were identified by applying the matrix to the list of scores obtained in the written examinations.

Selection of successful candidates and setting the passing score, therefore, were not determined by the number of places assigned by the Ministry, nor by using isolated top section scores. Only candidates meeting the composite standard set by the judges could be marked as having met the established criterion for a 'pass'. As required by law, public announcement of the successful candidates was made and the candidates were invited to participate in the oral examinations.

10. The GITIS Oral Scores

Each candidate went through the series of oral examinations in the presence of the jury. After all candidates had been tested, detailed discussion of each candidate's strength and weaknesses took place. The objective was to reach a consensus as to which candidates deserved selection. Once the collegial consensus on successful candidates was reached, each examiner rank-ordered all oral candidates on a scoring grid. The ranking scale followed a pass/fail continuum. Scores for passing candidates fell in the passing range; those for non-pass candidates in the 'no pass' range. This allowed for a clear distinction, point-wise, between passing and non-passing candidates. Each successful candidate received, in addition, a specific number of 'pass' points per rater. A candidate's oral test score equaled the composite total of these points.[9] A candidate's total examination score became the total sum of points obtained in the written and oral examinations.

Candidates who had failed the written examinations received a score of '0' for the oral part of the examination, but were rank-ordered in the final composite list reported to The College Entrance Examination Council.[10] Standard practice required that the written test score be counted as 50% of the total examination score. The final entrance examination score would be the average of the written and oral scores. The GITIS scoring system disallowed such weighted averaging. Only candidates passing the orals could obtain the points needed to pass the entrance examination. Non-passing oral candidates could not accumulate the necessary points to fall within the passing range. This left unfilled positions vacant, since no one could fall within their range.

11. Implications of the 'A'-'B'-'C' Language Classification System

As stated earlier, examinations are offered in four languages, namely, English, Spanish, Mandarin, and Japanese. It is important to realize that the candidates can have any of these languages as their 'A' language. The Mandarin-English program, for example, is composed of two sections. One section is made up of candidates who have English as their 'A' language, and the other, of candidates who have Mandarin as their 'A' language. The same is true for the other languages. Candidates in Japanese and Spanish must have English at least as a 'C' language.

The GITIS scoring system required, in any given language, different cut-off scores for those candidates who registered the language as either an 'A' or 'B' language. This approach strongly shook the traditional Chinese view for grading examinations. Evaluation of all candidates in terms of their language classifications meant cutting across traditional ROC and non-ROC citizenship classifications. To the Chinese mind, this implies a questionable and unfair manner of grading. Prolonged discussions were necessary before the proposed 'A'/'B' distinction was allowed. However, the second year, an ROC candidate with a Mandarin 'B' required ministerial-level meetings before the University accepted the different cut-off scores that meant his acceptance into GITIS.

The fact that achieving an 'A' level Mandarin, for example, is almost impossible for someone who has not had life-long education in the language, is not fully understood. By tradition, selection is made along citizenship lines and not according to linguistic proficiency. That proficiency has nothing to do with a person's registered citizenship was a difficult notion to accept. At GITIS, making this distinction became the subject of heated policy-making discussions. Fortunately for future candidates, acceptance of the 'A'-'B'-'C' classifications and the need for differential cut-off or passing scores is slowly gaining ministerial and institutional understanding.

12. The Need for a Psychometric Approach to Aptitude Testing

A psychometric approach to Translation and Interpretation student selection implies following a number of procedures to ensure construct validation, such as standardization of test administration procedures, proper pilot testing of instruments and adherence to standard principles of measurement and test construction. Rater training, for example, enhances reliability in the evaluation of candidates' performances. Perhaps equally important, a psychometrically sound approach enables us to evaluate whether we are, indeed, achieving our stated objective of identifying trainable students.

Translation and Interpreting schools are known for their high attrition rates. The social and economic usefulness of educating students in programs that pride themselves on high attrition rates is increasingly questioned and voiced. Although a student selection process 'à la Fu Jen University' is a rare luxury, the advantages of such a psychometrically sound approach are obvious. The first incoming class has completed the two-year programme. Three of its four incoming students were successful in their attempt to become academically qualified translators and conference interpreters (their certification was held before an international jury of top-level conference interpreters with impeccable professional credentials). The fourth student had dropped out after the first month of classes, having realized that Translation and Interpretation was not an appropriate career choice. High success rates are anticipated for the classes selected during the subsequent two test administrations. Though from one perspective, the restricted number of selected candidates places a financial burden on the educational institution, from another perspective, such selection implies optimal use of institutional resources. The GITIS experience provides significant proof of this. Of the 11 candidates selected during the first three years, 10 are scheduled for successful completion of their studies. This 91% success rate is as unusual as the highly selective process in use at Fu Jen University.

Selecting a student body with the requisite aptitude goes hand in hand with the development of a sound instructional program. Identifying the 'trainable' candidate constitutes the first step of the instructional design system. Cronbach and Snow (1977), in their now classic study of aptitude testing, consider aptitude as *any characteristic of a person that forecasts his/her probability of success under a given treatment*, and state that *psychologically, aptitude is whatever makes a person ready to learn in a particular situation*. For them, then, aptitude is a predictor or forecaster - a *facilitator* of learning and performance (Messick, 1980). The importance of aptitude testing in our field cannot be over-emphasized. Translation and Interpretation entrance screening examinations, largely classified as aptitude tests in our literature, must be based on sound, professional practice. In addition, they must be designed so that subsequent analyses and test data interpretations can provide reliable information about results. An understanding of the technical meaning of terms such as *aptitude*, *skills*, *constructs*, *reliability*, and *correlations*, as well as of the uses and limitations of test data interpretations, must guide test construction in our field. Without sound test construction principles, our intuitions about *aptitude* cannot be truly validated, nor can we obtain a better understanding of who our *trainable* students are.

It is hoped that the dissemination of information about selection procedures used in different Translation and Interpreting schools will improve our ability to identify the criteria needed to ensure optimal selection of our students.

This article first appeared in *Perspectives: Studies in Translatology* - 1993:1.

NOTES

1. The testing framework (also known as test blueprint, test matrix, or test table) serves to indicate the content structure of a planned test.

2. L_2 would be Japanese, Mandarin or Spanish, as the case may be.

3. The 14 places are distributed each year among the language sections by a complex decision-making process. Thus, the second year, the 14 places were assigned to English. The third year, 9 places to English and 6 to Japanese.

4. Fu Jen University is administered by three Catholic religious groups. GITIS is under the Divine Word Missionaries administration.

5. The written examinations were generated using a Macintosh computer system and LXR-Test generating software. Written test scoring and test item analyses were carried out with a Scanton OCR machine and test analysis software.

6. A 'back-up' list is necessary because candidates on the 'pass' list do not necessarily accept admission to the given programme, thereby leaving vacancies that can be filled by those on the 'back-up' list.

7. A criterion-referenced test may be defined as one which relates examinees' scores to a well-defined cut-off score or *level* of performance or mastery.

8. Norm-referenced measures may be defined as ones used to determine an examinee's performance in relation to the performance of other examinees taking the same measuring test.

9. The number of points per rank is determined by the number of places that the Ministry allots for admission in any given year. The minimum total possible points for the last

successful slot possible, plus the bonus passing points awarded per examiner, define the passing score for that year.

10. The College Entrance Examination Council is a university-wide academic body presided over by the University Dean of Academic Affairs and comprised of all deans, chairpersons (undergraduate deans) and directors (graduate deans). It is responsible for all examinations given by the University, and, as such, receives and approves the final results and admission reports.

References

AIIC 1978. "Research on Procedures for Selecting Students for the Postgraduate Course in Conference Interpreting at the Polytechnic of Central London". Geneva: AIIC.

Allen, M.J. and Yen, W.M. 1979. *Introduction to Measurement Theory*. Monterey: Brooks/Cole.

Anastasi, A. 1988. *Psychological Testing*. New York: MacMillan Publishing.

Arjona, E. 1984."Testing and Evaluation of Interpreter Performance". M. McIntire, ed. *Proceedings of the Fourth Annual CIT Conference, Silver Springs: Conference of Interpreter Trainers*. 111-139.

Arjona, E. 1985. "The Court Interpreters' Test Design". Olivares and Elias, eds. *Spanish Language Use in the U.S.A.* Mouton Press. 181-200.

Cronbach, L.J. & Snow, R.E. 1977. *Aptitudes and Instructional Methods*. New York: Wiley.

Cronbach, L.J. 1984. *Essentials of Psychological Testing*. New York: Harper & Row.

Ebel, R.L. & Frisbie, D.A. 1986. *Essentials of Educational Measurement*. Englewood Cliffs: Prentice Hall.

Gerver, D., Longley, P.E., Long, J. & Lambert, S. 1984. "Selecting Trainee Conference Interpreters: A Preliminary Study". *Journal of Occupational Psychology* 57:1. 17-31.

Lambert, S. & Meyer, I. 1988. "Selection Examinations for Student-Interpreters at the University of Ottawa, Canada". *Canadian Modern Language Review* 44:2. 274-284.

Messick, S. 1980. "Test Validity and the Ethics of Assessment". *American Psychologist* 35. 1012-1027.

Osterlind, S.J. 1989. *Constructing Test Items*. Norwell: Kluwer Academic Publishers.

Stansfield, C.W., Scott, M.E. & Kenyon, D.M. 1991. "The Measurement of Translation Ability". Available from ERIC Clearing House. 1-26.

Quality in Conference Interpreting: Some Pragmatic Problems

Andrzej Kopczynski
University of Warsaw

1. Definitions

1.1. Pragmatics

In his classic definition, Charles Morris (1946) contrasts the term *pragmatics* with *syntactics*, which deals with the relationships between signs, and with *semantics*, which deals with the relationships between signs and their referents. *Pragmatics* deals with the relationships between signs and their human users. Another area of research for which the concept of *pragmatics* is reserved is the performative analysis deriving from the writings of Austin (1962) and Searle (1969).

For the purpose of this paper, I wish to adopt a broad meaning when I say that *pragmatics* is the use of language in a goal-oriented speech situation, where the speaker is using language in order to produce a particular effect in the mind of the listener. In these terms, *pragmatics* deals with situated speech, and is akin to the concept of *communication* in general.

1.2. Quality

The other key concept in my paper is *quality*. For our purpose, it can be defined as *a degree of excellence* or *a degree of conformance to a standard* (*Webster's Third New International Dictionary* 1976).

I believe that *quality* can be viewed in at least two different ways, which I will call *linguistic* and *pragmatic*. In its linguistic sense, *quality* in translation is viewed as a set of rigid standards of equivalence in content and form between the spoken messages in L1 and L2. Concepts such as *equivalence* (identity or similarity of meaning), *congruence* (identity or similarity of meaning and form) and *correspondence* (formally closest translation overriding differences between two languages) have been developed to deal with texts in L1 and L2. Their common feature is to view T2 strictly in terms of T1 in order to measure the fidelity of translation. Furthermore, they do not make allowances for larger contextual variables in the act of translation. Nonetheless, I believe that these concepts are useful in investigating the interpretation process. For example, one provides the fullest possible translated text (correspondent text) as a reference to see what the interpreter omitted, added or replaced, and why. This procedure is similar to a well-known method in discourse analysis where one provides default elements to investigate presuppositions.

In its pragmatic sense, *quality* is not an absolute value, but rather contextually determined. In other words, context "complicates" the problems of quality in that it introduces situational variables that might call for different priorities in different situations of translation. Let us assume the following variables:

- the speaker, his status and the status of his receptors;
- the speaker's intention in issuing the message;
- the speaker's attitude toward the message and the receptors;
- the receptors' attitude toward the message and the speaker;
- the interpreter, his/her competence, judgements, attitudes and strategies;
- the form of the message;
- the illocutionary force of the message;
- the existing norms of interaction and interpretation of a speech community;
- the setting.

These variables can affect interpretation in the following ways:

1.2.1. The setting and the form and content of the message. If we assume that a minimum standard for the interpreter is to render the cognitive, affective, and appellative content of the text in L1 (T1), then what may vary is that each of these components may be given varying degrees of importance on different occasions. For example, at scientific congresses, the cognitive content is usually the most important, whereas in political or trade negotiations, the affective or appellative content may come to the fore because of the need to influence people (cf. representational, expressive and appellative text types [K. Reiss, 1976]).

Moreover, varying priorities in rendering content vs. form of T1 may occur. In some settings, rendering the style of T1 becomes very important, as when translating literary or diplomatic discourses.

1.2.2. The existing norms of interaction and interpretation of a speech community. Sometimes, conflicting situations may call for readjustments in translation on the part of the interpreter, otherwise the interpretation may activate a wrong schema or be considered impolite in the target culture. To this effect, I will mention two examples concerning the formality-informality scale and taboo words.

A university lecture in Poland is usually a more formal occasion than in the United States. Hence, a professor is expected to use a more formal style than that generally employed in the United States. I once heard an interpretation of a lecture given by an American professor in which the interpreter readjusted a number of English colloquial expressions using more formal ones in Polish.

The second example deals with an American film entitled *The Last Detail*, in which a sentenced marine is being escorted to a prison located across the U.S. by two other marines. The dialogue between these marines is peppered with four-letter words. At a showing of the film, the interpreter attenuated all vulgar expressions, fearing that they would shock the audience. He was probably right: unrestrained use of four-letter words at the movies is still unusual in Poland. From my experience, I have noticed that in similar drastic situations, I too tend to instinctively attenuate the expressions or the style.

One case comes to mind, however, when my clients did not appreciate my restraint. The clients in question happened to be diplomats. It turned out that they would have preferred a more drastic expression even if it was not very polite. Such examples only go to show that there is no hard and fast rule or recommendation. Rather, each situation should be assessed by the interpreter her/himself.

1.2.3. The participants. As mentioned above, the participants are the speaker, the receptors and the interpreter her/himself - their status, intentions and attitudes. The status, intentions and attitudes frequently vary across cultures and therefore constitute a formidable challenge for the interpreter who has to meet often conflicting requirements.

One such conflict is the frequently-quoted empathy with the speaker and/or the audience. *Empathy with the speaker* is a metaphorical term meaning rendering the speaker's communicative intentions, style, as well as the tone of his speech, including paralinguistic and nonverbal signals (tempo, intensity of voice, gestures). The questions that arise are: Is it necessary or possible to render all of them? Is it necessary or possible to render all of them on all occasions?

This raises the more general problem of the role of the interpreter - should s/he be the ghost of the speaker or should s/he intrude, i.e. omit, summarize or add portions of text? I suspect that the majority of speakers prefer the ghost role over that of the intruder. As bilingual and bicultural experts, however, we have a more or less conscious tendency to readjust or intrude (cf. several interesting studies on the subject by Kirchhoff 1976; Morris 1989; Kondo 1990). One reply may be that interpreters will usually try to please the target audience, a notion that is in keeping with the recent theory of translation (cf. the *skopos theory* of Reiss and Vermeer 1984) pointing to the *dethronement* of the original text, or speaker (Snell-Hornby 1988). But the question still remains as to whether or not interpreters should do it? How far can they go without committing errors?

Other aspects to be considered are the varying relationships between the participants during interpretation, as represented below:

Speaker(S) ----> Interpreter (I) ----> Receptors (R).

A study by David Snelling (1989) provides at least three such possibilities which can be presented as a) S = R; b) S = I; and c) I = R, where "=" denotes a similar set of presuppositions, values, and background.

a) S = R. An example of this situation can be a technical congress where the speakers and the audience get together to discuss the newest developments of a field of study. On the one hand, I believe one can assume that the receptors are primarily interested in the content of T1 and the precision of terminology rather than its style. On the other hand, the interpreter, even if s/he is thoroughly prepared, cannot possibly match the knowledge and background of the participants of the congress. S/he, therefore, has to adopt a different strategy to achieve the quality requirements from those cases when her/his knowledge matches the speaker and/or the receptors, e.g. keeping close to T1 and to the speaker.

b) S = I. In this case, the interpreter shares the same set of presuppositions, cultural values and language with the speaker. If s/he interprets for a far-removed culture, s/he may be expected to expand on what the speaker is saying in order to explain culture-specific phenomena and frequently readjust the style of T1 in order to comply with the target culture. In this case the interpreter probably plays more of an intruder role.

c) I = R. This case is a mirror image of the previous one in that the interpreter shares common presuppositions, culture and language with the receptors. Therefore, s/he is entitled to make shortcuts in rendering the meaning of T1, which is also considered as an intruder role.

The picture is somewhat simplified in that other important factors may come into play, such as the field of discourse (topic of conversation, theme of the congress, etc.), level of formality (e.g. interpreting for the top dignitaries), and individual tastes.

*   *   *

Inspired by similar studies in the field, notably Buehler (1984), Ilg (1988), Kurz (1989), Gile (1990) and Kurz (forthcoming), I conducted a survey among Polish users of our services to assess their attitudes and expectations towards conference interpreting. The criteria, however, are my own (the most important ones have been discussed above), as well as the responsibility for the statements and conclusions.

2. Respondents

The survey addressed two kinds of participants in conferences: the receptors and the speakers. The questions, although formulated in a different manner, were basically the same, in order to determine whether the point of view entails a difference of attitude to the same problem, as well as to ascertain whether there would be any differences in assessment and attitudes.

Three different professional groups were addressed: 20 respondents were involved in the humanities (H) and included philologists, historians, lawyers, and economists; 23 respondents dealt with science and technology (S&T) and included scientists, engineers, doctors; and lastly, 14 respondents were diplomats (D). In all, there were 57 respondents. The questionnaire was not administered to delegates at a conference but rather to people who attended international conferences as speakers or hosts, or who participated in negotiations in one or both of these roles.

3. Questionnaires

The questions addressed the three following main concerns:

1a) The respondents were asked what they considered to be the most important function of interpreting in a conference.

1b) The next question was the same as 1a), except that the respondent was asked to grade the priorities alongside the proposed suggestions along a three-point scare. These suggestions were:
- rendering the general content of T1
- rendering the detailed content of T1
- terminological precision
- style
- grammatical correctness of utterances
- fluency of delivery
- diction
- voice qualities

2a) The next two questions concerned issues which seemed the most irritating in conference interpreting. Again, I simply asked the respondents to mention whatever h/he considered as most irritating.

2b) The respondent was then asked to rank the suggestions which were provided below, namely:
- faulty terminology
- ungrammatical sentences
- stylistic mistakes
- incomplete sentences
- lack of fluency
- poor diction
- monotonous intonation
- monotonous tempo
- speeding up and slowing down
- too general rendition of content
- too detailed rendition of content

The next five questions concerned the more or less active role of the interpreter (the ghost role vs. the intruder role of the interpreter). The respondents had to check "yes" or "no".

The questions were:
3. Should the interpreter empathize with the speaker's intentions?
4. Should the interpreter imitate the dynamics of speech - tempo, intensity of voice, gestures?
5. Should the interpreter remain in the background or be visible?
6. Should the interpreter correct a speaker's mistakes?
7. Is the interpreter allowed to summarize the speech?
8. Is the interpreter allowed to add his or her own explanations to clarify what the speaker has said?

3. Results

3.1. Functions

3.1.1. Speakers vs. receptors. From the results provided in Table A1, both speakers and receptors considered *content* more important than *form* in interpreting, ranking *rendition of detailed content* as the most important (78.9% and 73.7%, respectively). The second most important criterion for both speakers and receptors was *terminological precision* (68.3% and 68.5%, respectively). *Form* ranked third: for speakers, the most important being *fluency*, and for receptors, *style and fluency*.

Table A1. *Functions of Interpreting (in percentages)*

Function	Speakers			Receptors		
	1	2	3	1	2	3
general content	21.1			13.2	2.6	2.6
detailed content	78.9	5.3		73.7	13.2	7.9
terminology		68.3	10.5	2.6	68.5	7.9
style		5.3	21.1	2.6		28.9
grammaticality		21.1	21.1	2.6	10.5	13.2
fluence			36.8		2.6	26.3
diction				5.3	2.6	5.3
pleasant voice			10.5			7.9

3.1.2. H vs.S & T vs.D. A similar pattern emerged among professions. *Detailed content* was followed by *terminology* (75, 73.9 and 71.4, and 80, 60.9 and 64.3, respectively). Formal preferences differed: the H group favoured *grammaticality* and *style*, whereas the S & T and D groups preferred *fluency*.

Table B1. *Functions of Interpreting (in percentages)*

Function	H			S & T			D		
	1	2	3	1	2	3	1	2	3
general content	20	5		13	4.3		14.3		7.1
detailed content	75	5	5	73.9	4.3	8.7	71.4	21.4	
terminology		80	5	8.7	60.9	8.7		64.3	14.3
style		5	25			26			21.4
grammati-cality	5	5	30	21.8		8.7		14.3	21.4
fluency			20	4.4		30.5			35.8
diction			5		8.7	4.4	14.3		
pleasant voice			10			13			

3.2. Irritants (Table A2)

3.2.1. Speakers and receptors. Both categories agreed that the greatest source of irritation was *incorrect terminology* (47.4% & 57.9%, respectively). Respondents clearly differed, however, as to the second and third most irritating items: the speakers were more sensitive to the *exact rendition of the content* of their speech (ranked 2nd and 3rd). The receptors were sensitive to *unfinished sentences* (ranked 2nd) and *grammaticality* (ranked 3rd).

Table A2. *Irritants (in percentages)*

Irritant	Speakers			Receptors		
	1	**2**	**3**	**1**	**2**	**3**
faulty terminology	47.4	21.1	21.1	57.9	15.8	10.5
ungrammatical sentences	15.8	21.1	15.8		13.2	21.1
poor style		5.2	5.2	2.6	7.9	10.5
unfinished sentences	5.2	10.5	15.8	18.5	36.8	10.5
lack of fluency	15.8		15.8	7.9	10.5	18.5
poor diction					2.6	7.9
monotonous intonation		10.5	5.2		5.3	2.6
monotonous tempo						
speed-up, slow-down						
too general content	15.8	31.6	21.1	10.5	7.9	10.5
too detailed content				2.6		7.9

3.2.2. H vs.S & T vs.D. Among the professional categories, the most irritating feature was also *incorrect terminology*. The S & T group seemed particularly concerned with this terminological aspect since they also ranked it as their second most irritating factor. For the H and D groups, the second most irritating phenomenon were *unfinished sentences*. The H group also ranked *incomplete sentences* as the third most significant irritant, whereas the S & T and D groups focused more on *lack of fluency* and of *ungrammaticality*, respectively.

Table B2. *Irritants*

Irritant	H			S & T			D		
	1	2	3	1	2	3	1	2	3
Wrong term	45	15	15	74	26.1	8.7	42.9	14.3	21.4
ungramm sentences		20	15		21.8	17.4	14.3	7.1	28.6
poor style		10	10			4.3	7.1	7.1	14.3
unfinished sentences	20	30	25	8.7	17.4	8.7	21.4	43	14.3
lack of fluency			15	8.7	4.3	30.5	14.3	7.1	
poor diction	10		10			4.3			
monotone tempo			5		17.4				
same tempo									
speed-up slow-down								21.4	14.3
content general	25	25	5	8.7	17.4				7.1
content detailed				4.3	4.3	8.7			

3.2.3. The role of the interpreter (Table A3). There were certain common choices among all categories: all were in favour of empathy with the speaker and considered the ghost role of the interpreter as preferable. This preference entailed further clarifications, namely:

- most claimed that the interpreter should imitate the tempo and the intensity of voice of the speaker, but not necessarily the gestures;
- most respondents would allow corrections of the speaker (with some reservation) and additional explanations, a reply which was in complete

contradiction with the ghost role of the interpreter! Surprisingly, the speakers themselves agree that they can be corrected, contrary to the receptors who opposed the idea. However, the great majority of respondents excluded the possibility of summarizing speeches.

As for the active (or intruder) role of the interpreter, the most liberal judges were the humanities group, and the most restrictive, the diplomats, possibly due to the highly formal environment of their profession.

Table A3. *Role of the Interpreter*

	Speakers		Receptors	
	Yes	**No**	**Yes**	**No**
Empathy?	89.5	10.5	94.7	5.3
Imitation: Tempo	68.4	31.6	68.4	31.6
Intensity of voice	52.6	47.4	36.8	63.2
Gestures	21.1	78.9	7.9	92.1
Interpreter: Ghost	57.9	42.1	84.2	15.8
Correct Speaker?	52.6	47.4	60.5	39.5
Summarize Speech?	42.1	57.9	31.6	68.4
Add Explanation?	52.6	47.4	52.6	47.4

Table B3. *Role of the Interpreter (in percentages)*

	H		H & T		D	
	Yes	No	Yes	No	Yes	No
Empathy	95	5	91.3	8.7	100	
Imitation: tempo	50	50	73.1	26.1	85.7	14.3
Intensity of voice	25	75	47.8	52.2	57.1	42.9
Gestures	15	85	4.3	95.7	14.3	85.7
Interpreter: Ghost	75	25	78.3	21.7	78.6	21.4
Correct Speaker?	50	50	69.6	30.4	57.1	42.9
Summarize speech?	35	65	26.1	73.9	50	50
Add explanations?	50	50	60.9	39.1	42.9	57.1

4. Conclusion

The following conclusions can be drawn from the results obtained in this questionnaire. There was a lot of uniformity in the opinions. All of the groups gave preference to *content* over *form* as the main functions of interpreting, and cited *detailed content* and *terminological precision* as their top two priorities. They considered *incorrect terminology* the most significant irritant. They differed in the choice of formal categories that are important in interpreting. All preferred the ghost role of the interpreter, but nonetheless favoured some intruder operations. Was this because they considered those intrusions natural in interpreting? There were slight differences in liberality, however, along the speaker-receptor and professional dimensions.

Obviously, additional statistical information is called for. Furthermore, other aspects of quality assessment by the user could be investigated in terms of scales of formality of interpreting situations, typology of conferences and, last but not least, interpreter strategies in order to achieve optimum quality in any given situation.

References

Austin, J.L. 1962. *How to Do Things with Words*. New York: Oxford University Press.

Buehler, H. 1984. "Pragmatic Criteria for the Evaluation of Professional Translation and Interpretation". J. den Haese and J. Nivette, eds. *AILA 1984 Proceedings*. Brussels. 4.

Gile, D. 1990. "L'Evaluation de la Qualité de l'Interprétation par les Délégués: Une Etude de Cas". *The Interpreters' Newsletter* 3. 66-71.

Ilg, G. 1988. "La Prise de Notes en Consécutive: les Fondements". *Parallèles* 9. 15-41.

Kirchhoff, H. 1976. "Das dreigliedrige, zweisprachige Kommunikationssystem Dolmetschen". *Le Langage et l'Homme* 31. 155-170.

Kondo, M. 1990. "What Conference Interpreters Should Not be Expected to do". *The Interpreters' Newsletter* 3. 59-65.

Kopczynski, A. 1980. *Conference Interpreting: Some Linguistic and Communicative Problems*. Poznaö: UAM.

Kurz, I. 1989. "Conference Interpreting: User Expectations". *ATA Proceedings of the 30th Annual Conference*. 143-148.

Kurz, I. "Conference Interpretation: Expectations of Different User Groups". [in press.]

Morris, C. 1946. *Signs, Language and Behavior*. Englewood Cliffs: Prentice Hall.

Morris, R. 1989. "Court Interpretation: The Trial of Ivan John Demjanjuk - A Case Study". *The Interpreters' Newsletter* 2. 27-37.

Searle, J.R. 1969. *Speech Acts*. Cambridge University Press.

Snell-Hornby, M. 1988. *Translation Studies: An Integrated Approach*. Amsterdam: John Benjamins.

SIMULTANEOUS INTERPRETATION

Simultaneous Interpretation: Contextual and Translation Aspects

Linda Anderson
Concordia University, Montreal

1. Introduction

Despite its frequently used misnomer, "simultaneous translation", simultaneous interpretation is neither translation, albeit in a paced and oral form, nor is it strictly simultaneous with the input speech. Its aim is not to establish linguistic equivalents between two languages, but to communicate the meanings of a speech being heard. It is a phenomenon of both cognitive and linguistic interest: cognitive, because of the information processing the task involves as well as the interpreter's ability to juggle several concurrent operations; and linguistic, because of the type of information processing being done--the recoding of a message heard in one language into speech in another language.

The simultaneous interpreter may be viewed as a complex information processing device confronted by a paced, auditory, tracking task. Sequestered in his soundproof booth, he must analyze and comprehend a continuous stream of speech, shape, coax and contort the message as he perceives it into the mould of his output language, then speak it. At the same time, he is analyzing the oncoming stream of new data bits into intelligible information and monitoring his own speech to ensure that it is properly paced, intelligible to his listeners, and conveys the original meaning as he understood it, fully cognizant of the fact that there is no possibility, when he is in doubt, of asking for repetition or clarification of any point.

Despite the fact that it has been in ever wider use since its inception over forty years ago, relatively little is yet known about the parameters involved in the simultaneous interpretation of speech or about how or under what conditions it works.

In much of the empirical research that has been conducted on simultaneous interpretation, the general strategy has been to manipulate some aspect of the input information and to observe the effects of the manipulation on the interpreter's output. One approach to the issue of measuring interpreter output has been to use a latency measure of the time lag or ear-voice span (EVS) separating words in the interpreter's speech from corresponding words in the source speaker's speech. This interval is considered to reflect the time involved in processing the incoming information (cf. Barik 1971, 1972, 1973, 1975; Gerver 1971; Oléron & Nanpon 1965).

The characteristic time lag interpreters show is, in information processing terms, considered to be due to the accumulation of source language items in some sort of buffer storage while the central processor is working on previously received information. Long lags presumably aid this processor as they afford larger chunks of input to operate on, but because of assumed limitations in capacity of the buffer store, a very long lag can lead to displacement of items from storage and result in omissions in output (Gerver 1974a). Conversely, short lags can reduce cognitive load, but may lead to errors in output, since interpreters may be working on too small a bit for proper apprehension of a message (Barik 1973).

Various investigators have found that simultaneous interpreters have their own "constructive" way of segmenting input speech: these segments, evidenced in the chunks of source language speech which the interpreter's ear-voice span encompasses, are considered to be the units of meaning which the interpreter is processing at any given time (Goldman-Eisler 1967, 1972; Oléron & Nanpon 1965; Treisman 1965). In most cases, when given the option, subjects seemed to wait to hear the syntactic and semantic structure of the phrase before beginning to interpret it (cf. Goldman-Eisler 1972).

A temporal measure of the interpreter output is useful, since the EVS has been shown to vary with input manipulations such as information presentation rates and speech/pause ratios (Barik 1973; Gerver 1971; Oléron & Nanpon 1965), speech length (Oléron & Nanpon 1965; Barik 1973, 1975), and input language (Oléron & Nanpon 1965; Treisman 1965). By itself, however, the time lag measure of input load conditions is insufficient. There appear to be limits to the lag in that there is both a characteristic lag, related to the task and the interpreter (Gerver 1971; Treisman 1965), and a maximum lag, presumably reflecting the limits of human short-term memory. If task difficulty is such that subjects are already operating at maximum ear-voice span, further increases in task difficulty will not further lengthen EVS, but will result instead in poorer interpretation quality (Barik 1975; Gerver 1971, 1974).

The quality of the interpreted output must therefore be quantified in some fashion. Investigators have refined the analysis of interpreter utterances by developing classifications of output into general categories of omissions, additions and substitutions together with words correct, in the hope that these divergences from the source speech would provide clues to the underlying processes of the task under different load conditions. Such classifications, however, suffer from the considerable subjectivity inherent in rater decisions about the equivalence of linguistic forms. They also tend to ignore a primordial facet of interpretation quality--whether the interpretations are readily understandable to the listeners for whom they are intended.

The present article is a summary of three experiments conducted into both cognitive and linguistic aspects of interpretation. The interpreter's task is not performed *in vacuo*, and yet no one has yet investigated the contextual conditions surrounding it. The first two experiments therefore look at contextual factors surrounding performance of the task; the third focusses on its central recoding or "translating" stage.

2. Experiments 1 and 2: Contextual Factors Surrounding Performance of Task

A number of aspects of the environment in which interpretation takes place are universally assumed to affect the quality in interpretation, so much so that they are expressly incorporated into the interpreter's working conditions as laid down in his contract. One is that if texts are to be read in the course of a conference, an abstract or the complete presentation must be made available to interpreters in advance of the conference. Another is that the interpreter must have a comfortable view of the speaker and audience.

Linguistic context at the sentence level can affect performance during interpretation, particularly semantic context (Treisman 1965), and interpreters have been found to make errors based on wrong expectations arrived at on the basis of linguistic and non-linguistic cues (Gerver 1976; Seleskovitch 1968). Yet context effects go much beyond the sentence level (Bransford & Johnson 1972). A message for interpretation could be considered to be not a sum of sentences, but an organic whole, in which each sentence is interpreted with respect to the broader linguistic as well as situational context in which it is uttered.

The presence or absence of linguistic context surrounding a message should be particularly important in simultaneous interpretation when the message is contained in a prepared text which is to be read aloud. Interpretation is properly intended for spontaneous speech and any professional interpreter will testify to the fact that interpreting written texts presented orally poses particular problems and is quite different from interpreting spontaneous speech. Written presentations are tighter and more formal in style than oral, and speakers who read texts generally speak faster and more fluently than when speaking extemporaneously (Oléron & Nanpon 1965; Seleskovitch 1968). The hesitations of spontaneous speech can afford respite, processing or catch-up time for interpreters. For all these reasons, if speeches are to be read during conferences, an abstract that sets them in context and provides a general view of the main points and progression of the arguments, or better still the complete text of the paper containing both form and content is thought to be invaluable to the person interpreting them.

The total content of communication acts extends beyond the linguistic level, however, and includes, in addition, the extra-linguistic context surrounding the speech being delivered--the audience, the speaker's relation to it, his background, the purpose of the conference, the "sociolinguistics" of the conference environment. This information is available in varying degrees to the interpreter, who can process it as background to his analysis of the foreground discourse. Non-verbal, visual information such as the speaker's facial expressions and gestures and his audience's reaction to what he is saying is an integral part of the overall communication system that supports and complements the verbal portion in complex ways (Argyle 1972). It gives rhythm and effective coloration to speech, contours and punctuates sentences, provides a whole range of nuances that can supplement, attenuate, modify, correct or contradict the meanings of the verbal portion (Lurçat 1972; Mehrabian 1971).

Experiments 1 and 2 of the present research series were designed to evaluate empirically the importance of these linguistic and extra-linguistic contextual factors in the performance of simultaneous interpreters.

The purpose behind Experiment 1 was to ascertain whether prior information about either the context or total content of a message would make any difference to the interpreter's rendering of the message. The effects could be felt broadly at the perception and/or encoding level of the input speech -

analysis of the speech - its rendition. Experiment 2 focussed on the effects of the visual context, over and above the verbal content, on interpretation performance.

3. Method

3.1. Subjects

Subjects were 12 professional English-French simultaneous interpreters who had been working actively for a minimum of five years and who each had English as their "A" or active (output) language.

3.2. Stimuli and Apparatus

The input material for interpretation in all the experiments was taken from videotaped recordings of an actual series of conferences conducted in both English and French on the topic of university research.

Passages for Experiment 1 were taken from the formal, prepared presentations read in French by three different speakers. Each passage was broken down into approximately 4 minutes of interpreting "warm-up" material, followed by about 6 minutes of material to be analyzed. In order to constitute the written texts of the speeches, the three presentations were transcribed with false starts, repetitions, etc., eliminated in order to simulate more closely the texts of speeches which interpreters frequently receive in real situations. One page summaries of these texts were made for use in the "précis" condition.

Input material for Experiment 2 consisted of 6 passages (6 minutes long on the average) of spontaneous French speech which were taken from six different panelists who spoke during the conference discussion periods. The first 4 minutes of each input speech were considered warm-up material, and therefore not included in the analysis.

3.3. Procedure

For Experiment 1, three conditions were used: a "text" condition, where subjects just before interpretation received a written copy of the complete speech; a "précis" condition, where subjects read beforehand a summary of the speech which set it in context, highlighted its main points and structure, but was devoid of any phrasing to be used; and a "no information" control condition, where no such information was available[1].

Two conditions were used for Experiment 2: a "video on" interpreting condition, where visual information of the conference setting was available to subjects through a videotape recording of the conference; and a "video off" condition, where the video portion was turned off and only auditory information was supplied.

The dependent variable being interpreter performance, it was decided to measure two separate aspects of performance, its intelligibility and its information content, by means of two scales developed by Carroll (1966), and used by Gerver in his 1971 experiments. The nine-point Intelligibility Scale assesses the degree to which the translated version sounds like normal prose and would be understandable in the same way as if it had been originally spoken in that language. Since interpretation can be both highly intelligible and the product of an interpreter's creative imagination, the second scale, Carroll's nine-point Informativeness Scale, was also used to measure the more conventional variable of "accuracy". This second scale turns the accuracy or "fidelity" questions around by asking how much new information the original message is perceived to convey after the translation has been evaluated by raters. If it is judged to contain information that is missing or totally different from the message in the translation, the original is scored as highly informative. Conversely, the original will be rated as uninformative if the original tells the rater nothing new or more than the translation did.

Neither scale was developed for interpretation and the assessment of performance they afford takes no account of types of translation disruptions or of style. Nevertheless, since the *raison-d'être* of conference interpretation is the effective transmission of a recoded message (intelligibility) and the preservation of information in the process (informativeness), both translation scales were considered suitable, with minor modifications, for use in the present study of simultaneous interpretation.

For a full account of the procedure and design used in all the experiments, the reader is referred to the author's unpublished master's thesis obtainable in the library of Concordia University, Montreal. For the purposes of this report, we will simply say that stimulus tapes were played individually to subjects over earphones from a videotape recorder, while subjects' oral output was recorded by means of a two-channel tape recorder on one track of subjects' tapes with the input speech simultaneously recorded on the other track.

4. Results

Means and standard deviations of the intelligibility and informativeness scores for each condition in Experiment 1 are presented in Table 1, whereas means and standard deviations for subjects' scores on the two scales in the "video on" and "video off" conditions of Experiment 2 are given in Table 2. High numbers on the 9-point Intelligibility Scale and low numbers on the 9-point Informativeness Scale denote superior performance.

As can be inferred from Table 1, analysis of the data indicate no significant effect of prior information about the content of the speech on either performance measure. As for Experiment 2, whereas scores on the two measures were both slightly better with the video on (as can be seen from the t values given in the Table), here again, in neither case was the difference statistically significant.

Table 1. *Means and Standard Deviations of Intelligibility and Informativeness Scores as a Function of Degree of Prior Information about Speech Content (Experiment 1)*

Measure	Prior Information Condition					
	Text		Précis		No Information	
	M	S	M	S	M	S
Intelligibility	6.50	1.30	6.71	1.37	6.67	1.48
Informativeness	3.24	1.50	3.27	1.32	3.41	1.52

Note: Highest intelligibility score = 9.
Highest informativeness score = 0.

Table 2. *Means and Standard Deviations of Intelligibility and Informativeness Scores as a Function of Viewing Condition (Experiment 2)*

Measure	Viewing Condition				
	Video On		Video Off		t^a
	M	S	M	S	
Intelligibility	7.09	.81	6.96	.69	.94 ns
Informativeness	3.20	1.08	3.35	1.14	.62 ns

Note: Highest intelligibility score = 9.
Highest informativeness score = 0.
[a]Critical value for $t_{11,\ .05}$ is 2.20

5. Discussion

The results of Experiments 1 and 2 are somewhat surprising in that they seem to suggest that the contract clauses requiring that interpreters have a good view of the speaker and audience and that they receive the texts of any prepared speech in advance, have no foundation in reality. In the first experiment, when interpreters had only a general idea of the topic of the speech beforehand, they were able to convey as much information and just as effectively as they could after having read the complete text of the speech. Similarly, interpreters receiving only auditory input, deprived of all visual context surrounding a conference, were also able to perform just as well as those who were privy to the full extent of the communication situation.

There are other possible explanations for the results. A problem often encountered in conference interpretation studies is the high subject variability which can overshadow real effects of experimental manipulations. There was great variability among the subjects used in this study, in spite of the five-year experience criterion. Some idea of this variability can be ascertained from the ranges in subjects' mean scores. In Experiment 1, scores for subjects across conditions ranged from 4.3 to 8.3 in regard to intelligibility of output, and from

1.97 to 5.86 in informativeness. In Experiment 2, scores ranged from 5.6 to 8.0 for intelligibility and from 2.12 to 5.52 for informativeness.

It would seem necessary, in future research into simultaneous interpretation, to include far larger samples of subjects or to provide a stricter control over their level of skills. There was no evidence in the data of the present experiment, however, to suggest that individual subjects were distorting the overall performance values for the different treatment conditions.

It is also conceivable that inter-passage variability might have obscured the effects of the experimental conditions used. Certain passages seem to have presented greater difficulty for subjects than others, as evidenced by both intelligibility and informativeness scores. Intelligibility of output seemed generally to follow the level of informativeness, but not everywhere. It would be of interest to pinpoint exactly where the greater difficulty in interpreting certain passages lay, and why information should, in some cases, be conveyed well by subjects, albeit not very intelligibly. A more detailed analysis of subject transcripts might reveal whether the effects of linguistic and extra-linguistic context are really as negligible on interpreter performance as they were found to be in the two experiments as gauged by the Carroll scales.

In regard to Experiment 1, the fact remains that interpreters are accustomed to plunging into source speeches "cold", in the sense of not being able to predict what is going to be said on a topic. It is not uncommon for interpreters to know nothing more about a conference than its title. Furthermore, subjects in the "no information" condition were not completely uninformed, since they knew the topic of the speech beforehand. It may be that it is only when formal presentations are particularly complex, technical or scientific, which was not the case in the present experiments, or differences in delivery particularly great that interpreters gain real benefit from reading copies or précis of speeches ahead of time. Future research could be usefully geared toward elucidating this question.

As far as Experiment 2 is concerned, it may be that, as has been stated categorically by a renowned interpreter (Thiéry 1974), closed circuit television cannot be considered an adequate substitute for direct viewing of the proceedings. Hence, the "video on" condition may not have been sufficiently naturalistic to reveal differences in performance due to the presence or absence of the normal visual input of a conference. It was not possible to control the scope and amount of information provided in the video condition either; the information was pre-determined by the videotapes previously made of the proceedings.

As it turned out, subjects were markedly different in their apparent need to see proceedings on the screen. Some mentioned having experienced difficulty or discomfiture throughout their interpretation when proceedings were not visible, some mentioned eventually becoming accustomed to it, others were observed occasionally not even to look at the screen when the visual information was available. While interpreting particularly fast or obscure passages, most interpreters in fact, closed their eyes to the screen, an instance likely of the potentially overloading effect that content, here visual, has been found to have (cf. Schwartz *et al.* 1973).

It might be that it is only when input conditions are particularly difficult, or when speakers draw abundantly from their store of non-verbal communication aids, or when there is substantial interplay between speakers and their situational context that interpreters in practice need the visual portion of the conference environment to maintain performance levels. Abundant information can be garnered from the auditory medium alone, if the effectiveness of radio communication is any indication.

6. Experiment 3: Central Recoding or "Translating" Stage

An information processing formulation of simultaneous interpretation would set forth a number of stages in the task: the source language is first perceived, then encoded, meaning is decoded, a code switch occurs, meaning is recoded into target language speech and then speech is produced.

In the descriptive and experimental literature on simultaneous interpretation, the recoding task of the interpreter has been viewed in two diametrically opposed ways. One considers the task essentially as one of establishing semantic hook-ups between the two dictionaries that are thought to be located in the interpreter's brain. Among the multiple tasks demanding the interpreter's attention, the stages where the "translation" takes places, "translating" in the context of the present experiment referring to this dictionary match-up procedure, are often assumed (cf. Gerver 1971) to require the most processing capacity.

Opposed to this conception is the view which holds that the interpreter's task is to give lexical expression to formless thought or "meaning", the notion being that thoughts in another language are in some sense irrelevant (Goldman-Eisler 1972; Seleskovitch 1976). According to this view, interpretation does not essentially involve any conscious operation of "translating" input or recoding languages at all, the "meaning" of a message being to all intents and purposes encoded non-verbally. Whereas in the former view, the principle processing task is that of translating the input, in the latter, the attention is considered to be devoted primarily to the task of analyzing and structuring the input message.

If the results of Experiment 2 are valid, perhaps, as some theorists assert, simultaneous interpretation can essentially be reduced to a task of listening comprehension. All listeners "interpret" speech against the background of their knowledge and experience, an activity involving essentially the monitoring, encoding and short-term storage of speech. The only difference with simultaneous interpretation may be the relatively incidental extra requirement that the listener reformulate the message and produce it in speech (cf. Seleskovitch 1968). If this is so, where does the "translation" operation fit in?

The third experiment in this article was an attempt to ascertain the significance of the language switch in the interpreters' recoding processes, the objective being to find out indirectly, whether interpreters are engaged in "translating" input at all. Does the interpreter devote any capacity or time to recoding from one language to another?

The paradigm for Experiment 3 was suggested by the common instances of distracted interpreters inadvertently interpreting into the same language as that used by the source speaker. In these instances, the interpreter is not generating an instant playback of the source speaker's words, he is indeed "interpreting" the speech, relaying the message as he apprehends it in his own words. It is as though the interpreter were hearing the ideas without their form, somehow extra-linguistically.

Performances were compared on two simultaneous interpretation tasks which differed only in the requirement to switch from one language to speak a different one. Both involved the search for words to express thoughts received. One of the tasks required the interpretation of French input into English output ("French Interpretation" condition), the other was the interpretation of English input into English output ("English Interpretation" condition). The two interpreting tasks involved the same tasks--monitoring, decoding, storage, recoding/output-word search, speech production and monitoring for correctness--but in the unilingual condition, the input and output languages were the same. If simultaneous interpretation is merely the expression of thoughts in words, the fact of restating the thoughts in another language should, arguably, be of little account.

Performance in the two interpreting tasks was further compared with performance in two "shadowing" tasks, shadowing being the parrot-like, paced repetition of auditory input. The shadowing tasks, in this case of speech in English and in French, were a control for the "peripheral" aspects of interpretation, that is, the "simultaneous" perception/production of English and French speech. It is known that interpreting takes more time than shadowing (Gerver 1971; Oléron & Nanpon 1965; Treisman 1965). It also seems reasonable to assume that the level of processing involved in shadowing as opposed to interpreting is minimal (cf. Cherry 1953; Gerver 1971, 1974; Treisman, 1965), although the evidence is not yet all in regarding the amount of semantic processing commonly performed in shadowing (Shaffer 1973).

Table 3 gives a breakdown of the constituent operations in the four experimental tasks. The two interpreting tasks are distinguished from the shadowing tasks in the additional processing they require of input. Any difference in output between interpretation and shadowing, therefore, should be attributable to processes that are central to the interpreting task, i.e. decoding and recoding meaning. Similarly, any differences between French and English interpretation should be due to the language-switching operation, rather than to the word search/recoding activity.

The experimental question was two-fold. First, we wished to know whether the act of crossing language borders, separate from the interpreter's other tasks, requires any processing time. Differences in response latencies among the four information processing tasks would be considered to reflect differences in the number of stages involved in processing the information (cf. Carpenter 1975; Trabasso 1972). The language switch operation in the bilingual interpretation condition could also logically be expected to result in an increase in response latencies. As we have seen, however, there seems to be a characteristic latency attached to the task of interpretation itself, such that any increase in task difficulty tends less to alter latencies than to increase disruption in interpreters' output (Gerver 1971).

The second question in Experiment 3 is therefore to determine if the language switch occupies any additional processing capacity, if not time. More specifically, it is hypothesized that if performance is significantly poorer (or latencies are longer) under the French interpretation condition than under the English, it would indicate that the requirement to switch languages was commandeering some of the channel capacity available for processing the speech.

The reader is referred to the "Method" section for Experiments 1 and 2 and to the same thesis for a full description of the experimental subjects, materials, procedure and design. Suffice it to say here that subjects were the same 12 interpreters as in the first two experiments, and input material was spontaneous speeches in English and in French from the same videotaped conference on university research.

Table 3. *A Comparison between Processing Stages as a Function of Combinations of Input language and Task (Exp. 3)*

	English Shadowing	French Shadowing	English Interpretation	French Interp.
	perceive Eng. speech	perceive Fr. speech	perceive Eng. speech	perceive Fr. speech
	encode English	encode French	encode English	encode French
			decode meaning	decode meaning
Processing stages				code switch
			encode English	encode English
	produce Eng. speech	produce Fr. speech	produce Eng. speech	produce English speech

In order to induce the somewhat unnatural condition of unilingual interpretation (unnatural if consciously produced), an attempt was made to simulate the actual conference conditions in which it has been observed to occur, that is where two languages alternate in rapid succession. For the two interpretation conditions, subjects were instructed to interpret throughout into English, regardless of the language they heard the passages in. They were also given preliminary practice in the unilingual interpretation until they reported feeling comfortable with it.

The subjects' speech output under the four treatment conditions--shadowing from English and French, interpreting from English and French--was transcribed and scored for Informativeness and Intelligibility. As the results of Experiments 1 and 2 raised some doubts about the sensitivity of the Carroll Intelligibility and Informativeness Scales, a second index--devised by the University of Ottawa School of Translators and Interpreters for the detailed evaluation of written translations--was used as a control, an additional measure of the quality of output in the two interpretation conditions.

Response latencies separating interpreter output from source input were measured by feeding each subject tape, containing interpretation and original, into a polygraph, yielding source speech tracing on the top track of the paper record and interpreted speech simultaneously on the bottom. (For a full treatment of exactly how the ear-voice span was obtained, see the above-mentioned thesis.)

7. Results

Table 4 contains means and standard deviations of response latencies, in seconds, for the four combinations of input language and task. Table 5 gives the mean scores and standard deviations on the two Intelligibility and Informativeness scales for the four treatment conditions. Remember that high Intelligibility and low Informativeness scores denote better performance.

Table 4. *Means and Standard Deviations of Ear-voice Span in Seconds (Experiment 3)*

Task	Input Language	EVS (Seconds)	
		M	S
Shadowing	English	1.35	.30
	French	1.44	.60
Interpretation	English	2.80	.69
	French	2.98	.88

The only significant difference among experimental conditions in terms of ear-voice span was between shadowing and interpretation, EVS in shadowing being significantly shorter. No significant differences were observed between the two experimental conditions of interest, the unilingual and bilingual interpretation. The assumption of the present experiment that EVS length reflects the number of processing stages required of a task would seem to be borne out, in relation to the shadowing versus interpretation tasks. Mean response latencies even in shadowing into French (which most subjects were unaccustomed to producing in a paced task) were still considerably shorter than those obtained in interpreting even into the same language as the original (1.44 seconds versus 2.80 seconds).

Table 5. *Means and Standard Deviations of Intelligibility and Informativeness Scores as a Function of Task and Input Language (Experiment 3)*

Task	Input Language	Measure			
		Intelligibility		Informativeness	
		M	S	M	S
Shadowing	English	8.01	.33	1.33	.19
	French	7.31	1.12	2.03	1.29
Interpretation	English	7.28	1.11	2.01	.79
	French	5.86	1.32	3.09	1.37

Information Congruence scores on the two interpretation conditions correlated highly with scores on the Intelligibility and Informativeness Scales; hence use of the Carroll scales seems to be vindicated. Shadowing was significantly better executed than interpreting on both measures of output quality. This would suggest that interpretation involves significantly more processing than shadowing. It would also suggest that the assumption that experienced interpreters possess such deeply ingrained dictionary hook-ups that they automatically trigger translation equivalents (cf. Treisman 1965) is unwarranted.

The Task X Input Language interaction for intelligibility scores in Table 5 shows that subjects did convey the message significantly less intelligibly during French interpretation than English. Output was also less informative, but not significantly so. Given the similar (and perhaps preferred) time lag applying to both interpreting conditions, the language switch of the bilingual condition would seem to have meant somewhat diminished processing capacity available.

8. Discussion

The results are not too surprising because investigators, as mentioned earlier, have revealed relatively constant EVS under a wide variety of stimulus conditions. Subjects in this experiment also seemed to exhibit their own preferred EVS in both bilingual and unilingual tasks.

What is more interesting here is that the characteristic between-subject EVS in interpretation holds up when subjects interpret both across and within language codes. The extra processing stage postulated for the language switch in the bilingual condition was not reflected in any appreciably longer processing time (2.98 seconds for bilingual interpretation versus 2.80 for unilingual).

The similar ear-voice span in the two interpreting conditions could be considered to suggest a similar processing load in the two tasks, indicating in sum that a code-switching stage imposes no extra burden on the information processor. Nevertheless, as EVS is constrained by immediate memory, maximum capacity of subjects' memory may have already been reached in both forms of interpreting. An interpreter's "preference" for a particular time lag might outweigh the effects on EVS of any manipulations of the interpreting task, including interpreting into the same language. In any case, EVS appears to provide only a rough indication of task burden, and the effects of language switching on interpretations would have to be sought elsewhere, in the quality of the interpreted output.

As regards interpretation quality in general, given that the task of interpretation is first and foremost to relay information with minimal delay, it may be that heightened levels of interpretation task load (as in the bilingual condition over the unilingual) may be reflected more in intelligibility losses than in information content. Subjects appear here to have been prepared to sacrifice the intelligibility, though not significantly the information content, of their renditions while interpreting bilingually. Perhaps in difficult situations, interpreters simply throw out the information bits in the hope that listeners will perform the further task of properly reconstructing the bits of information conveyed.

The language-switching effect seems to hold up within the individual passages interpreted in the two conditions, English input being consistently better executed on both performance measures than French, although again difficulty did not show up in measures of ear-voice span. A surprising finding was that output quality in the French shadowing condition was strikingly similar to the unilingual interpretation condition in terms of intelligibility and informativeness, although more akin to English shadowing in terms of latency. The subjects of the present experiment in fact were highly variable in their ability to shadow French input, pointing up again the need in studies of interpretation to control the level of input and output language skills, even among purportedly bilingual interpreters.

The results of the present experiment are consistent with the hypothesis that subjects do some "translating" of source input, but the extent to which they do so is not clear since only intelligibility measures were significantly affected in the language-switching condition. Certainly code switching or "translating" could reasonably be expected to present problems in practice when the interpretation is of arcane scientific material or technical jargons.

While the difference in interpretation results can plausibly be explained in terms of the language switch-effect, other explanations are possible. Performance differences might have been due to intrinsic characteristics of the two languages themselves (cf. Aaronson 1974; Macnamara 1967; Treisman 1965). Differences could also be due to subjects' varying abilities to decode speech in their first ("A") and second ("B") languages, as some investigators have suggested (Nott & Lambert 1968; Schwartz et al. 1973; Gerver 1971). It is unlikely, however, that such input language variables could account wholly for the different quality of output in the two interpreting conditions, particularly as the difference in output occurred in spite of the oft-mentioned lexical similarity of English and French (Barnett 1977; Taylor 1976), which might be expected to attenuate language-switching effects.

A more serious objection is that the English-French interpretation condition represents a situation that is too unnatural to be comparable to the normal interpretation done in real conference conditions. A few subjects did mention feeling ill at ease or tired while performing it. Perhaps the processing demands and the time required of the unilingual interpretation are due not to normal processes of interpretation but to subjects' relative lack of conscious practice or their difficulty in performing it.

It is possible too that the processing operations of unilingual interpretation, contrary to the bilingual, might have been primarily devoted to monitoring output in order to ensure that it was not mere shadowing. Certainly, the word-search operation could conceivably have been short-circuited--a source language unit having the potential of being plucked directly for use in target language speech--and this could have presented a problem to subjects who had been instructed to "interpret". There are three reasons, however, which would make it unlikely that the "testing for similarity" form of output monitoring during English-English interpretation was so consuming as to make it completely incomparable to French interpretation. Output monitoring regularly occurs in normal bilingual interpreting; the lexical and syntactic similarity between interpreter output and source input during the unilingual interpretation condition varied consistently between subjects (as does interpreter output during normal interpretation); and finally unconsciously unilingual interpretation is a frequent occurrence under real conference conditions.

If inhibitory factors were indeed operative during English-English interpretation as compared with the French-English, it could reasonably be expected to have taken longer or to be less intelligible or informative than French-English interpretation, which is a highly polished and practised skill with all subjects. The reverse was found, particularly in regard to intelligibility.

Two words of caution are in order as to how far the present findings may reasonably be generalized. First, only two input languages were used, and languages spoken by native French-speaking bilinguals at that. Second, despite every attempt to simulate "real-life" interpretation conditions throughout the study, the diminished situational context of the experimental conditions made the situation necessarily artificial for subjects, in the sense of not being experienced from an interpretation booth under actual conference conditions.

The research reported here can only be considered an exploratory attempt to gain an understanding of aspects of simultaneous interpretation performance which had been almost completely ignored by researchers, issues of practical and theoretical interest. It will be up to future research to determine the extent of the translation recoding in simultaneous interpretation, and to find out whether access to the full linguistic context or the rich visual context of a communication situation makes any difference in simultaneous interpretations of it. If researchers would turn toward the interpreters' "black box" to determine exactly what does occur between the moments of encoding input and of producing output, it could afford exciting insights into the way we process semantic information.

Notes

1. The first two conditions used are typical of the "real" interpretation situation.

References

Aaronson, D. 1974. "Stimulus Factors and Listening Strategies in Auditory Memory: A Theoretical Analysis". *Cognitive Psychology* 6. 108-132.

Argyle, M. 1972. "Non-verbal Communication in Human Social Interaction". R.A. Hinde, ed. *Non-verbal Communication*. Cambridge University Press.

Barik, H.C. 1971. "A Description of Various Types of Omissions, Additions and Errors of Translation Encountered in Simultaneous Interpretations". *META* 16. 199-210.

Barik, H.C. 1972. "Interpreters Talk a Lot, Among Other Things". *Babel* 3-10. (a).

Barik, H.C. 1973. "Simultaneous Interpretation: Temporal and Quantitative Data". *Language and Speech* 16. 237-270.

Barik, H.C. 1975. "Simultaneous Interpretation: Qualitative and Linguistic Data". *Language and Speech* 18. 272-297.

Barnett, G.A. 1977. "Bilingual Semantic Organization: A Multidimensional Analysis". *Journal of Cross-Cultural Psychology* 8. 315-330.

Bransford, J.D. & Johnson, M.K. 1972. "Contextual Prerequisites for Understanding: Some Investigations of Comprehension and Recall". *Journal of Verbal Learning and Verbal Behavior* 11. 717-726.

Carpenter, P.A. & Just, M.A. 1975. "Sentence Comprehension: A Psycholinguistic Processing Model of Verification". *Psychological Review* 82. 45-73.

Carroll, J.B. 1966. "An Experiment in Evaluating the Quality of Translations". *Mechanical Translation* 9. 55-66.

Cherry, E.C. 1953. "Some Experiments on the Recognition of Speech with One and with Two Ears". *Journal of the Acoustical Society of America* 25. 975-979.

Gerver, D. 1971. *Aspects of Simultaneous Interpretation and Human Information Processing*. Oxford University. [Unpublished Doctoral Dissertation].

Gerver, D. 1974. "The Effects of Noise on the Performance of Simultaneous Interpreters: Accuracy of Performance". *Acta Psychologica* 38. 159-167.

Gerver, D. 1976. "Empirical Studies of Simultaneous Interpretation: A Review and a Model. R.W. Brislin ed. *Translation: Applications and Research*. New York: Gardner Press.

Goldman-Eisler, F. 1967. "Sequential Temporal Patterns and Cognitive Processes in Speech". *Language and Speech* 10. 122-132.

Goldman-Eisler, F. 1972. "Segmentation of Input in Simultaneous Interpretation". *Journal of Psycholinguistic Research* 1. 127-140.
Lurçat, L. 1972-1973. "Du Geste au Langage". *Bulletin de Psychologie* 26. 501-505.
Macnamara, J. 1967. "The Bilingual's Linguistic Performance: A Psychological Overview". *Journal of Social Issues* 23. 58-77.
Mehrabian, A. 1971. *Silent Messages*. Belmont, California: Wadsworth.
Nott, C.R. & Lambert, W.E. 1968. "Free Recall of Bilinguals". *Journal of Verbal Learning and Verbal Behavior* 7. 1065-1071.
Oléron, P. & Nanpon, H. 1965. "Recherches sur la Traduction Simultanée". *Journal de Psychologie Normale et Pathologique* 62. 73-94.
Schwartz, J., Singer, J. & Macnamara, J. 1973. "An Analytic Comparison of Listening in Two Languages". *The Irish Journal of Education* 1. 40-52.
Seleskovitch, D. 1968. "L'Interprète dans les Conférences Internationales". Paris: Minard.
Seleskovitch, D. 1976. "Interpretation, a Psychological Approach to Translation". R.W. Brislin, ed. *Translation: Applications and Research*. New York: Gardner Press.
Shaffer, L.H. 1973. "Latency Mechanisms in Transcription". S. Kornblum, ed. *Attention and Performance IV*. New York: Academic Press.
Taylor, I. 1976. "Similarity between French and English Words - a Factor to be Considered in Bilingual Language Behavior?" *Journal of Psycholinguistic Research* 5. 85-94.
Thiéry, C. 1974. "Can Simultaneous Interpreting Work?" *AIIC Bulletin* 2. 3-5.
Trabasso, T. 1972. "Mental Operations in Language Comprehension". J.B. Carroll & R.O. Freedle, eds. *Language Comprehension and the Acquisition of Knowledge*. Washington, D.C.: V.H. Winston.
Treisman, A. 1965. "The Effects of Redundancy and Familiarity on Translating and Repeating Back a Foreign and a Native Language". *British Journal of Psychology* 56. 369-379.

A Description of Various Types of Omissions, Additions and Errors of Translation Encountered in Simultaneous Interpretation[1]

Henri C. Barik
University of North Carolina

1. Introduction

In simultaneous interpretation, the interpreter's version may depart from the original version in three general ways: the interpreter (henceforth abbreviated T for "translator," since it cannot conveniently be abbreviated "I") may omit some material uttered by the speaker (abbreviated S), he may add some material to the text, or he may substitute material, resulting in his saying not quite the same thing as the S. If the substitution is at considerable variance with the original version, we may speak of an "error" of translation.[2] This chapter presents a very general classification or coding scheme developed in relation to these three types of events, along with some relevant data. The work was carried out in the context of an investigation of simultaneous interpretation in which Ts of varying proficiency levels (professional Ts, "student" Ts and "amateurs") were required to simultaneously interpret several passages recorded on tape, which represented different types of materials (spontaneous, semi-prepared and fully prepared or "formal" material), the languages involved being English and French.[3] The coding system is necessarily subjective to a large extent since it was developed by one person only (the writer), though in consultation with another qualified person, and there was substantial agreement between the two judges in the codes assigned to a few sample texts. Still, it may be of some value to interpreters and to other researchers interested in the issue.

To arrive at the coding scheme, the recorded materials (there were 48 recordings altogether, each of 6 Ts interpreting 8 passages) were monitored several times and were followed at the same time on transcripts of the texts. The S and T versions, which were recorded on different tracks of the tape, could be considered either separately or simultaneously. All events judged to represent departures, however slight, of the interpretation from the original were noted and coded, being reported on the S transcript in the case of omissions, on the T transcript in the case of additions, and on both transcripts in the case of substitutions or errors, as shown in the brief example at the end of the present article.[4] The list of departures so produced was reconsidered a number of times, and items relating to the same type of event were combined. From this operation emerged the final coding scheme employed in the study, which we now describe.

2. Coding Scheme

2.1. Omissions

These, as stated, refer to items present in the original version which are left out of the translation by the T. Here we are dealing with clear omissions and not omissions resulting from the substitution of one thing for another by the T; the latter fall under the category of substitutions and errors. Omissions are determined on the basis of the final content of the original message, so that it is not considered an omission if the T does not translate a lexically irrelevant repetition or "false start" on the part of the S. Four main types of events fall under the heading of omissions (coded M, for "missing" material):

a) M1: skipping omission – omission of a single word or short phrase by T, who seems to skip over it. This type of omission usually refers to a qualifying adjective or some related event being left out of the translation by the T. The omission does not alter the grammatical structure of the sentence and results in minimal loss of meaning.

S version: ... un instrument *assez* difficile ...
T version: ... a difficult instrument ...

Such skipping omissions are of minor importance, and most of them are probably acceptable within the context of simultaneous interpretation. To these omissions were added some instances of other similar types of events, such as the omission of a preposition or a conjunction due to the restructuring of a sentence where there is little change in meaning.

S version: ... les garçons continuaient à grandir jusqu'à 18 ou 20 ans, *alors que* de nos jours ...
T version: ... boys continued to grow until 18 or 20. Nowadays...

b) M2: comprehension omission – omission where it appears that the T fails to comprehend or is unable to interpret part of the text. There is thus an interruption in his translation. This type of omission usually involves larger units of material, resulting in a definite loss in meaning. It may also result in disjointed speech on the part of the T, consisting of "bits and pieces" of translation.

S version: ... depuis l'époque où *il avait coutume de venir nous voir* il y a des années *à la Jamaïque*. Je n'ai jamais *admiré ou aimé personne plus que lui*...
T version: ... since the time when years ago ... I have never ...

Such omissions are obviously more serious than the first type.

c) M3: delay omission – as a possible subcategory of *M2*, we coded omissions which seemed to be due in large part to the delay of the T in his translation, as judged from listening to the tape. This would happen when, as the T was giving his translation of a segment of the text, the S resumed speaking, with the result that some of what S said did not seem to "register" with the T, who would then either wait until the beginning of a new unit of meaning or else simply bypass what had been said in order to "catch up." Whereas in *M2*, the T did not seem to comprehend what was said or was unable to convert it into the target language, in the present category, the assumption was that, had the T not lagged behind in his translation and had he been able to pay attention to what was being said, he may have been able to translate it. Of course, the T must necessarily lag slightly behind the S in his delivery, so that delay is a permanent factor to take into consideration; however, in this case, it appeared to be possibly the primary reason for the omission. There is, however, no hard and fast distinction between omission types *M2* and *M3*, and a large subjective element was involved when deciding which category was the more applicable in a particular instance.

d) M4: compounding omission – in the three types of omissions above, although disjointed speech may have resulted (*M2* and *M3*), the "logic" of the text or the relationship between the grammatical units was not altered. In some cases, however, the T seemed to recombine or compound elements from different clause groupings by omitting some material, with the result that the sentence had a slightly altered meaning, even if the gist of what was said was maintained.

S version: ... *J'étais à Londres* mercredi soir *lorsque* la nouvelle s'est répandue que ...
T version: ... Wednesday evening the news spread that ...

In this example, the T version carries the gist of the message but, through omitted material, compounds several units, giving the sentence a different meaning. This is not a case of disjointed material as in previous categories, since the T's delivery is smooth, and it appears that he selectively regrouped material from different constructions, forming a new entity. This type of omission, though not too common, is rather interesting. Such omissions sometimes seem to result from a lengthy delay on the part of the T: as the T is translating one segment of text, the S resumes speaking and it appears that part of what he says fails to register with the T, who may combine parts of different segments, if the contents permit it. Although such compounding omissions associated with delay were initially coded separately from those seeming to stem from selective encoding on the part of the T, the two instances were subsequently combined in the final coding scheme.

In addition to the above types of omissions, some other instances of omitted material were also coded at first and later discarded since they represent inconsequential omissions, some of which, as in *ii*) below, are even desirable. Among these were the following: *i*) omission of connective "and" (or French *et*) between words, phrases or sentences, where its omission is not disruptive; *ii*) omission of superfluous and often untranslatable material, in the form of fillers such as *well*, *now*, *you see*, in English, or *n'est-ce pas*, *eh bien*, in French. These occurred occasionally in spontaneous and semi-prepared texts; *iii*) omission of definite articles, etc., which should have been given; *iv*) omission of specification, as when, for example, *this young man* is rendered in translation as *the young man*, or when a specified item such as *children* is rendered by a corresponding pronoun such as *they*, where its reference is understood from the context.

These types of omissions are in fact quite acceptable within the context of simultaneous interpretation. Our concern was more with those departures of the translation from the original which to some degree affect the meaning of what is said. In some instances, such as omission type *M1*, this represents a very minor departure; in other cases it is more serious.

2.2. Additions

This category refers to material which is added outright to the text by the T. New material introduced by the T on account of an error of translation, even though it represents something which is not in the original, is not considered an addition but falls instead under the category of substitutions, to be discussed subsequently. Repetitions and false starts on the part of the T are not considered additions to the text. Four types of events constituting additions may be specified:

a) A1: qualifier addition – addition of a qualifier or a qualifying phrase not in the original version.

S version: ... ils gardaient tous deux enracinés en eux ...
T version: ... they both had *deeply* rooted within themselves ...

Here the T, possibly for emphasis, has added a qualifier not in the original text.

b) A2: elaboration addition – addition in the form of an elaboration or other straight addition to the text.

S version: ... je dois rester conscient de ce qui est juste ...
T version: ... I must be aware *and conscious* of what is just *and fair* ...

S version: ... he'll major in medicine, in pre-med, ...
T version: ... en se spécialisant ... au cours prémédical, *c'est-à-dire le ... MPC*

In these examples, the T further elaborates what the S is saying. In the second example the elaboration consists of quite extraneous, albeit helpful material, the T making reference to a specific program of studies (mathematics, physics, chemistry) directed at pre-medical students in France. Additions of types A1 and A2 refer essentially to the same sort of event and could in fact be combined, though they have not been in the study.

c) A3: relationship addition – addition of a connective or of other material which results in a relationship of elements or of sentences not present in the original.

S version: ... J'ai beaucoup apprécié aussi l'interprétation du film. Les deux grandes vedettes étaient ...
T version: ... I also enjoyed very much the performance of the actors ... *because* the two stars were ...

Here the T is introducing a causal relationship not explicitly stated in the original. This type of addition is somewhat more serious than the previous ones since it introduces some new meaning or relationship to what is being said, even if the gist is retained, whereas types *A1* and *A2* elaborate what is being said without altering the meaning.

d) A4: closure addition – addition which accompanies rephrasing, omission or misinterpretation on the part of the T and which serves to give "closure" to a sentence unit, without adding anything substantial to the sentence.

S version: ... et leur tour de poitrine augmente plus rapidement que leur tour de tête ...
T version: ... and their chest measurement *also* increases ...

Here the T has missed part of the original, and to give closure to his sentence he adds the word "also."

S version: ... des messieurs qui décident ... du choix des livres qu'ils vont publier et de la façon dont ils vont le faire ...
T version: ... men who decide ... the selection of the books which are going to be published and how they're going to be offered *to the public* ...

In this second example, although the gist of what is said is retained, it is surmised that the T has misinterpreted some of the text, since a more straightforward translation of *la façon dont ils vont le faire* would be *the way in which they are going to do it*, without any mention of *offering* or of *the public*. We assume that the T misunderstood something relating to *offert* in the place of *le faire*, resulting in his version: *how they're going to be offered....* To give closure to the sentence, the phrase *to the public*, which is clearly extraneous to the text, is added. The part which is added is of little consequence, but this is not the case for the part which is misunderstood or substituted, which represents a more serious departure.

In addition to the above, a few other types of additions were noted and excluded in the final coding scheme since they were judged inconsequential and, in most cases, too few in number. They may be described as follows: *i*) addition of connective *and* (or in French *et*) between phrases or sentences, resulting in a linking of separate units. This was fairly common with some Ts for certain passages; *ii*) addition of specification, substituting *this/that* for *the* or some similar event, or specifying an item referred to pronominally in the original; iii) translation of language-specific items not required in the target language, as when the definite article is carried over from French into English: e.g. *the* President Kennedy; *iv*) addition of preposition or other item resulting in an ungrammatical structure, but not contributing to or affecting the meaning of the material; *v*) addition on the part of the T of extraneous material or comment not related to the text. This is restricted to *amateur* Ts (persons fluently bilingual but with no training in interpretation) who occasionally, for example, "filled" a missing item by saying *the ... (blank)* or *the ... (something)* in place of the item, and who at times added remarks indicative of slight annoyance, to say the least!

3.3. Substitutions and Errors

This category refers to material which is substituted by the T for something said by the S. The substitution may involve a single word, or a whole clause; and whereas some substitutions hardly affect the meaning of what is being said, others alter it considerably and represent more serious "errors" of translation. A substitution necessarily represents a combination of omission and addition, but is considered as a category independently of these events. Five types of substitutions (errors) have been specified, some involving subcategories:

a) E1: mild semantic error – error or inaccuracy of translation of some lexical item, which only slightly distorts the intended meaning. Such errors may be associated with an awkward translation. The inaccuracy is restricted to the lexical item or expression, and does not affect the rest of the unit of which it is part.

S version: ... il n'a jamais montré de *malveillance* ni de *méchanceté* ...
T version: ... he never showed an *evil mind* or an *evil reaction* ...

Here the T's version is slightly awkward and inaccurate, but the gist of what is said is fairly well retained.

b) E2: gross semantic error – error of translation of some lexical item which substantially changes the meaning of what is said. Here again, the error is primarily limited to a specific item and does not affect the rest of the unit. Three types of events fall in this category:

i) E2a: error stemming from assumed misunderstanding by T of some lexical item because of a *homonym* or near-homonym, or because of confusion in reporting with a near-sounding word.

S version: ... l'autocritique est l'*arme* secrète de la démocratie ...
T version: ... (self-criticism is) the secret *soul* (of democracy) ...

Here the T apparently misunderstood *l'âme* for *l'arme*, resulting in his translation.

S version: ... la *diplomatie* parlementaire ...
T version: ... parliamentary *democracy* ...

Here it is assumed that in listening or in reporting, the T confused the words "diplomacy" and "democracy".

ii) E2b: error of false reference, possibly stemming from confusion and having its basis in the text (and thus differing from the error of "confused reporting" of type *E2a*, which brings an element extraneous to the text).

S version: ... nous savons qu'*il* avait foi ...
T version: ... we know that *we* had faith ...

Here it may be that the T has confused the subject of the subordinate clause with that of the principal clause, leading to an error or "false reference."

S version: ... ce qui n'empêche pas les enfants de la nouvelle génération d'être plus grands que leurs *parents* ...
T version: ... which doesn't prevent children ... from being taller than their *children* ...

Such errors are probably less damaging than those falling under *E2a*, since the listener probably realizes that the T has made a mistake of reference and can "correct" it, but this may be more difficult to do in the case of errors of type *E2a*.

Under this category are also included a few instances of displaced reference:

S version: ... I believe it was *anyway* — this is the comment made in *Time magazine* ...
T version: ... je crois qu'il s'agissait — *en tout cas*, c'est ce que disait *Time magazine* ...

Here, in the original version, *anyway* refers to *I believe it was*, as can be determined from S's delivery. The T has displaced it and incorporated it into the following unit, to give "anyway, that is what *Time magazine* said."
iii) E2c: error of meaning, not due to confusion:

S version: ... et [il] *se demande*, avec quelque angoisse ...
T version: ... and he looks, with some anxiety ...

Here it is judged that the translation of *se demande* as *looks* constitutes a substantial semantic error, which does not seem to be due to confusion with another word in the text.

Also included here are errors which appear to have no basis in the text and for which no suitable explanation can be found:

S version: ... je n'ai jamais *admiré* ni aimé personne plus que lui ...
T version: ... I have never *forgotten* or liked anyone else as much as I did like and admired him ...

Why the T initially translated *admiré* as *forgotten* is not known; it seems unlikely that *admiré* could be misunderstood as *oublié*. The T did in fact hear *admiré* since it enters into his translation, and it may simply be that T anticipated that S would say *je n'ai jamais oublié*. Such instances were very rare.

In addition, this category contains instances of clearly unintelligible material:

S version: ... in the *actual* presentation ...
T version: ... dans la présentation *dockswall* (?) ...

It may be surmised that the unintelligible word *dockswall* (?) is an approximation of the word *actual* or *actuelle*, but it defies comprehension.

There are thus two categories for semantic errors, one referring to mild errors or substitutions which more or less retain the meaning intended by the S, the other referring to more serious errors, with substantial change of meaning. Although three subcategories are specified in the latter case, they may be combined into one class or "gross" semantic errors.

The remaining categories of errors or substitutions refer to departures of the translation from the original which involve a whole phrase or unit, rather than a single lexical item. Three such categories have been specified, although here again they represent differing degrees of departure rather than distinctive categories.

c) E3: mild phrasing change, where the T does not say quite the same thing as the S, but the gist of what is said is not affected.

S version: ... *il aurait fort bien pu reprendre à son compte* les paroles de Shakespeare ...
T version: ... *we could very well say about him* the words of Shakespeare ...

Here the T makes a change in the subject of the sentence and alters the phrasing slightly, but the gist of what is said by S is retained.

S version: ... dans ce Conseil *qu'il a fortement marqué* de sa personnalité ...
T version: ... in this Council *to which he gave so much of* his personality ...

These phrasing changes are very mild and are generally acceptable within the context of simultaneous interpretation, where the T is allowed a certain latitude in his wording.

d) E4: substantial phrasing change – where the change in phrasing is more marked and leads to a difference in meaning, but the overall gist of what is said by the S is not too distorted.

S version: ... je trouve que ce film est une réussite, une manière de réussite...
T version: ... I would like to say that this is an excellent film, that it was a great success ...

As can be seen, the T has substantially rephrased what the S was saying, but the gist of the message is not too distorted.

Not all instances coded in this category were as substantial as the above example. There were in fact two subcategories, which were eventually combined. The phrasing changes considered in this category are more marked than those in *E3*, but less serious than those in the following category.

e) E5: gross phrasing change, resulting in a considerable difference in meaning. In this category are included all gross departures in meaning, which can arise on the basis of several factors. Among such causes were noted the following:
i) error of mistranslation:

S version: ... qui occupent dans cette maison un emploi salarié ...
T version: ... (who) ... are even paid by this publisher ...

ii) the T seems to *make up* something on the basis of some part of the text. This may be due to his lack of comprehension of what is said, or because of his lagging too far behind the S, which prevents him from fully understanding what S has said, and he consequently tries to "fib" his way through the text on the basis of some word in it.

S version: ... je dois garder enracinés en moi certains principes ...
T version: ... (substantial delay) ... and there are certain roots to this ...

iii) different meaning resulting from *omission* of some item:

S version: ... il a eu ... de grandes déceptions, et il y a été sensible.
T version: ... he had great disappointments, and he was sensitive.

iv) error due to *misunderstanding* of some item:

S version: ... (des écrivains qui) ... n'y occupent aucun autre emploi sinon celui de lecteur ...
T version: ... they have another job which is that of a reader ...

Here the T appears to have misunderstood *un autre* for *aucun autre*, resulting in a meaning almost opposite to what the S said. This type of error is similar to error *E2a*, but it affects the meaning of a whole unit rather than just the word involved.

Other events were also classified in category *E5*: meaningless or confused translations, reversals of meanings, transforming a question into a statement, etc. Some instances of confused translation were classified in either category *E4* or *E5* depending upon their seriousness. These various events were initially coded separately, but were subsequently incorporated into one or another of the phrasing changes categories. Essentially, we established three levels of phrasing changes or errors, exemplified by categories *E3*, *E4* and *E5*, and we determined which was the more appropriate in any one instance.

The above-description summarizes the main types of departures of the interpretation from the original noted in the course of the study, although we have by no means exemplified all the different variations of events associated with each category. The coding system had to be restricted so that events differing in some respects have been included in the same category, but the main classifications reflect different "types" of departures. As stated earlier, the system has obviously involved a good deal of subjectivity on the part of the coder, both in terms of the categories delineated and in the assignment of events to these categories, but this cannot be avoided when the basic dimension involved is that of "meaning" or meaning equivalence. The coding system is only meant to be an attempt at some systematization in the consideration of departures of translation occurring in simultaneous interpretation, and can no doubt be improved. Nor is the system intended to reflect except in a very gross way on the adequacy of "quality" of an interpretation since other critical factors such as delivery characteristics: voice intonation, appropriateness of pausing, etc., are not taken into consideration.

3. Some Relevant Data

We shall only very briefly comment on some findings of the investigation relating to departures of interpretation, since a detailed discussion of the data is beyond the scope of the present paper.

As stated earlier, six Ts were tested in the study: two fully qualified professional Ts, two "student" Ts who had recently completed an approved program in interpretation, and two "amateur" Ts who, as previously mentioned, were persons fluently bilingual in French and English but with no experience in simultaneous interpretation. These amateurs, however, had an active interest in languages, being affiliated with the language department of a university. (This may account in some measure for their, in fact, rather good performance in view of their total inexperience, though their performance would of course still be judged quite poor by professional standards.) In each category of Ts one was English dominant and the other French dominant, the alternate language constituting in all cases the "weaker" language of the T. The Ts were required to translate five passages from their weaker to their dominant language and three passages from their dominant to their weaker language.

Looking first at omissions, two basic measures may be considered: the number of instances of omissions and the amount of material omitted. Since the various texts used in the study differed in length, the number of instances of omissions had to be standardized to a common text length, which was selected as 100 words (of original text), not counting words associated with repetitions, false starts, etc. Of the six Ts tested in the study, three could be classified as "more-qualified Ts" (the two professional Ts and one of the student Ts) and three as "less-qualified Ts" (the two amateurs and the other student T, whose performance, in comparison with that of the more-qualified Ts, was rather poor). The more-qualified Ts make on the average from 2 to 4 omissions per 100 words and omit from 5 to 10% of the material, while less-qualified Ts make in the neighbourhood of 6 omissions per 100 words and omit from 20 to 25% of the material. These figures, of course, vary from text to text, and it is found that the measures of omission vary directly with rates of "input" – the proportion of speech associated with the messages, i.e. the extent to which the S is actually engaged in speaking in the course of his delivery (he may, for example, be actually speaking during 60% of the time that it takes him to deliver his message, while the other 40% is associated with halts and pauses in his delivery), and the speech rate of the S, i.e. the number of words or syllables that he utters in a fixed period of time. These findings offer support for the intuitively reasonable assumption that the more the S speaks in a fixed period of time, the more often and the greater the amount of material is likely to be omitted by the T.

Although the difference in the number of omissions associated with more-qualified and less-qualified Ts does not at first glance seem particularly striking (though it must be remembered that the measures are based on only 100 words of text, so that a difference of 2 to 4 omissions per 100 words does "add up" for an extended text), the two groups differ in the degree of "seriousness" of the omissions: whereas about 80% of the omissions of the more-qualified Ts are of the minor *skipping* variety (type *M1*) and thus only about 20% are more "serious," for less-qualified Ts roughly half or 50% of their omissions fall in the latter category. Whereas more-qualified Ts have about the same omission measures associated with interpretation in either direction (from their weaker into their dominant language or *vice versa*), less-qualified Ts, interestingly, usually do "better" when translating from the dominant into their weaker language, making fewer omissions and omitting less material in that situation than when translating from their weaker into their dominant language, which is the more "natural" direction.

Turning to *additions* of interpretation, two indices can likewise be calculated on the basis of the amount of original material effectively translated (i.e. excluding material omitted by the T), and the proportion of the translation (in terms of number of words) which constitutes added material (excluding words relating to repetitions, false starts, etc.). It may be said that in general there is very little addition of material in interpretation, some Ts making almost no additions, others making at the most 2 to 3 additions per 100 words (of original material effectively translated), and added material accounting for only 1 to 5% of the T's verbal output. Most additions are of the *qualifier* and *elaboration* types (*A1* and *A2*). There is a tendency for fewer additions to occur in relation to prepared texts (such as in the translation of a text initially intended for the written medium) than in relation to less structured passages. This may reflect the degree of formalism associated with such material, which may call forth a more rigid and set translation, whereas texts intended for oral delivery allow the T greater freedom of idiom, with a greater possibility of additions. With regard to the proficiency level of the T, there is possibly a tendency on the part of the more-qualified or professional Ts to add more material than less-qualified Ts; this may be attributable to their very expertise, which frees them from following the text too closely, in an almost literal fashion as is the case with amateurs, and hence increases the likelihood of slight changes and additions. Adding material in translation, it is evident, is not as "serious" an offense as omitting material or mistranslating part of the text, unless of course the added material is inappropriate to the context or leads to misinformation.

In considering substitutions and errors of translation, the number of errors must also be calculated on the basis of the amount of original material (number of words) effectively translated, i.e. removing from the word total, words associated with omitted material, since for such material, the possibility of concomitant errors is effectively removed. Due to a number of considerations, a measure relating to the amount of material associated with errors is not as readily calculable and is not in any case as pertinent as the number of instances of errors. More-qualified Ts commit approximately 3 errors per 100 words (of translated material) while less-qualified Ts make about 4 errors per 100 words (this figure is the result of an anomalously low error index for one of these Ts), but there are individual variations, and for some texts, embarrassingly enough, some less-qualified Ts make fewer errors than some more-qualified Ts. This finding is not really as disconcerting as it may appear at first: since less-qualified Ts omit considerably more material than more qualified Ts, they effectively have fewer possibilities of making errors since the error index is based on the amount of effectively translated material. It must also be recognized that the coding system probably favours the less-qualified T while penalizing the more-qualified T to some extent because of his very expertness. In coding errors, the main concern is with the "fidelity" of the translation, the issue being whether the meaning of what is said in the original text is conveyed. A distinguishing characteristic between more-qualified and less-qualified Ts is the degree of literalness of their interpretations: those by amateur Ts are typically very literal, being in many instances almost word-for-word "verbal transpositions" rather than translations, whereas those by professional Ts are substantially more in agreement with the idiom of the target language. Translations by amateurs are thus considerably more "awkward" and less intelligible or comprehensible than those of more-qualified Ts. The coding system, however, does not reflect too much on the overall intelligibility of the translation; its primary concern is with changes in meaning. Since professional Ts make an attempt at idiomatic expression, greater opportunity arises in their case for slight phrasing changes to occur than is the case with less-qualified Ts.

The data in fact generally indicate proportionally fewer "minor" errors (types *E1* and *E3*) for amateur Ts than for more-qualified interpreters.

Since the error index is not independent of the measure of omission and since both omissions and errors are disruptive of translation, these two categories of events can be combined to yield a general index of translation disruption. When this is done, the emerging pattern is quite consistent with expectations in establishing the superiority of the more-qualified Ts. Again, less-qualified Ts are characterized by generally better performance when translating from their dominant into their weaker language, showing on average fewer disruptions – and fewer "serious" ones (omission types *M2* and *M3* plus error types *E2*, *E4* and *E5*) – in that direction than when translating from their weaker into their dominant language. (Their translations, however, are to some extent even more literal when translating from dominant into weaker language).

The above remarks constitute only a very brief description of some of the findings of the investigation relating to departures of interpretation. The data presented above should not be taken too "literally." If the performance of less-qualified interpreters on the basis of the few measures reported here (though, as previously stated, the fact that the measures are based on a very restricted text length – 100 words – masks the overall difference in relation to actual text lengths), it must again be repeated that the indices developed do not give the "whole picture." They are meant only to quantify in a very general way the extent of departure between original and interpreted version, but do not reflect on other critical dimensions such as overall comprehensibility of the interpretation, degree of idiomaticalness, clarity of diction, among others, which are of obvious significance in simultaneous interpretation. Much work remains to be done in the area.

Appendix

Example of an application of coding system – (Omissions are reported on the S transcript, additions on the T transcript, and errors on both transcripts in sequential correspondence – the first error on the S transcript corresponding to the first error on the T transcript, etc.):
S version: J'étais à Londres mercredi soir lorsque la nouvelle s'est répandue dans les rues pleines de monde que (Monsieur X) était mort. Quand nous avons pu enfin y croire, nous avons ressenti tous comme un choc, une grande tristesse, un sentiment de deuil. Nous connaissions en lui un grand Américain, mais comme le Président Kennedy, nous sentions qu'il était à nous tous. J'ai ressenti moi-même un grande désolation, car je connaissais depuis longtemps, et fort bien, (Monsieur X), depuis l'époque où il avait coutume de venir

nous voir, il y a des années à la Jamaïque. Je n'ai jamais admiré ni aimé personne plus que lui.
T version: Wednesday evening the news spread throughout the world that (Mister X) was dead. When we learned this, we all felt a shock, a great sadness, a very deep feeling of mourning. We knew in him a great American, but, as President Kennedy, we all felt that he was one of us. I knew for a long time and very well (Mister X), since that time when years ago ... I have never ....

Notes

1. This paper is based on part of an unpublished doctoral dissertation submitted to the Department of Psychology of the University of North Carolina (Chapel Hill). The author is grateful to his thesis advisor, Samuel Fillenbaum, for his guidance. The study was supported by United States Public Health Service Research Grant M-10006 from the National Institute of Mental Health.

2. The terms *translation* and *to translate* are employed regularly in the present paper in the place of *interpretation* and *to interpret*, with the understanding that they refer to *oral* translation, i.e. interpretation, and not to formal or written translation.

3. Henri C. Barik. *A Study of Simultaneous Interpretation*, unpublished doctoral dissertation. University of North Carolina (Chapel Hill), 1969 (on file with University Microfilms, Ann Arbor, Michigan; Order no. 70-3192). For summary see: Henri C. Barik, "Interpreters Talk a Lot, among Other Things," *Babel*, 1972 (in press).

4. Transcripts of the texts employed in the study and of the interpretations obtained (full set of 8 translation for 2 Ts and sample of 3 translations for 4 Ts) have been deposited with the National Auxiliary Publications Service of the American Society for Information Science Inc., c/o CCM Information Sciences Inc., 909 Third Avenue, New York, New York 1022. These transcripts reproduce the texts only; omissions and other departures of translation are not indicated on them.

Message Redundancy and Message Anticipation In Simultaneous Interpretation

Ghelly V. Chernov
Moscow International School of Translation and Interpreting

1. Introduction

Objective studies of simultaneity in simultaneous interpretation (SI) began after the invention of the multichannel tape recorder and were carried out at approximately the same time by several researchers at the end of the sixties and in the beginning of the seventies (Henri C. Barik in the United States and Canada in 1971; David Gerver in the United Kingdom in 1974; Irina A. Zimnyaya and Ghelly V. Chernov in 1970; Anatoly F. Shiryayev in 1971; Ghelly V. Chernov in 1978 - in Russia). The results obtained by various methods and with different equipment were amazingly similar: it was found that interpreters speak and listen simultaneously for approximately 70% of the time, the total speaking time of the source language (SL) speaker being 100%. The time was ripe for psychologists and psycholinguists to sink their teeth into the whys and wherefores of a newly discovered phenomenon of a seemingly impossible human feat, namely, simultaneous interpretation.

2. The Russian School of Thought

The Russian school of thought on the underlying psycholinguistic machinery of simultaneity was based on the ideas of L. S. Vygodsky, A. R. Luria and A. N. Leontyev and their theory of activity in human behavior, including verbal behavior. Thus, the hypothesis was that simultaneous interpretation was a kind of verbal activity with specific features, carried out under specific conditions (Chernov 1978, 1987; Shiryayev 1979, 1982).

It would only be natural for me to concentrate on my own model of SI psycholinguistic machinery (Chernov 1978, 1979, 1980, 1987), which, as I dare to presume and will try to show, has a sufficient explanatory force. I call it the probability prediction model and regard the probability prediction of the verbal and semantic structure of the oral message in progress as the most essential psycholinguistic factor explaining the phenomenon of simultaneity in simultaneous interpretation.

I consider simultaneous interpretation as a complex type of bilingual, meaning-oriented communicative verbal activity, performed under time constraints and with a strictly limited amount of information processed at an externally controlled pace. Under such extreme circumstances, not all verbal messages, but only messages with an adequate degree of redundancy, can be interpreted simultaneously.

> ...Redundancy has its advantages, and a large degree of interdependence among the successive units of a language means that parts of the message can be lost or distorted without causing a disruption of communication. Any missing portions can be supplied by the receiver on the basis of the surrounding portions, on the basis of contextual clues (Miller 1963:103).

As purported by George Miller, redundancy in discourse boils down to 1) the iteration of message components and 2) their interdependence. Since both are objective factors, independent of the message recipient, that type of redundancy may be termed objective redundancy of the verbal message. At the acoustic level, or sound wave level, redundancy is represented mostly as phonotactical interdependencies, as well as the iteration of the verbal message's prosodic features. Within the framework of semantics (linguistic meaning), it should be appropriate to consider the level of the utterance and that of the complete communication (text, discourse), separately.

At the utterance level, the first aspect of objective (speech) redundancy is represented as the iteration of semantic components, ensuring semantic and grammatical agreement in discourse (Apresyan 1974), semantic interdependence being represented as semantic government. At the discourse or text level, the first aspect is represented as anaphoric repetitions and co-reference in discourse, and the second, as the coherence of the text. The first aspect reflects the topical, or thematic continuity of the text, and the second, a number of specific rules of semantic constraints of the type formalized by Chafe (1972). (See Table 1).

Table 1. *Types of Objective Redundancy*

redundancy factors information theory	representation in discourse by levels		philosophical essence of the phenomenon
	utterance	discourse	
repetition	iteration of semantic components and their configurations: agreement	co-reference	probability
interdependence	semantic interdependence: predicate-object and modifier relations	semantic constraints	certainty

On the other hand, a communication is subjectively redundant for the message recipient. To make the difference tangible, I propose to make the following distinction between the linguistic meaning and extralinguistic sense. I suggest that the process of language comprehension is based on a purely human capacity for making inferences. Whatever is inferred by the hearer is inferred about the meaning of the utterance and the part of discourse already produced. Considering the source of the inference, inferences can be broken down into their linguistic, cognitive, situational, and pragmatic nature.

I have been developing an unorthodox view that the notion of both presupposition and linguistic implicature are borrowed from one and the same source - the logical implication of the form "if A, then B", presupposing both the explicit antecedent A and the explicit consequent B. I suggest that a third term be introduced into the binomial formula of material implication in order to account for the difference between the linguistic presupposition and the linguistic implicature: (A) « B « (C), to be read "if A (implicit), then B (explicit); if B (explicit), then C (implicit)", where B is the explicit term to be found verbally expressed in the text of the message, whereas the terms A and C are only implied. In that case, (A) as an antecedent for B is its presupposition (which determines the meaning of the message) and (C) is its implicature, or the inference drawn by the recipient of the message from the explicit utterance of B (Chernov 1991).

Linguistic inferences can be drawn about the verbal form of the message, its linguistic meaning, as well as about the referential component of the semantic structure of the utterance (discourse). Pronominal co-reference may serve as one obvious example of the linguistic type of inferencing. Co-reference may be based on the common componential stock (for example, the term *sell* contains the semantic component *money;* hence, after the appearance of the verb *sell* in discourse, the noun *money* will follow with a definite article, and its appearance in discourse will be expected). The same may be said about semantic rules, as in the following example: *He left Moscow for St. Petersburg* implies that *he is no longer in Moscow,* and that *he is probably in St. Petersburg* or *...on his way there.* Any component of the semantic structure of the text could become a source of linguistic inference, as in *We have been impressed by...* infers that whatever impressed us must be "positive" or "good" (assessment); the linguistic inference *my delegation has worked towards an outcome...* must be followed by a non-factive proposition (Lyons 1977) *...reflecting a consensus,* or *...would reflect a consensus,* but not by **...which reflected a (the-?) consensus* (factivity).

The formalization of a semantic constraint, as suggested by Chafe (1972), may serve as a basis for a formal representation of a linguistic inference. Chafe's formula of X « Y - to be read "X entails Y"-, or consequently, "if X, then Y", also means that "the hearer's knowledge of X implies his/her knowledge of Y". Thus, a semantic constraint, as an objective factor of redundancy, becomes a subjective factor of linguistic inference for a given hearer, depending on, and drawn on the basis of, his/her knowledge of the language spoken. Chafe's semantic constraint forms a part of the following contextual rule

W : X « Y : Z

to be read "the presence of the semantic element W introduces the constraint X « Y, which remains in force up to the point where Z appears, where it will evaporate" (Chafe 1972).

The hearer makes cognitive inferences when the utterance makes sense, only when the semantic components of the utterance (or the portion of the discourse) already produced, interact with the listener's background knowledge. For example, in order to understand the utterances: *he studied at Eton,* or *he studied at Columbia,* one must have the appropriate background knowledge about Eton College in the United Kingdom, or Columbia University in New York. In fact, Searle (1979) argues that the notion of the literal meaning of a sentence only has application relative to a set of background assumptions, and... that these background assumptions are not all and could not all be realized in the semantic structure of the sentence (cf. also his example of *the cat is on the mat.*)

Linguistic and cognitive inferences are very often intertwined and sometimes even inseparable. Consider the following examples: *She couldn't come because of her mother* supplies a source of a linguistic inference about the reason of "her absence" which is rather vague, and a more specific cognitive inference depending on the circumstances: *...because her mother came to see her, ...was sick, ...asked her to do something,* etc.

At least one case of such dependence could be formalized in the form of a semantic (and sense) constraint:

W	:	X	--->	definiteness of X
object		part of W		
phenomenon		feature of W		
cause		consequence of W		

to be read as follows: if an object, a phenomenon, or a compelling reason are mentioned in a coherent discourse, any subsequent mention of an integral part of that object, or an inherent feature of the phenomenon, or an inescapable consequence of that cause, is normally accompanied by a sign of definiteness (a definite article in languages that have them at all), reflecting the presupposition of concurrent existence of the object and its parts, etc. This constraint would conveniently formalize Chafe's example about the bicycle (Chafe 1972).

There is distinct evidence to support positing separate entities as linguistic and cognitive types of inferencing performed during simultaneous interpretation. For instance the perception of the following utterance:

> This Assembly has increasingly turned its attention to the great problem of disparity between the standards of living of the developing and developed countries

is approximately such, as evidenced by three translations into Russian (out of eleven done during the experiment):

> "...problem of ... gap between level (1) of life ... in developed countries ... and level (2) of life of developing countries, ...and level (1) is high...(while)...level (2) is low" (cf. Chernov, 1987).

The situational inference about the meaning of the utterance (or the part of the discourse) already produced, has the communicative situation (or the situational context, for that matter) as the source of the inference. For example, from the speaker's address, *Mr. President...* an inference drawn situationally may establish a reference to the President of a country, or the president of a company, or the President of the UN Security Council, or the president of a college. In fact, it is the situational inference that turns the interrogative sentence *Could you pass me the salt?* into a speech act of making a request (cf. Searle 1979).

An analysis of the communicative situation of SI involves eight clearly identifiable factors:

- the characteristics of the source message, or speaker (S), obtained from a reply to the question "Who is speaking?"
- the theme of the message (Th): "What is he talking about?"
- the relation of the act of speech to the event that provoked it (E): "In what connection is he speaking?"
- the message recipient, or audience (A): "Whom is he addressing?"
- the place, or forum (F): "Where is he speaking?"
- the time (T): "When is he speaking?"
- the purpose of the communication (P): "What is he aiming at?"
- and its motive (M): "Why is he speaking?" (Chernov 1975, 1978, 1987).

The pragmatic inference from an utterance is made when the hearer draws conclusions about the speaker, and above all, about his/her social role, on the basis of the utterance's semantic contents, the hearer's own background assumptions, as well as his/her knowledge of the factors of the communicative situation. There are several excellent publications on the linguistic theory of pragmatics which are of direct relevance to this problem (cf. Leech 1983), yet there are hardly any directly related to simultaneous interpretation. I believe, however, that sociolinguistic studies of the social role played by the participants in an act of communication through SI and, specifically, experimentation in the deviation from the expected role, may prove to be quite revealing.

Redundancy at all levels, i.e. both objective semantic redundancy and subjective redundancy at the semantic level, allow for and, indeed, signify the predictability of meaning and sense in the message. Redundancy of normal verbal communication, at least in the languages that have been studied from that angle, is high enough to warrant the suggestion that the difference in message redundancy of dissimilar texts lies between 80 and 95 per cent and not between 0 and 100 per cent. A highly redundant text, such as an oral communication, is predictable. Hence, the psychological machinery of probability prediction entails some kind of correlation between the probability of certain linguistic (phonetic, prosodic, verbal and syntactic) or semantic (meaning and sense) developments in the utterance and coherent discourse at the stage of perception (communication between the speaker and the interpreter), and the anticipatory synthesis of the TL (target language) message. This machinery, in fact, makes it possible for a professional conference interpreter to perform simultaneous interpreting. In fact, the interpreter is engaged in concurrent perception and understanding (inferencing) of the SL communication, on the one hand, and reproduction (generation) of the TL message, on the other. This model is based on a fundamental methodological notion, according to which an organism tends to anticipate events in the outside world, as

> "a basic way of adjustment of all life forms to the spatio-temporal structure of the inorganic world in which sequentiality and iteration of events constitute the basic parameters of time" (Anokhin 1968,1978:18).

According to P.K. Anokhin,

> "the human central nervous system developed as a mechanism of maximal anticipation of sequential and iterative phenomena of the outside world at the greatest possible speed" (Anokhin 1978:19).

Anokhin presumes that the anticipatory reflection of reality is a universal natural law, the Pavlovian theory of conditioned reflexes being only a specific case.

Neither information content or redundancy is evenly distributed throughout the communication. Redundancy is concentrated in the thematic, or topical, part of each utterance, whereas information is at its greatest density at the rheme of the utterance. Hence, it is possible to compress speech in various ways in the thematic part of the utterance by reducing the number of syllables, or words, or semantic components, and by simplifying syntactical structures. In the following case, interpreting a chairman's announcement:

> I now give the floor to the distinguished delegate of the United Republic of Tanzania!

by a simple

> Tanzania!

exemplifies the situational compression which covers the reduction of the number of syllables, the number of words, deletion of the entire thematic part of the utterance and simplification of the syntactical structure to a single word. In fact, only the rheme of the utterance remains after the performance of an act of compression.

Comparison of the number of syllables in the original communication, uttered in Spanish, with the number of syllables in TL in the recorded passages of simultaneous interpretation, each interpreted by two interpreters during the 1978 United Nations experimental remote interpreting session via satellite, with the parallel control group of interpreters working in the conference room, indicates a strong tendency towards compression, as made evident by the following figures:

Table 2. *Syllabic Compression in SI*

A passage of 11 sentences.

	Spanish original	Russian		English		French	
		1	2	1	2	1	2
No. of syllables:	721	689	676	539	545	537	617

There is every reason to presume that in order to receive the information flow to the brain from the outside world, the brain must trigger a special neurophysiological mechanism ensuring the perception of the measure of information change, in the first place. It may be worth recalling, for example, that humans identify figures through the perception of stretches of maximum curvature, not of straight lines, and that moving objects are given priority in perception to stationary objects (*Perception,* 1972). Furthermore, phonemes are recognized not so much by a steady-state segment of the sound pattern, as by a transition stage; according to Massaro (1975), in order to perceive the CV type of syllable which averages 200 msec duration, one needs only 42 msec, 30 msec of which are transition, and a mere 12 msec, steady-state segment.

One can argue that comprehending meaning and sense is subject to a similar law of perception, and that attention is primarily focused on those semantic components that carry new information, which is exactly what the rheme is about. In other words, I believe (and there is plenty of supporting experimental and analytical evidence which are beyond the scope of this paper) that the interpreter's attention is focused on the rheme of the utterance. Any misperception or loss of item in the thematic, or redundant portion of the communication, can be easily restored; in the worst case, it is a matter of quality of interpretation, whereas the loss of a rhematic item may easily result in mistranslation.

The levels of probability prediction (PP) machinery are based on redundancy, from the level of the syllable to that of the word, phrase, utterance, communication (text) and situational context. The object of probability prediction (what is predicted) is a four-tiered source of classification, among which all the levels can be distributed.

Sound patterns (such as syllables encoding phonemes, intonation, stress, and other prosodic features) are perceived and anticipated at the "lower" tier (a) (see Chart on p. 150), and encompassing the levels of the syllable (I), the word (II), the phrase (III) and the utterance (IV). Redundancy at these levels has been quite extensively analyzed in psychology.

Grammatical (syntactical) and, more generally, categorial semantic features are anticipated and/or perceived at the next tier (b), encompassing the levels of the phrase (III) and the utterance (IV).

The third tier (c) - the semantic tier *per se* - encompasses the levels of the phrase (III), the utterance (IV) and the text (V), and constitutes the central or the pivotal tier of the probability prediction machinery in SI.

The highest tier of probability prediction (d), corresponding to the highest level of subjective redundancy, by inferring the sense and anticipating the probability of its further development in the message (the sense tier *per se*), consists in the levels of the utterance (IV), the text (V), and the situational context (VI).

Close interplay and interaction of such levels begin at the very moment preceding the beginning of the speech, when the speaker is given the floor.

If the speaker is known to the interpreter, as the speech begins, the interpreter forms a general outline of a probability prognosis of the meaning and sense structure of the forthcoming message, supported by some knowledge of other factors of the situational context. Such a prognosis may be called the top-to-bottom prognosis carried out at the fourth tier (d), (see Chart on Page 150) namely the sense tier.

The next step of the probability prediction process is carried out at the sound pattern tier (a), i.e., from the bottom upwards, after which the syntactical and semantic tiers become immediately involved.

If, on the contrary, the speaker is unknown to the interpreter and very little or nothing at all is known about the situational context in general, the probability prediction process begins in the bottom-to-top direction.

As the message develops (as a rule, in the course of the first several utterances), a general outline of a probability prognosis of the whole message (or its first thematic part) is formed in the mind of the interpreter, with the interaction of all the PP levels described. Without such interaction, errors and omissions appear in the TL communication. As the meaning and sense structure of the message develop, the scale of a forecast of the forthcoming semantic - and even of the purely linguistic features of the communication - narrows down at times to certainty (probability equaling 1). When a new subject is introduced by the speaker, the process begins anew.

Probability prediction is facilitated in that internal programmes (*plans*, in the terminology of Miller, Galanter and Pribram [1960]) of the utterances (as soon as they are ready) are carried out subconsciously as automatic operations and require little attention, if any, for the feed-back process. Attention is fully switched over to perception and comprehension and the TL communication produced by the interpreter becomes unchecked throughout if difficulties of perception occur. These may be due to a high level of noise or a rapid rate of speech resulting in low perceptional redundancy at the lower levels of the mechanism, or due to complicated syntactical structures or syntactical errors in the SL discourse, yielding low redundancy at the syntactical tier; or due to unknown terminology, or semantic gaps requiring more intense internal inferencing activity, or references to facts and events unknown to the interpreter, resulting in low redundancy at the semantic and sense tiers. In such cases, the simultaneous interpreter becomes unconscious of his/her own TL communications: he/she may interpret and speak without errors, but if errors and/or omissions do occur, they remain uncorrected (Gerver 1975; Chernov 1978). If, however, the overall level of redundancy is adequate and the conditions of perception are favourable, attention may be fully directed towards monitoring the process of speech production in the target language. Interpreters know that in such cases, they may lose awareness of the source language altogether.

The probability prediction model of SI models perception in discrete portions, by information density peaks, or points of reference at each level and tier. In fact, I have experimentally shown such points of reference in speech perception in SI for the level of the utterance (the rheme) and for the level of the situational context (factor S - "the speaker") (Chernov 1978, 1987). Lukanina (1974) has demonstrated syntactical points of reference in SI.

3. Model

My model presupposes 1) concurrent operation of the probability prediction machinery at several levels at each given moment, in time; 2) multichannel information processing; 3) heuristic interplay of levels from bottom to top and from the top down, as the message is scanned for information density peaks, above all at the sense tier. All these activities zero in on the sense of each utterance and of the communication as a whole, as it is perceived and transformed into the internal plan of the sense structure of the TL message.

The involvement of as many concurrent levels as possible, and as completely as possible, constitutes a major factor of reliability of the communication process via simultaneous interpretation. In order to be effective, this step-by-step machinery must operate at higher (semantic) levels, on the one hand, while the probability prediction steps should be sufficiently discrete, on the other.

The following conceptual chart illustrates theoretical results that could be obtained as a function of both separate engagement of each level and tier, and of the levels engaged concurrently.

Chart 1. *Hypothetical Results of SI as a Function of Engagement of PP Levels*

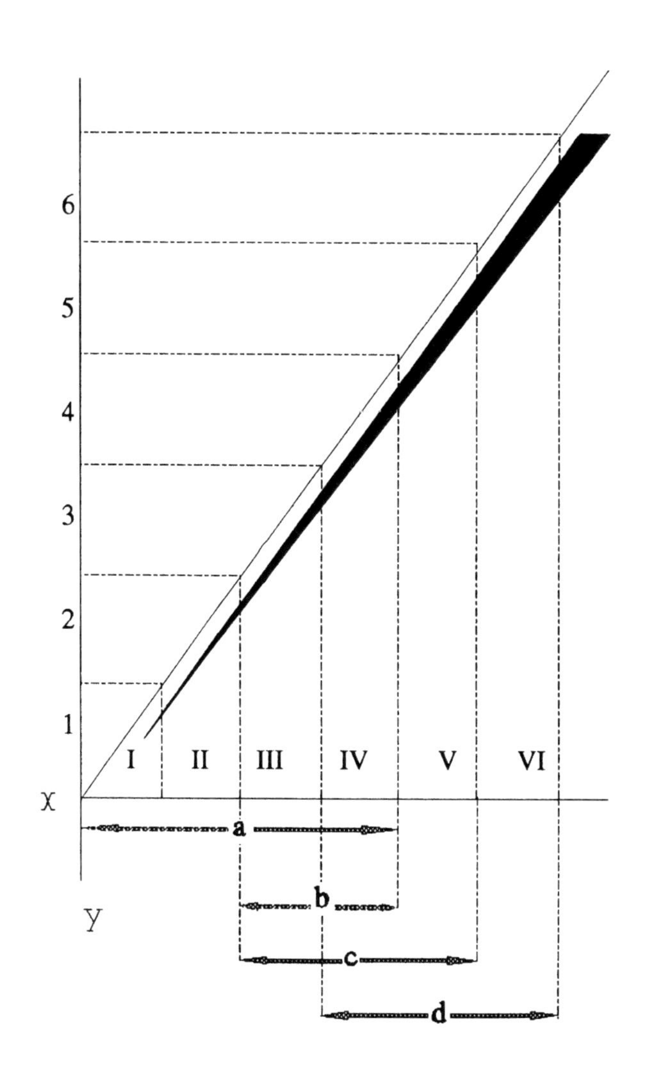

The chart illustrates the following notion: if, for the sake of argument, the interpretation could be carried out at the level indicated by the Roman numeral on the chart, alone and separately, this would produce a result indicated by the Arabic numeral. The Roman numeral indicates the step of the prognosis for a syllable (I), a word (II), a phrase (III), an utterance (IV), a communication (V), and the situational context (VI). The Arabic numeral indicates the results that could be obtained: 1) no translation, 2) rendering the prosodics of an unknown word (e.g. an unknown proper name) or unconnected words not forming a coherent utterance, whose sense was arrived at purely accidentally, 3) disconnected phrases, 4) incomplete rendering of disconnected utterances, 5) a mere summary of the message, 6) the explication of the theme, the purpose of the communication and its underlying motives. The letters indicate the tier of the prognosis: a) prosodic, b) syntactic, c) semantic, and d) sense.

It is curious enough that some of the hypotheses illustrated in the Chart have found both a willing and even unwilling experimental confirmation (cf. Benedictov, 1974 and Hendrickx, 1971 [plus comments by D. Seleskovich (1975)] for suggested "interpretation" of separate words; also see Chernov (1978) for experimental results of interpretation of proper names; see Shiryayev's (1979) experiment on interpretation of individual words, for levels I and II. cf. Chernov's (1978) experiments in interpretation at levels III and IV [undergraduates' course papers]). In fact, the cognitive activity performed by conference interpreters in the booth labelled as *transcodage* by D. Seleskovitch and M. Lederer (1986,1989) is also reflected in the chart: *transcodage* would produce the results indicated by Arabic numerals 1 through 4, concurrently engaged, with the exclusion of levels V and VI, and tier (d).

Our model explains why simultaneous interpretation can only be applied to communications characterized by an adequate level of redundancy, and why, for example, it cannot be applied to quality fiction and poetry or to legal documents, or purely numerical materials, usually requiring previous interpretation of background papers. Explaining as it does certain inherent limitations on SI, it allows for a number of applications both in the field of interpreter-training and in the field of SI management at international conferences by conference secretariats.

This article first appeared in META XXXVII:1, 1992, entitled "Conference Interpretation in the USSR: History, Theory, New Frontiers".

References

Anokhin, P.K. 1968. *The Biology and Neurophysiology of the Conditioned Reflex.* Moscow (in Russian).

Anokhin, P.K. 1978. *The Philosophical Aspects of the Functional System Theory.* Moscow (in Russian).

Apresyan, Y.D. 1974. *Lexical Semantics.* Moscow (in Russian).

Benedictov, B.A. 1974. *The Psychology of Learning Foreign Languages.* Minsk: Vysheyshaya Shkola (In Russian).

Chafe, Wallace L. 1972. "Discourse Structure and Human Knowledge". R.O. Freedle and J.B. Carroll, eds. *Language Comprehension and the Acquisition of Knowledge.* Winston and Sons: New York, Toronto. 41-70.

Chernov, Gh.V. 1975. "The Communicative Situation of Simultaneous Interpretation and Message Redundancy". *Tetradi Perevodchika* 12. Moscow. 83-101. (In Russian).

Chernov, Gh.V. 1978. *Theory and Practice of Simultaneous Interpretation.* Moscow (In Russian).

Chernov, Gh.V. 1979. "Semantic Aspects of Psycholinguistic Research in Simultaneous Interpretation". *Language and Speech* 22:3. 277-295.

Chernov, Gh.V. 1980. "Semantic Redundancy as a Key to Reliable Comprehension of a Verbal Message". *Comprendre le Langage: Actes du Colloque de septembre 1980.* Paris: Didier Erudition. 31-37.

Chernov, Gh.V. 1987. *Fundamentals of Simultaneous Interpretation.* Moscow: Vysshaya Shkola (In Russian).

Chernov, Gh.V. 1991. "Cognitive and Pragmatic Inferencing and the Intercultural Component in Translation". S. Tirkkonen-Condit, ed. *Empirical Research in Translation and Intercultural Studies.* Tübingen: Gunter Narr Verlag. 27-34.

Gerver, D. 1975. "A Psychological Approach to Simultaneous Interpretation". *META* 20. 119-128.

Hendrickx, P. 1971. *Simultaneous Interpreting: A Practice Book.* London.

Leech, G.N. 1983. *Principles of Pragmatics.* Longman: London and New York.

Lukanina, S.A. 1974. "On a Mechanism of Handling Syntactic Information in Simultaneous Interpretation". *Tetradi Perevodchika* 11. 87-91. (In Russian).

Lyons, J. 1977. *Semantics II.* Cambridge University Press,816-818.

Massaro, D. 1975. *Understanding Language: An Information-Processing Analysis of Speech Perception. Reading and Psycholinguistics.* New York: Academic Press.

Miller, G.A. 1963. *Language and Communication.* New York, Toronto: McGraw-Hill.

Miller, G.A., Galanter, E. and Pribram, K.H. 1960. *Plans and the Structure of Behaviour.* New York: Holt, Rinehart and Winston.

Held, R. and Richards, W. 1972. *Perception: Mechanisms and Models.* MIT. San Francisco: W.H. Freeman and Co.

Searle, J.R. 1979. *Expression and Meaning.* Cambridge: Cambridge University Press.

Seleskovitch, D. 1975. *Langage, Langues et Mémoire.* Paris: Minard.

Seleskovitch, D. & Lederer, M. 1986. *Interpreter pour Traduire.* Paris: Didier Erudition.

Seleskovitch, D. & Lederer, M. 1989. *Pédagogie Raisonnée de l'Interprétation.* Opoce: Didier Erudition.

Shiryayev, A.F. 1979. *Simultaneous Interpretation: The Activity of a Simultaneous Interpreter and Methods of Teaching Simultaneous Interpretation.* Moscow.

Shiryayev, A.F. 1982. "The Picture of Verbal Processes and Translation". N. K. Garbovsky, ed. *Translation as a Linguistic Problem.* Moscow University Press. 3-12 (In Russian).

Comprehension during Interpreting: What do Interpreters know that Bilinguals don't?

Mike Dillinger
*McGill University**

1. Introduction

A fundamental question for professionals involved in the selection, training, evaluation and hiring of simultaneous interpreters is that of what interpreters know that bilinguals do not. Do simultaneous interpreters know different strategies for allocating attentional and memory resources? For making sentence processing more efficient? For bringing prior knowledge to bear on comprehension? Answers to these questions are important in that they can provide the principles on which to base assessment of proficiency and aptitude, planning of training, and on-going improvement of professional performance.

Although simultaneous interpreting has received increasing attention as an object of study (Mackintosh 1985; Henry & Henry 1987; Gile 1988), unfortunately little of it has been in the form of reliable experimental research (Gile 1988). Consequently, precious little is known about the differences between experienced and novice interpreters' performance, and nothing at all is known about any possible differences in the way they go about carrying out the task (Dillinger 1989). Two sets of opinions, however, have emerged on this issue.

In most studies, it is assumed and/or asserted (without evidence) that the skills of interpreters are not characteristic of bilinguals in general (e.g., Gerver 1976), and hence that the models developed of skilled interpreting do not apply to novice interpreters (e.g., Moser 1978). On this view, then, there are important but still unidentified differences in the ways that novice and experienced interpreters perform the task. An important implication of this view is that experience and training are of great importance because they lead to qualitative differences in how the task is carried out.

More specifically, Nida (1969, cited in Gerver 1976) predicts that "experienced simultaneous translators may often short circuit the deeper [semantic] level of analysis". Although there is no evidence either for or against Nida's hypothesis, nor is it clear just what he meant, experienced interpreters have been found to add more information and delete less (Barik 1969), process larger chunks of the input, and give less literal translations (McDonald & Carpenter 1981), as well as being less sensitive to whether translation is from or into the dominant language (Lawson 1967; Barik 1969).

The second position holds that translation ability in general (e.g., Harris & Sherwood 1978) and interpreting skill in particular (e.g., Longley 1978:47) are natural consequences of bilingualism. On this view, then, there are few or no differences in the ways that novice and experienced interpreters (as distinct groups) perform the task: there are only individual and quantitative differences in text processing skill. This implies that experience and training have little effect on how the task is carried out. There is apparently no experimental evidence available either for or against this second position.

The research reported here was carried out in an attempt to address, in a systematic fashion, the question of whether there are qualitative differences in processing between novice and experienced interpreters, and thus to provide strong evidence in favor of one or the other position as well as an empirical base for characterizing the nature of interpreting skill. Rather than attempting to study interpreting in all its complexity, however, this research focussed only on the interpreters' comprehension processes to permit more detailed consideration of them. Translation and production processes were left for further research.

To address the issue of possible differences in comprehension processing, bilinguals with no interpreting experience were contrasted with experienced conference interpreters with respect to the degree to which their interpreting performance reflected different degrees of comprehension of the source text. The general question about this half of interpreting skill was broken down in to more specific questions about the different kinds of syntactic and semantic processing going on in comprehension during interpreting.

2. Method

2.1. Subjects

The experienced interpreters (n=8) were professional conference interpreters from the Montreal area with an average of 3830 hours[1] of active interpreting experience. The group was predominantly female (75%), and the average age was estimated at 45 years.

The inexperienced interpreters (n=8) were bilingual graduate students attending one of the two English-language universities in Montreal (McGill or Concordia). These subjects had never attempted simultaneous interpreting before. Males were more numerous in this sample (69%), and the average age was 29 years.

Other than self-evaluation, no assessment of subjects' bilingualism was attempted, since in several studies self rating proved most highly predictive of performance, especially among highly educated subjects (see Albert & Obler 1978). All subjects were quite obviously very proficient in both languages (i.e., balanced bilinguals), and all subjects used both languages on a day-to-day basis (overall, English 53% and French 47% of the time), so there is reason to believe that subjects' self-evaluations of dominance reflected only small differences in their functional language skills, especially with respect to comprehension. Of the experienced interpreters, 25% of the subjects gave English as their better language, 50% gave French, and 25% said they were equally fluent in both. The responses were the same for the language they preferred to translate into. Of the inexperienced subjects, 69% of them gave French as their better language, 6% gave English, and 25% reported that they were equally fluent in both.

Some authors (e.g., Gile 1990) consider a "major methodological problem" with experimental research that the data acquired are not "representative" because the samples are small and non-random, which "severely limits the validity of statistical tests performed on them". This is quite correct, but only when inappropriate use is made of the statistical analysis techniques. Samples are in fact usually small, but there are a variety of statistical techniques that were developed or adapted for the analysis of small samples (such as the repeated-measures ANOVA or profile analysis used here). The sample used here is not non-random – that would imply some systematic selection of subjects – but no sampling method using human subjects is truly random. Sampling from human subjects is always biased by their willingness to cooperate and by their spatial distribution, hence convenience for the experimenter. Thus, it is not realistic to expect perfectly random sampling for any experiment. The consequences of this deviation from randomness are well-known and many statistical techniques are insensitive to all but very gross deviations. The worst scenario in any case is that one would not be able to generalize beyond the subjects used — but even then the information is still perfectly valid for those subjects. Gile's preoccupations are well placed, even if exaggerated: the inappropriate use of statistics is not only uninformative, but can yield misleading results.

2.2. Materials

Two 580-word texts in English (see Appendix A), a narrative and a procedure, were used as stimuli.

To assess the processes dealing with high-level semantic ("frame") information which is often associated with text type, it was very important to isolate frame-level properties as the only important difference between texts. This was to permit the interpretation that text differences were due primarily to differences in these frame properties. To assure the reliability of this contrast, a multidimensional profile of some thirty lexical, syntactic, and semantic properties was constructed and the two texts were equated along each dimension (see Dillinger 1989; Ch. 4). This strategy yields a finer-grained, much more reliable comparison across texts than the similar-length-and-content comparison usually found in comprehension and interpreting studies using more than one text.

In an attempt to neutralize the effects of prior knowledge on comprehension, texts on a topic unfamiliar to the subjects (positron emission tomography) were used. Rate of presentation was controlled at 145 words per minute, for all subjects (see Gerver 1976 for the effects of rate of presentation on interpreting accuracy).

It should be made perfectly clear that the texts were **not** "artificially composed with the aim of obtaining certain linguistic characteristics" (Gile 1990). The texts were written with the express intention of making them "communicative", natural texts; they were written to be read to an audience. The linguistic characteristics of the texts were measured afterwards. Even so, some might consider them "artificial", but it is not clear what that might mean or how it might affect interpreters' performance. It might mean that the prose is turgid or stilted; but that is merely a question of taste. It might also mean that they are not the sorts of texts that one would find as "conference speeches given to delegates," but one could conceive of a science education conference from which these texts could have been excerpted. In any case, what sort of conference with what sort of delegates would have to be involved for one to speak of a "natural" text and more valid interpreting data? It might also mean that the texts are "artificial" because they were not excerpted from actual conference proceedings. One might ask, however, why this would make a difference. No one knows what the differences are (if there are any) between the texts used here and the sorts of texts found in actual conference situations. The hypothesis that the texts are different and the processes involved in comprehending and interpreting them are qualitatively different because one text was presented to an audience and the other was not is not only unsupported by any evidence, but also seems entirely implausible. In sum, there seem to be no objective criteria to judge the "artificiality" or "naturalness" of the texts used, and more importantly, there is no evidence that the "artificiality"of the texts makes any difference in how interpreters interpret.

2.3. *Tasks*

Subjects were instructed to interpret, and afterwards to recall, each experimental text. They were explicitly instructed not to worry about remembering the text but to concentrate on interpreting it. Both texts were presented in English; interpreting was from English into French. Presentation of each text lasted approximately four minutes. A short practice text on a related topic was also presented to all subjects for warm-up.

2.4. *Procedure*

Subjects were seated individually in a small, quiet room which was very similar in appearance to an interpreter's booth, equipped with a Fostex X-15 series II four-track cassette tape recorder and full-sized enclosed headphones with an unobtrusive Radio Shack 33-1063 miniature lapel microphone clipped to the headphone wire. After a short introduction presented on tape, subjects interpreted a two-minute warm-up text, then the first experimental text. After the first experimental text, they were asked to provide a recall of it, and took a short break while the experimenter readied the equipment for the second text. Finally, they interpreted the second experimental text and provided a recall. All instructions and stimuli were presented binaurally from the left channel (channel

1) of the stimulus tape. Subjects' interpreting performance, as well as their recalls, were recorded on the right channel (channel 2). After the task was completed, subjects were given a short debriefing session to get information on their training, experience and reactions to the experiment.

2.5. Deviations from Standard Interpreting Practice

Much ink is wasted in the literature on interpreting to decry experimental research as irrelevant and uninteresting. Most of the experimental research admittedly does not address the questions that interpreters and interpreter-trainers would like answered. Some of it is even flawed methodologically. This, however, is to be expected in a field with no experimental tradition and little theoretical development, and does not justify the view implying that it should not be undertaken. The current situation, in which practitioners and experimenters have become polarized around pseudo-issues such as the "validity" or "representativity" of experimental data, has had the single effect of stunting the growth of research on interpreting. Everyone, practitioners and experimenters alike, loses when research on interpreting is not done: practitioners lose the opportunity to acquire reliable information about how to identify and develop interpreting skills, and experimenters lose the opportunity to investigate one of the most complex linguistic processes known. It is not enough to encourage interpreters to do research, because they commit basic errors of experimental design and statistical analysis, not having in-depth training in them. Nor is it sufficient to encourage experimenters to study interpreting, because they commit basic errors of interpreting practice, not having the necessary experience with the task. The only rational solution, of course, is to do cooperative research, since neither has the necessary experience with the others' expertise.

Out of respect for practitioners' concerns about how well laboratory data corresponds to real-world interpreting, the following task analysis is offered in an attempt to show that the data obtained here are to no small extent "valid" and "representative". The experimental task used in a laboratory setting for this study seemed to deviate from standard interpreting practice in several ways:

1) The task was decontextualized. That is, the text interpreted was not presented in the context of a particular audience, on a particular social occasion such as a conference of specialists. These communicative parameters were left undefined, and constitute the major difference between laboratory and natural conditions. The extent to which this may affect actual interpreting performance

has not been studied in any detail, although its importance has been repeatedly emphasized by Seleskovitch (1984) and colleagues. It is important to bear in mind, however, that their theorizing is based almost entirely on the interpretation of spontaneous speech, in particular dialogue. In a conversational situation, context is obviously much more important than in interpreting prepared text, so that their theorizing may be less relevant for the present interpreting task.

2) It was not possible to see the speaker. This is a particular instance of the difference pointed out in (1), and subject to the same *caveats*. Note that all of the examples used by Seleskovitch & Lederer (1984) to emphasize the importance of contextual variables are cases in which either deictic reference to the immediate physical situation or speaker/addressee identity are important, and that neither of these is important in the presentation of a prepared text. Thus, the kind of text chosen and type of social situation (lecture) that was presupposed here both acted to reduce the importancc of contextual variables, thus making this laboratory task much more similar to one kind of natural setting than would initially seem to be the case. Moreover, Anderson (in this volume) found no differences in accuracy between interpreting with or without a view on the proceedings.

3) The interpreters were not allowed to prepare for the task, nor were they allowed to choose the topic. Interpreters sometimes specialize in, or develop a preference for, given topics, and in most cases are given the opportunity to do some preparation before interpreting about a given topic. This difference refers to the role of prior knowledge in interpreting performance, a clearly important, although entirely uninvestigated, factor. This does not, however, make the experimental task very different from normal practice, for the following reasons.

On the one hand, interpreters rarely have technical knowledge of topics they are called upon to interpret; at best they have some general awareness of the area under discussion, at least in Canada where the market does not make great demands on technical specialization. On the other hand, it is unlikely that in a few days' time an interpreter untrained in physics, math or chemistry (i.e., the majority) will be able to understand very much of any technical topic. Moreover, preparation time is used (according to experienced subjects) to become familiar with the vocabulary of the area, rather than attempting to understand theory. This emphasis on the lexical characteristics of a given type of technical text is also reflected in the widespread use of terminology databases and specialized dictionaries. The difference, then, between preparing and not preparing for an interpreting session seems to be one of increasing the subjective frequency of rare words – presumably with a consequent facilitation of access to them, rather than increasing prior knowledge *per se*.

4) There was no audience. One subject reported that an important difference of the laboratory setting was the absence of an audience. She found the tension and pressure to perform an important stimulus that was missing in the laboratory. The consequences for processing are unknown, but one might expect little more than a slight (if any; see Anderson 1979) decrement in overall performance because of this difference, rather than a major qualitative difference in how the task is carried out.

5) Subjects were not paid. The consequences of this difference are, unfortunately, quite unpredictable, but again might entail a slight decrement in performance. However, it is unlikely that subjects will be able to perform such an enormously complex task in more than one way.

In sum, the main deviations from standard interpreting practice bear on context and prior preparation. The setting and type of text used here (pre-prepared material read in a lecture or radio broadcast setting) reduced the importance of contextual variables. Preparation would have emphasized correct terminology, rather than increasing prior theoretical knowledge. Since the translations produced were analyzed for content, correct or incorrect terminology (*cycloscope* for *cyclotron*, for example) made little difference in coding. Thus, the differences between the experimental task and normal practice have been minimized as much as was possible.

2.6. Data Manipulation

The steps described above yielded 16 interpreting protocols for each text. All of the protocols were transcribed including false starts, hesitations, etc. and were divided into syntactic units to facilitate subsequent analyses. French-language protocols were transcribed by a French-native-language linguist. Only the analyses of these 32 protocols are reported here.

In all comprehension research some assessment is made of the degree to which the response protocols – in this case, the subjects' translations – match or mismatch the input text (Ericsson & Simon 1984); this is the fundamental step of generating data from the observations. One typical, but more detailed than usual, form of this analysis (recall/inference coding, see Bracewell, Frederiksen & Frederiksen 1982) proceeds by categorizing the propositional information units of the original text as absent, recalled, inferred, or recalled with inference in the response protocol. This coding technique has proved to be very useful, and is in fact more detailed and reliable than many more widely used techniques (e.g., simple presence vs. absence of propositions judged without reference to explicit criteria). Since a proposition – the unit of meaning used in this analysis – represents preferentially the "structural meaning" of a sentence, it is made up of a head concept (or predicator), a list of concepts ("fillers"), and their relations ("slots") to the head concept. For example, the structural meaning of "John translated two baroque poems this month", would be represented with the following slot-filler pairs, which constitute two propositions:

HEAD:translate
AGENT:John
OBJECT:(two) poems
TEMPORAL:(this) month
HEAD:(two) poems
ATTRIBUTE:baroque

The slots (in capital letters) are basic semantic relations derived from the work of Fillmore (1968), Gruber (1976) and others, as defined in Frederiksen (1975). This sort of analysis is standard practice for representing sentence meanings in linguistics (where the slots are called "theta roles"), cognitive psychology and computer science. Of course, this notation is understood to represent only a part of the meaning of a given string of words, and it is this structural meaning and the relative synonymy of the words involved that are analyzed in the Bracewell *et al.* coding technique, as well as that used here.

The attempt in the present study to measure subtle processing differences using a small number of subjects made a more refined adaptation of this method necessary. Rather than matching entire propositions, here the units of comparison were the individual slot-filler pairs that constitute each proposition. That is, each slot-filler pair of each proposition in the input text received a score according to the degree of similarity between it and the segment of the subject's response being analyzed, using the following ordinal scale of similarity:

0 if the slot-filler pair was not present in the segment (absent); least similar.
1 if there was a change of meaning in either the slot or the filler (semantic change).

2 if there was a change in surface form of either the slot or the filler, without a change in meaning (paraphrase).
3 if the slot-filler pair appeared in the segment verbatim (verbatim); most similar.

For each proposition, the difference/similarity between the response protocol and the propositions of the input text was represented with three measures: (a) the proportion of the original proposition's slot-filler pairs reproduced with semantic changes, (b) the proportion paraphrased, and (c) the proportion reproduced verbatim.

The response type called verbatim merits some comment in dealing with translation protocols. Obviously, translations are never verbatim, but are meaning-preserving paraphrases in another language. However, in this study, verbatim was used to indicate that in translation the same sentence structure and direct translation-equivalent lexical items were used. Paraphrased responses were those in which there were other meaning-preserving surface changes (for example, use of passive voice instead of active). Perhaps more accurate names for these response types might be "strictly meaning preserving" and "loosely meaning preserving"; the relative proportions of each type, however, show that this is not an important difference in the present data.

One question that arises with respect to this coding method is that of its applicability across languages. The semantic relations in terms of which sentence meanings are described were proposed as language universals, and have been used in the analysis of a wide variety of languages. The applicability of such concepts as Agent, Affected Object, Instrument, Location, Time, etc. is hardly controversial; quite the contrary, it would be of great interest to discover a language to which they do not apply. This sort of semantic analysis, as does any other, has its limitations; it does not, for example, capture the connotations of different synonyms, of stylistic differences between roughly synonymous sentences, nor the presuppositions or entailments of different constructions. Such aspects of meaning have been systematically excluded so as to better concentrate on the aspects of interest at the moment.

2.7. Design and Analyses

For each of the experimental texts a database was constructed, using Microsoft® Excel, in which each record (row) corresponded to a text proposition, and each field (column), to information about the linguistic properties of the text. This made it simple to generate information about propositions with a given property (e.g., those found in matrix or non-matrix clauses, that were root or non-root propositions, those found in a segment with n clauses, etc.), as well as to classify propositions by these properties. Once the raw data matrices were appended to these databases as new fields, generating dependent measures by performing calculations on classes of propositions became simple with the database calculation functions built into Microsoft® Excel. The matrices of dependent variables generated by the methods described above were subjected to mixed between and within repeated-measures multivariate analyses of variance using the Multivariance VII statistical analysis package (Finn & Bock 1985). The between-subjects factors were Experience and Text Order; the within-subjects factors tested were Clause Density, Clause Embedding, Proposition Density, Directness of Mapping, Frame/non-Frame propositions, Frame component, and Text Frame type. See Dillinger (1989, Chapter 4) for details of the within- and between-subjects statistical models used to analyze the data, as well as complete results of the analyses.

3. Results

3.1. The Effects of Experience on Interpreting

This section deals with the differences in interpreting performance associated with the subjects' experience with the task. Recall that the difference in experience between the two groups was intentionally large (3830 hours, or some 8.5 years), precisely so that the differences would show up unambiguously. The interest of identifying these differences is clear: they will indicate what skills the experienced interpreters have acquired over the years. It may be that with experience interpreters come to comprehend more efficiently (quantitative differences) or even in different ways (qualitative differences) than the inexperienced subjects. These differences, of course, are what interpreter training is all about.

3.2. Overall

Accuracy of interpreting overall was, as expected, better for the experienced interpreters than for the inexperienced subjects, and this difference was statistically significant (See Table 1 for a summary of the significant statistical tests). Quantitatively, experienced subjects interpreted accurately approximately 17% more of the text than the inexperienced subjects (M^{exp} = 57.6%, M^{inexp} = 41.0%). The difference, although rather smaller than expected, was not at all surprising.

Table 1. *Summary of Effects of Experience on Interpreting*

Contrast name	*F* (1,12)	*p*
Experience	6.9911	.0215
Exp x RT3-2	5.7652	.0335
Exp x Text x RT2+3-1	5.3876	.0387
Exp x RM2-1	7.9886	.0153
Exp x RM2-1x Text	6.1834	.0287
Exp x RM2-1 x RT3-2	5.6753	.0347
Exp x RM2-1 x RT2+3-1x Text	12.3588	.0043

The important, qualitative, questions now arise: What is this advantage due to? What do experienced interpreters know how to do differently or more efficiently than inexperienced bilinguals? Is the difference one of syntactic processing, i.e., having to do with the operations performed on a sequence of words to generate one or more sentences? Is the difference to be found in proposition generation, i.e., the operations that generate propositional meaning units from the grammatical information in clauses and sentences? Or perhaps the difference lies in the ways in which these propositions are linked together to form the more complex meaning structures characteristic of different kinds of texts, i.e., a difference in "frame" processing. Finally, the differences between experienced and inexperienced interpreters might lie in all of these processes, or even in none of them, which would lead to the conclusion that the differences are not to be found in comprehension but in the processes of translation or production. These are the questions dealt with here: rather than just investigate whether and to what extent there is a difference in overall accuracy, the differences in specific processes that underlie this difference — just how this difference is obtained — are studied.

3.3. Syntactic Processing

A given item of information might appear in a simple sentence or in a complex one, or in syntactically different places in the sentences; if this affects subjects' ability to interpret, we can conclude that this difference is an indication of the importance of syntactic processing in interpreting. Moreover, if the experienced subjects are more or less sensitive to this syntactic distinction, then we can conclude that their syntactic processing is different from that of the inexperienced subjects. Two such syntactic properties were investigated: *Clause density* and *Clause embedding*.

Clause density designates the total number of clauses per segment – roughly the proportion of subordinate clauses to main clauses –, and as such is a measure of the syntactic complexity of the segment. Each proposition was classified as to whether it was found in a segment with 1, 2, or 3 or 4 clauses (i.e., simple, somewhat complex, and more complex clauses).

Clause embedding designates the syntactic "prominence" of the clause: whether it was a main ("matrix") or subordinate ("non-matrix") clause. Each proposition was classified as to whether it was found in a matrix or a non-matrix clause.

Both of these measures are associated with the assumption that clause density and embedding lead to more "effort" in syntactic processing and consequently to a higher probability of errors in interpreting performance.

None of the tests of the joint effects of experience and either of these syntactic properties revealed any systematic differences (i.e., the interactions of experience with clause density and with clause embedding were not significant). The same was true even when the comparisons were made taking the different kinds of texts into account (i.e., there were no significant interactions of experience and text type with clause density or embedding – See Table 1). This strongly suggests that experienced and inexperienced interpreters are analyzing the grammatical properties of the texts in the same ways during interpreting. The differences between experienced and inexperienced interpreters apparently lie elsewhere.

3.4. Proposition Generation

A given item of information (proposition) might appear in a sentence that contains a lot of other information or might be less directly related to the grammatical characteristics of the sentence in question, thus making it more difficult to construct propositional information units from the grammatical information provided. If these affect the subjects' ability to interpret, we can conclude that this difference is an indication of the importance of proposition generation in interpreting. Again, if the experienced subjects are more or less sensitive to this distinction, then we can conclude that their processes of proposition generation are different from those of the inexperienced subjects. Two text properties were investigated that were indicative of this sort of processing: *Proposition density* and *Directness of mapping*.

Proposition density designates the total number of propositions per segment – roughly the number of propositional information units in the segment –, and as such is a measure of the complexity of comprehending each segment. Each text proposition was classified as to whether it was found in a segment with 1 to 3, 4, or 5 to 7 total propositions (i.e., low, medium and highly informative segments).

Directness of mapping designates the correspondence or non-correspondence between the syntactic "importance" the clause and the semantic "importance" of the information in the same clause: if a given unit of information was found in a main (matrix) clause and in a main ("root" or "unembedded") proposition, then the correspondence between clause and proposition was considered direct. The same was the case if both clause and proposition were subordinate ("embedded"). If one was embedded and the other not, then the correspondence was considered indirect.

Both of these measures are associated with the assumption that proposition density and more indirect mappings lead to more "effort" in semantic processing and therefore to a higher probability of errors in interpreting performance.

As was the case with syntactic processing, the tests of the joint effects of experience and proposition density revealed no systematic differences. However, the tests involving experience and directness of mapping showed clear differences, in particular of processing main clauses that corresponded to embedded and unembedded propositions. (See Table 1).

Figure 1 shows that for both texts, unembedded (root) propositions were processed better than embedded propositions, and that this difference was greater for the experienced interpreters. The figure is broken down by text to show that the same *qual*itative pattern of results was found for both experienced and inexperienced interpreters; the experienced interpreters apparently carried out the appropriate processes more efficiently, hence interpreted more accurately, leading to the *quan*titative difference shown in the graph. This pattern of results strongly suggests that experienced and inexperienced interpreters are analyzing the texts in the same ways during interpreting, although the experienced interpreters are more accurate in their analyses. This, then, is one difference in what experienced and inexperienced interpreters seem to be doing – a very specific one that deals with giving special treatment to constructing propositional information units from *main* (matrix) clauses. Note that there were no systematic differences having to do with other kinds of clauses, or with the amount of information per segment.

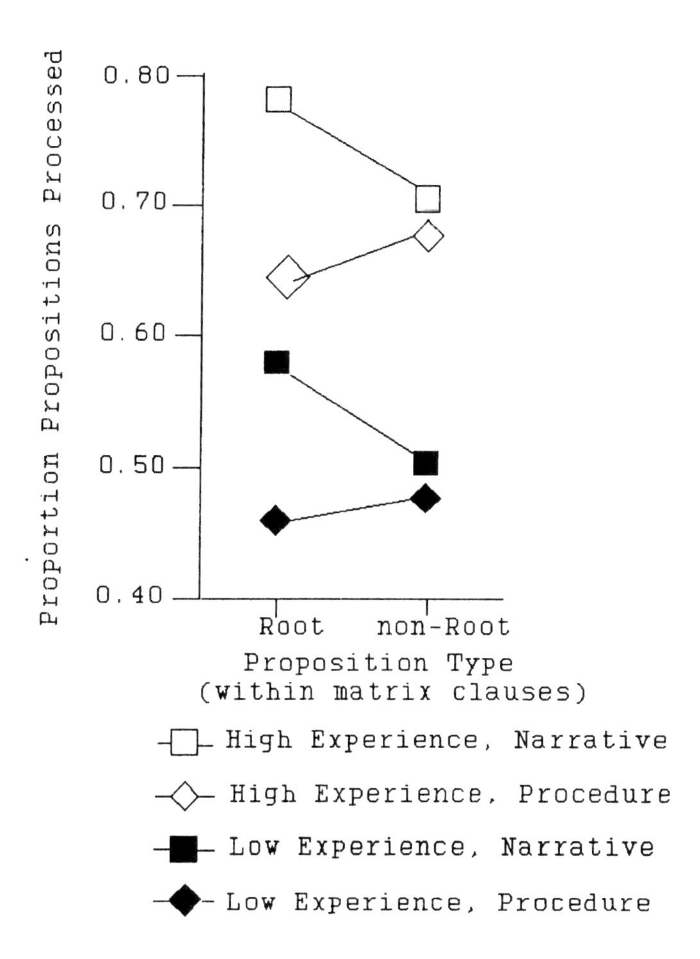

Figure 1. *Joint effects of Experience, Text Type and Directness of mapping on interpreting performance.*

3.5. Frame Processing

A given item of information (proposition) might be more or less important to the kind of text in question or might belong to a part of the text (to an episode, or subprocedure, for example). If either of these properties affects subjects' ability to interpret, we can conclude that this difference is indicative of the importance of linking together propositional information units into what are called "frames", "scripts" or "schemata" – the more complex information structures that characterize texts, rather than sentences. Again, if the experienced subjects are more or less sensitive to these distinctions, then we can conclude that their processes of frame processing are different from those of the inexperienced subjects. Two text properties were investigated that were indicative of this sort of processing: *Proposition type* within the frame and *Frame component.*

Proposition type refers to whether a given proposition belongs to the main frame structure ("frame" propositions) or not ("non-frame" propositions), and as such is an indicator of the relative "importance" of that proposition to the kind of text frame structure that needs to be built to understand the text.

Frame component refers to the part of the text frame that a given proposition belongs to. The *Narrative text* contained three episodes, so the propositions in that text were classified as to whether they belonged to episode1, episode2, or episode3. Likewise, the *Procedural text* contained three subprocedures, and the propositions in that text were classified as to whether they belonged to subprocedure1, subprocedure2, or subprocedure3.

These measures are associated with the hypothesis that similar parts of a frame are processed in similar ways: that frame propositions are more likely to be interpreted in the same way, and that the propositions belonging to episodes or subprocedures are more likely to be treated together and related.

The tests of the joint effects of experience and these frame-related factors revealed no systematic differences (See Table 1). This once again strongly suggests that experienced and inexperienced interpreters are structuring the propositions of the texts in the *same* ways during interpreting. The differences between experienced and inexperienced interpreters are apparently not to be found here.

3.6. The Effects of Text Structure on Interpreting

The results above dealt with the *differences* between experienced and inexperienced interpreters. This section deals with the *similarities* between them: in particular, what aspects of text structure influence interpreting performance, regardless of the subjects' experience? This is of importance because it characterizes the interpreting process in more detail, as well as providing a base for predicting interpreters' performance as a function of text characteristics, and for scaling the difficulty of texts used in training interpreters. A methodological note is in order at this point: the effects of text-structure variables were assessed "within subjects", that is, the statistical tests were carried out with each subject serving as his own "control". This is important because it makes the test much more sensitive than a "between subjects" assessment.

3.7. Text Type

Two text types were contrasted in the present study: *Narrative* and *Procedural*. The types were defined in terms of the different ways in which propositional information is structured in each text. If this difference affects subjects' ability to interpret, we can conclude that they are making use of this type of information about the high-level conceptual structure of the text, even in the very limited time they have available. Recall that the two texts were very carefully controlled to be very similar with respect to thirty or so other characteristics, so that text-induced differences can be unambiguously interpreted as being due to the different ways in which propositional information is organized in them. Effects of text type also serve as evidence that interpreters go beyond more or less literal sentence meanings to integrate them into a text structure as they go.

There was a very strong effect of text type on interpreting performance: subjects interpreted significantly more of the narrative text than of the procedure (See Table 2 for a summary of the significant statistical tests involving text type). That is, in spite of the fact that both texts had the same number of words, clauses, cohesive elements, and propositions, as well as similar distributions of the amounts and types of each of these, there was a systematic difference in how well interpreters performed with them. This difference can be attributed to the different ways in which propositional information was organized to form an informational structure, or frame, for the text.

Table 2. *Summary of Effects of Text Frame Type on Interpreting*

Contrast name	F (1,12)	p
Text	40.6818	.0001
Clause density		
Text x Cls 2-1	8.2180	.0142
Clause embedding		
Text x Mtx-NMtx	17.1142	.0014
Text x Mtx-NMtx x RT3-2	6.5773	.0248
Proposition density		
Text x DenMid-Lo	12.6654	.0040
Text x DenHi-Mid	67.7256	.0001
Text x DenHi-Mid x RT3-2	37.7185	.0001
Text x DenHi-Mid x RT2+3-1	52.6748	.0001
Directness of mapping		
Text x RM2-1	244.9252	.0001
Text x RM4-3	11.9140	.0048
Text x RM2-1 x RT2+3-1	7.9555	.0155
Text x RM4-3 x RT2+3-1	6.5147	.0254

Besides an overall effect of text type on interpreting performance, there were systematic joint effects of text type and each of the text-structure variables (Table 3). In other words, syntactic processing and especially proposition generation varied systematically as a function of the different text types. This is quite a surprising result, since it suggests that similar syntactic and propositional units are dealt with *differently* when they are used to build information structures of different types, which is the opposite of what is often assumed to be the case. The effects of these syntactic and propositional characteristics of the texts will be examined next.

Table 3. *Summary of Effects of Text-structure Variables on Interpreting*

Contrast name	*F* (1,12)	*p*
Clause Density		
Cls 3-2	7.60671	.0174
Cls 2-1 x Text	8.2180	.0142
Clause Embedding		
Mtx-NMtx x Text	17.1142	.0014
Mtx-NMtx x Text x RT3-2	6.5773	.0248
Proposition Density		
DenMid-Lo	134.7180	.0001
DenHi-Mid	11.7727	.0050
DenMid-Lo x Text	12.6654	.0040
DenHi-Mid x Text	67.7256	.0001
DenMid-Lo x RT3-2	131.3964	.0001
DenMid-Lo x RT2+3-1	104.9934	.0001
DenHi-Mid x Text x RT3-2	37.7185	.0001
DenHi-Mid x Text x RT2+3-1	52.6748	.0001
Directness of Mapping		
RM2-1	184.7604	.0001
RM4-3	131.7132	.0001
RM2-1 x Text	244.9252	.0001
RM4-3 x Text	11.9140	.0048
RM2-1 x RT3-2	178.0147	.0001
RM4-3 x RT3-2	18.0132	.0012
RM2-1 x RT2+3-1	101.5333	.0001
RM2-1 x Text x RT2+3-1	7.9555	.0155
RM4-3 x Text x RT2+3-1	6.5147	.0254
Frame Processing Variables	Narrative	Procedure
Contrast name	*F* (1,12) *p*	*F* (1,12) *p*
Frame/non-Frame Information	66.7674	.0001 <1.0
FNF	14.6537	.0025 <1.0
FNF x RT3-2	<1.0 ns	6.9552 .0217
FNF x RT2+3-1		
Frame Components	6.4072	.0264 5.3365
Frco2-1	6.1986	.0285 6.5224
Frco2-1 x RT2+3-1		

3.8. *Syntactic Processing*

The same syntactic variables as discussed above (*Clause density* and *Clause embedding*) were tested for their influence on interpreting performance. When assessed independently of text type, only one test proved significant: the difference between information found in segments with high and medium clause density. This is indicative of a weak overall effect of syntactic characteristics on interpreting performance, one that only begins to appear when there are at least three clauses per segment. Note that segments with more than three clauses are apparently not characteristic of spoken texts, only of complex texts written to be read. This suggests that the normal syntactic characteristics of spoken texts do not affect interpreting performance systematically.

When assessed with text type, the role of syntactic processing appeared in a different light. The joint effects of text type and clause density were weak, but this time affecting the simpler segments with 1 or 2 clauses each. On the other hand, the joint effect of text type and clause embedding was very strong. As shown in Figure 2 below, more of the propositions in subordinate (non-matrix) clauses were interpreted accurately, but more of the propositions in main (matrix) clauses were used as the basis for inferences, in particular for the Narrative text.

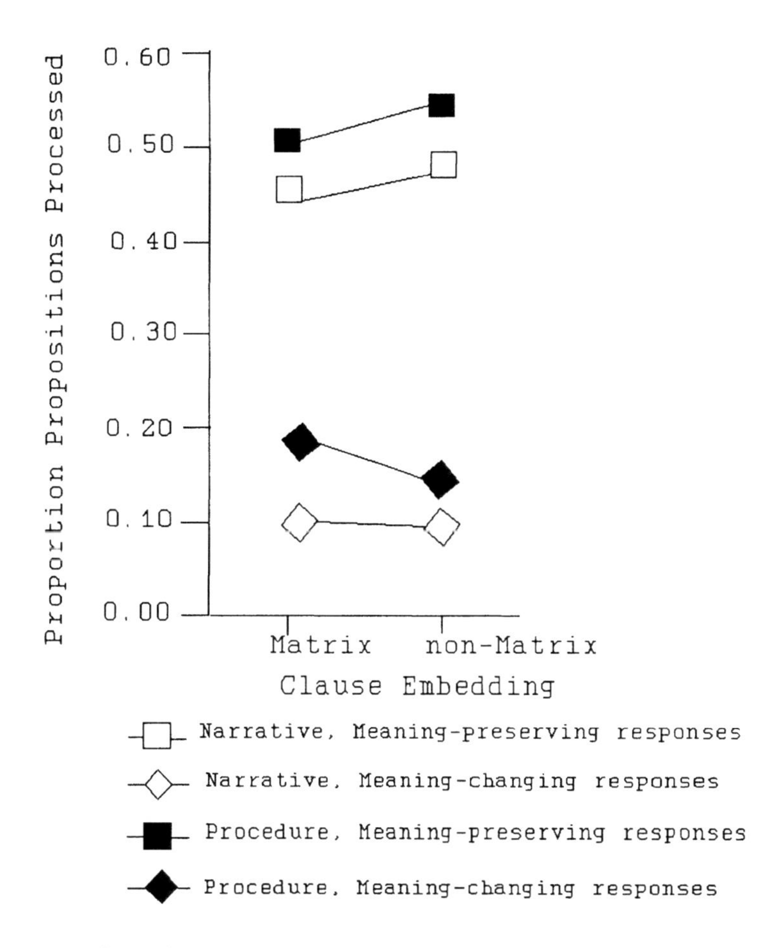

Figure 2. *Joint effects of Clause embedding, Text type and Response type on interpreting performance.*

In sum, there was little effect of syntactic complexity on interpreting, and more of an effect of embedding, in particular in the context of the different text types. This is most likely due to the fact that more of the information in the narrative appeared in matrix clauses, whereas more of the information in the procedure appeared in embedded clauses.

3.9. Proposition Generation

The same variables relating to proposition generation as discussed above (*Proposition density* and *Directness of mapping*) were tested for their influence on interpreting performance. When tested independently of and together with text type, the effects of both variables were very strong and systematic. This is indicative of the central role that this stage of processing – the step of generating propositional information units from grammatical information – plays in interpreting.

Independently of text type, accuracy of interpreting decreases with increasing propositional density (see Figure 3); this reproduces Treisman's (1965) report of decreasing "efficiency" in translation with increasing information rate. The effects of directness of mapping were also very strong, both for matrix and embedded clauses: in general, the embedded propositions were interpreted less accurately than root (unembedded) propositions.

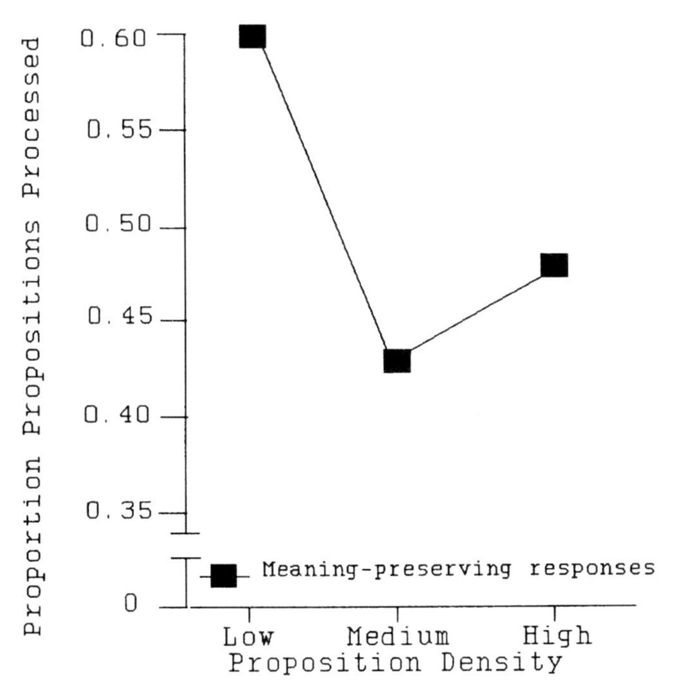

Figure 3. *Effects of proposition density on interpreting performance.*

The joint effects of these variables with text type were also very strong. In Figure 4 below, it is clear that the propositions found high-density segments were more important for understanding the procedure than for the narrative.

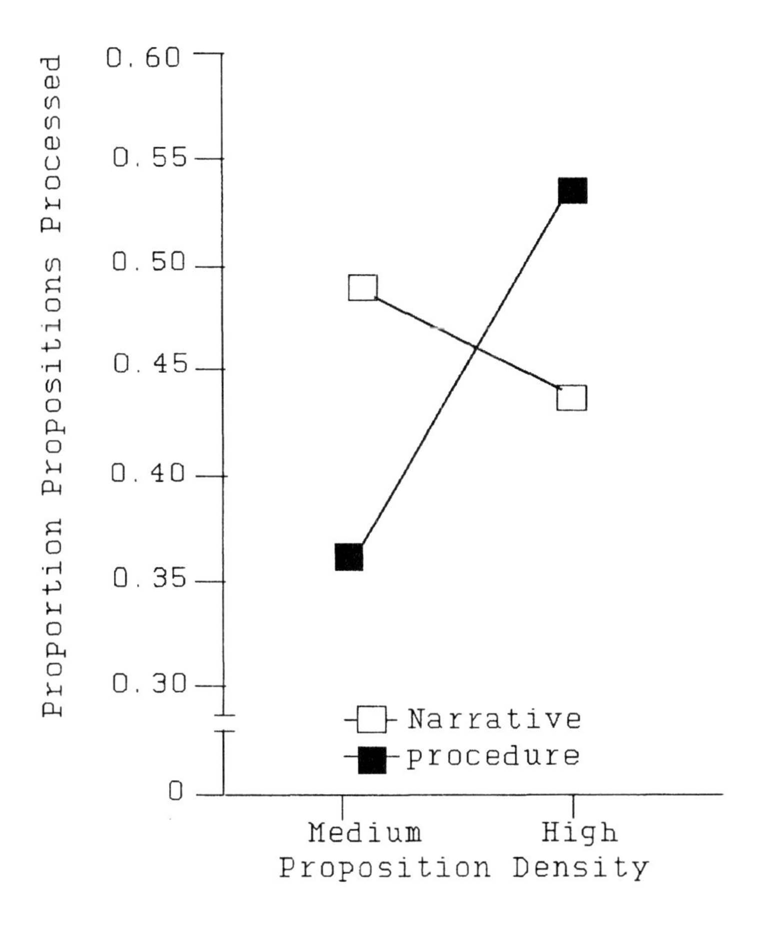

Figure 4. *Joint effects of proposition density and Text Type on interpreting performance.*

The next Figure (5) shows that understanding the Procedure entailed emphasizing the non-root propositions in matrix clauses and the root propositions in non-matrix clauses, whereas the opposite was the case for the Narrative.

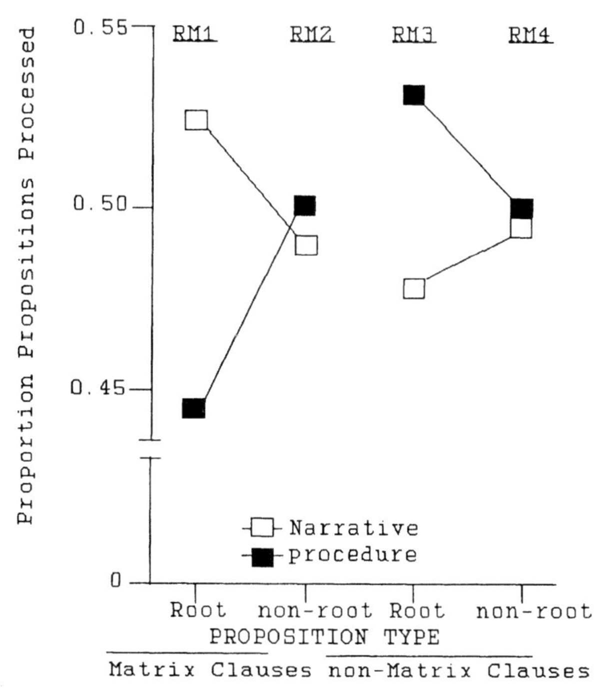

Figure 5. *Joint effects of Directness of mapping and Text type on interpreting performance.*

3.10. Frame Processing

The same variables relating to frame processing as discussed above (*Proposition type* and *Frame component*) were tested separately for each text-type for their influence on interpreting performance. The effects of the frame/non-frame distinction were strong for the *Narrative text*, but not present for the *Procedure* (with one exception). The effects of the differences between *Frame component* were only present for the first two components, and were equally weak for both texts.

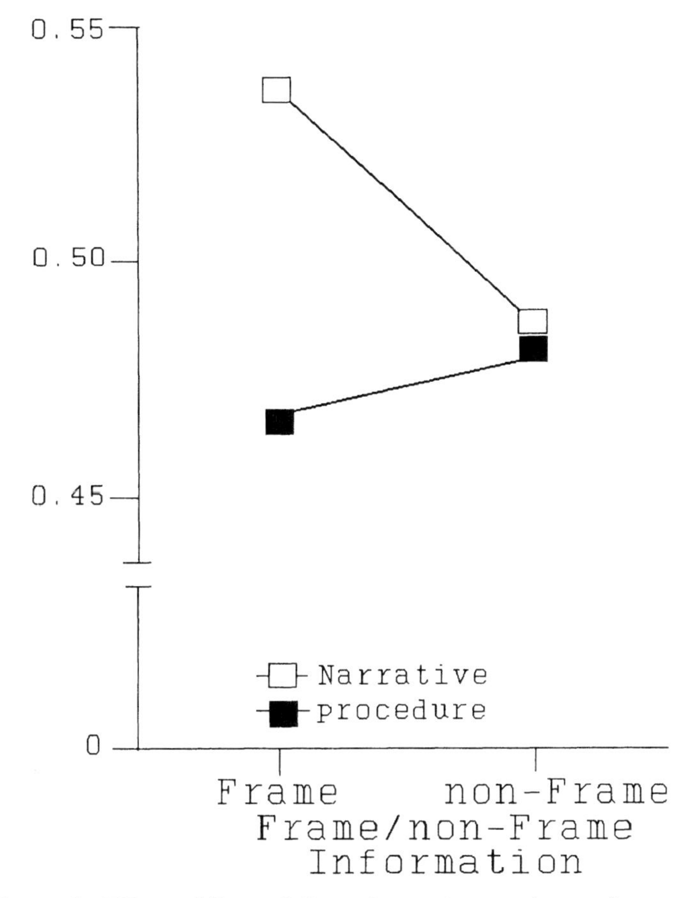

Figure 6. *Effects of Frame information on interpreting performance by Text type.*

The difference between Frame and Non-frame information (Figure 6) was very strong for the *Narrative*, but not significant for the *Procedure*. This suggests that interpreters (regardless of experience) were able to comprehend the event structure of the Narrative, but were unresponsive to the hierarchical structure of procedure and subprocedure in the *Procedural text*. This suggests that interpreters were treating the procedure as if it were a mere sequence of events — as a narrative.

The difference between the *Frame components* (episodes for the *Narrative* and subprocedures for the *Procedure*) was present but weak for both texts and only referred to the difference between the first and second components (Figure 7). The general trend of decreasing performance from component to component as the text progressed may be due to fatigue or waning interest, but it is clear that an understanding of the gist of the text is much more dependent on the first component of the text. This suggests that interpreters were processing the frame component information for both texts in the same ways, and were more successful for the narrative apparently because it is a simpler or more common genre.

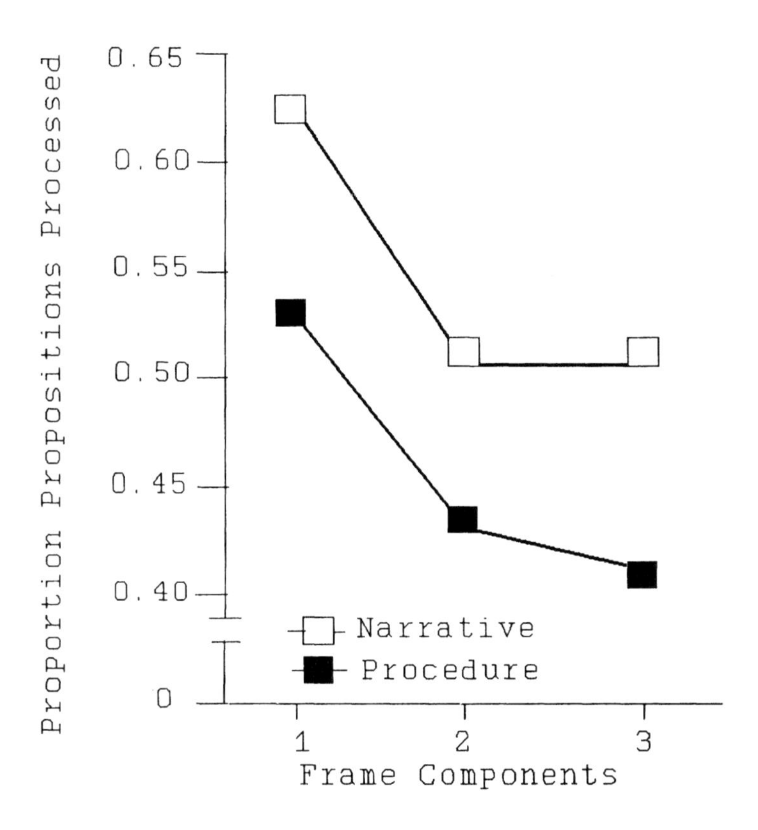

Figure 7. *Effects of Frame component on interpreting performance by Text type.*

To summarize, in processing both texts, interpreters, regardless of experience, were similar in that they were not sensitive to variations in syntactic complexity, but were very sensitive to how directly the text's syntactic properties (in particular clause embedding) reflected the importance of the information it contained. Processing the *Procedural text* entailed much more attention to information in more complex and denser segments, as well as to embedded propositions. Understanding the *Narrative text* entailed more attention to matrix clauses and root propositions in simple segments. These differences can account for the differences in subjects' performance: in processing the procedure, apparently more "effort" was expended with syntactic analysis and proposition generation, creating an extra processing load that was reflected in less accurate performance.

Differences due to experience only arose with respect to the crucial step of proposition generation: experienced interpreters seemed to perform this subprocess more efficiently, independently of any of the other variables investigated.

4. Discussion

The present study was concerned, in most general terms, with how simultaneous interpreting is carried out, in particular with the similarities and differences between experienced and inexperienced interpreters' comprehension processes during interpreting. This general question about the nature of interpreting expertise was broken down into more specific questions about the extent and relative importance of syntactic processing, proposition generation and frame-structure processing – component processes of comprehension in general.

Experience had a weak quantitative effect on interpreting overall, reflecting the fact that the experienced interpreters performed 16.6% more accurately than the inexperienced bilinguals across the board. There were few qualitative differences as would be indicated by interactions of *Experience* with *Text-structure* variables, and the order of presentation of the texts had no important effects at all. The only exception to this pattern was a weak interaction of *Experience* with *Directness of mapping*: experienced interpreters were apparently more selective in their processing of non-root propositions in the matrix clauses of the procedural text. This suggests that the experienced subjects may have learned to be more selective in the surface information they will process semantically, as a function of the text frame structure that is to be built with it. That is, the subprocess of proposition generation may be more closely tailored to the needs of subsequent frame processing for the experienced interpreters.

The pattern of results found here is consistent with the view that experienced interpreters have not acquired any special set of abilities, rather that normal comprehension processes are more flexible than previously believed. This is supported in particular by the presence of main effects of experience and text-structure variables in the absence of systematic interactions between them. Experienced subjects apparently performed the same sorts of processing in the same ways, but with a slight quantitative advantage.

Figure 8 provides a summary of the results, depicting *Performance* by *Experience group* as a function of the text-structure variables assessed. The parallelism of the two sets of lines reflects the absence of major group differences; the deviations from parallelism indicate the small, unsystematic differences in processing that were found. Note that experience-related differences only began to appear for the processing of the procedural frame information, and the only statistically significant interaction of experience was with the directness of mapping variables (RtMtx). Two kinds of responses are shown as well: meaning-preserving responses (accurate translations), and meaning-changing responses (modifications to the meaning of the original text) to show that the relation of both response-types to the different text-structure variables and to experience are similar.

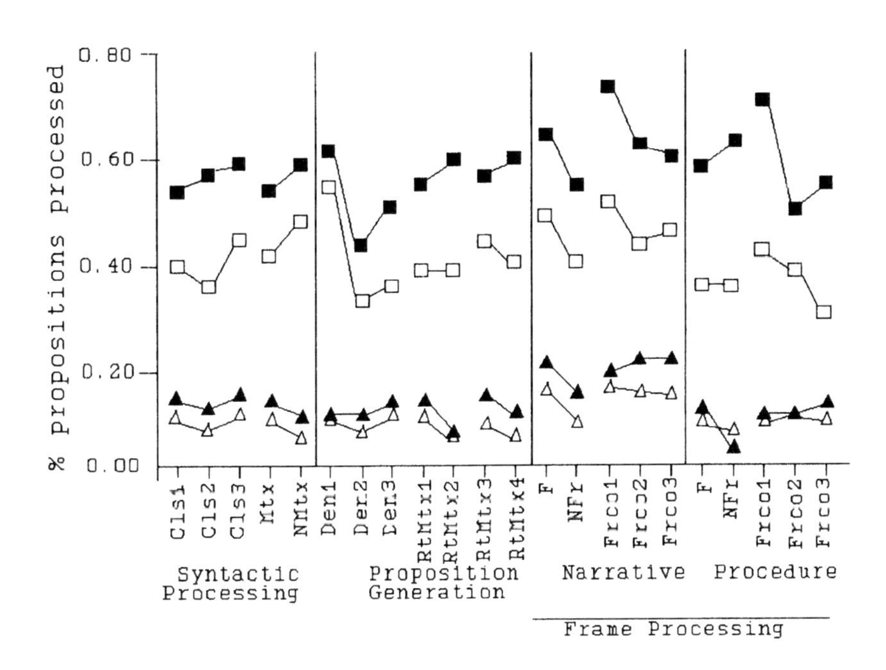

Figure 8. *Interpreting performance (means) by Experience, Text-structure and Response-type variables.*

These results, then, constitute support for the view that translation ability and interpreting skill are natural consequences of bilingualism (see Harris & Sherwood 1978; Longley 1978), and as a result that the differences between experienced and inexperienced interpreters will be mainly quantitative. It is very important to note, however, that the results discussed here refer to the simultaneous interpreting of prepared texts in a conference setting, and may not be generalizable to interpreting more spontaneous dialogue or debates. Conversational text is different from the materials used here in that it is generally less explicit and less predictable, so its processing makes greater demands on prior knowledge and inference generation. Moreover, Frederiksen (1989) argues that the processing of different text types is independent of general comprehension skill (as reflected here in the quantitative differences in understanding the two texts), so that it is possible that an interpreter may work well in the booth with the types of pre-prepared materials used here, but not perform so well with conversational dialogue, or *vice versa*.

Furthermore, it must be made clear that although there were only very subtle differences in the comprehension processes used by experienced and inexperienced subjects, this does not mean that they may not be important. Some of the differences appeared in relation to the more difficult procedural text, and showed up under very specific conditions, which suggests that any special comprehension abilities of experienced interpreters may only appear clearly with more difficult materials or at faster rates of presentation. The variables indexing proposition generation interacted with Experience and this suggests that the possible differences may bear on this poorly understood component of comprehension.

Perhaps even more importantly, it would be misleading to conclude that there are no differences at all between expert and novice interpreters: the main finding of this study bears on their comprehension processes only, and the importance of production processes is not to be underestimated. Quite clearly, "it is one thing to have comprehended a passage in the original and quite another to reproduce it within the given time constraints in the target language" (B. Moser-Mercer, personal communication). It is quite possible that expert interpreters may differ from novices principally with respect to their production processes, which have not been studied here. For example, it may be the case that experienced interpreters will show more independence in their production; that is, the novices will tend to follow the surface features of the original, whereas the experts will produce target-language texts whose formal features are nearly independent of those of the original. Answers to this await further research. The point of the present study was to discover whether the apparent differences between experienced and inexperienced interpreters are due to differences in comprehension; of course to complement these findings, differences in production ability also have to be studied.

5. Conclusion

The fact that simultaneous interpreting is possible at all provides evidence for the modularity and parallel execution of the component processes of discourse comprehension.

The present study has provided evidence that:

(a) comprehension in interpreting is not a specialized ability, but the application of an existing skill under more unusual circumstances;

(b) comprehension in interpreting is characterized by all of the same component processes as listening – processing is not curtailed [as Nida (in Gerver 1976) suggested] – with an emphasis on semantic processing, in particular proposition generation.

The findings suggest that it is not a special, acquired skill, but an ability that seems to accompany bilingualism naturally, and this supports the view that this same modularity and parallelism are features of text processing generally.

These findings may also have some important practical and methodological consequences. They provide principled, empirical support for the intuition current in interpreter training programs that selection is of the utmost importance. If interpreting skill is a function more of general text processing ability than of specific training (i.e., the view that "interpreters are born, not made"), then selection is more important than course work. In particular, if 8.5 years' experience only affords a 17% improvement in accuracy of interpreting, then how much of that is provided by formal training, and how much by experience with the task itself? Indeed, the results reported here suggest that a program of training in simultaneous interpreting (assuming the necessary language skills) need be neither extensive nor complex.

These findings also suggest that interpreters' performance is limited by the same broad parameters that limit text comprehension in general: the nature of the text itself and the prior knowledge that they can bring to bear on understanding it. If, in general, the main factor limiting the efficiency of communication is the difference between the knowledge of the comprehender and the knowledge presupposed by the text, then there are at least two ways to improve communication involving an interpreter: (a) the interpreter has to have the same knowledge as presupposed by the speaker, which suggests greater specialization of interpreters and the inclusion of specific domain knowledge in their training, and (b) the speaker/writer has to design the text so that the interpreter, rather than the speaker's equally knowledgeable peers, can understand it.

Finally, these findings raise a series of new questions to be answered. Will the results be the same with more complex materials or at higher rates of presentation? Will they be replicated with other text types? How does the process of proposition generation work during interpreting? Is interpreting so demanding as to interfere with memory for the text that was interpreted? Is this interference greater for inexperienced interpreters? What sorts of differences in translation or production processes characterize experienced and inexperienced interpreters? How can one best go about studying production?

* This research was carried out at McGill University's Laboratory of Applied Cognitive Science as part of the author's doctoral dissertation. Current mailing address:
Fundação de Ensino Superior de São João del-Rei — FUNREI
Departamento de Artes, Letras e Cultura — Campus Dom Bosco
36.300 São João del-Rei, MG BRASIL.
I thank Sylvie Lambert (University of Ottawa), Joseph Danks (Kent State University), Barbara Moser-Mercer (Université de Genève) and Daniel Gile (ISIT, Paris) for their useful comments on this work.

Notes

1. Given that under normal conditions professional interpreters work 20 minutes on, 20 minutes off during a six-hour working day, that is 3 hours of interpreting per day, and that a reasonably active interpreter might work some 150 days per year, the subjects who participated here therefore had an average on 8.5 years' interpreting experience.

References

Albert, M. and Obler, L. 1978. *The Bilingual Brain*. New York: Academic.

Anderson, L. 1979. *Simultaneous Interpretation: Contextual and Translation Aspects*. Department of Psychology, Concordia University, Montreal, Canada [Unpublished Master's Thesis.]

Barik, H. 1969. *A Study of Simultaneous Interpretation*. Psychology Department, University of North Carolina, Chapel Hill. [Unpublished Doctoral Dissertation.]

Bracewell, R. J., Frederiksen, C., Frederiksen J. 1982. "Cognitive Processes in Composing and Comprehending Discourse". *Educational Psychologist* 17:3. 146-164.

Dillinger, M. 1989. *Component Processes of Simultaneous Interpreting*. Department of Educational Psychology, McGill University, Montreal, Canada. [Unpublished Doctoral Dissertation.]

Ericsson, K. and H. Simon. 1984. *Protocol Analysis: Verbal Reports as Data*. Cambridge, MA: MIT Press.

Fillmore, C. 1968. "The Case for Case". E. Bach and R. Harms, eds. *Universals in Linguistic Theory*. New York: Holt, Rinehart & Winston. 1-88.

Finn, J. and Bock, R. 1985. *Multivariance VII.* Mooresville, IN: Scientific Software.
Frederiksen, C. 1975. "Representing Logical and Semantic Structure of Knowledge Acquired from Discourse". *Cognitive Psychology* 7. 371-458.
Frederiksen, C. 1989. "Text Comprehension in Functional Task Domains". D. Bloom, ed. *Learning to Use Literacy in Educational Settings*. Norwood, NJ: Ablex.
Gerver, D. 1976. "Empirical Studies of Simultaneous Interpretation: A review and a Model". R. Brislin, ed. *Translation: Applications and Research.* New York: Gardner. 165-207.
Gile, D. 1988. "An Overview of Conference Interpretation Research and Theory". D. Hammond, ed. *American Translators Association Conference 1988.* Medford, NJ: Learned Information. 363-372.
Gile, D. 1990. "Observational Studies and Experimental Studies in the Investigation of Interpretation". Presented at the Scuola Superiore di Lingue Moderne, Trieste, Italy.
Gruber, J. 1976. *Lexical Structure in Syntax and Semantics*. Amsterdam: N. Holland.
Harris, B. and B. Sherwood. 1978. "Translating as an Innate Skill". D. Gerver and W.H. Sinaiko, eds. *Language Interpretation and Communication.* New York: Plenum Press. 155-170.
Henry, R. and D. Henry. 1987. *International Bibliography of Interpretation*. Sudbury, Ontario, Canada: Laurentian University.
Lawson, E. 1967. "Attention and Simultaneous Translation". *Language and Speech* 10. 29-35.
Longley, P. (1978). "An Integrated Programme for Training Interpreters". D. Gerver and W.H. Sinaiko, eds. *Language Interpretation and Communication*. New York: Plenum Press. 45-46.
Mackintosh, J. (1985). "The Kintsch and van Dijk Model of Discourse Comprehension and Production Applied to the Interpretation Process". *Meta* XXX:1. 37-43.
McDonald, J. and Carpenter, P. (1981). "Simultaneous Translation: Idiom Interpretation and Parsing Heuristics". *Journal of Verbal Learning and Verbal Behavior* 20:2. 231- 247.
Moser, B. (1978). "Simultaneous Interpretation: A Hypothetical Model and its Practical Applications". D. Gerver and W.H. Sinaiko, eds. *Language Interpretation and Communication.* New York: Plenum Press. 353-368.
Seleskovitch, D. & Lederer, M. (1984). *Interpréter pour Traduire*. Paris: Didier.
Seleskovitch, D. (1984). "Les Niveaux de Traduction". D. Seleskovitch and M. Lederer, eds. *Interpréter pour Traduire*. Paris: Didier. 124-135.
Treisman, A. (1965a). "The Effects of Redundancy and Familiarity on Translating and Repeating Back a Foreign and a Native Language". *British Journal of Psychology* 56:4. 369-379.

Appendix A: Experimental Texts

Narrative

I have a friend named Alex who is a nuclear physicist, but he works in a public hospital instead of at some big university's reactor. He spends a lot of his time shooting protons at glucose and other things. Alex makes several different isotopes with the old cyclotron which is in his lab, and he often helps one of the computer programmers who works in the hospital's brain scanning center. Yesterday I visited Alex at the hospital.

When I found the right office, it was already 10 o'clock. Alex was reading a collection of technical articles, but he put his book on a nearby shelf when I arrived and he showed me all around the lab. He turned on the small cyclotron which was in one corner and made some fluorine isotope to demonstrate how simply it worked. The small machine made noises while Alex explained what it was doing. Afterwards, Alex made some terrible coffee. We talked about the local news for a little while, until a staff doctor asked for some carbon-eleven glucose in a hurry. He said he would call as soon as he was ready for it. Then he prepared the next patient for her scan. Alex explained that since the glucose isotope was only hot (or radioactive) for about a half an hour, he could just set up what was in the lab. He would only start to make the isotope itself when the doctor called again. Not long after Alex was all ready, the doctor called back to confirm his previous request and Alex began to prepare his magic potion right away. When he had finished it, he checked whether it was hot (or radioactive) enough for the scanner. Then we ran up to the scanner room on the third floor, with the solution in a lead bucket.

The scanner was a big aluminum ring with millions of wires connecting it to a big computer in the next room. The patient was waiting nervously for an injection on a long table, with her head inside the ring. As we walked back down the stairs together, Alex explained that scanners detect gamma rays coming from inside the patient's brain. I didn't really understand very much of what he was talking about. It sounded really crazy to me.

After lunch, Alex checked in at the lab. Then we visited his friend Yoshio who ran the brain scanner's computer system. Even before he greeted us, Yoshio pointed at the two TV screens on a large desk and then asked which image was clearer. Yoshio was working on a new program to make the images sharper. Then he pointed at another screen with the same brain image, but it had two handles connected to it, like a video game. He suggested how we should play around with the handles, and when we moved them, the image changed in color and brightness. Yoshio explained that it was better for the doctors to manipulate the color and brightness of the important parts of the image.

The telephone rang, interrupting him. The call was for Alex. He had to go back to the lab, and it was time I left, too. We thanked Yoshio for his explanation of the new program, and walked to the main entrance together. Then Alex went to make some other kind of isotope and I went to the bank to pay some bills. It was a very interesting visit.

Procedure

A man goes to visit his doctor. He complains that his head often aches. He feels weakness in his arms and nausea. The symptoms make the doctor suspect that the patient has a brain tumor. He cannot be sure, though, without finding out what's happening inside the patient's skull. How is it possible to discover, causing no damage, what's going on inside someone's brain? Technology has provided us with a safe way of getting this information: the PET scanner. Let me explain how it works.

First, the patient is prepared: he lies on his back, his eyes and his ears are covered by wrapping them with gauze, and his head is secured with plastic pins so it can't move at all. Finally, his head is placed inside a donut-shaped machine and he is given an injection of a radioactive solution. This is made from a kind of glucose with a radioactive marker attached to some of its molecules. The marker is usually a carbon isotope produced in a cyclotron. This apparatus shoots protons into the nuclei of carbon atoms so they end up with an extra proton. This makes the atoms unstable, but only for a while: after half an hour most of them are normal again. These unstable atoms are attached to the glucose and injected into the patient's neck.

After the injection, scanning begins. The scanner has gamma ray detectors around the patient's head. That's why it's shaped like a donut: so his head can fit in the middle. The unstable atoms eject positrons to become stable again. The positrons each emit two gamma rays when they hit electrons in the patient's tissue, and this is called annihilation. The gamma rays leave the annihilation site in opposite directions and they have enough energy to leave the brain through the skull. When they hit two detectors simultaneously, a signal is sent to a computer. Because each of the detectors has a tube in front of it, it can only see straight ahead. Thus each pair of these detectors only gives information about a small area of tissue. The scanner then collects these signals and registers which of the detectors they came from.

When the scanner finishes its job, the computer starts reconstructing an image of the region that was scanned. A program compares the number of signals sent by each pair of detectors and those sent by all the others, and then it calculates the number of gamma rays emitted by each of the regions of the brain. The image appears on a screen as some colored squares that represent a cross-section of the brain, and this image is what the doctor interprets to perform his diagnosis.

Since the different colors represent different amounts of gamma rays and the rays are produced by the radioactive glucose, he can see where the glucose concentrated. Doctors already know that tumors consume more energy than normal tissue, and that they get this energy from glucose, so the doctor can spot the tumor because it will have a brighter color. Other disorders also show typical patterns on the image, and with different isotopes we can get information about the processes happening in the brain. The isotopes are safe, since they're only radioactive for a short while. The doctor doesn't have to open the skull, so he doesn't cause any damage. Thus, this technique allows him to see what's happening inside the brain easily and safely.

Memory For Sentence Form After Simultaneous Interpretation: Evidence Both For And Against Deverbalization

William P. Isham[1]
Department of Linguistics
University of New Mexico

1. Introduction

In international forums, such as the United Nations or UNESCO, participants from different countries do not communicate directly, but through the services of simultaneous interpreters. Using earphones, these professionals listen to the sentences produced in one language and deliver, a few seconds later, new sentences in a different language that are equivalent in meaning.

Consider the mental processes that are involved with this task. Minimally, incoming sounds in the "source" language must be perceived, segmented, and categorized into words; the appropriate lexical equivalents are then chosen from the "target" language lexicon and produced. Many lay people think that identifying the incoming words and producing their equivalents is a sufficient explanation of the simultaneous interpretation task. There are several reasons, however, to believe otherwise. First, target-language (TL) words cannot be produced in the same order in which they appeared in the source language (SL), for this would often result in an ungrammatical sentence in the target language. For example, if an interpreter working from English into French heard the sentence *I feel like going to the movies*, and produced for each English word a French word that is equivalent in meaning, the following would result: *Je sens comme allant à le cinéma*. This is clearly ungrammatical in French. To produce a grammatical translation, such as *J'ai envie d'aller au cinéma*, often requires understanding the sense of a phrase in order to choose the correct lexical items. Without understanding the sense of "to feel like," for example, it is difficult to explain how the English verb "to feel" could activate the unrelated French verb "avoir" (literally, "to have"). Often, a translation requires more than a "sophisticated" lexical search. In another possible rendition of the same sentence, *Ça me dirait bien d'aller au cinéma*, the syntax has been radically altered, as it transforms the subject of the English sentence into an indirect object, and uses the conditional tense.

From examples such as these, we know that interpreters must, in addition to performing lexical processing, use their knowledge of the grammar of the target language, for the target sentence plan is not necessarily provided by the word order of the input. However, we can presume little else, for many questions cannot be answered by logic alone. Do interpreters use their syntactic knowledge of the source language as a source of information for planning the TL sentence, or is syntactic knowledge used only for the original parsing of the input, such that once comprehension has been achieved, the structure of the SL input has no further role during simultaneous interpretation? Seleskovitch (1975; cited in Gile 1990), an influential interpreter educator in Paris, has formalized the latter view, stating that the input is "deverbalized" before it is restructured according to the dictates of the TL grammar. This stage of deverbalization is explained by Gile as "a stage at which only the meaning remains in the interpreter's mind without any trace of its linguistic vehicle" (1990:33). Little experimental work, however, has been performed that tests these claims (Gile 1990); most of the literature is either theoretical or descriptive in nature (see Gerver 1976 for a review, and Gran & Dodds 1989 for a sampling of more recent work).

Nevertheless, there is evidence of a sort that supports the notion that comprehension plays a central role. It is not rare for an interpreter to anticipate the speaker, that is, to produce in the target language the end of a sentence before the source-language speaker has done so. Another example: when no good equivalent for a word exists in the TL, the interpreter may produce to a short phrase -- or sometimes even several sentences -- to replace the word. Such observations would seem to require some level of comprehension by the interpreter.

Some experimental work also points to the importance of comprehension. If comprehension is indeed a necessary stage to interpretation, then we would expect that interpreters would not begin their TL rendition until sufficient information has arrived to form a meaningful unit. Interpreters do not produce their output instantaneously, rather, they lag behind the SL speaker, on average from 2-6 seconds (Cokely 1986; Gerver 1976). Several investigators have searched for the best predictor of lag times, or "ear-voice spans." Goldman-Eisler (1972) and Davidson (1992) both examined the amount of input received before interpreters began speaking. They both concluded that interpreters waited for a subject NP and a predicate, that is, a clause. A clause is sufficient to form a proposition, a unit of meaning that can take a truth value (Mckoon & Ratcliff 1980; Isham & Lane 1993), and thus, this finding is consistent with the belief that interpreters attend to meaning.

That is not evidence, however, that the propositions are in fact actively processed, only that they would be available before TL production begins. Isham and Lane (1992) investigated the comprehension of interpreters more directly, by examining their performance with an on-line cloze task. Professional interpreters interpreted passages from English into American Sign Language (ASL); these passages had certain words of phrases deleted and replaced by a tone. Subjects were told that upon encountering a tone, they were to figure out what was missing, and to "fill the gap" in the TL rendition. Deleted portions, called "clozes," either required simple recall of information presented explicitly in the preceding portion of the text, or they required subjects to make inferences. Subjects who interpreted the passages found the inferences easier to perform than when they provided a word-for-word rendition of the SL input. Word-for-word translation seemed to interfere with the processes involved with making inferences, processes said to begin and end at the conceptual level of processing (Jackendoff 1987).

The experiment reported here is not an investigation of comprehension itself, but rather the processes that would lead to comprehension; the processing of the incoming sentences. Are incoming sentences treated any differently when the objective is to interpret them than when the goal is simply to understand them? One way to investigate this question is to examine what kinds of information about sentences is retained after the processing has finished. In a now classic experiment, Sachs (1967) showed that we generally retain the "gist" of the sentences we have recently heard, rather than the particular words and syntactic relations that formed their surface structure. A few years later, Jarvella (1971) showed that this shift from form to meaning generally occurs at sentence boundaries.

He did this in the following way. Subjects listened to passages which were interrupted at unexpected intervals. Subjects then recalled as many of the words preceding the interruption as they could. Subjects received one of two versions of each passage, which were differentiated only by the last two sentences before each recall trial. The last thirteen words were identical in both versions, but differed in whether they belonged to the same or to different sentences in the surface structure. Consider this example:

A: The confidence of Kofach was not unfounded. To stack the meeting for McDonald, the union had even brought in outsiders.

B: Kofach had been persuaded by the officers to stack the meeting for McDonald. The union had even brought in outsiders.

The last two clauses, underlined, are identical, but in version A, they belong to the same sentence whereas in version B, they do not. Jarvella showed that verbatim recall for the most recent clause (e.g., *the union had even brought in outsiders*) was better than for the previous clause, and that this clause (*to stack the meeting for McDonald*) was recalled better in A than in B, that is, when it is part of the most recently heard sentence at time of testing. This result demonstrated that it is not an absolute number of words that predicts verbatim recall, but rather the location of syntactic boundaries. Subjects generally paraphrased previous sentences, even though verbatim recall had been emphasized. This shows that it is not the meaning or "gist" of previous sentences that has become lost, but the information about the particular form of the sentence itself.

Performance on the Jarvella task, then, shows whether or not information about the sentence form -- the particular lexical items employed and their relative ordering -- is available to subjects at a given point in time. Normally, such information will be available for only the most recent sentence. If interpreters process incoming sentences in much the same way as listeners do, we would expect the same pattern of verbatim recall. If, however, interpretation requires more (or less) focus on the SL structure, this should be reflected by better (or poorer) recall. Note that this paradigm allows us to test Seleskovitch's (1975) claim that a complete "deverbalization" of the input occurs prior to TL production. If no trace of the SL sentence remains, interpreters should show poorer recall overall, and less of a difference between the two versions of a given test item.

Isham and Lane (1993) replicated Jarvella's result with native speakers of English, and obtained exactly the same pattern of recall as had Jarvella. In addition, a group of professional interpreters interpreted the passages into American Sign Language, and like the listeners, recalled the English words preceding the tone that signaled each test trial. The interpreters showed the same pattern of recall, that is, an advantage for the final clause, and superior recall for the previous (hereafter: the "critical") clause when it had been part of the most recent sentence. However, verbatim recall for the critical clause in the clause boundary condition (version A in the above example) was poorer than that of the listeners. Interpreters tended to paraphrase the initial clause in two-clause sentences more often that listeners did. Thus it would seem that, contrary to Seleskovitch (1975), information about the form of the SL sentence was available, at least for this group of interpreters. In partial support of Seleskovitch, however, these interpreters appeared to lose the memory trace for sentence form sooner than the listeners did, that is, at clause boundaries rather than at sentence boundaries. This indicates a greater tendency to process clause by clause, rather than sentence by sentence. This may be yet another indicator, like the results of Goldman-Eisler (1972) and Davidson (1992), that interpreters use the clause as their default unit of processing.

The experiment reported here replicates the experiment with signed language interpreters, this time with professional interpreters who regularly interpret from English into French. If the process of interpretation requires, *a priori*, a clause by clause approach, then like the ASL interpreters, these subjects should also show poorer performance for the critical clause when compared to subjects who listened to the passages.

In addition, each text was followed by a quiz containing 12 True-False questions. Half of the questions on each quiz were in English, the other half were in French. The quizzes were employed mainly to motivate subjects to understand the passages. Both English and French questions were included in order to test comprehension independently of the source or target languages.

2. Method

2.1. Subjects

Twelve French/English bilinguals and nine professional interpreters were recruited from the Paris metropolitan area to serve as subjects. All were native speakers of French, and had achieved a high level of fluency in English. Participation was voluntary.

2.2. *Materials*

The two passages created by Jarvella (1971) for his original experiment were used in this study. There were sixteen matched pairs of test items. Each test item was 20 words in length, and consisted of three complete clauses of seven, six and seven words, in that order. Across each matched pair, the critical and final clauses were identical, while the initial clause varied between the pairs. These initial clauses were designed by Jarvella so that the critical clause either completed the sentence begun by the context clause, or began a new sentence completed by the final clause.

Thus, the 20 words of each test item formed two sentences in which the last thirteen words were identical between matched pairs and formed the same two clause-type constituents. For this study, the crucial difference between the matched pairs lay in whether the critical and final clauses were separated in the surface structure by a clause boundary or by a sentence boundary. The two conditions will be identified by which boundary type is in this position. The two variations are diagramed here (an example was given previously).

(A) Clause Condition: [Context$_1$] [Critical Final]

(B) Sentence Condition: [Context$_2$ Critical] [Final]

Four test items of each condition were embedded into both of the passages: their matched counterparts created the other version of each passage. In addition, each passage had four dummy items, identical across passage versions, used as controls to prevent subjects from identifying a pattern among the test items. The two sentences in each dummy item varied in length and sentence structure and, like test items, occurred just before a tone prompting recall.

Each of the four experimental texts (two versions each of two passages) was taped on a separate audiocassette, allowing for counterbalancing the order in which passages were heard. The passages were recorded at a moderate rate of speech (130 words per minute).

Twelve True/False questions were constructed in English for each text, and a French translation made of each question. Two versions of each quiz were then assembled such that the first six questions were in English and the last six in French in one version; the other version was made of the opposite combination. In this way, for each subject who received a particular question in English, there was another who received it in French.

3.3. Procedure

Half of the subjects in each group received one version of each passage, the other half received their matched counterparts. Half of the subjects listened to Passage One first, the other half received Passage Two first. Thus, Group, Passage Version, and Order of Passages were all between-subjects variables, and Passage and Boundary (sentence vs. clause boundary) were within-subjects variables. Version and passage order were randomly assigned.

All subjects were run individually. Subjects sat at a writing table with pen and paper in front of them, wearing earphones. Subjects first read the instructions, which were to listen to (or interpret) the passage normally, "as if they were listening to (interpreting) a lecture." They were told that the passages would be interrupted from time to time by a tone. Upon hearing this signal, they were to immediately write down as much as they could remember from the passage just prior to the interruption, word-for-word. Verbatim recall was emphasized. Subjects used one side of a separate sheet of paper for each answer, and turned the page face down to signal that they had finished.

The experimenter, sitting out of view of the subjects, controlled the tape player, stopping it when a tone occurred. Subjects were allowed an unlimited amount of time to write down their response.

Subjects rested for two minutes between passages. Sessions lasted approximately one hour. For each subject, the session resulted in eight clause, eight sentence, and eight dummy responses.

4. Results

The words correctly recalled within each clause were tallied and expressed as a proportion of the number of words within its clause. Control variables such as Passage, Passage Version, and Order of Passage were analyzed to ensure that they did not interact significantly with Group. This was confirmed, and observations were then collapsed across these control variables for the remaining analyses, which included Clause (critical vs. final) and Boundary (clause boundary vs. sentence boundary) as within-subjects variables, and Group (listeners vs. interpreters) as a between-subjects variable.

As can be seen in Figure 1a, the listeners demonstrated the classic pattern of verbatim recall first shown by Jarvella (1971). The serial position of each word is shown on the x-axis, beginning from the first word of the critical clause and counting down to the last word of the final clause. The mean proportion correct recall is plotted on the y-axis for both boundary conditions; the dashed line shows the location of the clause boundary (unfilled circles) or the sentence boundary (filled circles). Recall for the final clause is almost perfect, and better than recall for the critical clause regardless of the syntactic boundary condition. Recall for the critical clause appears to depend on the syntactic boundary that separated it form the final clause. When it was followed by a clause boundary, making it part of the most recent sentence, verbatim recall of the critical clause was superior to when the clause was followed by a sentence boundary.

Analyses conducted on each group independently revealed that the variance between the interpreters was almost eight times greater than the variance between the listeners. Therefore, the serial position curves for each individual interpreter were examined to see how the interpreters' scores were distributed.

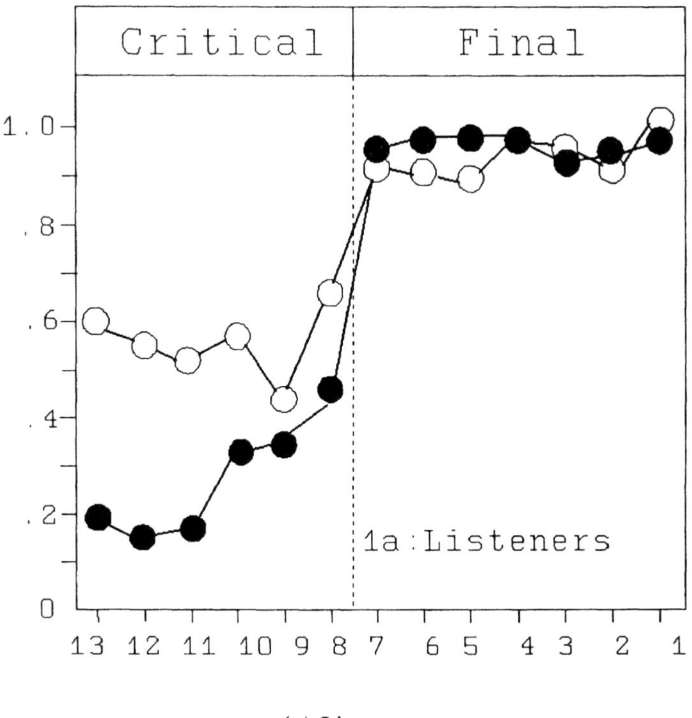

(a) Listeners

Rather than the recall scores being scattered haphazardly, it was discovered that the interpreters split into two groups of about equal size (4 and 5 subjects), each having its own distinctive pattern of recall. Figures 1b and 1c show these two patterns, which have been arbitrarily labeled Type I and and Type II. Each group was compared with the 12 listeners. Analyses using both subjects (F_1) and items (F_2) as the random variable were conducted, and are reported as min F' (Clark 1973).[2]

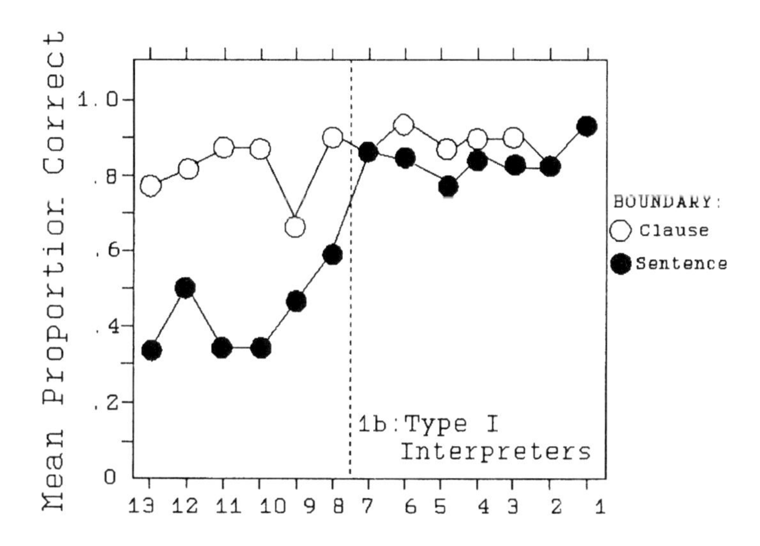

(b) Type I Interpreters

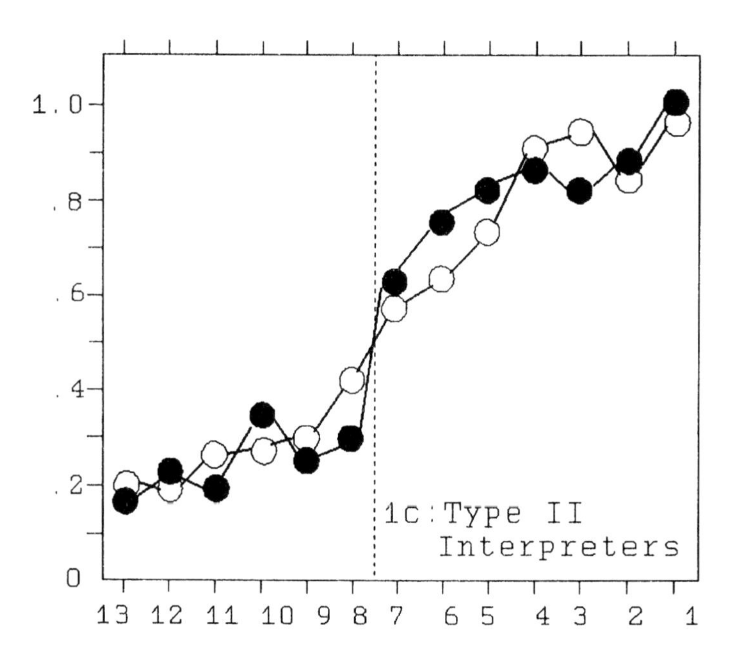

(c) Type II Interpreters

Figure 1. *(a), (b), and (c) Word serial position*

4.1. Listeners Versus Type I Interpreters

We first examine the Type I interpreters in comparison with the listeners. There was no main effect of group [both Fs, $p>.45$]. As expected, the main effects of clause and of boundary were both significant [min $F'(1,22)=54.1$; and min $F'(1,24)=14.6$, respectively, both $p<.001$]. Thus, for both groups, recall was better in the final than the critical clause, and better when a clause boundary intervened between these two clauses than when a sentence boundary did. The interaction between clause and boundary was also significant [min $F'(1,28)=17.6$, $p<.001$], indicating that recall depended on the particular combination of clause and boundary: recall in the final clause was equivalent in both syntactic boundary conditions, but was better in the critical clause in the clause boundary condition than in the sentence boundary condition. Each of these results is clearly visible in Figures 1a and 1b.

The interactions between the within-subjects factors and Group are more relevant to our concerns, however. The Clause by Group interaction was significant [min $F'(1,26)=6.7$, $p<.025$]. Figure 2, which displays the mean proportion correct recall for the two groups within each clause, clarifies the nature of this interaction. While the difference between the final and critical clauses is significant for each group [both min F's, $p<.001$], this advantage of the final clause over the critical clause is attenuated in the Type I interpreters when compared to the listeners. These interpreters recalled more words from the critical clause than the listeners did [min $F'(1,29) = 6.8$, $p<.025$], but fewer words from the final clause [$F1(1,14)=6.1$, $p<.05$; $F2(1,15)=6.15$, $p<.05$] although we should regard this difference in the final clause with some caution, since min F' was not significant [$p<.10$].

The interaction between boundary and group was significant at the .06 level by both subjects and items [both $Fs=4.0$]; this reflected a trend for the difference between the clause and sentence boundary conditions to be larger in the Type I interpreters than in the listeners. The three-way interaction of Clause, Boundary, and Group was not significant [both $Fs<1.0$].

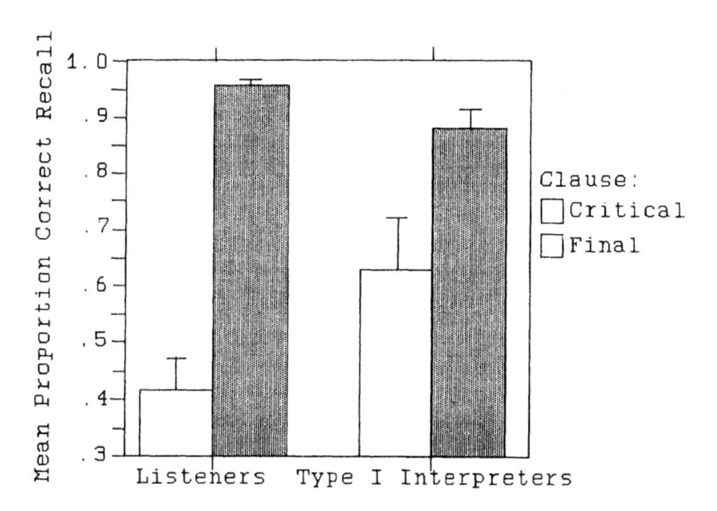

Figure 2. *Mean proportion correct recall as a function of group and clause. Error bars represent one standard error of the mean.*

4.2. Listeners Versus Type II Interpreters

The differences between listeners and Type II interpreters are evident in Figures 1a and 1c, and the analyses support the conclusions drawn by the eye. There was a significant main effect of Group [min $F'(1,16)=8.8$, $p<.025$]; listeners recalled more words overall than did the Type II interpreters. The advantage of the most recent clause was intact: the final clause was recalled better than the critical clause [min $F'(1,26)=91.5$, $p<.001$]. The main effect of boundary, however, was significant by both subjects and items, but not min F' [$F_1(1,15) = 8.5$; $F_2(1,15) = 7.2$, both $p<.02$; min $F'(1,30)=3.9$, $p<.10$]. The Clause by Boundary interaction was significant [min $F'(1,29) = 7.5$, $p<.025$], again showing that performance (of both groups combined) on the critical clause depended in part on the syntactic boundary that followed it.

The interaction between Clause and Group was not significant [for both Fs, $p>.33$), as it was for the comparison for the Type I interpreters; this indicated that Type II interpreters recalled less than the listeners in both the final and critical clauses. The Boundary by Group interaction was significant by both subjects and items, but not by min F' [$F_1(1,15)=8.8$, $p<.01$; $F_2(1,15)=6.7$, $p<.02$; min $F'(1,29)=3.8$, $p<.10$]. Figure 3 shows that boundary influenced recall of the listener group, but had no effect for the Type II interpreters.

Finally, the three-way interaction between Clause, Boundary, and Group was also significant in both analyses, but not by min F' [$F_1(1,15)=9.9$, $p<.01$; $F_2(1,15)=5.1$, $p<.05$; min $F'(1,27)=3.4$, $p<.10$]. This reflected the fact that Type II interpreters recalled the critical clause in the clause boundary condition no better than listeners recalled it in the sentence boundary condition.

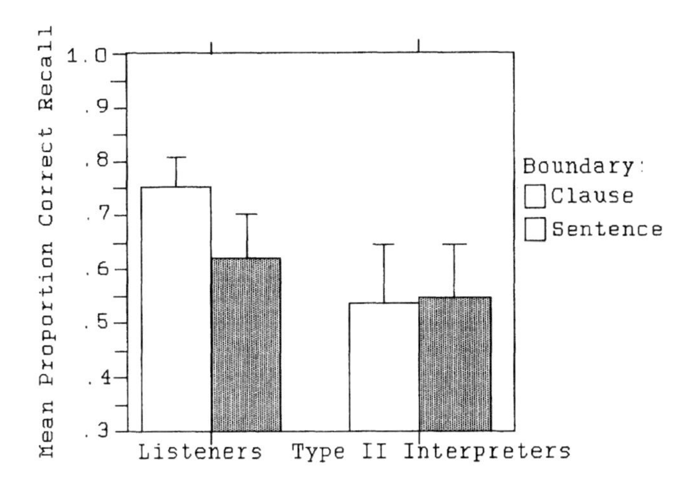

Figure 3. *Mean proportion correct recall as a function of group and boundary. Error bars represent one standard error of the mean.*

4.3. Quiz Results

No significant effects were obtained for Group or for Language (English vs. French) or for their interaction (all $p > .14$). Thus, the level of comprehension measured by the quizzes was the same for all three groups, regardless of whether they were tested in English or in French.

5. Discussion

The one result that is common to both Type I and II interpreters will be addressed first: recall of the final clause is poorer in both interpreter groups than in the listeners. The listeners recalled 96% of the final clause, while the Type I and Type II groups recalled 88% and 83%, respectively. This finding was a bit of a surprise. Generally, our ability to recall the last clause of a sentence is extremely good; recall performance in the final clause has been virtually perfect in many replications of the Jarvella task (see Jarvella 1979 for a review). Isham & Lane (1993) replicated this result with native speakers of English, as well as with subjects who had interpreted the texts into American

Sign Language. The control subjects in the present study show that even when we listen to sentences from a non-native language, recall for the most recent clause is equal to that of native listeners. The interpreters in this study are the first group to show a marked disadvantage for the final clause (albeit recall remained quite good).

It is relevant that the ASL interpreters showed no disadvantage in the final clause, for it suggests that the effect is not due to the interpretation process itself. This is also suggested by the fact that in spite of clearly different patterns employed by Type I and Type II interpreters, there was no statistical difference between their recall in the final clause [$F_1(1,7)=1.55$, $p>.25$]. Thus we must explain this difference between the interpreters and the listeners in terms of a factor that is impervious to task (i.e., listening vs. interpreting) and impervious to strategy employed while interpreting (Type I vs. Type II).

French/English interpreters share one experience that neither the listeners nor ASL/English interpreters do: French/English interpreters are working with two spoken languages. These subjects listened to the source-language input in the presence of the noise that they themselves were creating by producing their TL output. We know that interpreters monitor their own voice as well as to that of the SL speaker, for they frequently correct their own speech errors (Barik 1975; Gerver 1974). In fact, many interpreters displace one earphone of their headset, in order to facilitate this process (Fabbro, Gran, & Gran 1991). Thus, two phonological streams are entering the speech perception system simultaneously.

Isham and Lane (1993) suggested that differing sources of information can be used during verbatim recall, and that every available source will be garnered in the recall effort. One such source may be a phonological memory, that is, a memory of the perceptual experience of hearing a series of speech sounds. Baddeley and Hitch (1974) have proposed a "phonological buffer" which has a fixed capacity; this has been determined to be about 1.5 to 2 seconds of speech input (Besner, Davies & Daniels 1981; Baddeley 1986). If used during this verbatim recall task, memory of the sounds of the words should be available only for the most recently heard words; this would correspond to the final clause of these materials. Other sources of information, such as memory for the words themselves, or memory for the meaning of the phrase, would be unaffected, and remain available to guide recall.

It may be, therefore, that the inferior recall of the final clause in the spoken language interpreters is due to "phonological interference", caused by the two speech streams encountered by this group alone. This is quite plausible, since speaking while listening is known to interfere with immediate memory for speech sounds (Levy 1978; Besner *et al.* 1981).

As to the previous clause, the division of the interpreters into two distinct groups was unexpected. Each group displayed interesting differences from the listener group; unfortunately, the data do not allow us to explain the predictor variable that determines why some subjects behaved in one way, and other subjects in another way. Nevertheless, the results make clear that there is more than one way in which to process incoming sentences during simultaneous interpretation: one that leaves behind a memory trace for the form of the source-language sentence; and another that does not. Evidence for this claim will be discussed first, after which a possible explanation for the difference between Type I and Type II interpreters will be considered.

In general, Type I interpreters displayed the same basic pattern as did the listeners. This pattern reflects a tendency to group incoming words into clause-size units, and in turn, to group clause units into sentence units. This can be seen in Figures 1a and 1b by the sharper drop in recall performance at the sentence boundary than at the clause boundary in both groups. Verbatim recall for previous sentences is very poor, indicating that the representations for these sentences have been transformed into an abstract conceptual code that provides little help in recalling the exact wording of the original sentences. Thus, information about the lexical items and their relative ordering remains available only for the most recent sentence. The advantage of the Type I group over the listeners in the critical clause seems to support that sentence-sized units are actively sought, for as can been seen in Figure 1b, there appears to be no advantage of the final clause in the clause-boundary condition: the level of recall remains steady through both the critical and final clauses. After interpreting until an unexpected interruption, Type I interpreters can remember the most recent sentence with a high degree of accuracy, regardless of whether that sentence has one clause (the sentence boundary condition) or two (the clause boundary condition). From this we conclude that these interpreters were translating the input on a sentence-by-sentence basis, and that their manner of processing source-language sentences involved attention to their surface form. This focus resulted in a mental representation that included surface information, and thus aided verbatim recall.

The pattern of results of the Type II interpreters is quite different: their overall recall is inferior; there is no distinction made between the two types of syntactic boundary; and recall of the critical clause in the clause boundary condition is no better than in the sentence boundary condition. Furthermore, there is no sudden drop in recall between the words in positions 7 and 8; rather, recall declines in a more or less steady manner (compare this with the listeners in Figure 1a). These interpreters appeared to be oblivious to the presence of syntactic boundaries in their verbatim recall: no distinction is evident between the final and the previous sentence. This indicates that Type II interpreters processed incoming sentences in a manner that drew attention away from their surface form, thus leaving little trace in memory of the original parsing of words into clause or sentence units.

Let us consider how we might explain the difference between the Type I and Type II interpreters in terms of strategies employed during interpretation. Many factors are thought to influence interpreting performance: the rate of speech input (Gerver 1969; Darò, 1990); the grammatical similarities and differences between the source and target languages (Spiller-Bosatra, Darò, Fabbro, & Bosatra 1990); the familiarity of the interpreter with the subject matter (Taylor 1990); the semantic density of the input (Gile 1990); many more could be listed. However, such differences in the relation between the interpreter and the interpreting assignment have been reduced in this experimental setting. All subjects worked between the same two languages, experienced the same prerecorded speaker (and thereby rate of speech, density, etc.), and were unfamiliar with the narratives presented to them. The two patterns of recall, then, cannot be explained by such setting-specific factors. Instead, they reflect an "internal" difference, that is, a difference that resides within the interpreters and not in such external factors as those listed above.

Several researchers have noted that interpreters speak of using either a "word-based" or "meaning-based" approach (Darò, 1990; Fabbro, Gran, Basso & Bava 1990). According to these authors, the meaning-based approach is generally preferred, reserving a word-based approach for specific situations, as in translating a list of nouns or numbers, or when interpreting highly technical material. What exactly is meant by these terms remains somewhat vague in terms of the cognitive processes involved, although we may presume that a word-based approach involves attempting to interpret word-for-word as much as the similarities between the source and target languages allow.

One might hypothesize that the Type I interpreters were using a word-based approach, thus improving verbatim recall, while the Type II interpreters used a meaning-based approach, and thus leading to inferior recall that is unaffected by syntactic boundary. That Type I interpreters may indicate a word-based approach is supported by the results in recall made by "transliterators" in the previous experiment (Isham & Lane 1993). This group of professional interpreters performed a strictly word-for-word translation task, and they showed a pattern similar to Type I interpreters here. Thus a group that we know -- rather than hypothesize -- were using a word-based approach behaved much like the Type I interpreters.

In contrast, the performance of the Type II interpreters is much like what one would expect to result from the complete "deverbalization" hypothesized by Seleskovitch (1975). Even with such complete deverbalization, we would not expect recall to be at absolute zero. Having no individual representation of the form of the most recent sentence to guide verbatim recall, subjects employ whatever bits and pieces of information they can locate to aid in the recall effort. Information concerning the most recent word would be the most likely to remain available, while the amount of information regarding each of the earlier words diminishes as the distance between it and the final word increases. Therefore, we would expect a "recency effect": the more recent the word, the more likely the subject is to recall it. This recency effect is indeed evident in Figure 1c, as can be seen by the linear trend in recall increasing toward the most recent word.

Thus, the pattern of recall for the Type II interpreters does support the idea of "deverbalization," insofar as there does seem to be a strategy for simultaneous interpretation that leaves behind very little information about source-language sentences. However, it is also clear that this is not a mandatory stage through which all interpretation must pass. The strategy of the Type I interpreters resulted in improved verbatim recall for the critical clause, showing that if anything, these subjects had more information about incoming sentences available than would normally be expected. Clearly, these subjects did not deverbalize any more than the listeners did, yet they too produced a fluent, comprehensible French rendition of the source-language input. It may well be true that one approach or the other results in a product of higher quality, in terms of fewer errors overall, but that does not change the fact that interpretation can transpire in these two modes.

Thus, we should understand deverbalization as one possible stage of interpretation, rather than a required one, at least when interpreting between English and French. As was pointed out in the introduction, however, a strictly word-for-word transcoding of the source language is not possible, due to the differences in grammar that will be found between any two natural languages (for this reason, "form-based" may be a better term for this strategy than "word-based," and will be used hereafter). It follows, then, that as the difference in grammars between language pairs becomes greater and greater, the form-based approach becomes less and less an option. If true, we should expect that interpreters working between English and Mandarin Chinese, for example, to have no option but to use a meaning-based strategy, and to show evidence of deverbalization.

We have been using the word "strategy" loosely, but its correct meaning in cognitive terms denotes conscious control. To date, no one has tested whether interpreters do have conscious control over the technique they use, and so we do not know if the form-based and meaning-based approaches to simultaneous interpretation should actually be labeled "strategies," or whether we should be using the more generic term "processes" in describing them. We also do not know why these subjects used one technique or the other. The difference between Type I and Type II interpreters may reflect the only process known by each individual, or each may be a strategy preferred in general by each interpreter. It may also be that the Type I interpreters normally use a meaning-based approach, but switched strategies for the purposes of this experiment, in an effort to be better able to meet the demands of the verbatim recall task. These questions are peripheral, however, to our main point: as has been claimed by practitioners, interpreter educators and researchers (e.g., Darò, 1990; Gile 1990; Fabbro *et al.* 1991), the manner of processing incoming sentences is not predetermined, a priori, by the need to produce equivalents in another language.

Nevertheless, the issue of conscious control is an interesting one. A future experiment might instruct subjects to use a meaning-based approach for one text, and a form-based approach for the another text. In this way, we could determine two things: first, whether the resulting patterns of recall mirror those of the Type I and Type II interpreters, thus providing support for the hypothesis that the two patterns of recall reflect the difference between "form-based" and "meaning-based" approaches; and second, whether they have conscious control over the approach they use.

In sum, recall in spoken language interpreters is poorer in the final clause, which may be an effect caused by the interference with a phonological memory of receiving two streams of speech simultaneously. Secondly, there is more than one way to process incoming sentences when interpreting from English into French. Whether or not this difference is a matter of strategy -- a conscious choice -- remains to be determined. In any case, all of the interpreters delivered fluent output in a continuous manner, and hence, were able to perform the interpreting task. Thus, this study has shown that interpretation should not be conceived of as a single process, made up of so many sub-components, but as at least two processes, differentiated by the sub-components they contain.

Notes

1. I thank the Fyssen Foundation for funding my research in France, and the University of Paris V for providing housing for my research. I would like to express my deep appreciation to Dr. Juan Segui who welcomed me into his laboratory, offered support and guidance, and, in general, helped to make my stay in France so worthwhile. I also thank M. Barry Jaggers for his assistance in locating the interpreters who participated in the study. Finally, I am gratefull to the interpreters themselves, professionals who were willing to take time from their busy schedules in order to be part of this experiment.

2. The results from the analysis-by-subjects may be questioned on the grounds that the difference in sample sizes between the listeners and each interpreter group, combined with the fact that the interpreter groups are now small, may affect the analyses. Note, however, that the problem of unequal samples increases the likelihood of making a beta error, that is, of wrongly accepting the null hypothesis (Rosenthal & Rosnow 1984). Therefore, the difference in sample sizes will make significance harder to achieve, not easier. Note also that the items analysis retains the same number of cells: only the number of observations that make up the mean in each cell has changed.

References

Baddeley, A. D. 1986. *Working Memory*. Oxford: Clarendon Press.

Baddeley, A. D. and Hitch, G. 1974. "Working Memory". G. Bower, ed. *The Psychology of Learning and Motivation*. New York: Academic Press. 47-90.

Barik, H. C. 1975. "Simultaneous Interpretation: Qualitative and Linguistic Data". *Language and Speech* 18. 272-297.

Besner, D., Davies, J. and Daniels, S. 1981. "Reading for Meaning: The Effects of Concurrent Articulation". *Quarterly Journal of Experimental Psychology* 33. 415-437.

Clark, H. H. 1973. "The Language-as-Fixed-Effect Fallacy: A Critique of Language Statistics in Psychological Research". *Journal of Verbal Learning and Verbal Behavior* 12. 335-359.

Cokely, D. 1986. "The Effects of Lag Time on Interpreter Errors". *Sign Language Studies* 53. 341-376.

Darò, 1990. "Speaking Speed during Simultaneous Interpretation: A Discussion of its Neuropsychological Aspects and Possible Contributions to Teaching". L. Gran and C. Taylor, eds. *Aspects of Applied and Experimental Research on Conference Interpretation*. Udine: Campanotto Editore. 83-92.

Davidson, P. M. 1992. "Segmentation of Japanese Source Language Discourse in Simultaneous Interpretation". *The Interpreters' Newsletter*, Special Issue 1. 2-11.

Drewnowski, A. and Murdock Jr., B. B. 1980. "The Role of Auditory Features in Memory Span for Words". *Journal of Experimental Psychology: Human Learning and Memory* 6. 319-332.

Fabbro, F., Gran, B. and Gran, L. 1991. "Hemispheric Specialization for Semantic and Syntactic Components of Language in Simultaneous Interpretation". *Brain and Language* 41. 1-42.

Fabbro, F., Gran, L., Basso, G. and Bava, A. 1990. "Cerebral Lateralization in Simultaneous Interpretation". *Brain and Language* 39. 69-89.

Gerver, D. 1969. "The Effects of Source Language Presentation Rate on the Performance of Simultaneous Conference Interpreters". *Proceedings of the 2nd Louisville Conference on Rate and/or Frequency Controlled Speech.*

Gerver, D. 1974. "Simultaneous Listening and Speaking and Retention of Prose". *Quarterly Journal of Experimental Psychology* 26. 337-342.

Gerver, D. 1976. "Empirical Studies of Simultaneous Interpretation: A Review and a Model". R.W. Brislin, ed. *Translation: Applications and Research.* New York: Gardner Press. 165-207.

Gile, D. 1990. "Scientific Research vs. Personal Theories in the Investigation of Interpretation". L. Gran and C. Taylor, eds. *Aspects of Applied and Experimental Research on Conference Interpretation*. Udine: Campanotto Editore. 28-41.

Goldman-Eisler, F. 1972. "Segmentation of Input in Simultaneous Translation". *Journal of Psycholinguistic Research* 1. 127-140.

Gran, L. and Dodds, J. 1989. *The Theoretical and Practical Aspects of Teaching Conference Interpretation*. Udine: Campanotto Editore.

Gran, L. and Taylor, C. 1990. *Aspects of Applied and Experimental Research on Conference Interpretation*. Udine: Campanotto Editore.

Isham, W. P. and Lane, H. 1992. *A Common Conceptual Code in Bilinguals: Evidence from Simultaneous Interpretation*. [Unpublished manuscript.]

Isham, W. P. and Lane, H. 1993. "Simultaneous Interpretation and the Recall of Source-Language Sentences". *Language and Cognitive Processes*. [in press.]

Jackendoff, R. 1987. *Consciousness and the Computational Mind*. Cambridge, MA: MIT Press.

Jarvella, R. J. 1971. "Syntactic Processing of Connected Speech". *Journal of Verbal Learning and Verbal Behavior* 10. 409-416.

Jarvella, R. J. 1979. "Immediate Memory and Discourse Processing". H. Bower, ed. *The Psychology of Learning and Motivation: Vol. 13. Advances in Research and Theory*. New York: Academic Press. 379-421.

Levy, B. A. 1978. "Speech Analysis during Sentence Processing: Reading versus Listening". *Visible Language* 12. 81-101.

McKoon, G. and Ratcliff, R. 1980. "Priming in Item Recognition: The Organization of Propositions in Memory for Text". *Journal of Verbal Learning and Verbal Bahavior* 19. 369-386.

Rosenthal, R. and Rosnow, R. L. 1984. *Essentials of Behavioral Research: Methods and Data Analysis*. New York: McGraw-Hill.

Sachs, J. S. 1967. "Recognition Memory for Syntactic and Semantic Aspects of Connected Discourse". *Perception and Psychophysics* 2. 437-442.

Seleskovitch, D. 1975. *Langages, Langues et Mémoire*. Paris: Minard Lettres Modernes.

Spiller, E. and Bosatra, A. 1989. "Role of the Auditory Sensory Modality in Simultaneous Interpretation". L. Gran and J. Dodds, eds. *The Theoretical and Practical Aspects of Teaching Conference Interpretation*. Udine, Italy: Campanotto Editore. 37-38.

Spiller-Bosatra, E., Darò, V., Fabbro, F., and Bosatra, A. 1990. "Audio-phonological and Neuropsychological Aspects of Simultaneous Interpretation". *Scandinavian Audiology* 19. 81-87.

Taylor, C. 1990. "Coherence and World Knowledge". L. Gran and C. Taylor, eds. *Aspects of Applied and Experimental Research on Conference Interpretation*. Udine, Italy: Campanotto Editore. 21-27.

Putting one's Heart into Simultaneous Interpretation[1]

Tatiana Klonowicz
University of Warsaw

1. Introduction

That linguistic communication contributes to a wide variety of phenomena studied in psychology and is itself a subject matter of psychology, is obvious to the point of banality. Communication holds individuals and societies together. According to a dictionary definition,

> In order to have communication, both the transmitter and the receiver must share a common code, so that the meaning or information contained in the message may be interpreted without error (Reber 1986:136).

To remedy communication difficulties among people who are considered to share the same language, psychologists propose and implement various training techniques. To enable people to share other cultures, an additional element must often be incorporated into the communication process, i.e., a translator whose role consists in rendering the meaning of information according to the rules of a target language.

Decoding a message presented in one language and encoding it in another appears to be a challenging task. The demands, as well as the responsibility associated with this task make it an interesting object for psychological study. However, so far, translation has been analyzed almost exclusively as a linguistic or psycholinguistic process (cf. Brislin 1976; Even-Zohar and Toury 1981; Gilewski 1986; Koller 1979). Although such research has helped to provide a better insight into certain aspects of translation, we are still far from understanding the more complex processes and mechanisms involved. Perhaps it is the complexity of the task which has led most authors to refer to the translator not in terms of a human being, but rather in terms of abstract constructs. The term "black box" became an all-inclusive label which seemed to absolve the researcher from looking into the intricacies of the work carried out by a translator.

Psycholinguistic research, concerned mostly with the degree of equivalence of target and source languages, has achieved little to correct this bias. Perhaps the only concession to the human factor is the attention paid within this approach to the nature and character of encoding and decoding operations performed by translators (Barik 1975; Goldman-Eisler 1972; Goldman-Eisler and Cohen 1975).

The present research[2], which is part of a broader research project (Klonowicz 1992) is focused on the translator whose skill and effort make it possible to cope with the complex requirements of being a decoder and a conveyor of meaning. The project deals with simultaneous interpretation as a variation of translation mediated by the communication process. SI is the process of orally converting a message from one language into another as the message is being received (Barik 1975). An appraisal of the process (Klonowicz 1992) suggests that at any moment, the interpreter may be engaged - either simultaneously or in very rapid succession - in the following actions: 1) listening to what is being said by the speaker, i.e., receiving the message; 2) understanding the meaning, i.e., decoding the message; 3) converting the meaning into the target language, i.e., encoding the message; 4) delivering the translated version, i.e. emitting the message. Each of the actions has a complex hierarchical structure. All of them must be performed in real time and under considerable time pressure since the interpreter must reasonably keep pace with the speaker in delivering the translated version.

The crucial task characteristics of dual information processing, the necessity to store for subsequent processing the continuation of the message as the speaker delivers it, the time pressure, audience influence and social responsibility, all combine to make SI an ideal potent naturalistic stimulus condition for stress research in general, and for the study of information processing under stress, in particular.

The aim of the present study was to investigate the performance of simultaneous interpreters from the perspective of management of energy resources involved in information processing. Perhaps the most elegant way of studying information processing has been proposed within the cognitive psychophysiological approach (cf. Ciarkowska 1992). Unfortunately when applied to the investigation of information flow in terms of the processing stages occurring between presentation of an utterance by a speaker and completion of a response (interpreting the utterance into a target language), this appoach, based on measurement of the separate stages, will inevitably lead to oversimplification. The requirement, by this approach, to divide the process into separate stages, leads to the loss of the view of the process as a whole. A cruel caricature of the interpreter is one of a "speaking dictionary", i.e., someone performing very tiny bits of interpretation (e.g., word by word). This sham characterization has little in common with the real demands of the task. The artificiality of this research paradigm is all too obvious. Interpretation thus conceptualized becomes a test of the most elementary switches between the two languages, but provides no information whatsoever on more complex mechanisms and feedbacks (Klonowicz 1992).

There is, however, another way to investigate the allocation of resources in information processing in general, and in SI in particular. This approach, adopted in the present study, is centered on the concept of processing capacity. Its main assumption is that the human being is a limited processor which can be loaded to varying degrees and which responds to this load. Investigations carried out within this framework focus on the search for capacity limits and the measurement of processing load, on the one hand, and on the allocation of resources, on the other.

The main argument in favour of this approach stems from the model proposed by Sanders (1983). Motivated by the need to explain the physiological consequences of psychological stress, Sanders succeeded in bridging the two approaches - cognitive and capacity - to information processing. In brief, the model assumes that the processing stages at the cognitive level are coupled with, and depend upon, resources or energy supplies which guarantee that the effort will be deployed to meet the task demands. The energy supply mechanisms responsible for the input and output processing stages as well as the response choice stage can be investigated within the cognitive psychology paradigm. However, since their functioning is supervised and coordinated by a higher order mechanism, information about their stages can also be gathered at a more general level, i.e. within the "sandwich paradigm" (Linden & McEachern 1985), without probing into more specific mechanisms.

The validity of this approach to the evaluation of changes in resource strategy as a consequence of stress associated with SI has been demonstrated in previous research (Klonowicz 1990, 1992). The data indicate that SI requires allocation of considerable effort as measured by cardiovascular activity and that the effort deployed in order to meet the demands of SI depends on task difficulty as well as on individual differences in skill and basic personality (temperament).

Perhaps the most interesting result was that cardiovascular activity increased significantly before an interpretation 20 to 30 minute shift (henceforth referred to as a "turn") and that in a subjectively easier task, this mobilization was followed by the normalization of systolic blood pressure and heart rate, but not of diastolic blood pressure. After completion of such a turn, systolic blood pressure and heart rate dropped back almost to the baseline level, whereas diastolic blood pressure remained significantly elevated.

Appearance of the "mobilization wave" was interpreted in terms of exaggerated resources activation caused by anticipated task difficulty, whereas the "normalization wave" was hypothesized to reflect the process of adjustment of resources to a task which gradually becomes more familiar. In view of the fact that this interpretation was based on data aggregated across several turns, i.e., over different periods of the day, it should be regarded as a tentative explanation only. If this interpretation is true, recurring cycles of resource mobilization-normalization can be expected during a day's work. Previous attempts to investigate this issue (Klonowicz in press) indicated sustained mobilization, while normalization was demonstrated only in the first and second shifts. However, the above-mentioned study did not control for task difficulty which was later shown to considerably influence the process of normalization of cardiovascular activity. Subjective perception of high level of task difficulty blocked the normalization (Klonowicz 1992). The present study was devised as a further test of the hypothesis of resource mobilization adjustment according to task demands. The experiment was focused on patterns of cardiovascular activity as a measure of effort. Level of performance - another measure of adequacy of resources allocation - was not investigated. It has been argued elsewhere that this line of research not only presents enormous technical difficulties, but also is fraught with errors of subjective judgment (Klonowicz in press). The current experiment is based on the assumption that, since the participants in the study are top-ranking simultaneous interpreters, they either "deliver the best quality product" or quit, i.e., signal for a replacement. Just as performance level was semi-controlled by means of subject selection, the processing load was controlled by the choice of conferences with balanced levels of difficulty.

2. Method

2.1. Subjects

Subjects were 16 (7 male, 9 female) professional interpreters who volunteered to participate in the study. None of them showed borderline hypertension nor had a parental history of hypertension.

2.2. Design

Subjects were individually tested in a factorial ANOVA design involving factors Subjects and Situation. The latter factor comprises 9 levels: a baseline and 8 measures of cardiovascular activity before and after each of four 30-minute turns (from the beginning of the conference until the lunch break). Since the full mobilization-normalization pattern was shown to appear only for interpretation **into** a foreign language[3], interpreters who in the course of a working day had to switch directions, i.e., interpret into Polish, were not included in the study. Also excluded were those subjects who - for a variery of both objective and/or subjective reasons - worked shorter turns.

2.3. Procedure

The experiment was carried out in a natural setting, i.e., during a conference. All measures were taken immediately prior to and after a 30-min turn in a booth. All subjects were familiar with the procedure (2 habituation sessions were run for this purpose in an experimental setting). Moreover, cardiovascular readings were taken for each interpreter on three separate, mildly active, semi-social occasions which did not involve interpreting. The averaged values of the obtained measures served as baselines.

2.4. Apparatus

Cardiovascular activity measures were taken with a Timex automatic blood pressure and heart rate monitor. This is an electronic cuff device which gives a digital display of blood pressure and heart rate. The cuff is initially deflated to 140-160 mm Hg and then deflates to arrive at a systolic blood pressure (SBP). Subsequent readings give diastolic blood pressure (DBP) and heart rate

(HR). The cuff was placed on the upper left arm. The monitor was checked as an accurate automatic measure of cardiovascular activity.

3. Results

The results are presented in Figures 1 and 2. The figures depict the mean scores of blood pressure and heart rate in the control baseline condition (BL), at the beginning (Pre) and at the end (Post) of the 4 turns. Vertical bars in Figure 1 are divided to represent two sets of data each: SBP and DBP. Bars in Figure 2 represent one set of data: HR.

ANOVAs with repeated measures were run on these data. Greenhouse-Geisser-adjusted degrees of freedom were used to control for biased F-tests. ANOVAs revealed a significant effect of Situation on all three sets of data: SBP -F (5,81)=4.67; DBP-F (4,72)=3.54; HR (5,76)=4.33; p (lower limit) < 0.05. This outcome indicates that SI produced reliable changes from baselines in all three cardiovascular measures.

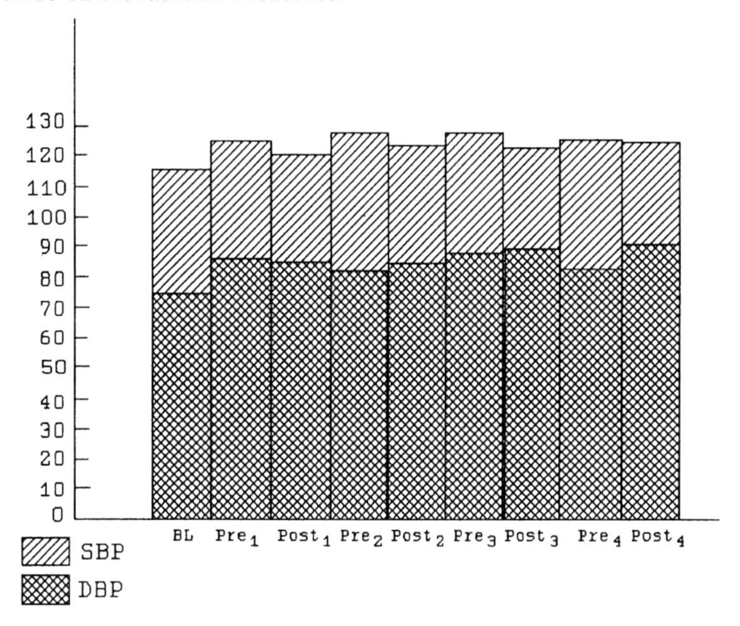

Figure 1. *Mean scores of SBP and DBP during baselines and two task periods for each turn Pre (Post) - measurements taken before and after each turn (from 1 through 4)*

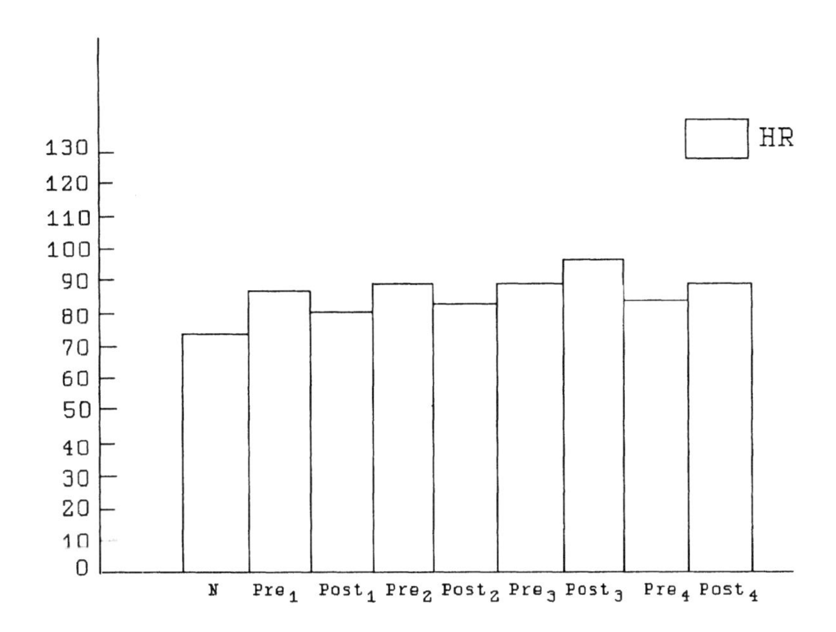

Figure 2. *Mean scores of HR during baseline and two task periods for each turn Pre (Post) - measurements taken before and after each turn (from 1 through 4)*

Inspection of the pattern of results in Figures 1 and 2 indicates that only SBP and HR seem to be sensitive to the task period, whereas the increase in DBP is relatively stable across time periods. The planned comparisons more specifically identify where the differences across time periods lie. These comparisons are of special interest because they indicate differential effects of the two periods of work - the beginning and the end - on allocation of resources throughout a day. Changes in cardiovascular activity associated with the two time periods were assessed by comparing the readings obtained before and after each shift with the baseline (BL). The first step consisted in assessment of the mobilization wave (Pretest values numbered 1 through 4), and in the second step, the normalization wave was evaluated (Posttest values numbered 1 through 4). Table 1 contains the *t* values obtained in specific comparisons of baseline vs. various task periods. This table has to be looked at in connection with Figures 1 and 2 which show the mean values for each of the 9 conditions.

As the data in Table 1 indicate, the mobilization wave is manifest in all three measures of cardiovascular activity. Commencement of each turn causes significant elevations of SBP, DBP, and HR over the baseline levels. Comparisons of levels of baseline cardiovascular activity with the cardiovascular activity at the end of the turns indicate that normalization occurs systematically for SBP only (none of the *t* values reached the level of significance). DBPs recorded at the end of each shift were significantly higher than the baseline DBP value, indicating that after initial mobilization, this parameter of cardiovascular activity is not subject to normalization. For HR, the data indicate initial good recovery (the first two "Post" HR values do not differ significantly from the baseline), but with time, this pattern is broken and in the two following shifts, the once elevated HR is sustained.

Table 1. *Pair-Wise Comparisons of the Effects of Task Conditions (t values)[a] for Three Measures of Cardiovascular Activity*

Comparison	SBP	DBP	HR
1. Mobilization			
BL *vs.* Pre_1	2.86**	2.53*	2.91**
BL *vs.* Pre_2	2.75**	2.63*	3.03**
BL *vs.* Pre_3	3.03**	2.83**	2.74*
BL *vs.* Pre_4	3.80**	2.92**	2.86**
2. Normalization			
BL *vs.* $Post_1$	0.18	2.05*	0.76
BL *vs.* $Post_2$	0.08	2.03t	1.19
BL *vs.* $Post_3$	0.60	2.07*	2.09*
BL *vs.* $Post_4$	1.08	2.49*	2.68*

The level of significance for these comparisons was adjusted according to Bonferroni statistics: α multiplied by 2, *df* 31

$^{t}p<0.10$

$^{*}p<0.05$

$^{**}p<0.01$

4. Discussion

Subjects responded differently to two - beginning and end - turns. The beginning of a turn produced a large increase on all three cardiovascular measures. By the end of a turn and throughout a given day, SBP normalized regularly, whereas HR normalization took place only through the first turns. No normalization was demonstrated for DBP. The question arises as to the functional significance of these changes in cardiovascular activity.

Recent studies produced evidence that tasks such as mental arithmetic or video games elicit cardiovascular activity seemingly in excess of that expected on the basis of concurrent energy expenditure (Carroll, Turner & Hellawell 1986; Gliner, Bunnell & Horvath 1982; Turner and Carroll 1985). Although the situational determinants of this excessive mobilization of the cardiovascular system remain unclear, the data point to the role of task difficulty and its challenging nature. The results of the present study are consistent with the hypothesis that people exhibit exaggerated cardiovascular responses to stress of an unfamiliar mental task. The present results replicated previous reports of the occurrence of a mobilization wave, and the cardiovascular findings were largely consistent with previous work (cf. Klonowicz 1990, 1992, in press). Thus it can be concluded that elevations of SBP, DBP, and HR observed at the beginning of each work shift represent a period of "active preparedness" to face the challenge.

In the present experiment, longer time-on-task periods were investigated than is usually the case in psychophysiological research. Time-on-task is supposed to be the main factor in adjustment of cardiovascular activity to real task demands which become more familiar as an interpreter gains knowledge of the speaker: the topic, speech rhythm, accent, vocabulary, and so forth. Consequently it may be concluded that the appearance of the normalization wave reflects a better match between demand and capacity, i.e., energy resources needed to cope with the task. Similar reasoning would apply to the role of a concomitant factor in SI; accelerated responses of the cardiovascular system to public speaking were also shown to decrease following performance (Knight & Borden 1979; Long, Lynch, Machiran, Thomas and Manilow 1982).

Further extension of the temporal frame of the experiment beyond one turn made it possible to detect that with time the normalization pattern is broken; once elevated, cardiovascular activity tends to remain high (the only exception being SBP). Since the initial activation reported in this and in an earlier study (Klonowicz in press) remains massive, this may indicate that longterm performance causes deficits in matching resources to task demands or else elicits a counteraction against growing fatigue that would lead to performance decrements. The two explanations are consistent with Sanders' (1983) model of resources allocation and his research which demonstrated overextension of resources under stress of high activation. Although neither of these hypothetical explanations could be tested in the present study, both seem to indicate an increasing amount of stress that disrupts the proper functioning of the energy allocation mechanism.

Thus the results reported in this study indicate the functional significance of the pattern of changes in cardiovascular activity. It is generally recognized that preparedness for a future task is highly adaptive because it allows a precursive tuning. As Epstein (1967:105) states,

> "it is at times necessary to pay the price of momentary increase of arousal if one is to later be able to respond at a reduced level of arousal".

However, there remains a problem of the consequences of this arousal.

The present study demonstrated that arousal - as evidenced by increases in cardiovascular activity - recurs systematically and even increases. A task which regularly overtaxes a mechanism responsible for resource allocation leads to a protracted reaction. It is noteworthy that at the beginning of each shift SBP and DBP immediately increased and that over the course of the shift SBP dropped while DBP remained elevated. This patterning of cardiovascular events resembles a miniature of the time course of blood pressure changes often seen in the development of essential hypertension.

The findings reported in the present study may have clinical importance for the development of hypertension and heart disease. The full clinical significance of these data remains to be demonstrated. At present, it can be said that SI is indeed an effortful task. The workload and the high external demand for successful performance may constitute a health risk factor.

The question arises as to why people take up this hazardous occupation. One answer may be that it is creative as well as challenging - and unlike many other creative activities - provides immediate reinforcement in terms of knowledge of results. According to Carruthers (1980), the hidden mechanism underlying the search for hazardous occupations is that they cause norepinephrine secretion, which is usually pleasurable. The wheel spins: SI increases arousal and stimulates norepinephrine release, which brings pleasurable sensations, but also has an excitatory effect on the sympathetic nervous system and hence accelerates cardiovascular activity.

Notes

1. The article was published in the "Polish Psychological Bulletin".

2. This research was supported by grant RPBP III. 25 and by a grant to the author from the Ministry of National Education, Project No. 40.

3. In Poland, simultaneous interpreters are required to interpret either into a foreign language or into Polish (the language of the country). As a rule, professional interpreters - who are at least bilingual - consider the latter task to be more difficult (Klonowicz 1992). It can be speculated that the reason why interpreting into Polish is perceived as more difficult as compared with interpreting into a foreign language is that the situation undergoes considerable change. When interpreting into a foreign language, the interpreter associates the speaker with a portion of the audience speaking this language, i.e., the interpreter is in control of one communication channel only. When interpreting into Polish, the interpreter becomes additionally a source for his/her colleagues (other interpreters) who - more often than not - prefer to rely on the Polish input. Hence, there is an immediate increase in responsibility, because several other language versions delivered to conference participants depend on the person interpreting into Polish. Thus, the "Polish booth" assumes the role of the principal communication channel between speaker and audience as a whole, and it is in this event that the "maintenance synergy" of the communication system becomes a one-person responsibility.

References

Barik, H.C. 1975. "Simultaneous Interpretation: Qualitative and Linguistic Data". *Language and Speech* 18. 272-297.

Brislin, R. 1976. *Translation: Application and Research*. New York: Gardner.

Carroll, D., Turner, J.R. & Hellawell, J.C. 1986. "Heart Rate and Oxygen Consumption During Active Psychological Challenge: The Effects of Level of Difficulty". *Psychophysiology* 23, 174-181.

Carruthers, M. 1980. "Hazardous Occupations and the Heart". C.L. Cooper & R. Payne, eds. *Current Concerns in Occupational Stress*. New York: Wiley.

Ciarkowska, W. 1992. *Psychofiziologiczna analiza aktywnosci poznawczej* (Psychological Analysis of Cognitive Activity). Wroclaw: Ossolineum.

Epstein, W. 1967. *Varieties of Perceptual Learning*. New York: McGraw-Hill.

Even-Zohar, J. and G. Toury, eds. 1981. *Theory of Translation and Intercultural Relations*. Tel Aviv: The Porter Institute for Poetics and Semiotics.

Gilewski, W. 1986. *Psycholingwistyczne aspekty procesu tlumaczenia* (Psycholinguistic Aspects of the Translation Process). University of Warsaw, Poland. [Unpublished Doctoral Dissertation.]

Gliner, J.A., Bunnell, D.E. & Horvath, S.M. 1982. "Hemodynamic and Metabolic Changes Prior to Speech Performance". *Physiological Psychology* 10, 108-113.

Goldman-Eisler, F. 1972. "Segmentation of Input in Simultaneous Translation". *Journal of Psycholinguistic Research* 1, 127-140.

Goldman-Eisler, F. & Cohen, M. 1975. "An Experimental Study of Interference Between Receptive and Productive Processes Involving Speech". *International Journal of Psycholinguistics* 1, 5-6.

Klonowicz, T. 1990. "A Psychological Assessment of Simultaneous Interpretation: The Interaction of Individual Differences and Mental Workload". *Polish Psychological Bulletin* 21, 37-48.

Klonowicz, T. 1992. *Stres w wiety Babel* (Stress in the Tower of Babel). Wroclaw: Ossolineu.

Klonowicz, T. (in press). "The Effort of Simultaneous Interpretation: It's Been a Hard Day..." *Babel. Revue Internationale de la Traduction.*

Knight, M.L. & Borden, R.J. 1979. "Autonomic and Affective Reactions of High and Low Socially-Anxious Individuals Awaiting Public Performance". *Psychophysiology* 16. 209-213.

Koller, W. 1979. *Einfuhrung in die Ubersetzung-wissenschaft*. Heidelberg: Quelle & Meyer.

Linden, W. & McEachern, H.M. 1985. "A Review of Physiological Prestress Adaptation: Effects of Duration and Context". *International Journal of Psychophysiology* 2, 239-245.

Long, J.M., Lynch, J.J., Machiran, N.M., Thomas, S.A. & Manilow, K.L. 1982. "The Effect of Status on Blood Pressure During Verbal Communication". *Journal of Behavioral Medicine* 5, 165-172.

Reber, A.S. 1983. *Dictionary of Psychology*. London: Penguin Books.

Sanders, A.F. 1983. "Towards a Model of Stress and Human Performance". *Acta Psychologica* 53, 61-97.

Turner, J.R. & Carroll, D. 1985. "Heart Rate and Oxygen Consumption During Mental Arithmetic, a Video Game, and Graded Exercise: Further Evidence of Metabolically-exaggerated Cardiac Adjustment". *Psychophysiology* 22, 261-267.

Intonation In The Production And Perception Of Simultaneous Interpretation

Miriam Shlesinger
University of Tel-Aviv

1. Introduction

One of the central themes in the study of intonation has been its role in the creation of meaning, and the relevance of intonational contrasts to the grammar. Attempts at analyzing the paralinguistic and intonational elements have included frequent reference to the importance of establishing the potential of two given utterances which differ in nothing other than intonational features to carry two different meanings (Ladd 1980; El-Menoufy 1988). The functionality of intonational choices and their role in facilitating (or obstructing) communication is by now a universal point of departure in the literature.

> English intonation contrasts are grammatical: they are exploited in the grammar of the language. The systems expounded by intonation are just as much grammatical as are those, such as tense, number and mood, expounded by other means (Halliday 1967).

Frequent reference is also made to the pragmatics of intonation and the effect of differences in the communicative situations. Thus, for example, a pronounced "build-up" before a pause is a feature of fiery oratory (Pike 1945); an increase in the number of tone groups per clause typifies formal speech (Halliday 1970), as does the prevalence of level tone (pitch movement 3) (Halliday 1985); the tendency towards regular beat marks casual spontaneous speech, as opposed to the self-conscious, monitored variety (Halliday 1985); strict correlations between breaths and grammatical junctures are a feature of reading aloud, as opposed to spontaneous speech (Crystal 1969, citing Henderson *et al.* 1965a, 1965b); and a preponderance of the emphatic "held effect" may be expected in sports commentary and television advertising (Crystal 1969).

Clearly, the study of intonational markedness as it correlates with different genres and situations is as yet largely sporadic. One setting in which virtually no attempt has yet been made to isolate the salient intonational features is that of simultaneous interpretation. To wit, in the literature on simultaneous interpretation *per se* and in psycholinguistic studies using simulated interpretation-like tasks, considerable reference has been made to the manner in which the intonation of the original (source-language) utterance affects the interpretation output (Shillan 1968; Varantola 1980; Enkvist 1982a; Kopczynski 1980; Alexieva 1988; Barik 1972). Discussion has centered on certain prosodic features; chiefly, the interpreter's use of the speaker's pauses (Goldman-Eisler 1980; Varantola 1980; Seleskovitch 1982); and the delivery rate of the source text (Bowen and Bowen 1985; Cartellieri 1983; Massaro 1978; Gerver 1975; Jumpelt 1985; Dejean le Féal 1982; Seleskovitch 1982).

In a situation involving SI, the interpreter is but an intermediate addressee. The implications of this status for comprehension and subsequent transmission of the speaker's message are self-evident: the more exophoric the piece of discourse; i.e., the more it refers directly to the extralinguistic situation, the less it is apt to be comprehended by any but the intended addressee(s). In other words, the more assumptions the speaker makes about his speaker's prior knowledge of the situation, the more difficult it will be for the interpreter to reconstruct the message. For example, it is vis-à-vis the intended, rather than the intermediate addressee that the speaker will apply the Gricean maxim of quantity, whereby the contribution should be as informative as required - no more, no less. One of the devices which the interpreter will use in compensating for this handicap is the intonational system, which appears to be *sui generis*; i.e., the intonation used in simultaneous interpretation appears to be marked by a set of salient features not found in any other language use.

Little has been written on the intonation of the interpreter's own output, and its effect on the ultimate addressee has yet to be discussed. In one of the very few references to the subject thus far, Mossop notes that

> Listening to a simultaneous interpretation through a headset... one is constantly aware of listening to a translation - not principally because the source speaker is visible, but because the characteristic 'interpreter's intonation' and the stop-

and-start pattern of the interpreter's voice tell us so. A similar awareness is obtained in written translation only when the text contains a certain amount of unidiomatic writing, especially word-for-word or literal translations of 'faux amis' (Mossop 1987).

In a rare reference to the direct effects of intonation, interpreters are admonished to maintain good rhythm and intonational patterns, since these are "conducive to information retrieval" (Alexieva 1988).

The present paper describes a twofold experiment designed, first, to isolate the salient features of intonation in interpretation as a distinct mode of language use, and second, to examine the cumulative effect on these features on how well a text is perceived (in terms of comprehension and recall).

2. Procedure and Apparatus

Ten excerpts were taken at random from the recorded, real-time output of professional interpreters in actual conference settings. Each excerpt was approximately 90 seconds long (15-20 typed lines). Six were in Hebrew (interpreted from English); four were in English (interpreted from Hebrew). Two of the English excerpts were the output of non-native speakers, whose Hebrew (native-language) interpreting output is also included in the corpus; i.e., the ten passages were the output of eight professional interpreters.

2.1. Production: Isolating the Salient Features

Repeated listening to the interpreted output revealed a set of features which seemed to differ markedly from those of spontaneous discourse. To validate the intuitive judgements on intonation in the interpreted passages, elicitation of the same passage by the same speakers in a non-interpreting setting was called for; i.e., ideally, it would have been useful to obtain the same texts from the same informants. Since it was not feasible to elicit these in the form of spontaneous speech, a second-best option was chosen: the passages were transcribed, and each interpreter was asked to read "his/her" passage aloud. It should be noted that a minimum of three years had elapsed between the actual interpretation and the experiment in question; only two of the ten interpreters recognized the passage - and this only as a result of marked lexical cues. Thus, it may safely be assumed that the reading, for all intents and purposes, was *prima vista* and was in no way expected to reveal those features which typify intonational interpretation.

2.2. Perception: Effect of Interpretational Intonation on Comprehension and on Recall

Once the features characteristic of simultaneous interpreting *production* had been pinpointed, their effect on *perception* could be assessed. Towards this end, recordings of three passages were played to two groups of subjects (eight in Group A and seven in Group B), matched for fluency in the languages concerned, and for familiarity with interpreting.

Both groups of judges listened to recordings of the same three passages. Group A listened to the interpreted version, whereas Group B heard the read-aloud one. Since the text, the speaker (interpreter/reader) and the format (a recording) were identical for each passage, it was assumed that the sole distinguishing factor would be the intonation, and that by comparing the test results of the two groups, it would be possible to establish the differential effect of interpretational intonation.

After each recording had been played, three questions on each of the three passages were presented in written form to each of the two groups of judges. (The same nine questions were presented to both groups.) The nine questions were meant to determine the effect of the mode of delivery. The passages did not lend themselves to inferential questions, but rather to a straightforward test of recall and comprehension, given that they averaged no more than fifteen lines and were presented out of context.

3. Results

3.1. Production

The salient features of interpretational intonation, described in the analysis below, have been grouped into four broad categories: (1) tonality - the distribution of an utterance into distinctive contours, or information units; (2) tonicity - which syllable carries maximum pitch prominence in the tone group; (3) tone - the means of marking the opposition between certain and uncertain polarity. If polarity is certain, the pitch of the tonic falls; if uncertain, it rises (Halliday 1967); (4) prosody - duration and speed.

All but one of the features described below - acceleration - was found in the output of at least four different interpreters; i.e., only one of the three features was possibly idiosyncratic. Moreover, although languages (and even dialects) do differ in various aspects of intonation (Ladd 1990; Cutler 1987; Rameh 1985), the features which came to the fore in the present study seemed to cut across (at least these two) languages.

The data below refer to occurrences of the given feature in the interpreted passage only; i.e., whenever the feature appeared in the read-aloud mode as well, it was not counted. It should be noted that each of the interpreted texts in the corpus was longer in duration than its read-aloud counterpart; i.e., the interpretation was slower (took more time) than the reading.

Passage 2 and passage 6 were produced by interpreters who, although working into English, are native speakers of Hebrew. The same two interpreters also produced the Hebrew passages 1 and 7, respectively. The data below do not reveal a significant pattern of differences between the two passages in the case of either interpreter, though further study is needed to determine whether directionality does in fact play a role in interpretational intonation.

3.1.1. Tonality (Chunking, Pauses, Division into Tone Groups). The range of grammatical structures which pauses tend to separate is relatively small and constant (Crystal 1969). Functional pauses serve to divide discourse into tone groups and organize it into information units (Halliday 1985; El-Menoufy 1988). Nonfunctional pauses caused by hesitations, on the other hand, tend to lower the congruence between chunking and syntax, since the ensuing junctures are nongrammatical.

The data below would seem to indicate that pauses *within* grammatical structures are by far the most salient feature of tonality in interpretation; i.e., interpreters are prone to introduce a disproportionate number of pauses in "unnatural" positions, which are liable to impede understanding (Alexieva 1987).

As for pauses at the clause or sentence boundary, while the interpreted passages did generally include pauses at sentence boundaries (in conformity with the original), these tended to be tentative rather than final, and were often coextensive with a low-rise intonation (pitch movement 3). Tentative pauses are frequently used in the middle of a primary contour, usually serving a parenthetic function (Ladd 1978; Pike 1945); thus, a high incidence of such pauses in nonparenthetical position is anomalous. Moreover, since the tentative pause correlates with an attitude of uncertainty, the cumulative pragmatic effect is bound to be altered. As in other instances of introducing an element which runs counter to the listener's expectations, understanding is likely to be affected.

Table 1. *Incidence of Salient Features of Interpretational Tonality (Total Number of Occurrences in the Passage)*

Passage	Pause within constituent	Tentative pause in final position
1	5	3
2	8	6
3	1	7
4	2	1
5	4	2
6	3	2
7	3	1
8	4	5
9	4	4
10	7	-

3.1.2. Tonicity (Stress, Assignment of Tonic Syllable). Tonicity has an important cohesive function (El-Menoufy 1988) in that it indicates, through contrast, which information is new.

> ...we may refer to a 'grammatical' function of tonicity when we find two otherwise identical structures being differentiated by tonicity alone, as long as the contrasts made may be seen to function analogously to the 'closed system' concept in grammar (Crystal 1969).

In other words, there is a very restricted number of contrasts at this point in the grammar, as opposed to the number of contrasts available elsewhere, which is limited only by the number of words in the utterance. The greatest potential for misunderstanding an utterance as a result of anomalous tonicity would seem to lie in the incompatibility of stress with semantic contrast (Brown 1974), i.e., a misperception of new vs. given information.

Table 2. *Incidence of the Salient Feature of Interpretational Tonicity*

Passage	Stress incompatible with semantic contrast
1	5
2	3
3	4
4	3
5	6
6	1
7	2
8	2
9	7
10	3

3.1.3. Tone (Pitch Movement). Changes in pitch are an important cue, to which listeners are particularly sensitive; in fact, they are considered a more powerful cue than either duration or volume (Bolinger 1986). It has been shown that when listeners' expectations are proven wrong, perception is temporarily disrupted (Cutler 1987). Thus, the preponderance of the low-rise nonfinal pitch movement, conveying the tentative, provisional attitude of an afterthought (Halliday 1985) in positions where a final (usually falling) one would be expected, is likely to impede comprehension. Tone, moreover, plays a key role in inferencing and in the disambiguation of otherwise identical utterances; unnatural placement of tone is bound to detract from its disambiguation potential as well.

Table 3. *Incidence of the Salient Feature of Interpretational Tone*

Passage	**Nonstandard matching of pitch movement and discourse pattern: low-rise, non-final pitch in final position**
1	4
2	6
3	8
4	1
5	2
6	2
7	5
8	2
9	11
10	1

3.1.4. Other Prosodic Features (Duration and Speed). Duration plays an important role in both the production (Brown 1974) and the perception (Ladd 1978) of stress. Since listeners tend to use speech rhythm predictively, and since salient syllables tend to occur at roughly regular intervals, any nonstandard alteration of speed is liable to encumber comprehension.

> Duration, however, refers to a different function of time: given a syllable with a perceived pitch, loudness and timbre, perceptually distinct variation in overall speed of utterance may take place... which may be linguistically significant (Crystal 1969).

Cutler (1987) cites several studies which have shown that lengthening or shortening a single vowel in a recorded utterance could cause a perceptible momentary alteration in tempo, and increase listeners' reaction time to detect phoneme targets.

The speeding up or slowing down of syllables creates an auditory effect of "clipped" or "drawled"/"held" speech, each of which has a correlate in terms of meaning: a drawl creates the effect of emphasis or of hesitation; held syllables lend prominence to the segment, and often convey greater tension. Length is ultimately a matter of pragmatics as well; e.g. an overall reduction of syllabic length is an indication of familiarity (Crystal 1969).

Table 4. *Incidence of the Salient Features of Intonational Prosody*

Passage	Lengthening/holding of segment	Acceleration (sometimes preceded by false start)
1	8	-
2	-	-
3	1	-
4	2	1
5	-	-
6	1	-
7	3	-
8	1	-
9	4	-
10	-	2

3.2. Perception

A test was devised to determine the extent of comprehension and recall by each of the two groups of subjects. The same test was administered to both groups. It consisted of three questions on each of three passages (a total of nine questions). The total number of correct answers in Group A (8 subjects) was 15 out of a possible 72 (21%) and in Group B (7 subjects) 26 out of a possible 63 (41%). The difference between the proportions of correct answers in the sample was 20%; i.e., the proportion of correct answers in the second group was approximately double that of the first.

4. Summary

That interpretation has an intonation all its own is intuitively apparent to anyone using this medium. The parameters and effects of its markedness merit further study. Replication should involve larger samples. Moreover, some contextualization (e.g. a brief description of the setting and speaker) would seem warranted. In the perception test described here, the subjects were given no prior information about the setting. The total absence of frame is bound to impede perception whether the passages are interpreted or read aloud; in the case of those listening to interpretation, however, this may have been a compounding factor. It stands to reason that perception of interpreted texts by conference participants, who are aware of the frame and familiar with the background, is considerably higher.

Further research is also needed to ascertain the relative weight of the different salient features of interpretational intonation in recall, comprehension, inferencing and other tasks.

The fact that intonation may affect meaning and perception is referred to extensively in the literature. The present study, however limited in scope, does indicate that in the case of interpretation this is indeed the case.

References

Alexieva, B. 1988. "Analysis of the Simultaneous Interpreter's Output". P. Nekeman, ed. *Translation, Our Future: Proceedings of the XIth World Congress of the FIT*, Netherlands: Euroterm Maastricht. 484-488.

Barik, H.C. 1972. "Interpreters Talk a Lot, Among Other Things". *Babel* 18. 3-11.

Bolinger, D. 1986. *Intonation and Its Parts: Melody in Spoken English*. Stanford: Stanford University Press.

Bowen, D. and M. 1985. "The Nuremberg Trials (Communication Through Translation)". *Meta* XXX. 74-77.

Brown, G. 1974. "Practical Phonetics and Phonology". J.P.B. Allen and S. Pit Corder, eds. *Techniques in Applied Linguistics*. Oxford: Oxford University Press. 24-58.

Cartellieri, C. 1983. "The Inescapable Dilemma: Quality and/or Quantity in Interpreting". *Babel* 29. 209-213.

Crystal, D. 1969. *Prosodic Systems and Intonation in English*. Cambridge: Cambridge University Press.

Crystal, D. 1975. *The English tone of voice: Essays in intonation, prosody and paralanguage*. Bristol: Edward Arnold.

Cutler, A. 1987. "Speaking for Listening". A. Allport, D.G. Mackey, W. Orinsz and E. Scheerer, eds. *Language Perception and Production*. London: Academic Press. 23-40.

Déjean-le Féal, K. 1982. "Why Impromptu Speech is Easy to Understand". N. Enkvist, ed. *Impromptu Speech: A Symposium*. Abo Akademi. 221-230.

El-Menoufy, A. 1988. "Intonation and Meaning in Spontaneous Discourse". M. Cummings Benson and W.S. Greaves, eds. *Linguistics in a Systemic Perspective* Amsterdam: John Benjamins. 1-26.

Enkvist, N. (ed). 1982a. *Impromptu Speech: A Symposium*. Abo Akademi.

Enkvist, N. 1982b. "Impromptu Speech, Structure, and Process". *Impromptu Speech: A Symposium*, 11-32. Abo Akademi.

Gerver, D. 1975. "A Psychological Approach to Simultaneous Interpretation". *META* 2. 119-128.

Gerver, D. and Sinaiko, H.W. eds. 1978. *Language, Interpretation and Communication: NATO Symposium on Language, Interpretation and Communication, Venice, 1977*. New York: Plenum Press.

Goldman-Eisler, F. "Psychological Mechanisms of Speech Production as Studied Through the Analysis of Simultaneous Translation". B. Butterworth, ed. *Language and Speech Production 2 - Speech and Talk*. London: Academic Press.

Halliday, M.A.K. 1967. *Intonation and Grammar in British English*. The Hague: Mouton.

Halliday, M.A.K. 1970. *A Course in Spoken English: Intonation*. Oxford: Oxford University Press.

Halliday, M.A.K. 1985. *An Introduction to Functional Grammar*. London: Arnold.

Henderson, A., Goldman-Eisler, F. and Skarbek, A. 1965a. "Temporal Patterns of Cognitive Activity and Breath-Control in Speech". *Language and Speech* 8. 236-242.

Henderson, A., Goldman-Eisler, F. and Skarbek, A. 1965b. "The Common Value of Pausing Time in Spontaneous Speech". *Quarterly Journal of Experimental Psychology* 17. 342-5.

Jumpelt, R.W. 1985. "The Conference Interpreter's Working Environment Under the New ISO and IEC Standards". *META* XXX. 82-90.

Kopczynski, A. 1980. *Conference Interpreting: Some Linguistic and Communicative Problems*. Poznan: Institute of Applied Linguistics, Warsaw University.

Ladd, D.R. Jr. 1978. *The Structure of Intonational Meaning: Evidence from English*. Bloomington: Indiana University Press.

Massaro, D.W. 1978. "An Information-Processing Model of Understanding Speech". D. Gerver and W.H. Sinaiko, eds. *Language, Interpretation and Communication: NATO Symposium on Language, Interpretation and Communication, Venice, 1977.* New York: Plenum Press. 353-368.

Mossop, B. 1987. "Who Is Addressing Us When We Read a Translation?" *TEXTconTEXT* 2. 1-22.

Pike, K.L. 1963. *The Intonation of American English.* Ann Arbor: University of Michigan Press.

Poyatos, F. 1987. "Nonverbal Communication in Simultaneous and Consecutive Interpretation: A Theoretical Model and New Perspectives". *TEXTconTEXT* 2. 73-108.

Prince, E. F. 1982. "Language and the Law: Reference, Stress and Context". D. Schiffrin, ed. *Meaning, Form and Use in Context: Linguistic Applications*, Washington D.C.: Georgetown University Press. 240-252.

Rameh, Clea A. 1985. "Intonation and Topic in Portuguese". K.R. Jankowsky, ed. *Scientific and Humanistic Dimensions of Language.* Amsterdam: John Benjamins.

Seleskovitch, D. 1982. "Impromptu Speech and Oral Translation". N. Enkvist, ed. *Impromptu Speech: A Symposium.* Abo Akademi. 241-254.

Shillan, D. 1968. "Phrasing and Meaning". *META* XIII. 47-51.

Varantola, K. 1980. *On Simultaneous Interpretation.* Turku: Turku Language Institute.

NEUROPSYCHOLOGICAL RESEARCH

Lateralization for Shadowing Words versus Signs: A Study of ASL-English Interpreters

David P. Corina
University of Washington, Seattle
and

Jyotsna Vaid
Texas A & M University

1. Introduction

Research on language organization in the brain has until recently focused on users of a single language, and specifically on users of a single *spoken* language. Such studies, while providing important information, offer at best a limited view of cerebral organization of language. To arrive at a more fundamental understanding of the nature of hemispheric functional asymmetry, it is important to consider how different language experiences can affect cerebral lateralization.

Towards this end, investigators in the past ten years have studied bilingual speakers to examine whether there is differential lateralization when more than one language is acquired. A separate line of research has investigated patterns of lateralization for signed languages (e.g., American Sign Language-ASL) in deaf persons to assess the extent to which language modality may influence brain organization. The present study chose to look at the intersection of these two endeavours, namely, language lateralization in bimodal bilinguals, that is, in hearing bilinguals who are fluent in ASL and English. Previous studies of hemispheric specialization comparing bilinguals and unilinguals have occasionally yielded significant group or subgroup differences. Patterns of language lateralization *within* bilingual groups are thought to be influenced by such factors as relative language proficiency, the manner of second language acquisition, and the age of onset of bilingualism (Vaid 1983). While the particular contribution of any of these factors varies (see Hall and Vaid 1989 for a meta-analytic review), the bilingual laterality literature as a whole demonstrates that factors external to innate biological endowments may, under certain circumstances, alter the pattern of cerebral functional asymmetry for language.

Early studies of language lateralization in the deaf have suggested differences between deaf and hearing persons. Some of these studies claimed a right-hemisphere (RH) dominance for sign language, in comparison to left-hemispheric (LH) dominance for spoken languages, while others claimed that deaf persons lack cerebral specialization altogether. However, methodological problems such as heterogeneity of subject populations and the use of static, line drawings of signs rather than dynamic, videotaped presentations of actual signers, may account for the varied findings (see Poizner & Battison 1980; Kettrick & Hatfield 1986; and Vaid & Corina 1989 for further discussion). Recent tachistoscopic studies which have controlled for some of these confounds generally show a greater right visual field (RVF) advantage for identification of moving signs in brain-intact deaf adults who are native signers of ASL (Poizner 1984; Neville, Lawson & Corina 1989). These studies are in accord with evidence from neuropsychological studies of deaf persons who have incurred brain damage due to stroke who manifest discrete sign aphasias following left but not right hemisphere damage (Bellugi, Poizner & Klima 1983; Poizner, Bellugi & Klima 1987). This converging evidence (see also Corina, Vaid & Bellugi 1992 for a study using a dual-task paradigm) would suggest that sign language, despite its spatial nature, is primarily mediated by the left hemisphere.

While the studies mentioned above indicate left hemisphere specialization in *deaf* users of ASL, it is not clear whether this pattern of lateralization in deaf persons may be the result of the effects of early auditory deprivation rather than being due to an inherent property of language *per se*. Thus, it becomes important to consider whether *hearing* users of ASL will show a similar left hemisphere specialization for sign. In addition, the use of hearing signers enables a comparison of lateralization for a signed language and that for a spoken language, inasmuch as hearing signers are essentially bi-modal bilinguals.

Since hearing signers may have acquired ASL at birth from deaf parents, or may have become proficient in signing only in adulthood, to communicate with the deaf community, the factor of age of exposure to ASL was incorporated into the research design. Indeed, even in studies of deaf signers, this variable has received some attention (see Newport & Supalla 1980). To date only a few studies have (either directly or indirectly) considered the effect of age of onset of bilingualism for ASL-English bilinguals in relation to cerebral specialization of either language (see Kettrick 1986). Neville, Lawson and Corina (1989) recently conducted a series of event related potential studies of tachistoscopically shown moving signs in which both native and non-native hearing ASL-English bilinguals served as subjects. Preliminary analyses suggested an overall right visual field-left hemisphere (RVF-LH) advantage in accuracy of report, although the brain wave measures suggest some group differences which are currently being explored further.

In summary, an investigation of cerebral lateralization for sign in hearing bilinguals allows us to address the following questions:

1) Do hearing users of ASL show a left hemisphere specialization of sign language?
2) Are there qualitative differences in the degree of lateralization for a signed versus a spoken language?
3) What effects does the age of onset of bilingualism have on cerebral lateralization of language in ASL-English bilinguals?

2. Dual Task Paradigm

A dual task paradigm was used to investigate these questions. This paradigm, originally used by Kinsbourne and Cook (1971), involves a comparison of subject performance in two conditions. In one, subjects are required to perform a simple manual task, such as repeated finger tapping. In the second condition, subjects are asked to perform a cognitive task in addition to the manual task. As we might expect, performance in the dual task condition is worse than that in the single task condition. This usually results in slower and less frequent tapping. When the amount of manual output (in this case, number of taps) for each hand under concurrent versus control conditions is compared, findings generally indicate greater right hand interference in right handers for tasks involving verbal production.

Dual task studies have been used to examine differences between unilinguals and bilinguals (see Green & Vaid 1986), and have demonstrated more bilateral language representation within bilinguals (Hynd, Teeter & Stewart 1980;

Sussman, Franklin & Simon 1982). A dual task measure also appears to be sensitive to differences between groups who differ in degree of second language proficiency (Green 1986). However, not all studies have reported group differences whether between bilinguals and unilinguals (Soares & Grosjean 1984) or between bilingual subgroups (Hall & Lambert 1988) using this paradigm. The present study is the first to use a dual task paradigm to consider bilingual subgroup differences as well as modality differences (i.e., signed vs. spoken language; see also Corina *et al.* 1992). The specific cognitive task chosen in this study involved shadowing signed or spoken lexical items. As discussed elsewhere (see Green *et al.* 1989), shadowing is a skill that is sufficiently attention demanding and therefore likely to produce measurable interference in the concurrent task.

3. Functional Cerebral Distance Principle

Two assumptions underlie the interpretation of asymmetric interference found in dual tasks. First, it is assumed that limb movements are controlled at the cortical level primarily by the contralateral hemisphere. Second, other factors being equal, it is assumed that interference between two concurrent activities will be greater when both are controlled by a different hemisphere. From these two assumptions, it follows that an activity for which the left hemisphere is specialized will interfere mainly with right hand performance and an activity for which the right hemisphere is specialized will mainly interfere with left hand performance. This within versus between hemisphere comparison may be construed as a special case of a more comprehensive model based on the principle of functional cerebral distance. In brief, the functional cerebral distance principle states that the degree to which two simultaneous activities affect each other varies inversely with the functional distance between the cerebral regions in which the respective processes are represented (Hiscock 1986).

The functional cerebral distance principle makes specific predictions about patterns of observed interference of simultaneous executed tasks as a function of cerebral lateralization. Thus, in the present study, we would expect that, if sign and spoken language differ in their distribution of lateralization, a different pattern of tapping interference should be observed while signing as compared to that while speaking. Whether interference patterns will also vary as a function of age of onset of bilingualism was of further interest.

4. Method

4.1. Subjects

A total of 32 right-handed hearing adults participated in the experiment. Subjects were classified into two groups according to their onset of bilingualism: early bilinguals were those who had acquired both ASL and English before the age of 5 years, whereas late bilinguals had acquired their second language (ASL) after the age of 12 years. All subjects were either pending certification or were certified sign language interpreters. The mean length of certification was 7.5 years for the early bilinguals and 3.7 years for the late bilinguals. Mean number of years reported interpreting were 17.9 and 6.4 years for the early and late bilinguals respectively.

4.2. Stimuli and Apparatus

Stimuli consisted of blocked sets of common English words, ASL signs, pseudo signs, and a list of ASL signs alternating with English words. English stimuli were presented on an audio tape at the rate of one word per second. The English and ASL stimuli were all common nouns. The pseudo signs were meaningless signs that obeyed the phonological constraints of ASL signs.

Subjects were to tap a telegraph key that was mounted on a board with a velcro strap fastened around their wrist to prevent unnecessary arm movement. The telegraph key set-up was connected to an Apple 2e computer, which recorded the number of taps during each 30 second trial.

4.3. Procedure

Prior to testing, all subjects were given a speeded sign test. The test required them to sign a list of 24 single, one-handed signs or one-hand dominant signs as quickly as possible using their right hand followed by their left hand, for half the subjects, and the reverse order for the remaining. Two parallel lists of signs were used, taken from Vaid, Bellugi & Poizner (1989). All responses were videotaped. A score for each hand, based on the number of signs produced in ten seconds, constituted a measure of hand dominance for sign production.

Following the speeded sign test, baseline tapping rates were measured. During test trials, subjects were to tap a telegraph key as quickly as possible while concurrently shadowing (copying) spoken or signed lexical stimuli. All subjects participated in four test conditions in which they were required to shadow lists of pseudosigns, ASL signs, English words, and a combination word and sign list. Order of hand used to tap was counterbalanced across subjects as was the order of conditions (with the constraint that the combination condition was presented last for all subjects). Percent decrement in tapping rate was measured for each hand and served as an index of interference, with greater right than left hand disruption taken to signal greater left hemisphere activation of the concurrent activity. Subjects were instructed to tap as quickly as possible while performing the shadowing task. All subjects received practice trials to acquaint them with the tasks.

4.4. Data Analysis

Percentage decrement of tapping rate in the concurrent relative to the baseline condition was calculated for each hand for each condition (see Kinsbourne & Hiscock 1983). Scores for each subject were entered into a five-way analysis of variance. The variables were Group (early vs. late bilingual), Sex (male vs. female), Hand (right vs. left hand used for tapping), Condition (ASL signs, pseudo signs, English words, and ASL and English), and Condition Order (signing first vs. speaking first). A preliminary analysis had revealed no effect of Hand Order so this variable was dropped from the analysis. The independent measure of hand dexterity obtained from each subject on the speeded sign test served as a covariable for analysis of sign and pseudo-sign data.

5. Results

The analysis of variance revealed a main effect of Condition [$F(3,84) = 53.92$, $p < .01$], a main effect of Sex [$F(1,28) = 5.43$, $p < .03$], a main effect of Hand [$F(1,28 = 5.35$, $p < .03$], and a three way Condition x Condition Order x Hand [$F(3,84) = 3.41$, $p < .03$] interaction. There was no significant effect of early vs. late onset of bilingualism ($F < 1$).

The main effect of sex revealed that women showed more tapping interference than men. The hand effect indicated greater right than left hand interference. The condition effect revealed that the pseudosign condition produced the largest interference, followed by the sign condition, with the voice and combination voice/sign conditions producing much lower levels of interference (see Figure 1).

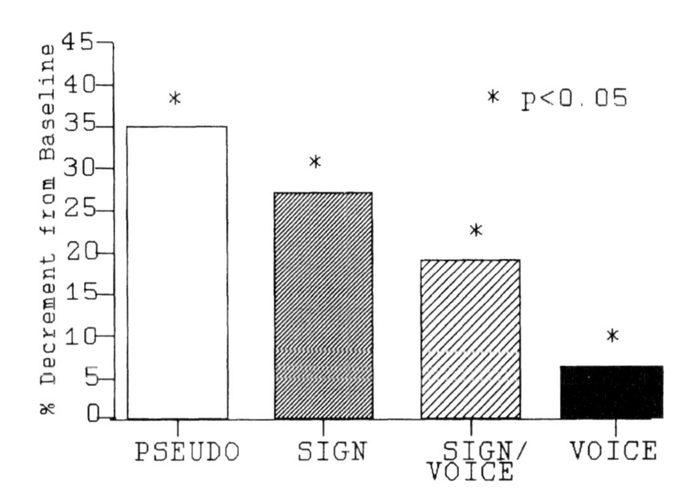

Figure 1. *Relative degree of manual interference across conditions*

The three-way interaction of Condition x Condition Order x Hand qualifies the above results in the following way. Significant hand differences for any condition were observed only when the condition was presented first. When it was not the first condition of the study, a significant hand difference was not obtained. Thus, greater right than left hand interference for sign was found only when the sign condition was first (Tukey's hsd = 4.50, k = 2, $p < .05$) while greater right than left hand interference for English words was obtained only when the words were first (this effect was near significant, $D_{critical}$ = 4.50, $D_{observed}$ = 4.04). A similar result characterized the remaining two conditions, with the combination voice-sign condition showing a near-significant hand effect ($D_{critical}$ = 4.50; $D_{observed}$ = 4.16). See Table 1.

Table 1. *Mean Percent Decrement in Tapping as a Function of Condition, Hand, and Condition Order*

	Sign first		English first	
	Rt Hand	Lt Hand	Rt Hand	Lt Hand
ASL Signs	32.6	25.8*	26.4	24.2
Pseudo Signs	41.6	33.2*	33.2	31.4
English Words	5.4	3.2	10.5	6.5*
ASL/English Combined	21.4	17.3	21.8	17.8

* The difference in right and left hand decrement scores is significant at $p < .05$.

It may be argued that the greater right hand interference for sign and pseudosign shadowing is an artifact arising from the necessity for subjects to be signing with their non-preferred hand when tapping with their right hand. To investigate this possibility, a separate analysis for sign and pseudo sign conditions was carried out collapsing over nonsignificant variables, using hand dexterity scores obtained from the speeded sign test as covariables. The use of covariables in this way allows one to equate right and left hand performance by factoring out initial differences that may be present. The hand effects from this analysis were still statistically significant [$F(1,29)=4.35$, $p<.05$], indicating greater right than left hand interference.

6. Discussion

This study revealed a number of interesting findings. Most importantly, it clearly revealed a significant right hand interference effect for signing, when the sign condition preceded the other conditions. This effect was still present after taking hand dexterity into account and, as such, argues strongly for left hemisphere mediation of sign language production, at least in hearing, fluent signers. This finding is important in that it is consistent with recent findings of left hemisphere mediation of sign language in deaf persons (see Poizner *et al.* 1987; Corina *et al.* 1992). Our results imply that left hemisphere lateralization characterizes all human languages, whether they are spoken or signed.

It is of interest that pseudo-signs also produced greater right than left hand interference. This finding is not altogether surprising given that the pseudo-signs chosen obeyed phonological constraints of American Sign Language. It is important to note that in dichotic listening studies, nonsense syllables reliably show greater left hemisphere processing (Kimura 1972). The present study is thus the first to show that pseudo-signs, like pseudo-words, involve LH processing.

A particular striking finding of this study relates to the hierarchy of interference effects found for the first four experimental conditions. Specifically, the pseudo sign and sign shadowing conditions produced significantly more interference than the English word or the combination English-ASL conditions. The English word condition in fact turned out to be much easier than either of the sign conditions[1]. However, despite the overall elevation of interference effects across both hands during the signing conditions, the direction of asymmetry of the signing and speaking conditions is the same.

It is illuminating to view the above findings in relation to the functional cerebral distance principle (FCD). Recall that the FCD principle predicts the greatest amount of interference for two tasks which are functionally related. In this model, functional relatedness is determined by the degree of similarity between underlying action patterns controlling the respective activities. In the present study, two types of functional relatedness are noted across sign and speech conditions. In the first case, it is predicted that signing and tapping will be more interfering than will speaking while tapping. This follows from the fact that cortical areas controlling manual-manual outputs (as in signing and tapping) are more functionally related than oral-manual outputs (as in speaking and tapping). That is, the motor control apparatus for tapping and signing is more similar than that for tapping and speaking, and of course, such motor interference would be equal for both right and left hands. Thus, we suspect that it is this greater overlap of effect or output during the signing and tapping conditions that gives rise to the overall greater interference found for these conditions in comparison to the speaking conditions. However, a second type of interference is predicted by the Kinsbourne and Cook model (1971). To the extent that both signing and speaking are functionally equivalent linguistic manipulations, we might expect a qualitatively similar degree of interference. We would argue that it is precisely this functional relatedness that gives rise to the nearly equivalent asymmetric interference patterns found in both signing and speaking conditions (see Figure 2).

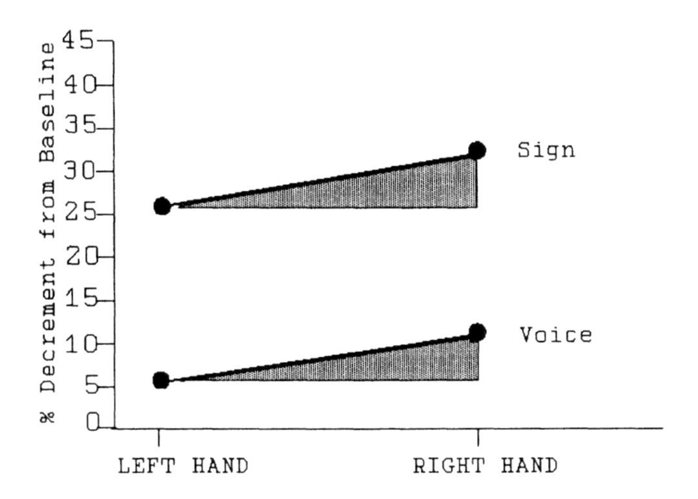

Figure 2. *Relative interference as a function of Condition, Hand, and Order*

With regard to the bilingual group variable, the present study did not uncover any difference in asymmetry between early and late ASL users. This finding runs counter to a result reported by Sussman and colleagues (1982) which indicated greater left hand disruption for late bilinguals as compared to early bilinguals (but see Green, Schweda-Nicholson, Vaid, White & Steiner 1990 for a different outcome). Procedural factors, such as task differences, may have contributed to the inconsistency of the results across the studies. For example, the present study used a shadowing task, while the Sussman *et al.* study involved reading, picture description and reciting automatisms (e.g. counting), and the Green *et al.* (1990) study used an interpretation task in addition to shadowing.

In summary, the present study has been successful in demonstrating a left hemisphere contribution to the mediation of sign language in hearing ASL-English bilinguals. As such, this research suggests language lateralization may arise from inherent characteristics of human languages, regardless of the modality in which that language is expressed. The study also demonstrates the utility of a dual task measure for investigating cerebral lateralization in signers. This measure was sensitive in detecting modality differences between sign and speech, that is, the surface level articulator differences, as well as the modality-independent similarities between sign and speech, arising from the fact that both are linguistic codes.

Notes

1. This finding may reflect the fact that the subjects were highly practised in monitoring English or English/sign input given their profession as interpreters. In a follow-up study we are conducting using English unilingual non-interpreter controls, the hand asymmetry effect for shadowing English words is in fact larger.

References

Bellugi, U., Poizner, H., and Klima, E.S. 1983. "Brain Organization for Language: Clues From Sign Aphasia". D. Kimura, ed. *Human Neurobiology* 2. 155-170.

Corina, D., Vaid, J. & Bellugi, U. 1992. "The Linguistic Basis for Left Hemisphere Specialization". *Science* 255. 1258-1260.

Green, A. 1986. "A Time Sharing Cross-Sectional Study of Monolinguals and Bilinguals at Different Levels of Second Language Acquisition". *Brain and Cognition* 5. 477-497.

Green, A., Schweda-Nicholson, N., Vaid, J., White, M. & Steiner, R. 1990. "Hemispheric Involvement in Shadowing vs. Interpreting: A Time-Sharing Study of Simultaneous Interpreters and Matched Bilingual and Unilingual Controls". S. *Brain and Language* 39. 107-133.

Green A. and Vaid, J. 1986. "Methodological Issues in the Use of the Concurrent Activities Paradigm". *Brain and Cognition* 5. 465-476.

Hall, G. and Lambert, W.E. 1988. "French Immersion and Cerebral Language Processing: A Dual-Task Study". *Canadian Journal of Behavioral Science*. 20:1. 1-14.

Hall, G. and Vaid, J. 1989. "Bilingualism and Cerebral Lateralization: A Meta-Analysis". Paper presented at annual meeting of the International Neuropsychological Society, Vancouver.

Hiscock, M. 1986. "Lateral Eye Movements and Dual Task Performance". H.J. Hannay, ed. *Experimental Techniques in Human Neuropsychology*. New York: Oxford University Press. 264-308.

Hynd, G., Teeter, A. and Stewart, J. 1980. "Acculturation and Lateralization of Speech in the Bilingual Native American". *International Journal of Neuroscience* 11. 1-7.

Kettrick, C. 1986. "Cerebral Lateralization for ASL and English in Deaf and Hearing Native and Non-Native Signers". Paper presented at conference on "Theoretical Issues in Sign Language Research", Rochester, N.Y.

Kettrick, C. and Hatfield, N. 1986. "Bilingualism in a Visuo-Gestural Mode". J. Vaid, ed. *Language Processing in Bilinguals: Psycholinguistic and Neuropsychological Perspectives*. Hillsdale, N.J.: Lawrence Erlbaum.

Kimura, D. 1973. "The Asymmetries of the Human Brain". *Scientific American* 728:3. 70-78.

Kinsbourne, M. and Cook, J. 1971. "Generalized and Lateralized Effect of Concurrent Verbalization on a Unimanual Skill". *Quarterly Journal of Experimental Psychology* 23. 341-345.
Kinsbourne, M. and Hiscock, M. 1983. "Asymmetrics of Dual-Task Performance". J. Hellige, ed. *Cerebral Hemispheric Asymmetry: Methods, Theory and Application*. New York: Praeger. 255-224.
Neville, H., Lawson, D. and Corina, D. 1989. "Event Related Potential Recordings in Response to Digitized ASL Signs in Deaf Subjects". The Salk Institute.
Newport, E. and Suppalla, T. 1980. "Clues From the Acquisition of Signed and Spoken Language". U. Bellugi and M. Studdert-Kennedy, eds. *Signed and Spoken Language: Biological Constraints on Linguistic Form*. Dahlem Konferenzen, Weinheim: Verlag Chemie GmbH.
Poizner, H. 1984. "Hemispheric Specialization for Computer Synthesized Signs". Paper presented at annual meeting of the Psychonomics Society, Houston.
Poizner, H. and Battison, R. 1980. "Cerebral Asymmetry for Sign Language: Clinical and Experimental Evidence". H. Lane and F. Grosjean, eds. *Recent Perspectives on American Sign Language*. Hillsdale, NJ: Lawrence Erlbaum.
Soares, C. 1984. "Left Hemisphere Language Lateralization in Bilinguals: Use of the Concurrent Activities Paradigm". *Brain and Language* 23:1. 89-96.
Sussman, H., Franklin, P. and Simon T. 1982. "Bilingual Speech: Bilateral Control". *Brain and Language* 15:1. 125-142.
Vaid, J. 1983. "Bilingualism and Brain Lateralization". S. Segalowitz, ed. *Language Function and Brain Organization*. New York: Academic Press.
Vaid J., Bellugi, U. and Poizner, H. 1989. "Hand Dominance for Signing: Clues to Brain Lateralization of Language". *Neuropsychologia* 27:7. 949-960.
Vaid, J. and Corina, D. 1989. "Visual Field Asymmetries in Numerical Size Comparisons of Digits, Words, and Signs". *Brain and Language* 36. 117-126.

Author Notes

We are grateful to Marina McIntyre and Dennis Cokeley for allowing us to set up our apparatus during the annual Registry of Interpreters for the Deaf Conference held in San Diego, Ca. We thank Lucinda O'Grady for serving as a sign model and Richard Batch for programming assistance. This research was first reported at the conference, "Theoretical Issues in Sign Language Research," sponsored by the Cognitive Sciences Program, University of Rochester, Rochester, N.Y., June 1986. The conference talk was entitled "Tapping into bilingualism: A concurrent activities study of ASL and English." This work was supported in part by National Institutes of Health Grants NS 15175, NS 19096, NS 22343, HD 13249, and by National Science Foundation Grant BNS 83-09860 to Drs. Ursula Bellugi and Howard Poizner at the Salk Institute for Biological Studies. The illustration was made by Frank A. Paul, copyright Dr. Ursula Bellugi, The Salk Institute.

Reprint requests should be sent to Jyotsna Vaid, Department of Psychology, Texas A & M University, College Station, Texas 77843.

Non-Linguistic Factors Influencing Simultaneous Interpretation

Valeria Daró
Graduate Interpreters' School
University of Trieste

1. Introduction

Simultaneous interpretation is considered a rather complex cognitive task. It was only after World War II, during the trials against Nazi criminals in Nuremberg that simultaneous translation came to the fore as a real profession, although interpretation as verbal mediation between two different languages practically came into existence when people of different communities started trading. With the setting up of the first interpretation departments at European and American universities, the mere teaching of simultaneous and consecutive interpretation techniques was soon flanked by theoretical studies on interpretation, most of them falling within the domain of linguistics or psychology (Gerver & Sinaiko 1978). In recent times, however, other scientific disciplines started taking interest in the study of interpretation with experimental techniques. As a result, much research work was carried out in the fields of neuropsychology, neurolinguistics, neurophysiology, cognitive psychology, not to mention computer science and electronic engineering.

One of the basic findings of neuropsychological experimental research, still a premise for any further investigation on linguistic skills, is that in more than 90% of human beings, language functions tend to be organized in the left cerebral hemisphere (Taylor-Sarno 1981), whereas the right cerebral hemisphere apparently controls the emotional aspects of speech (Code 1987). However, polyglots and bilinguals, especially coordinate bilinguals who learned their second language late in life, generally show a more symmetrical cerebral organization of languages as opposed to monolinguals (Albert & Obler 1978; Vaid 1983, 1986; Fabbro 1990b). The organization of languages in the brain of simultaneous interpreters was the subject of several experimental works based on neuropsychological techniques. Fabbro *et al.* (1990b) as well as Green *et al.* (1990) pointed out that during simultaneous interpretation, both hemispheres are substantially activated, thus reducing the cerebral asymmetry for linguistic functions that was evidenced during simple linguistic tasks (Sussman *et al.* 1982). Other neurological and psychological studies attested to the influence of biological factors, e.g. sex, on linguistic functions and their cerebral organization in polyglots. A general superiority of female versus male subjects in carrying out sequential motor tasks and in linguistic skills was thus evidenced (Hampson & Kimura 1988). Apparently males and females differ from each other even with respect to their cerebral organization of languages, whereby women tend to show better results in tests involving speech performance or motor abilities (Ojemann & Creutzfeldt 1987).

In the fields of electronic engineering, computer science and artificial intelligence, researchers are trying to develop a highly efficient automatic translation system (Cirilli 1989). Moreover, research in the field of automatic speech recognition will undoubtedly give an important contribution to the study of simultaneous interpretation from a physical point of view and perhaps even succeed in realizing a fully automatic translation unity. Such a system would require the creation of computerized models of voice recognition, translation and synthesis of acoustic verbal messages, so as to obtain the same kind of performance on the part of a good simultaneous interpreter. At present, this goal is still at an experimental level, though several extraordinary results have already been achieved. For example, with a computerized system, it is now possible to correct the pronunciation of a speaker talking in a foreign language, so as to make it sound similar to that of a native speaker, without changing its original characteristics (Abe *et al.* 1988). This means that phonetic and prosodic features of languages can be described by means of a mathematical model, and that they can be converted according to the correct pronunciation of a native speaker. It is not difficult to imagine what kind of impact the results of these experiments may have on the practice and teaching of simultaneous interpretation.

Although investigations in this field are still at an initial stage, they give a clear example of the importance of interdisciplinary research, i.e., of the synergy resulting from different disciplines such as linguistics, neurophysiology, neuropsychology, electronic engineering and artificial intelligence. A description of some experimental works that have been carried out in the last few years aimed at investigating simultaneous interpretation with interdisciplinary approaches will follow. These works concern a) neuropsychological aspects, such as memory and attention during a complex cognitive task such as simultaneous interpretation (Darò 1989); b) non-linguistic aspects of verbal communication, such as speaking speed and its effects on the performance of a simultaneous interpreter (Darò 1990a); as well as c) emotional, suprasegmental aspects of speech in polyglot subjects (Darò 1990b).

2. Attention and Memory

In a recent experimental study (Darò 1989; Spiller-Bosatra *et al.* 1990), the method of "complex auditory shadowing" (cf. Mowbray 1964) was adopted to investigate the effects of training, acquired in the practice of simultaneous interpretation, on the improvement of the so-called long-term memory (cf. Squire 1987). The experimental paradigm of shadowing was adopted several times to study simultaneous interpretation as a cognitive task. Treisman (1965) and Gerver (1974 a,b) evidenced that simultaneous interpretation is more complex than shadowing. The results of their research showed that during simultaneous interpretation, subjects made more mistakes and had a longer delay (i.e., "décalage") than during shadowing. Several authors suggested that shadowing can be a useful propaedeutic practice to simultaneous interpretation (Gerver 1974 a,b; Bosatra and Spiller 1984). Recently, Green *et al.* (1990) evidenced that shadowing tasks are predominantly processed by the hemisphere that is specialized in language, whereas -as it has been already pointed out (cf. Fabbro *et al.* 1990b; Fabbro, 1990)- during simultaneous interpretation, both hemispheres are activated, and the assessed cerebral asymmetries for linguistic functions tend to be reduced.

Auditory shadowing consists in the presentation of lists of words sent to one ear at a time through earphones; the words must be repeated aloud by the subject immediately. In this experiment (Darò 1989), subjects were instructed to listen to and immediately repeat lists of Italian words, as well as to listen to and immediately translate into Italian lists of German words (<u>control lists</u>). The complex paradigm of auditory shadowing consisted in repeating (or translating) lists of words that were sent to one ear, and at the same time in listening to and memorizing 1-3 target words which were sent to the opposite ear and were to be correctly reported at the end of each list (experimental lists). Each list of words (30 lists with 50 words each for each ear) included 1 to 3 target words in the same language as the words of the list, which were synchronized so as to always coincide with a word of the list. Thus, each subject had to shadow 1500 Italian words sent to the right ear (RE) and as many sent to the left ear (LE); and then she had to translate into Italian 1500 German words sent to the right ear and 1500 sent to the left. The same number of words was then presented together with a total amount of 240 target words (60 target words in Italian to the left ear and 60 to the right, and the same in German).

The subjects of this experiment were divided into two groups. The control group was formed by three right-handed female students attending the 3rd year of the SSLM (Scuola Superiore di Lingue Moderne per Interpreti e Traduttori, Trieste, Italy) who were just beginning their training in simultaneous interpretation. The second group, the interpreters' group, was formed by five female students (four right-handed and one non right-handed; cf. Briggs and Nebes 1975) attending the 4th year of the same School for Translators and Interpreters, who had been training in simultaneous interpretation for at least one year. The subjects were aged 22-24 (average age 23.12), their mother tongue was Italian (L1) and they had a very good knowledge of German (L2) and a good knowledge of one or two other European languages.

2.1. *Results*

The statistical analysis (ANOVA) of the number and type of errors showed interesting results: the 3rd year students made significantly more errors than the 4th year students (3rd y. = 406; 4th y. = 162; $p<0.01$). Both groups generally made more mistakes when listening to the lists of words with their left ear (LE) as opposed to the right ear (RE): (LE = 271.41; RE = 235.97; $p<0.05$). In both languages, Italian (It) and German (Ger), the 3rd year students made significantly more errors when listening with their left ear than with their right ear (RE = 362.33, LE = 449.67; $p<0.02$; It RE = 417.5, It LE = 467.33; Ger RE = 307.17, Ger LE = 432), whereas this difference between the two ears was not displayed in the 4th year students (RE = 160.15, LE = 164.45; It RE = 132.6, It LE = 156; Ger RE = 187.7, Ger LE = 172.9); (cf. Figure 1).

As regards the target words, there was no significance concerning any factor or any interaction, that is to say, either between ears or between groups or languages. The 3rd year students' average score of correctly reported Italian target words was 48.33 with the right ear and 48.33 with the left ear; in German, 43.0 with the right ear and 47 with the left. The 4th year students correctly reported an average of 44.60 Italian target words with the right ear and 41.20 with the left; 39.4 German target words with the right ear and 39.60 with the left ear.

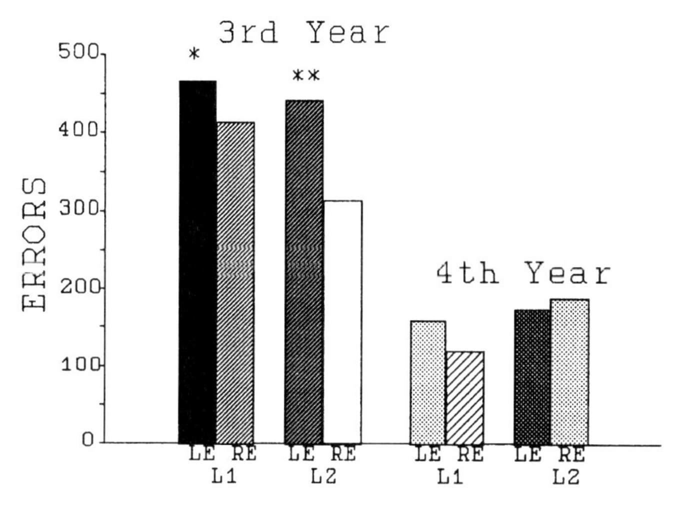

Figure 1. *Number of errors for each group (3rd and 4th year), for each language (L1 = Italian, L2 = German) and for each ear (RE = right ear, LE = left ear). Only the 3rd year students made significantly more errors with their left ear, both in Italian (* $p<0.007$) and in German (** $p<0.03$). The 4th year students did not show any significant difference between ears in the two languages.*

2.2. Discussion

When practising, a simultaneous or consecutive interpreter needs to acquire specific neurophysiological and cognitive strategies that go beyond the mere knowledge of languages. Generally speaking, the acquisition of these techniques requires more than one year of academic training. During this training period, the future interpreter learns to develop different skills. Apart from re-organizing his selective attention that must be diverted to different concurrent tasks (listening to the source language, understanding/analyzing, summarizing and talking in the target language), he must develop peculiar strategies in order to extend his verbal short-term memory, especially during an unnatural situation requiring simultaneous listening and verbal production. This unnatural situation was to some extent reconstructed with the experimental paradigm of complex shadowing, which enabled us to analyze both shadowing abilities (i.e., distribution of selective attention on different simultaneous tasks and verbal short-term memory) and verbal long-term memory (memorization of target words). The gradual development of verbal short-term memory is partly demonstrated in our experiment by the fact that the 4th year students made significantly fewer errors in both conditions (control and experimental lists) and in both languages than the 3rd year students, who were less trained in simultaneous interpretation.

Moreover, this experiment confirmed the advantage of the right ear (left hemisphere) during auditory shadowing of verbal material in right-handed subjects, as had already been pointed out (cf. Trevarthen 1984). However, subsequent studies (cf. Vaid 1986; Fabbro 1990) have shown that in polyglots, and especially in interpreters, the cerebral organization of linguistic functions is far less asymmetrical than in monolinguals, and that this decrease in asymmetry gradually develops with improved proficiency and practice of foreign languages (L2, L3 etc.). This observation partly applies to the experimental work already described. Actually, whereas the 3rd year students still showed a superiority of the right ear (left hemisphere) evidenced by fewer errors in both languages, the 4th year students showed a rather balanced performance between the two ears and thus a symmetrical behaviour of the two hemispheres (cf. Fabbro *et al.* 1987; Lambert 1990, 1993; cf. Figure 1).

We tried to find an explanation for such a rapid change in the cerebral organization of linguistic functions leading to this difference between the two groups of students. Given that the mechanism underlying cerebral asymmetry for linguistic functions is still unknown, we based our interpretation on several recent studies stressing different features. Geschwind and Galaburda (1985) insist on the importance of neuroanatomical differences in the two hemispheres that lead to functional differences; other studies underline the supremacy of neurophysiological differences (cf. MacNeilage 1982). However, the organization of attention seems to be of the utmost importance in the performance of difficult cognitive tasks (cf. Broadbent 1971; Tucker 1988). In our opinion, the greater symmetry of linguistic functions in simultaneous interpreters may in some degree also depend on a modification of their attentive strategies. The simultaneous interpreter, who listens to an incoming message and at the same time has to translate it into another language as well as control his/her own output, must learn to give up his/her preferential right-ear lateralization for verbal material, and try to focus his/her verbal attention on both ears. Moreover, in simultaneous interpreters, the left ear (right hemisphere) is apparently more involved in the recognition of the content of the source language (cf. Gran & Fabbro 1987; Lambert 1990).

A further interesting aspect suggested by our results regards verbal long-term memory, which was studied through the additional task of memorizing and reporting the target words after shadowing (with or without translation) each list of 50 words. Our data show no significant difference in the number of correctly reported target words when comparing the two groups. The acquisition of the techniques of simultaneous interpretation apparently does not affect long-term verbal memory. Forgetting (amnesia) is likely to be a very important function in the life of a simultaneous interpreter, who would be otherwise seriously disturbed if he recalled the contents of all the speeches he has already translated. Moreover, according to the most recent theories on the consolidation of long-term memory in the brain (cf. Squire 1987), the acquisition of good long-term memory can occur with specific strategies (i.e., association of an event with specific objects or items of a particular room, road, scene, etc; cf. Luria 1981; Squire 1987) which have nothing in common with the classic training of simultaneous or consecutive interpretation. Last but not least, these strategies cannot be easily applied during a whole session of simultaneous interpreting, where the interpreter is already trying to divide his attention on the many different concurrent tasks he is confronted with.

2.3. Speaking Speed

One of the outstanding characteristics of a simultaneous interpreter is his/her ability to talk rather quickly. The speaking speed of an interpreter mainly depends on the pace of the incoming message, which, if very fast, forces the interpreter to accelerate his/her own output so as not to miss too much of the message (cf. Darò 1990a). However, the interpreter's speech rate not only depends on i) the speaker's speed, but also ii) on the direction of translation (it has been demonstrated that one and the same concept can be expressed with more or less phonemes according to which language is used; cf. Miller 1951), as well as iii) on the type of the text to be translated (e.g. technical versus rhetorical texts), iv) on the strategies used by the interpreter (word-for-word versus meaning-based translation), v) on the level of language proficiency of the interpreter, and vi) on his/her physiological abilities.

As regards speaking speed, two preliminary statements should be made: 1) children generally speak more slowly than adults, whose mean rate is of 7 syllables per second (cf. Lenneberg 1967); 2) women can be more rapid and efficient in performing repetitive and complex motor skills as well as in verbal production. As one of the physiological characteristics in favour of a good simultaneous interpretation is speech fluency, this may be another explanatory factor for the "natural selection" of more female than male subjects in the interpreters' schools (one example being the SSLM in Trieste, Italy, with a female population of about 90%) and in the interpreters' departments of international organizations (EEC Commission, European Parliament). Some experiments carried out on simultaneous interpreters should be reconsidered in light of the concurrent presence of some specific biological and physiological features in simultaneous interpreters, such as i) female gender, ii) the ability of to develop a consistent speech fluency, and iii) a more symmetric representation of linguistic functions in both hemispheres.

2.3.1. Speaking Speed as a Determinant Factor in Three Experiments.

A. A group of 16 monolingual right-handed male subjects (average age=26; L1=Italian) was submitted to a verbal-manual interference paradigm (tapping) which consisted in carrying out two different tasks with two different speech rates (cf. Fabbro *et al.* 1990a). Each subject was asked to carry out four trials (of 20 sec. each) of silent finger tapping for each hand, once at normal speaking speed (7 syllables per sec.), and once at increased speaking speed (12 syllables per sec.). The concurrent verbal task consisted in reciting aloud a well-known prayer (the Lord's Prayer) for four trials of 20 sec each both at normal and at increased speaking speed, with the right and with the left hand. According to the formula suggested by Sussman *et al.* (1982; cf. also Gran & Fabbro 1988), the percentage of disruption for each hand (RH=right hand; LH=left hand) and each condition (normal = NSS versus increased speaking speed = ISS) was calculated. In the condition with normal speaking speed, subjects showed a greater disruption with the right hand as opposed to the left hand (RH=7.46%, LH=0.97%; $p<0.003$), thus indicating a left-hemisphere lateralization of linguistic functions. In the condition with increased speaking speed however, there was no significant difference in the verbal-manual interference rate between the right and the left hand (RH=5.30%, LH=3.97%; $p>0.1$, cf. Figure 2). These results indicate that the cerebral organization of linguistic functions may show different patterns with respect to specific parameters, such as speaking speed. Apparently, the faster speech production is, the more symmetric the involvement of the two hemispheres.

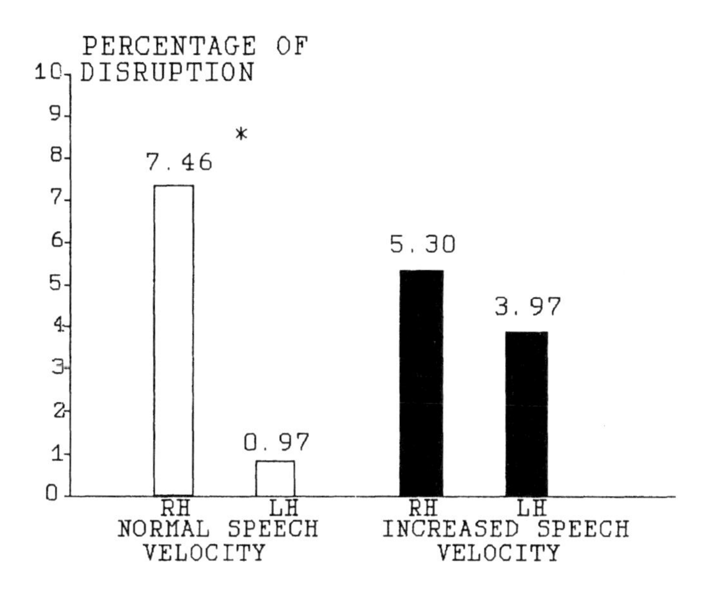

Figure 2. *Mean percentage of verbal-manual disruption with the right hand (RH) and wih the left hand (LH) at normal speech velocity and at increased speech velocity (asterisk indicates a significant difference between right-hand and left-hand finger tapping: $p<0.003$).*

B. A previous similar experiment had been carried out on bilingual subjects (L1=Friulian, L2=Italian) of different ages (cf. Fabbro *et al.* 1988). A paradigm involving a verbal-manual interference task, where the concurrent verbal tasks consisted in reciting aloud four common proverbs, two in Friulian and two in Italian, one rhythmically articulated and the other normally expressed, was performed by 12 right-handed girls attending the first year of elementary school (group 1), 12 right-handed girls attending the fifth year of elementary school (group 2) and 7 university female students (group 3). Group 1 showed a greater right-hand (left-hemisphere) disruption for both languages; in group 2, this difference between the two hemispheres decreased and finally disappeared in group 3. According to this result, the laterality effect related to linguistic functions tends to decrease as the subjects grow older. In this experiment, speaking speed was not measured in terms of syllables per second, but it was noted that the youngest girls (group 1) spoke more slowly than the girls of the second age group (group 2), who, in turn, spoke more slowly than the oldest subjects (group 3). Most probably, therefore, this gradual decrease in speech laterality in bilingual female subjects may also depend on a gradual increase in speaking speed, which develops with age.

C. In a recent study on cerebral lateralization during simultaneous interpretation (Fabbro *et al.* 1990b), attention was focussed on the development of cerebral lateralization of languages in interpreters. A verbal-manual interference paradigm where the concurrent verbal task consisted in reciting the days of the week in the three different languages known by the subjects was used. The subjects, who were student interpreters, showed a symmetric representation of their mother tongue (L1 = Italian) during automatic speech, whereas L2 (English) and L3 (German or French or Russian or Spanish) appeared to be lateralized, though not significantly, in the left hemisphere. Although in this experiment speaking speed was not analyzed, it can be stated that all the subjects generally spoke rather quickly, especially when reciting in Italian. We may thus infer also from this third experiment that the more symmetrical distribution of linguistic functions for L1 may in part depend on speaking speed, which again was rather high.

2.3.2. Discussion. All the experimental studies described above suggest that a high speaking speed is at the same time a typical feature of a simultaneous interpreter and a decisive factor for the hemispheric organization of linguistic functions. The fact that simultaneous interpreters (and to some extent women in general) have a more symmetric hemispheric representation of linguistic functions may also partly depend on their tendency to speak faster than other groups of subjects. In addition, the functional application of specific physiological and cognitive strategies in carrying out particular tasks brings about lasting changes in the structures and functions of the brain (cf. Bakker 1984; Akoi & Siekewitz 1989). We suggest that the tendency of interpreters to increase their speech rate, especially during their work, leads to a more symmetric organization of linguistic functions in the two hemispheres of their brain.

Speaking speed thus might be seen as another important factor influencing simultaneous interpretation also from a neurological point of view. It should be therefore taken into consideration in the discussion of the results of the experimental studies on the cerebral organization of linguistic functions in simultaneous interpreters. The first experiments with the verbal-manual interference paradigm carried out on interpreters (cf. Gran & Fabbro 1987; 1988) as well as the following experiments based on the same technique (cf. Green *et al.* 1990) should be evaluated also with respect to speaking speed. Actually, the results of all these inquiries showed a symmetric representation of linguistic functions in simultaneous interpreters, but this symmetry may depend in part also on the high speaking speed required during the task. Future experiments should consider speech rate as an additional parameter to be measured (cf. Fabbro *et al.* 1990a).

2.4. Fundamental Frequency of Speech

Verbal communication occurs through the vocal-auditory channel. Speech is the product of the concurrent interaction of three different anatomical systems: a) the pulmonary system supplying energy by means of air exhalation, b) the laryngeal system which serves as a source of vocal signals, and c) the supralaryngeal vocal tract which acts as a filter on the signal produced by the vocal cords (Lieberman 1984; Borden & Harris 1984). The vocal cords determine the "sonority" of a vocal signal: a voiced sound is produced when the vocal cords vibrate, on the contrary a voiceless sound occurs when the vocal cords are open and there is no vibration. Vowels (V) and some consonants (C) are produced with vocal cord vibration, whereas so-called voiceless consonants only occur when the vocal cords do not vibrate (Malmberg 1977). The modification of the supralaryngeal vocal tract (pharyngeal cavity, oral cavity, and nasal cavity) determines the sound shape of vowels and consonants of human languages (Jakobson & Waugh 1979).

Obviously, verbal communication does not only imply linguistic aspects, but also analogical aspects, that are predominantly controlled by nervous structures of the right hemisphere (Code 1987). Moreover, voice intonation is an important analogical feature of speech and depends on several different factors: fundamental frequency, vocal signal intensity, pauses in the word chain and rhythm (Di Cristo 1986). It also reveals several analogical features of the speaker, e.g. sex, age, persuasive power, fatigue, stress, etc. (Scherer 1986).

The fundamental frequency (Fo) is determined by the rate at which the vocal cords open and close during phonation. Adult male speakers' fundamental frequency is on average 120 Hz, whereas adult females normally phonate at a Fo of 225 Hz and children under 10 years of age phonate at about 300 Hz (Perkins & Kent 1986). During speech production the fundamental frequency does not always remain the same: it generally increases in sudden stressful circumstances or situations of emergency. In most human languages the fundamental frequency progressively decreases at the end of a verbal statement, whereas it generally increases at the end of an interrogative sentence (Lieberman & Blumstein 1988).

A description of a simple experimental research to assess fundamental frequency in one and the same speaker producing the same vocal signal throughout different statements in five different languages will follow (Darò 1990b). The aim of this experiment was to determine whether the fundamental frequency of a polyglot (female) subject was the same for all the languages she knew, or whether and how it changed according to the spoken language.

2.4.1. Material, Methods and Results. The subject of this experiment was a female, right-handed polyglot simultaneous interpreter aged 25 years. Her task was to read aloud a coherent text of about 300 words in the five different languages she knew (L1=Italian; L2=German, learned at school from kindergarten onwards up to her university degree; L3=English, learned from age 10 up to her university degree; L4=Dutch, learned at university; and L5=French, learned for 7 years at high school). At the end of each of the five texts the subject had to conclude by saying "This sentence was read by X." in the language of the spoken text, thus respectively in L1: "Questa frase è stata letta da X"; in L2: "Dieser Satz wurde von X gelesen"; in L3: see above; in L4: Deze zin is door X gelezen"; and in L5: "Cette phrase a été lue par X" (where X stands for the subject's first name and family name, composed as follows: CVCVCVV CVCV). All the phonemes of her names were voiced sounds, thus produced with vocal cord vibration. Each text was read three times, the order of languages being random. The subject was not told about the purpose of the experimental session.

The subject's speech production was recorded by means of a Sony analog recorder TC-277-4 with an AIWA unidirectional microphone held at a distance of 10 cm from her mouth. The fundamental frequency (Fo) of the last spoken sentence at the end of each text was analyzed by means of a computerized automatic system (Mumolo 1980; 1985; Lieberman & Blumstein 1988). Figure 3 shows respectively the oscillographies of the vocal signal (top) and the fundamental frequency tracings (bottom) of the final sentence for all five languages.

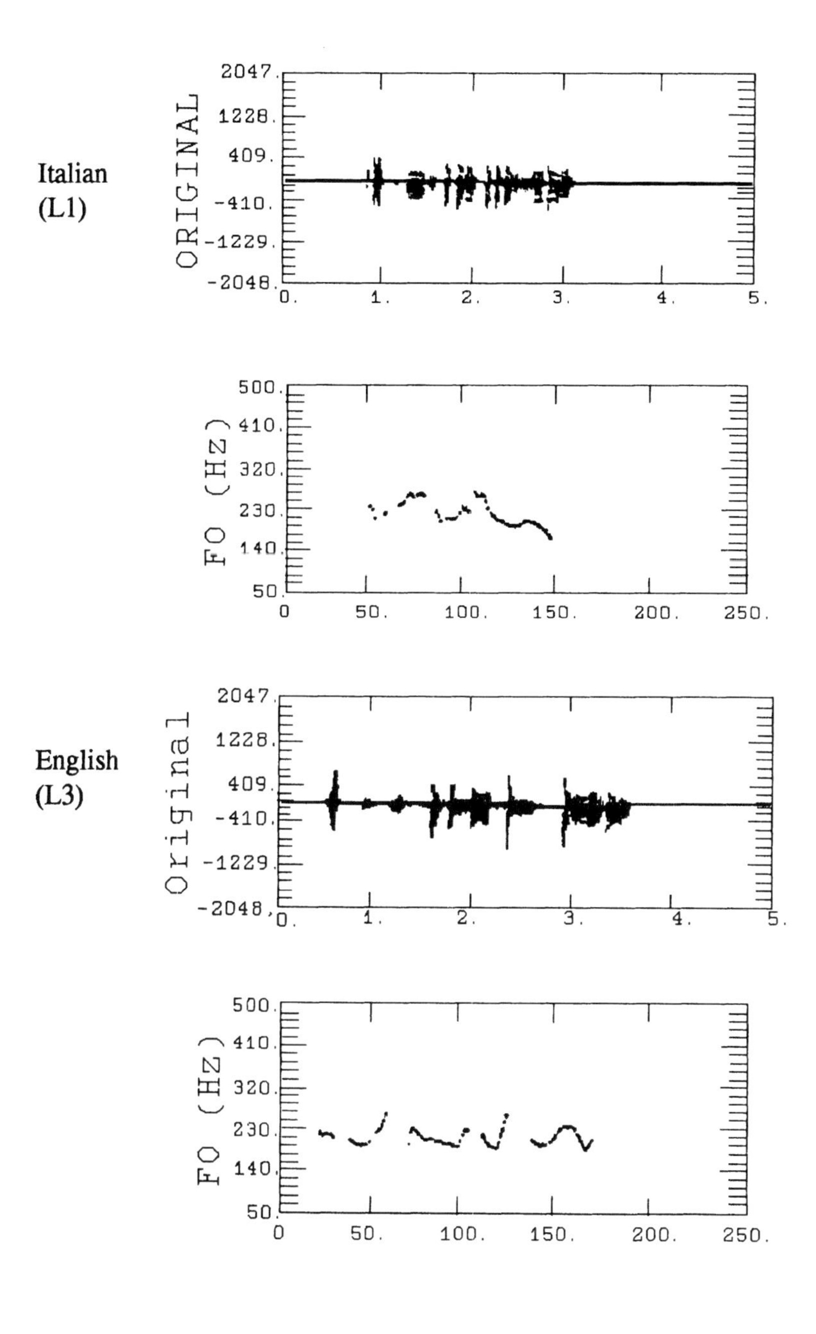
Italian
(L1)
ORIGINAL
2047.
1228.
409.
-410.
-1229.
-2048.
0.
1.
2.
3.
4.
5.
FO (Hz)
500.
410.
320.
230.
140.
50.
0
50.
100.
150.
200.
250.
English
(L3)
Original
2047.
1228.
409.
-410.
-1229.
-2048.
0.
1.
2.
3.
4.
5.
FO (Hz)
500.
410.
320.
230.
140.
50.
0
50.
100.
150.
200.
250.

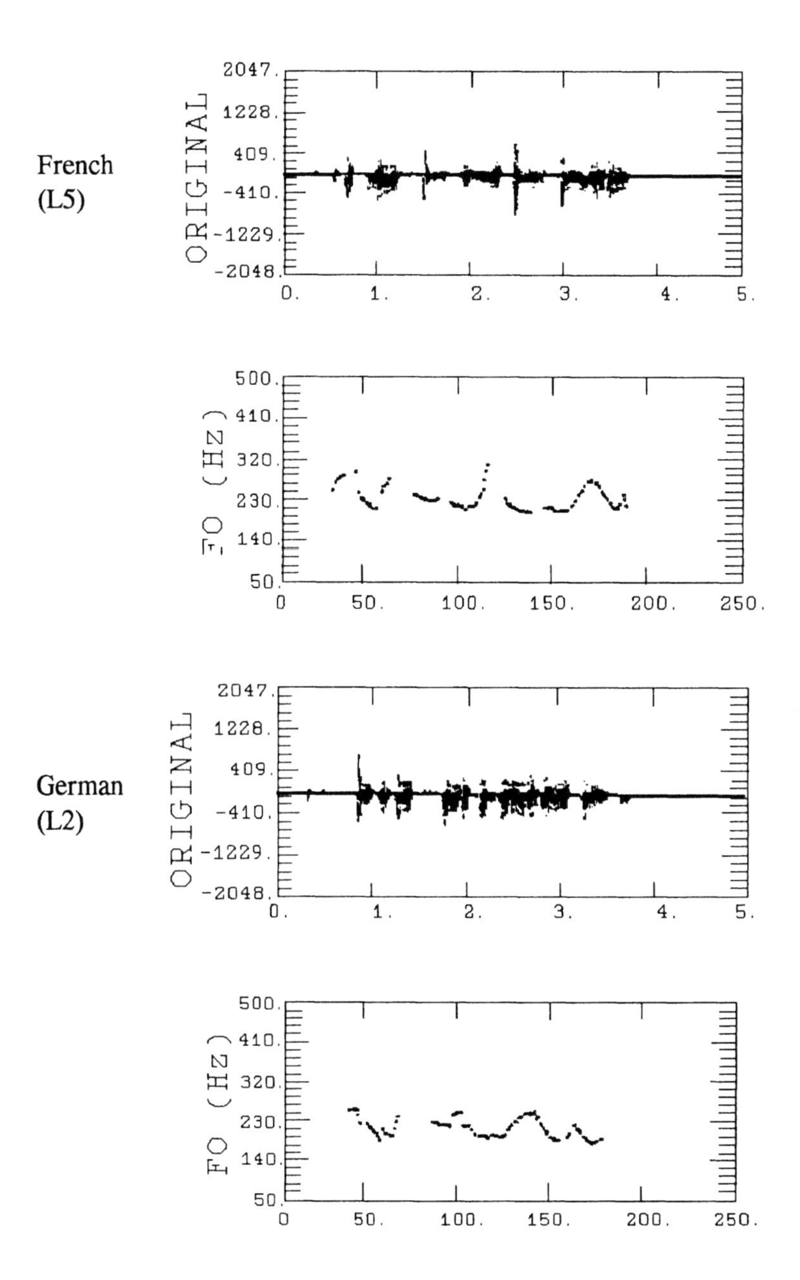
French
(L5)
ORIGINAL
2047.
1228.
409.
-410.
-1229.
-2048.
0.
1.
2.
3.
4.
5.
F0 (Hz)
500.
410.
320.
230.
140.
50.
0
50.
100.
150.
200.
250.
German
(L2)
ORIGINAL
2047.
1228.
409.
-410.
-1229.
-2048.
0.
1.
2.
3.
4.
5.
F0 (Hz)
500.
410.
320.
230.
140.
50.
0
50.
100.
150.
200.
250.

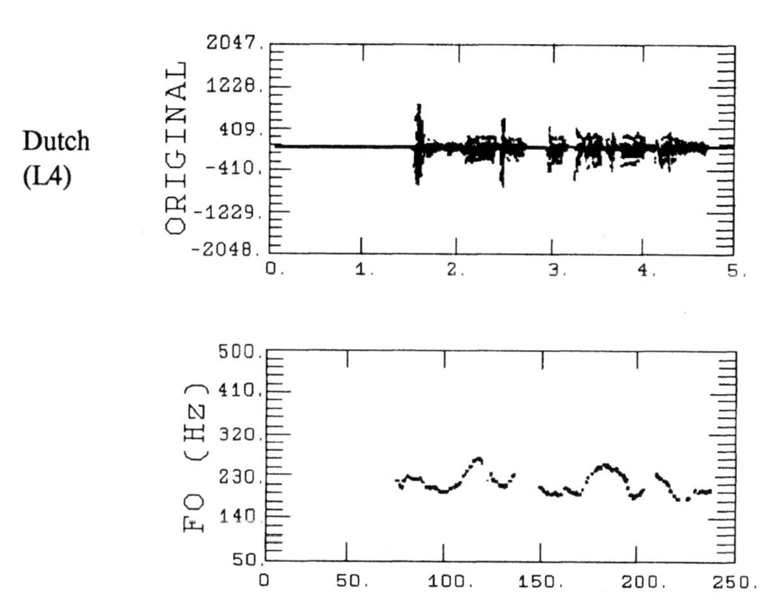

Figure 3. *Oscillographies of the vocal signal (top) and fundamental frequency tracings (bottom) of the final sentence in Italian, English, French, German and Dutch, respectively.*

A statistical analysis of the fundamental frequency during the production of name and surname in all 15 (3 texts x 5 languages) final sentences was carried out in order to compare identical phonological features within five different language contexts. In Italian (L1) the fundamental frequency was on average 182.5 Hz, and turned out to be <u>the lowest</u> of all ($p < 0.001$). Average Fo in French (L5) was 211.2 Hz, thus significantly higher than in Italian ($p < 0.01$), in English (L3, $x=202.8$ Hz, $p < 0.002$) and in Dutch (L4, $x=204.99$, $p < 0.02$). As regards German, Fo was on average 209.5, thus significantly higher than in Italian ($p < 0.001$), in English ($p < 0.05$) and in Dutch ($p < 0.03$; cf. Fig. 2), with no significant difference with French.

2.4.2. Discussion. Human speech conveys linguistic information (e.g. phonemes, morphemes, logical and grammatical rules) as well as suprasegmental or emotional information through prosody, rhythm and accents. The latter depend on many different factors, such as pauses, intensity and fundamental frequency of the voice (Kristeva 1977; Di Cristo 1986; Lieberman & Blumstein 1988). Suprasegmental features inform the listener about the level and "type" of emotional tension of the speaker. In fact they tend to express the speaker's attitude towards the content of the spoken message, i.e., whether he is convinced or sceptical, whether he lies or tells the truth etc. (Scherer 1986; Ekman 1985). Moreover, suprasegmental features most probably also reveal some aspects of the speaker's personality, such as self-confidence, insecurity or psychopathological disorders that can make the voice sound pleasant or unpleasant. It is therefore crucial that people whose profession is based on verbal communication, such as actors, speakers and conference interpreters, be aware of the theoretical and practical characteristics of the suprasegmental features of speech and learn how to improve the quality of their voice (cf. Gran & Dodds 1989).

Recent studies showed how effective communication among human beings, reaching high levels of information exchange, seems to involve imitation. The listener generally tends to assume the speaker's non-verbal attitude and behaviour (muscle contraction, respiratory cycles, posture etc.), and this unconscious imitation is even more marked with a growing interest of the listener towards the speakers' message and personality (Erikson 1980; Scherer 1986). During simultaneous or consecutive interpretation it is often very important for the interpreter to also express the non-verbal aspects of the speaker's message. This can be achieved only a) if the interpreter is able to recognize these aspects of verbal communication, b) if s/he is able to keep a neutral, unbiased attitude towards the contents of the message, and c) if s/he decides to imitate or to interpret the non-verbal aspects of the speaker's communication. If the non-verbal features of the message are to be rendered also into the target language, the interpreter will not use a standard voice quality which usually sounds boring and unpleasant. Instead, s/he will modulate and modify the non-verbal aspects of his or her own voice according to the speaker and to the situational context. In order to achieve this result, an interpreter should be aware of the unconscious and/or conscious emotional attitude that s/he has towards each one of the various languages s/he knows, because there may be particular relations between his or her emotional, non-verbal sphere and the languages s/he knows and uses in his or her profession (Minkowski 1963; Paradis 1989). For example, the interpreter's unconscious attitude towards a language learned in a formal context (e.g. at university), may completely differ from that towards another language learned in an affective context (family, love experience, etc.).

In the above-mentioned experimental, the subject's lowest fundamental frequency was recorded when she spoke in her mother tongue (L1=Italian: Fo x=182,5 Hz). This means that when speaking this language the subject's laryngeal muscles, and perhaps the muscular system of the whole body, reached the highest level of relaxation in comparison with the other languages. For the above-mentioned reasons, it may be assumed that while listening to an interpretation by this subject from any source language towards her L1, the listener tends to be influenced and therefore more relaxed than while listening to her in a language other than L1.

As regards the syntactic position of name and surname within each final sentence spoken by the subject during the experiment, the author is well aware of its importance (cf. Lieberman 1967), though it was not determinant. In fact, in French (L5), the fundamental frequency turned out to be the highest of all, most probably because it was the weakest language of the subject, even though its syntactic structure was similar to that of Italian and English (final position of name and surname) as opposed to the German and Dutch sentence construction (semi-final position of name and surname).

3. General Discussion

It can be generally stated that scientific experimental research in the field of simultaneous interpretation is rather a recent event. Beside scientific observations and descriptions of the different processes implied in this complex cognitive task, several papers on personal empirical considerations have been written by professional interpreters. As significant as these contributions may be, they must nevertheless be regarded with great caution for different reasons: a) they usually express personal opinions depending on a personal history and tend to be generalized, sometimes inappropriately; b) they often are derived from "consolidated professional ideologies", such as the idea that a good interpretation necessarily implies the complete understanding (and cognitive elaboration) of the contents of the incoming message. In our opinion professional modesty may help to distinguish between having, on the one hand, limited knowledge of the basic elements of a huge and perhaps complex discipline or of scientific matters and, on the other hand, claiming to grasp the complete meaning of the speaker's message. The hypothesis that a simultaneous interpreter often does not understand the real contents of a message, though he succeeds in translating the "surface structure" of the input, is far more realistic. In fact he cannot know all the possible implications of the speaker's statements, as he rarely is an expert of that precise matter. When the content of the message to be translated falls within a domain requiring a specific subject-related knowledge, a simultaneous interpreter who is aware of the limitations of his encyclopaedic knowledge is far more preferable than one who believes that s/he understands or should try to understand most of the meaning and runs the risk of misinterpreting or overinterpreting such a complex message. Neurolinguistic data support this hypothesis, which accepts the possibility of producing a good simultaneous interpretation without understanding the contents. In fact, literature reports clinical cases of polyglot aphasic patients, who could not understand the meaning of sentences or phrases, but were nevertheless able to translate them into another language (cf. Paradis 1984).

Even in simultaneous interpretation, a cautious approach, with a good dose of doubts, upon which the western scientific thought since Galileo is based, should be considered necessary. What is the need for personal considerations of simultaneous interpreters, then? Of course, they may be used for different purposes, e.g. as cues for a biography, or as suggestions for devoted followers or pupils. From a scientific point of view, however, they can merely serve as hints to set up theoretical hypothesis, which must be verified through experimental methods. Only a "verifiable, repeatable" experiment can corroborate or contradict a hypothesis. A systematization of the data obtained with experiments will form the scientific groundwork of a true discipline which may be used both for the teaching and practice of simultaneous interpretation (cf. Gran & Fabbro 1988; Gran & Dodds 1989).

The present work aimed at presenting some experimental studies concerning some non-linguistic aspects of simultaneous interpretation, which may have the following practical implications:

1. The cerebral organization of attention is one of the main points in performing simultaneous interpretation. Monolinguals probably tend to process linguistic communication through the right ear, whereas professional interpreters distribute their attention towards verbal inputs to both ears.

2. The gradual learning of simultaneous interpretation techniques probably has a decisive influence on verbal short-term memory with a possible reinforcement of verbal short-term memorization strategies, whereas long-term memorization strategies seem to remain unaffected. This again raises a basic problem of the psychology and neurobiology of memory, i.e., that not only remembrance and recall of stored information is important, but also memory decay or at least "non-storage" of irrelevant data. A sort of unconscious selection of important vs. nonessential information to be memorized probably occurs also during simultaneous interpretation, otherwise a professional

interpreter who has to translate all sorts of issues and topics would be gradually storing far too many notions, or s/he would recall information at the wrong moment.

3. Speaking speed is another non-linguistic feature of verbal communication. While working, simultaneous interpreters generally speak very quickly, which implies a rapid articulation ability. Most probably this leads to a major involvement of the cerebral structures which control verbal expression, and in particular, to a greater participation of the right hemisphere in the control of speech production. The right hemisphere is generally known for controlling the suprasegmental features of language, therefore a higher speaking speed, as occurring during simultaneous interpretation, could be partly responsible for difficulties in controlling, say, intonation, prosody, pronunciation etc., because of a sort of interference with or overcharge of the right hemisphere. In fact the first evident symptoms of time stress in unexperienced or student interpreters are uncontrolled prosody and pronunciation, wrong intonation coupled with an extremely loud voice.

4. In our opinion, more attention should be devoted to suprasegmental features of verbal expression during simultaneous interpretation. Our knowledge of the significance and implications of these aspects should be applied in order to improve pronunciation or prosody while interpreting, so as to avoid hesitations and monotonous speech tones which some interpreters unfortunately still consider as sounding "terrifically professional" to the detriment of the whole professional category and of the ears of the poor listener!

Moreover, this knowledge should first of all open a scientific discussion on the implications of the non-verbal aspects of speech in general, and in particular for simultaneous interpretation. There are still too many open questions in this regard. For example, should an interpreter be aware of his emotional attitude towards the speaker? Is it really possible to "keep cool", i.e., neutral towards the speaker's message and behaviour? What happens if something hurts the interpreter's ethical and moral belief? As verbal communication also conveys non-linguistic information, the interpreter him or herself is not completely neutral in his utterances, even while speaking from a booth through a microphone. Interpreters should at least be aware of the power of verbal expression, without deluding themselves about their being dettached or completely neutral. They themselves may also conjure some information which is not verbally expressed, but mediated by the (unconscious) choice of their words or, more frequently, by the way of presenting them.

Another topic for wider discussion concerns the interpreters' emotional attitude towards the languages they know and work with. Both, at the conscious and at the unconscious level, all the different languages they know may in fact bear positive or negative connotations which may greatly and specifically influence their performance and ultimately the way in which they interpret a message.

References

Abe, M., Nakamura, S., Shikano, K. and Kuwabara, H. 1988. "Voice Conversion Through Vector Quantization". Proceedings of *1988 IEEE*. 655-658.

Albert, M.L. and Obler, L.K. 1978. *The Bilingual Brain*. New York, Academic Press.

Akoi, C. and Siekewitz, P. 1989. "La Plasticità del Cervello". *Le Scienze* 246. 24-32.

Bakker, D.J. 1984. "The Brain as a Dependent Variable". *Journal of Clinical Neuropsychology* 6. 1-16.

Borden, G.J. and Harris, K.S. 1984. *Speech Science Primer*. Baltimore, London: Williams & Wilkins.

Bosatra, A. and Spiller, E. 1984. "Aspetti Audiofoniatrici Dell'Interpretazione Simultanea". *Riv. Orl. Aud. Fon.* 2. 209- 211.

Briggs, G.C. and Nebes, R.D. 1975. "Patterns of Hand Preference in a Student Population". *Cortex* 11. 230-238.

Broadbent, D.E. 1971. *Decision and Stress*. London, Academic Press.

Cirilli, C. 1989. "Traduzione Automatica: Problemi e Prospettive". *L'Elettrotecnica* 11. 957-965.

Code, C. 1987. *Language Aphasia and the Right Hemisphere*. Chichester: Wiley & Sons.

Darò, V. 1989. "The Role of Memory and Attention in Simultaneous Interpretation: A Neurolinguistic Approach". *The Interpreters' Newsletter* 2. 50-56.

Darò, V. 1990a. "Speaking Speed During Simultaneous Interpretation: A Discussion on its Neuropsychological Aspects with Possible Contributions to Teaching". Proceedings of the *Round Table on Theoretical and Experimental Research on Conference Interpretation*, University of Trieste, Nov. 16, 1989, Campanotto, Udine.

Darò, V. 1990b. "Voice Frequency of Languages During Simultaneous Interpretation". *The Interpreters' Newsletter* 3. 88-92.

Di Cristo, A. 1986. "Aspetti Fonetici e Fonologici Degli Elementi Prosodici". L. Croatto, ed. *Aspetti Fonetici Della Comunicazione*. Padova, La Garangola. 267-321.

Ekman, P. 1985. *Telling Lies*. New York, London: Norton & Co.

Erikson, M.H. 1980. *The Collected Papers of Milton H. Erikson on Hypnosis*. Vol. 1. New York: Irvington Publishers, Inc.

Fabbro, F. 1990. "Cerebral Lateralization of Human Languages: Clinical and Experimental Data". B. Chiarelli, P. Lieberman and J. Wind, eds. *The Origin of Human Language*. NATO Advanced Study Institute: Kluwer.

Fabbro, F., Gran, L., Bava, A. 1987. "Modifications in Cerebral Lateralization during the Acquisition of a Second Language (English) in Adult Italian-Speaking Females: An Experimental Dichotic Listening Study". *Neuroscience* 22. 748.

Fabbro, F., Darò, V., Bava, A. 1988. "Cerebral Lateralization in Early Learning of a Second Language". *Atti del VI Convegno di Primatologia*. Trieste, June 15-18, 153.

Fabbro, F., Clarici, A., Darò, V., Bava, A. 1990a. "Speech Velocity affects Cerebral Lateralization of Motor Functions of Language". *Int. J. Anthropol*. 5. 174.

Fabbro, F., Gran, L., Basso, G., Bava, A. 1990b. " Cerebral Lateralization during Simultaneous Interpreting". *Brain and Language* 39. 69-89.

Geschwind, N., Galaburda, A. 1985. "Cerebral Lateralization". *Arch. Neurol*. 42. 428-459, 521-552, 634-654.

Gerver, D. 1974a. "The Effect of Noise on the Performance of Simultaneous Interpreters: Accuracy of Performance". *Acta Psychologica* 38. 159-167.

Gerver, D. 1974b. "Simultaneous Listening and Speaking and Retention of Prose". *The Quarterly Journal of Experimental Psychology* 26. 337-341.

Gerver, D. and Sinaiko, H.W., eds. 1978. *Language Interpretation and Communication*. New York: Plenum Press.

Gran, L. and Fabbro, F. 1987. "Cerebral Lateralization in Simultaneous Interpreting". K. Kummer. ed. *Across the Language Gap: 28th American Translators Association Conference*. Medford N.J., Learned Information Inc. 323-335.

Gran, L. and Fabbro, F. 1988. "The Role of Neuroscience in the Teaching of Interpretation". *The Interpreters' Newsletter* 1. 23-41.

Gran, L. and Dodds, J. 1989. *The Theoretical and Practical Aspects of Teaching Conference Interpretation*. Udine: Campanotto Editore.

Green, A., Schweda Nicholson, N., Vaid, J., White, N. and Steiner, R. 1990. "Hemispheric Involvement in Shadowing vs. Interpretation: A Time-Sharing Study of Simultaneous Interpreters with Matched Bilingual and Monolingual Controls". *Brain and Language* 39. 107-133.

Hampson, E. and Kimura, D. 1988. "Reciprocal Effects of Hormonal Fluctuation on Human Motor and Perceptual-Spatial Skills". *Behav. Neurosci*. 102. 456-459.

Jakobson, R. and Waugh, L. 1979. *The Sound Shape of Language*. Bloomington and London: Indiana University Press.

Kristeva, J. 1977. *Théorie d'Ensemble et Poylogue*. Paris: Edition du Seuil.

Lambert, S. 1990. "Simultaneous Interpreters: One Ear may be Better than Two". *The Interpreters' Newsletter* 2. 11-16.

Lambert, S. 1993. "The Effect of Ear of Information Reception on the Proficiency of Simultaneous Interpretation". *META* XXXVIII. 198-211.

Lenneberg, E. 1967. *Biological Foundations of Language*. New Jork: John Wiley & Sons.

Lieberman, P. 1967. *Intonation, Perception, and Language*. Cambridge, Mass.: MIT Press.

Lieberman, P. 1984. *The Biology and Evolution of Language*. Cambridge, Mass.: Harvard University Press.

Lieberman, P. and Blumstein, S.E. 1988. *Speech Physiology, Speech Perception, and Acoustic Phonetics*. Cambridge, Mass.: Cambridge University Press.

Luria, A.R. 1981. *Neuropsicologia della Memoria*. Roma: Armando Editore.

MacNeilage, P.F. 1982. *The Production of Speech*. New York: Academic Press.

Malmberg, B. 1977. *Manuale di Fonetica Generale*. Bologna: Il Mulino.

Miller, G.A. 1951. *Language and Communication*. New York: McGraw-Hill.

Minkowski, M. 1963. "On Aphasia in Polyglots". L. Halpern, ed. *Problems of Dynamic Neurology*. Jerusalem: Hebrew University. 119-161.

Mowbray, G.H. 1964. "Perception and Retention of Verbal Information Presented during Auditory Shadowing". *JASA* 36. 1459-1464.

Mumolo, E. 1980. *Sviluppo di un Sistema di Analisi e Sintesi della Voce*. Tesi di Laurea in Ingegneria Elettronica, Università di Trieste, Italy.

Mumolo, E. 1985. *L'Ambiente di Elaborazione Vocale Utilizzato per lo Studio della Fonoarticolazione Umana ed Animale*. Rome: Face Standard.

Ojemann, G.A. and Creutzfeldt, O.D. 1987. "Language in Humans and Animals: Contribution of Brain Stimulation and Recording". V.B. Mountcastle, F. Plum and S.R. Geiger, eds. *Handbook of Physiology*. Bethesda: American Physiological Society 1.5:2. 657-699.

Paradis, M. 1984. "Aphasie et Traduction". *META* XXIX. 57-67.

Paradis, M. 1989. "Bilingual and Polyglot Aphasia". F. Boller and J. Grafman, eds. *Handbook of Neuropsychology*. Amsterdam: Elsevier 2. 117-140.

Perkins, W.H. and Kent, R.D. 1986. *Textbook of Functional Anatomy of Speech, Language, and Hearing*. London: Taylor and Frances.

Scherer, K.R. 1986. "Vocal Affect Expression: A Review and a Model for Future Research". *Psychological Bulletin* 99:2. 143-165.

Spiller-Bosatra, E., Darò, V., Fabbro, F., Bosatra, A. 1990. "Audio-phonological and Neuropsychological Aspects of Simultaneous Interpretation: Role of Auditory Shadowing". *Scand. Audiol.* 19. 81-87.

Squire, L.R. 1987. *Memory and Brain*. New York: Oxford University Press.

Sussman, H.M., Franklin, P., Simon, T. 1982. "Bilingual Speech: Bilateral Control?" *Brain and Language* 15. 125-142.

Taylor-Sarno, M. 1981. *Acquired Aphasia*. New York: Academic Press.

Treisman, A. 1965. "The Effects of Redundancy and Familiarity on Translation and Repeating Back a Foreign and Native Language". *British Journal of Psychology*. 56. 369-379.

Trevarthen, C. 1984. "Hemispheric Specialization". J.M. Brookhart, V.B. Mountcastle, I. Darian-Smith and S.R. Geiger, eds. *Handbook of Physiology*. Bethesda: American Physiological Society 1:3. 1129-1190.

Tucker, D.M. 1988. "Hemisphere Specialization: A Mechanism for Unifying Anterior and Posterior Brain Regions". D. Ottoson, ed. *Duality and Unity of the Brain*. London: Macmillan. 180-192.

Vaid, J. 1983. "Bilingualism and Brain Lateralization". S. Segalowitz, ed. *Language Functions and Brain Organization*. New York: Academic Press.

Vaid, J. 1986. *Language Processing in Bilinguals: Psycholinguistic and Neuropsychological Perspectives*. Hillsdale, N.J.: Lawrence Erlbaum & Associates.

Neurological and Neuropsychological Aspects Of Polyglossia and Simultaneous Interpretation

Franco Fabbro
Istituto di Fisiologia, Università di Trieste, Italy

and

Laura Gran
Scuola Superiore di Lingue Moderne per Interpreti e Traduttori Università di Trieste, Italy

1. Bilingual and Polyglot Aphasia

Nowadays, about half of the human population of the world is either bilingual or polyglot (Grosjean 1982), and therefore clinical cases of bilingual or polyglot subjects who become aphasic after cerebral lesions are quite frequent. Although the percentage of bilingual or polyglot aphasics is rather high, no systematic, thorough study on aphasia has been conducted on such patients as yet (Paradis 1977; Albert & Obler 1978). If compared to monolingual aphasic patients, bilingual or polyglot aphasics may reveal *specific impairments* that have already been reported in early studies dating back to the last century as well as in more recent surveys on this issue (Minkowski 1963; Albert & Obler 1978; Vaid 1983; Paradis 1989).

1.1. Selective Aphasia

In a bilingual or polyglot subject who has become aphasic following a cerebral lesion, all the languages he/she knows are not necessarily impaired. Such a clinical situation is known as selective aphasia. In addition to many cases reported in the literature, we had the opportunity to follow a bilingual girl (L1= Friulian, spoken in the family environment; L2=Italian, spoken at school and started at about 4-5 years of age) who became aphasic at age 8 after a cerebral infarction of the left-hemisphere fronto-temporal region. Shortly after the pathological event, this girl showed good comprehension of both languages with total impairment of expression; after about one month she started talking only in Italian (L2) even with her parents who addressed her in Friulian (L1), and three months later she recovered Friulian as well. Four years have passed since the infarction and the girl now speaks both languages fluently, except for slight impairments (rare anomias and a few syntactic errors which can only be detected with language tests; Fabbro & Darò 1992; see also Voinescu *et al.* 1977; Nilipour & Ashayeri 1989).

1.2. Selective Crossed Aphasia

Paradis and Goldblum (1989) described a case of a right-handed trilingual patient aged 27 (L1=Gujarati, L2=Malagasy, both acquired in infancy; L3=French, in which he was schooled; all three languages were used daily in different social contexts). The subject underwent a surgical operation for the removal of a parasitic cyst in the right prerolandic area. Before the operation, the patient was found to have non-fluent aphasic deficits *only* in Gujarati. When tested post-operatively, he showed a recovery in this language with parallel impairments in Malagasy (morphological and syntactic errors both in expression and in comprehension). Four years later, the patient showed good recovery in all three languages. The pre-operative speech impairments with Gujarati (L1) revealed a representation of the patient's mother tongue in the right hemisphere. Speech impairments occurring in right-handers after lesions of the right hemisphere are generally described as *crossed aphasias* (Kertesz 1985), and the above-mentioned case is an example of selective crossed aphasia in a polyglot subject.

1.3. Different Aphasic Syndromes in Polyglot Aphasia

A bilingual or polyglot aphasic patient may show the same kind of impairments with the same degree of seriousness in all the languages he knows (Gastaldi 1951; Watamori & Sasanuma 1978). In some cases of polyglot aphasia, however, a different aphasic syndrome may be observed for each language (Albert & Obler 1978; Silverberg & Gordon 1979).

1.4. Polyglot Aphasia with Mixing Problems

Bilingual and polyglot aphasics may suffer from another kind of syndrome known as *mixing*, whereby the patient mixes up languages by borrowing the lexical or syntactic structures of one language while speaking in another language (Perecman 1984).

1.5. Translation Impairments

Gastaldi (1951) reported a case of a 42-year-old bilingual (L1=German, L2=Italian) male patient with non-fluent aphasia in both languages as a result of a luetic vascular disease. After having pronounced a word in one language, the patient was not able to translate it into the other language. Moreover, being addressed in one language, he always answered in the same one, but never succeeded in translating his own reply into the other language.

1.6. Alternate Antagonism

Two cases of temporary impairment in the access and use of one of the two languages known to two different bilingual aphasic patients were reported by Paradis and co-workers (1982). While comprehension of both languages was generally good, one patient was observed to alternate languages every 24 hours on 4 consecutive days, and the other patient suffered from complete impairment in the production of one language during one week, and complete impairment in the production of the other language during the following week.

1.7. Paradoxical Translation in Aphasics

Both patients reported by Paradis and co-workers (1982) as exhibiting alternate antagonism phenomena also showed paradoxical translation behaviour. They could translate, without hesitation or mistakes, words and even difficult sentences from the language in which on that day they were fluent into the language in which they could not speak spontaneously. Oddly enough, they could not perform the opposite task of translating from the language they understood (but did not speak spontaneously) into their fluent language.

1.8. Spontaneous Translation

A few cases of polyglot patients with an unusual, immediate compulsion to translate words or sentences from one language into another with no real need, have been reported in neurolinguistic literature. One of them was the self-analysis of a syndrome suffered by the famous linguist Roman Jakobson (1964), who became aphasic for a few hours after a car accident and kept on translating spontaneously all his inner thoughts into four or five languages. A similar case was reported by Perecman (1984) who observed a trilingual (L1=German, L2=French, L3=English) aphasic patient who spontaneously translated the sentences he himself pronounced: if, for example, he produced a sentence in German, he would spontaneously translate it into English or French. Both paradoxical and spontaneous translation suggested the theory that, from a neurolinguistic point of view, translation processes may be different and independent from the comprehension and production processes of a specific language (Paradis *et al.* 1982; Paradis 1984; Perecman 1984).

1.9. Liturgical Language Conservation

Durieu (1969) described the case of an aphasic syndrome with right hemiplegia in a Catholic priest aged 59 whose mother tongue was French, but who also knew Latin and New-Testament Greek as well as rudimentary biblical Hebrew. This patient suffered severe impairments of expression and object-naming in French, yet he could say Mass in Latin without difficulty. The conservation of fluency in a liturgic language with parallel aphasia in one's own mother tongue is known as *automaticity of prayer language* (Kraetschmer 1982).

1.10. Specific Impairments of Reading and Writing

Streifler and Hofman (1976) reported a case of an ambidextrous bilingual (L1=Hebrew; L2=Polish) woman who showed writing impairments in her first language as a result of a brain concussion due to a car accident: she started writing Hebrew script from left to right whereby each letter was in mirror image, and she could read Hebrew only if the script was written in this way or reflected in a mirror. Another case is that described by Wechsler (1977) concerning a right-handed bilingual (L1=English, L2=French) male patient aged 57 who, after an infarct of the left occipital lobe, presented reading impairments mostly in English. Furthermore, Albert and Obler (1978) reported a case of a left-handed bilingual (L1=Hebrew; L2=English) young female patient who underwent a neurosurgical operation to remove a bilateral frontal destruction following a car accident. A few weeks later she wrote in English from right to left, as if she were writing in Hebrew or Arabic.

1.11. Aphasia with Tonal Languages

As is generally known, voice pitch, which depends on the frequency at which vocal cords vibrate and is therefore better defined as *fundamental frequency* (Fo), participates in the prosodic features of the verbal production of several Indoeuropean languages. For example, in these languages, statements (affirmative sentences) end with a lowering in fundamental frequency, whereas questions (interrogatives) are generally expressed with an increase in tone at the end of the sentence (Lieberman & Blumstein 1988). Among right-handed Indoeuropean-language speakers, the fundamental frequency of voice is generally controlled by the right hemisphere (Code 1987). However, there are also languages where tones, i.e. voice pitch, correspond to a distinctive feature defining two different phonemes: the pronunciation of two identical syllables with two different contours of fundamental frequency produces two different words and meanings (Lieberman & Blumstein 1988). Several studies point out that in tonal languages (e.g. Chinese), the left hemisphere is far more involved in the perception of tones. Chinese-speaking aphasics with a lesion of the left hemisphere showed impairments in the perception and production of consonants and phonemic tones. Chinese aphasic patients with left-hemisphere lesions generally confuse tones with a phonemic value as well as consonants (Packard 1986).

1.12. Reading and Writing Impairments in Phonetic and Ideographic Script Systems

The Japanese generally use two different script systems: a phonetic (*Kana*) and an ideographic (*Kanji*) system. In the phonetic system, each syllable corresponds to a Kana character, whereas in the Kanji system, each ideogram corresponds to a whole word or meaning. Among Japanese aphasics, selective impairments in the use of Kana characters vs. Kanji ideograms were reported by Sasanuma (1975). As a result of lesions to of the most central areas of language (Broca's and Wernicke's areas, *fasciculus arcuatus*), Japanese patients may suffer impairments in the use of Kana characters, whereas impairments in the use of Kanji ideograms are frequently related to non-phonological (lexical and/or semantic) speech impairments due to lesions of the peripheral language areas (Vignolo 1982; Luria 1978; Damasio & Geschwind 1984).

2. Patterns of Recovery in Polyglot Aphasia

Even as regards recovery, bilingual and polyglot aphasic patients reveal peculiar recovery patterns in comparison to monolingual aphasics (Basso 1987; Lecours & Lhermitte 1979; Taylor-Sarno 1981). Eight different patterns have been observed so far in the recovery of languages in polyglots (Paradis & Lecours 1979; Paradis 1987, 1989): i) all the languages known to the subject and impaired in a similar way may have a *parallel recovery*; ii) if the type and severity of impairments differ from language to language, a *differential recovery* may occur; iii) recovery is said to be *successive* if one language starts improving only after full recovery of another language; iv) when one language regresses as the other progresses, there is *antagonistic* recovery; v) when not all the languages are regained, the patient has a *selective* recovery; vi) a *mixed* recovery occurs when the patient systematically shows interferences, confusion and mixing phenomena at all linguistic levels (phonological, morphological, syntactic, lexical and semantic) in one or all languages; vii) when the patient has access to speech production in one language and not in other languages at different, alternating time periods, he is said to have a *recovery with alternate antagonism*; and viii) when one and the same patient shows different aphasic syndromes for different languages (e.g. fluent aphasia for one language and non-fluent aphasia for another language), a *recovery of different types of aphasia* occurs.

3. Cerebral Representation of Languages in Bilinguals and Polyglots

An aphasic syndrome in a polyglot subject presenting different types and degrees of impairments for different languages may be explained in several ways.

A) Differing types of aphasia for different languages within the same subject may be due to differential recovery varying from language to language at the moment of clinical testing.

B) This phenomenon may depend, however, on different levels of proficiency in the various components characterizing the languages known to the subject. Some linguistic impairments observed in the patient may be due to his/her low proficiency regarding the grammar of one particular language rather than to the effects of the pathological event.

C) Another interpretation would suggest a cerebral representation of languages in *partially* different anatomical areas of both hemispheres. Ojemann and Whitaker (1978) as well as Rapport and co-workers (1983) studied the cerebral organization of Indoeuropean and Oriental languages in bilingual and polyglot subjects by means of cortical electrical microstimulation techniques during neurosurgical operations. They demonstrated that stimulation of perisylvian areas accounting for motor speech production, heavily impaired verbal expression in all the languages known to the patient. Sometimes stimulation of the same cortical areas, both in pre- and post-rolandic regions, affected naming ability in all languages known to the subject, whereas stimulation of other brain areas would impair just one language in different ways. These studies also showed that the first language (i.e., the mother tongue, L1) tends to have a rather centralized, perisylvian representation, whereas the other languages known to the subjects (L2, L3, L4 etc.) tend to have a wider cortical representation. As the first language tends to be represented in the brain by a kind of focal pattern, one would expect that a perisylvian lesion would mostly impair L1, and that a lesion to marginal areas would impair the other languages to a greater extent. Moreover, as the second, third and fourth (etc.) languages tend to have a more widely distributed cortical representation, a posterior lesion would be likely to produce non-fluent aphasic syndromes for these languages, as happens in children (Taylor-Sarno 1981; Paradis 1989). These studies with cortical electrostimulation suggested that the cortical areas underlying the neural organization of a language may undergo structural changes following intensive use of that language. These changes also include a reduction in the size of the cortical areas (Ojemann and Creutzfeldt 1987).

D) A fourth explanation is based on the hypothesis that each language is represented in a different cerebral area. If so, a focal lesion would disrupt a restricted cortical area and thus impair just one single language.

E) Another hypothesis postulates the existence of a specific cortical area accounting for the control of the switching mechanisms to select verbal production in one language instead of another. A lesion of this area would suppress or alter the switching mechanisms, thus preventing a polyglot patient from correctly selecting the context-related language. He may for example be able to speak just one language, or show interferences between all or some of the languages he knows (cf. *mixing* in the section *Polyglot Aphasia with Mixing Problems*). According to some authors (Pötzl 1925; Leischner 1948), this area is probably located in the left supramarginal gyrus, though some polyglot patients with lesions to the left temporo-parietal region have been reported to use and alternately select different languages without difficulty, whereas other patients with no apparent lesions of this area were unable to switch from one language to another (Paradis 1989). In a study on bilingual subjects using Wada's test, Zatorre (1989) suggested that the frontal lobe plays a relevant role in controlling the switching from one language to another.

F) A further possibility would imply different neuronal circuits for every single language only at a microanatomical level and not at a macroanatomical level. As regards macroanatomical structures, all languages may be represented in the same cerebral areas, whereas at a microanatomical level different languages may be organized in separate neuronal circuits (Paradis 1977, 1989).

G) According to another hypothesis, the inability to use a language does not necessarily imply complete neuronal destruction of this language, but a mere inhibition of access to it. Both clinical evidence of aphasic patients presenting alternate antagonism (Paradis *et al.* 1982) and the results of experimental investigations by means of hypnosis (As 1963; Fromm 1970) point to the fact that in some cases verbal performance may be partially or completely inhibited whereas linguistic competence for all languages remains unimpaired. On the other hand, in some cases not only verbal expression but linguistic competence in general may be inhibited (Fabbro 1989b, 1990).

H) Finally, other authors assume that each language known to a subject may present a specific cerebral lateralization differing from the representation of the other languages (Albert & Obler 1978).

A crucial and ongoing controversial aspect is whether nervous functions and neuronal structures underlying language skills in bilinguals and polyglots differ from those in monolinguals (e.g. the existence of peculiar structures accounting for the co-ordination of specific mechanisms underlying linguistic functions in polyglots, such as language switching). Paradis (1977, 1984, 1987) suggests quantitative rather than qualitative differences between bilinguals and monolinguals as regards the neuronal mechanisms of language. In addition, when a bilingual subject speaks one of his two languages, both languages are concurrently activated with parallel, though partial, inhibition of the language not being spoken at that point in time. After voluntary selection of one language for the purpose of verbal expression, the activation level of the same language increases, whereas the other language(s) are inhibited, though only partially, so as not to preclude comprehension of the non selected language(s). Paradis' theory is supported also by D.W. Green (1986) who points out that more energy is required to produce or select a word in different languages than to understand the same word in any of the familiar languages. These two authors suggest that the inhibiting mechanisms for one language, which are activated when a polyglot subject speaks another language, are similar to the mechanisms for the selection of words within one single language in the case of monolinguals. When a monolingual subject selects a specific word, the cerebral structures underlying it are activated together with the cerebral structures underlying other semantic fields, though the latter are partially inhibited (Luria 1978; Crowder 1986).

4. Cerebral Asymmetries in Bilingual and Polyglot Subjects

In an exhaustive review of the existing literature on polyglot aphasia, Albert and Obler (1978) found that about 10% of bilingual or polyglot aphasic patients had suffered an injury to the right cerebral hemisphere, whereas crossed aphasia (aphasia due to lesions of the right hemisphere) generally occured in only 1-2% of monolingual subjects (Kertesz 1985). The authors thus concluded that, apparently, in bilingual and polyglot subjects, involvement of the right hemisphere in linguistic functions is greater than in monolinguals. Later, Chary (1986) studied linguistic functions in right-handed polyglot and monolingual aphasic patients and found that 13% of his polyglot patients (3 out of 27) suffered from aphasia following a lesion of the right hemisphere. Moreover, he found a high percentage of aphasic syndromes (12.82%) even among monolingual illiterate subjects after lesions of the right hemisphere.

Several years ago, Fabbro (1989a) reported on linguistic competence in bilingual (L1=Friulian, L2=Italian) patients with left or right hemisyndrome. Two different versions of the *token test* (De Renzi and Faglioni 1975) were administered once in Italian and once in Friulian, to 15 right-handed Friulian-Italian bilingual patients with a left hemisyndrome and to 13 patients with a right hemisyndrome. The token tests revealed impaired comprehension in 59% of the patients (8/13) with a right hemisyndrome (token test results: < 27), whereby 7 patients displayed comprehension impairments in both languages and only one patient merely in Italian. As regards the patients with a left hemisyndrome, only 20% (3/15) showed impaired language comprehension, two of them in both languages and one only in Friulian. The results of this study on bilingual aphasic patients support both Chary's (1986) as well as Albert and Obler's (1978) reports. At the current state of research on bilingual aphasia, however, there is *no certain* clinical evidence of greater right-hemisphere involvement in linguistic functions in bilingual and polyglot subjects (Solin 1989).

Following the first review on cerebral asymmetries of linguistic functions in bilinguals and polyglots by Albert and Obler (1978), several hypotheses on cerebral asymmetry in the representation of linguistic functions in bilinguals and polyglots have been put forward. Paradis (1987, 1989) schematically summed up the possible hypotheses in five points: i) both or more languages are lateralized to the hemisphere that is specialized for linguistic functions (in most cases the left hemisphere); ii) one or some languages are lateralized to the left hemisphere, whereas the other(s) is (are) represented in the right hemisphere; iii) only the first language (mother tongue) is lateralized to the left hemisphere, whereas the other(s) is (are) bilaterally represented in both hemispheres, and this happens especially when the additional language(s) is (are) acquired in adulthood; iv) in bilinguals and in polyglots the hemisphere that is not dominant for linguistic functions (generally the right hemisphere) is more involved in the linguistic functions of all languages than it is in monolinguals; v) all the languages known to the subject are represented bilaterally. Several researchers who were interested in the neuropsychology of bilingualism and polyglossia tried to identify the role of specific biological, psychological and linguistic *critical factors* (type of bilingualism, age of language acquisition, stages of language acquisition, specific features of language, sex) accounting for the hemispheric specialization of languages (Obler *et al.* 1982).

5. Research with Neuropsychological Experimental Techniques

5.1. Experimental Studies with Electroencephalographic Techniques

Rogers and co-workers (1977) examined the EEG-activity in bilingual children (L1=Hopi; L2=English) while they were listening to short stories told to them in their two languages. The authors found greater right-hemispheric involvement when the children were listening to Hopi than when they were listening to English. By means of a similar technique, Tenhouten (1981) studied cortical activity in Chinese-English adult bilinguals while they were listening to stories in both languages. A strong desynchronization of the alpha rhythm in the left hemisphere was observed only for the subjects' mother tongue (Chinese). These data suggest that the second language is less lateralized. Genesee and co-workers (1978) tested three groups of bilingual subjects subdivided according to the age of second-language acquisition (infancy, school-age and adolescence) on their ability to recognize words in French or in English. Both the correctness of their answers and EEG-activity of the left and right hemispheres where recorded during this task. The first two groups (early and school-age bilinguals) presented greater activation of the left hemisphere, whereas the third group of subjects (late bilinguals) exhibited greater right-hemisphere activation with "*gestaltisch*" or melody-based recognition strategies. Waggoner (1987) studied event-related evoked potentials during the acquisition of a language invented for the purpose of the test and found constantly higher left-hemisphere involvement. By means of a unilateral electroconvulsive technique, Chernigovskaya and co-workers (1983) studied the cerebral lateralization of language components in a bilingual psychiatric patient. On the basis of their findings, the authors suggested that the cerebral organization of specific language components differs according to the subject's type of bilingualism. In bilinguals who have acquired the second language with an analytical metalinguistic method, the right hemisphere controls the physiological mechanisms accounting for the production of the semantic structures of the mother tongue, whereas the left hemisphere controls the production of the semantic structure of the second language and the surface structures of both languages. However, in bilinguals who have acquired their second language in a natural communication context, the semantic structures of both languages are represented in the right hemisphere, whereas the surface structures of both languages are controlled by the left hemisphere (see also Jakobson & Waugh 1984).

5.2. Experimental Studies with Tachistoscopic Techniques

The tachistoscopic technique consists in a brief (generally less than 250 msec) exposure of verbal or spatial stimuli to the right visual field (RVF) for direct projection to the left cerebral hemisphere, or to the left visual field (LVF) for direct projection to the right cerebral hemisphere. Various tests carried out on monolingual subjects involving tachistoscopic presentation revealed a RVF (left-hemisphere) superiority in the recognition of verbal stimuli written with phonetic characters, versus a LVF (right-hemisphere) superiority in the recognition of physiognomical or spatial stimuli (Bryden 1982; Tassinari *et al.* 1988; Fabbro *et al.* 1989). Moreover, with the tachistoscopic presentation of pictures to be named as fast as possible, monolingual subjects generally exhibited shorter reaction times than bilingual subjects and polyglots, independently of the visual field to which objects were presented (D.W. Green 1986). Coordinate bilinguals have shorter reaction times with visual material presented in their first language as opposed to their second language (Mägiste 1979). Shanon (1982) examined three different groups of bilingual subjects (Israelis with good knowledge of English, Anglo-Saxons with good knowledge of Hebrew and Hebrew-English bilinguals) who had to recognize Hebrew and English words written vertically. The author found right-visual-field superiority for both languages in all groups, though the second language seemed to be less lateralized than the mother tongue (see also Soares 1982). Sewell and Panou (1982, 1983) studied French-English and German-English late bilinguals with matched monolingual controls. In tasks requiring recognition of words, the bilingual subjects exhibited a general right-visual-field (left hemisphere) superiority that was even more evident in the first language than in the second language (see also Walters & Zatorre 1978). In a task requiring the recognition of tachistoscopically presented numbers, only the group of monolingual subjects showed left-visual-field (right hemisphere) superiority, whereas no such asymmetry was displayed in the other two groups (see also Vaid & Corina 1989). In another experiment with tachistoscopic presentation of words in English and Hebrew, Bentin (1981) studied hemispheric lateralization of languages in a group of Israeli boys with limited knowledge of English. In the first experimental session, this author observed a left-visual-field (right hemisphere) superiority with English words, whereas in the second session, this superiority shifted to the right-visual field (left hemisphere). According to Bentin's explanation, the left-visual-field superiority during the first session was due to a spatial analysis of the presented stimuli at the initial stage of the experiment. With a tachistoscopic presentation of words in Hebrew to a group of Japanese subjects, no significant difference between visual fields was found (Yoshizaki & Hatta 1987). The experiment was repeated after instructing some of the subjects on the pronunciation of these words, and others on their meaning, whereas a third group did not receive any further information. Only the subjects who knew how to pronounce the unknown words presented a right-visual-field superiority (left hemisphere), thus suggesting a possible plastic modification of the hemispheric involvement in a specific cognitive task as well as a modification of cerebral lateralization following the acquisition of a new strategy for the solution of a cognitive task. Recently, Vaid (1987) studied visual field asymmetries for L1 and L2 during tasks of rhyme and syntactic category judgments, both in early and in late bilingual subjects. She found early bilinguals to be likely to adopt semantic strategies, whereas late bilinguals tend to use surface strategies in order to perform the task (Vaid 1987; Vaid & Lambert 1979).

5.3. Experimental Studies with Dichotic Listening Techniques

The dichotic listening technique consists in the simultaneous presentation through earphones of two different acoustic stimuli, such as numbers, words, syllables, or sentences, sent separately to each ear. Although each one of the two cerebral hemispheres normally receives acoustic information through both ears, with dichotic listening, the crossed auditory paths become more effective than the ipsilateral auditory paths. By means of this experimental technique, right-ear (left-hemisphere) superiority in the recognition of verbal acoustic stimuli versus left-ear (right-hemisphere) superiority in the recognition of environmental sounds has been shown in Indoeuropean monolinguals (Kimura 1961; Studdert-Kennedy & Shankweiler 1970; Fabbro *et al.* 1987). The dichotic listening technique is one among the most frequently used experimental paradigms for the purpose of studying cerebral asymmetries for language in bilingual and polyglot subjects. Usually, words in two (or more) different languages are presented simultaneously. The hemispheric specialization for the different languages known to a subject can be determined by analyzing the number of correctly recognized words sent separately to each ear (left and right). Several studies implying dichotic listening tasks have been carried out on various groups of bilingual subjects of different ages, different languages and different levels of second language proficiency, and most of them showed a significant right-ear (left-hemisphere) superiority for both languages (Gordon

1980; Galloway 1980; Piazza *et al.* 1981; Mohr & Costa 1985; Galloway & Scarcella 1982; Albanese 1985; see also Albert & Obler 1978; Vaid 1983; Genesee 1987). Moreover, other peculiar characteristics of the cerebral organization of linguistic functions in bilingual subjects have been observed: 1) females generally present a less marked asymmetry between ears, i.e. between hemispheres (Gordon 1980); 2) in fluent bilingual subjects, an interlinguistic paradigm (dichotic presentation of acoustic material in two different languages) shows that the right hemisphere is likely to be more involved in second language functions (Albanese 1985).

Another experimental paradigm of dichotic listening for the assessment of cerebral asymmetries for languages in bilingual subjects consists in the presentation of pairs of syllables including a vowel and a stop, a voiced or a voiceless consonant (e.g. /ba/, /da/, /ga/, /pa/, /ta/, /ka/) to be repeated by the subjects immediately after presentation. Two similar studies showed left-ear (right-hemisphere) superiority in a group of right-handed Navajo-English bilingual children (Scott *et al.* 1979; Hynd & Scott 1980) and in a group of right-handed Crow-English bilingual children (Vocate 1984); whereas right-handed monolingual (L1 = English) controls showed right-ear (left-hemisphere) superiority. Recently, McKeever and co-workers (1989) repeated this experimental paradigm with three different groups of subjects: a) American children who were addressed in English during the experiment, b) Navajo children who were addressed in Navajo, and c) Navajo children who were addressed in English. Group a) and b) displayed significant right-ear (left-hemisphere) superiority, whereas the third group showed symmetric performance between ears. These results where similar to those reported by Scott and co-workers (1979) and by Vocate (1984), thus suggesting that the language used for the purpose of communicating with the bilingual subjects during an experimental session with a dichotic listening paradigm may have a specific influence on the subjects' cerebral organization. Fabbro and co-workers (1988b) studied cerebral lateralization for L1 (Italian, mother tongue) and L2 (English, second language) in three groups of right-handed female subjects: a) monolingual students of the faculty of medicine with a very poor knowledge of English (control group), b) bilingual students attending the 1st year at the School for Translators and Interpreters of the University of Trieste (SSLM) and c) bilingual students attending the 4th year at the SSLM. All the subjects were submitted to a dichotic listening test with an interlinguistic paradigm (concurrent administration of numbers in both languages). The control group and the group of 1st-year SSLM students showed a significant right-ear (left-hemisphere) advantage for both languages, whereas in the group of 4th-year SSLM students, only the first language (Italian) was found to be lateralized to the left hemisphere, while English (L2) was apparently more symmetrically represented in the brain. A possible explanation of these data is based on the hypothesis of greater right-hemisphere involvement following second language acquisition at high proficiency level. These results may also depend on a partial modification of the strategies of selective attention for L2 (English), which the 4th-year students had learnt to divert onto both ears (Treisman 1965; Bryden 1982).

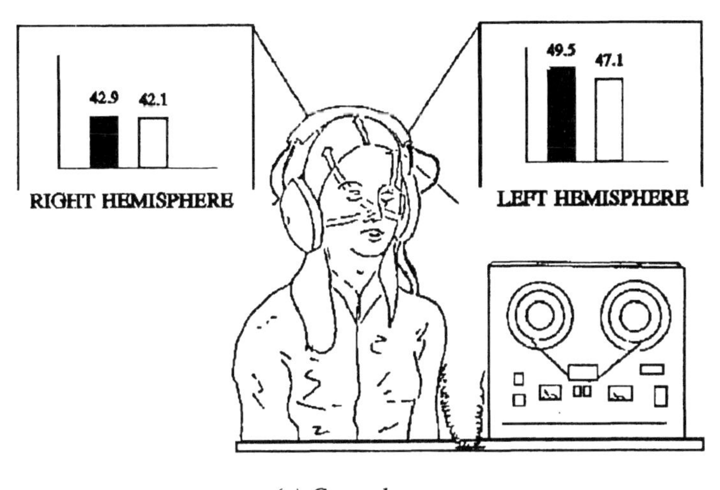

(a) Control group

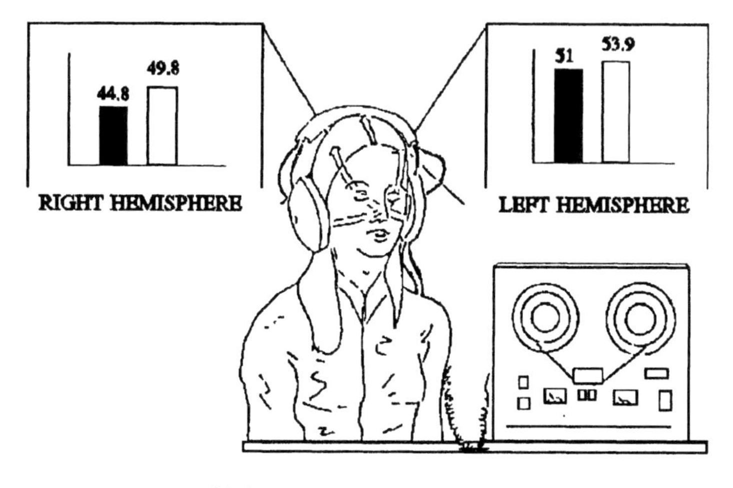

(b) 1st year student interpreters

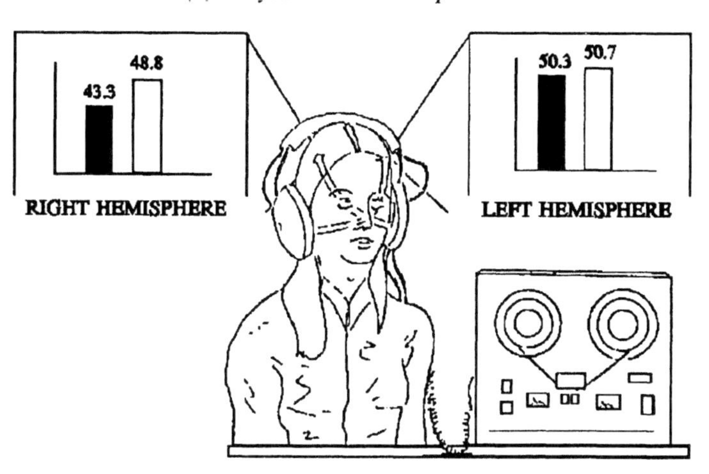

(c) 4th year student interpreters

Figure 1. *This figure shows the results of an experiment with the dichotic listening technique (L1: Italian, black histograms; L2: English, white histograms) in three groups of female subjects: (a) controls (university students at the Faculty of Medicine), (b) students attending the 1st year of the Interpreters' School and (c) student interpreters in the 4th year of the same School. Only the 4th-year students did not show the usual right-ear superiority for L2. The average number of correctly reported digits for each group and each language are recorded on each histogram.*

5.4. *Experimental Studies with Verbal-Manual Interference Paradigms*

The verbal-manual interference paradigm (also known as *finger tapping*) was developed by Kinsbourne and Cook (1971) in order to study the cerebral lateralization of specific superior cognitive functions, such as speech production and perception. The subjects are instructed to remain silent while tapping a key connected to a digital counter as fast as possible for a given number of trials, first with their right index finger (which is controlled by left-hemisphere motor structures) and then with their left index finger (which is controlled by right-hemisphere motor structures). Then the subjects are asked to carry out the same motor task while concurrently performing a verbal task, such as repeating lists of words, telling a short story, describing a picture, reading aloud, etc. The percentage of disruption in a motor task (tapping), due to a concurrent cognitive task (verbal production), assessed according to a specific formula, indicates the cerebral-functional distance between the two concurrent tasks. The percentage of disruption is inversely proportional to the functional distance between the cerebral areas controlling the movements of the right or the left index finger and the cerebral areas accounting for speech production (Hicks *et al.* 1975; McFarland & Geffen 1982; Kamhi & Masterson 1986). In right-handed monolinguals, the concurrent verbal task provokes greater disruption in the right hand because speech as well as motor functions are controlled by the left hemisphere. The left hand, being controlled by the right hemisphere, is less disrupted by the verbal functions, which are performed by the left hemisphere (Simon & Sussman 1987; Green & Vaid 1986; Clark *et al.* 1985; Kefee 1985; Fabbro *et al.* 1990b). The first studies on the cerebral lateralization for different languages (L1 and L2) by means of this technique were carried out by Sussman and co-workers (1982). The authors divided their subjects into a group of 9 early bilinguals (with acquisition of the second language prior to age 9) and a group of 31 late bilinguals, each subject having different combinations of L1 and L2. They found left-hemispheric lateralization for both languages in early bilinguals, whereas late bilinguals displayed left-hemispheric lateralization only for the first language and symmetric representation of the second language in both hemispheres. Both groups of bilingual subjects presented less marked cerebral asymmetry in the representation of linguistic functions with respect to a group of monolingual controls. A similar experiment was carried out by Soares (1984) who studied a homogeneous group of 16 right-handed bilingual male subjects (L1=Portuguese; L2=English). The results showed clear left-hemispheric lateralization of linguistic functions for L1 and L2 in all bilingual subjects. Hoosain and Shiu (1989) found greater right-hand (left-hemisphere) disruption for L1 and L2 in a group of Chinese-English bilingual subjects, too. On the other hand, Green (1986) obtained different results with a verbal-manual interference paradigm aimed at assessing cerebral lateralization for L1 (English) and L2 (Spanish) in three groups of English-speaking non-Hispanic male adults at three levels of second language acquisition: a) beginning Spanish learners, b) intermediate Spanish learners, and c) fluent English-Spanish bilinguals. Groups a) and b) showed left-hemisphere lateralization of both languages, whereas in the third group, L1 seemed to be more symmetrically distributed in both hemispheres than L2, thus suggesting a different cerebral representation of L1 in bilinguals as opposed to monolinguals.

5.5. Further Experiments

1) A few years ago, cerebral lateralization for L1 (Friulian) and L2 (Italian) was studied in three groups of right-handed bilingual female subjects: a) 12 girls attending the first grade at elementary school aged 6, b) 12 girls attending the fifth grade of elementary school aged 12, c) seven young women attending university, and in three control groups of monolingual (L1=Italian) subjects with matching ages (Fabbro *et al.* 1988a; Fabbro 1992). This study aimed at assessing the effects of intensive second language acquisition in a formal environment (school) on the cerebral organization of both languages. The paradigm included three different sessions of finger tapping, one to be performed in silence and two with a concurrent verbal task (reciting proverbs in Italian and in English). The controls performed the concurrent verbal task in their mother tongue (Italian) only. The first two groups of bilingual girls showed a left-hemispheric lateralization for both languages which seemed to be less marked in the twelve-year-old girls, whereas the university students, who were fluent in both languages, tended to have a more symmetric representation of linguistic functions in both hemispheres. The monolingual university students did not show significant left-hemisphere advantage either, whereas in both groups of younger monolingual controls (aged 6 and 12, respectively), language seemed to be lateralized to the left hemisphere. These results suggested that the cerebral lateralization of L1 and L2 to the left hemisphere tends to be modified with the progression of age and with improved second language proficiency towards a more symmetric representation in the brain. There are other factors, though, which could participate in this progressive

modification of linguistic function representation, such as verbal fluency, speaking speed, etc. (Fabbro *et al.* 1990a; Darò 1990a; see also Kinsbourne & McMurray 1975; Kee *et al.* 1986).

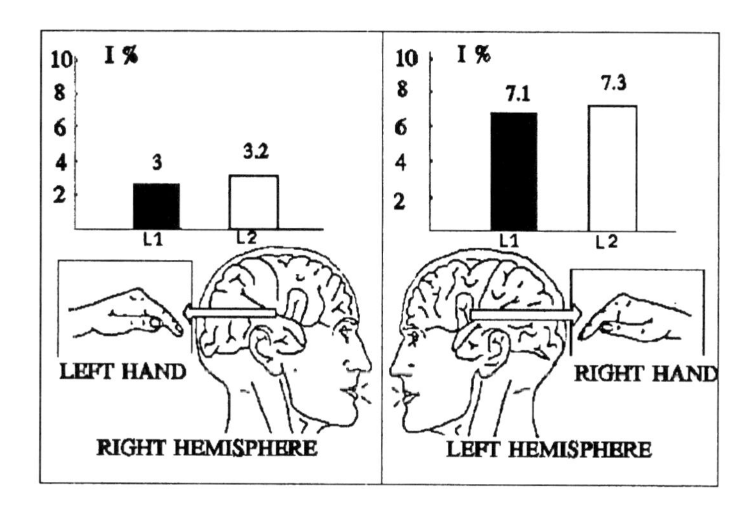

(a) Bilingual girls (1st year elementary school)

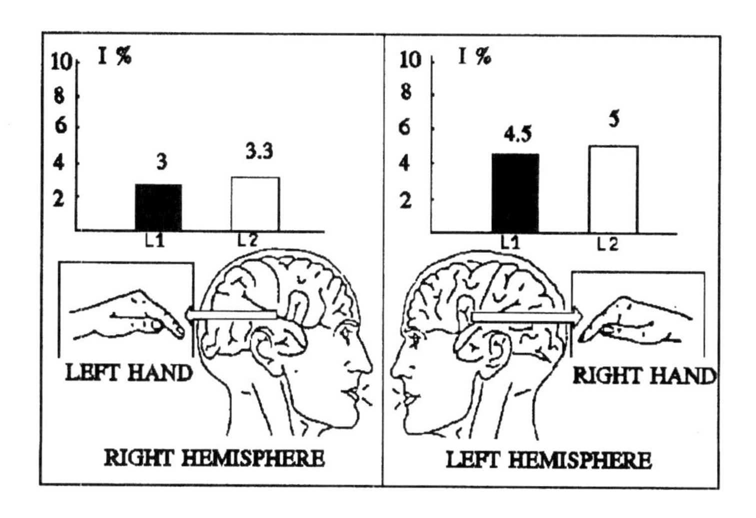

(b) Bilingual girls (5th year elementary school)

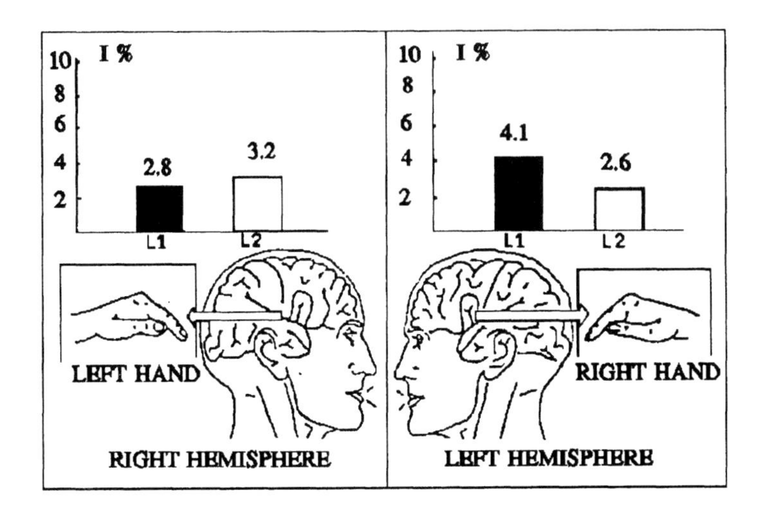

(c) Bilingual female university students

Figure 2. *This figure shows the results of an experiment with a verbal-manual interference paradigm in three groups of bilingual subjects (mean age: 6, 12; and 20 years, respectively, L1: Friulian; L2: Italian). In the first two groups (a) & (b)(age 6 and 12, an expected greater right-hand (left-hemisphere) disruption was found, whereas the group of older subjects (c) (average age 23) did not show any significant difference between hands.*

2) In another experiment (Fabbro 1992), cerebral lateralization was examined for L1 (Italian) and L2 (another Indoeuropean language) in four groups of polyglot students attending the 4th year of the School for Translators and Interpreters (SSLM) at the University of Trieste. The first group included 7 right-handed student translators (3 males and 4 females); the second group was made up of 10 non right-handed student translators (6 males and 4 females); the third group of 7 right-handed student interpreters (4 males and 3 females); and the fourth group of 7 non right-handed female student interpreters. Their task was to perform 8 sessions of finger tapping with each hand, either in silence, while reciting the Lord's Prayer in Italian (L1) and while reciting the Lord's Prayer in their second language. The results showed that the right-handed subjects (translators plus interpreters) generally showed left-hemisphere lateralization for linguistic functions, whereas the non right-handed subjects showed a more symmetric representation of languages. However, when the

translators were considered separately from the interpreters, only the right-handed translators were found to have significant left-hemisphere lateralization of linguistic functions both for L1 and L2, whereas the other three groups of subjects tended to show a more symmetric cerebral representation of both languages. Despite the reduced number of subjects available for this experiment, the authors drew the following conclusions: i) as happens in right-handed monolinguals, right-handed polyglots tend to show stronger left-hemispheric lateralization for linguistic functions as opposed to non-right-handed polyglots (i.e. with left-hand or mixed-hand preference); ii) translators, who translate written texts, and conference interpreters, who translate verbal material orally, may have a different cerebral organization of linguistic functions depending on the way in which they generally use their working languages.

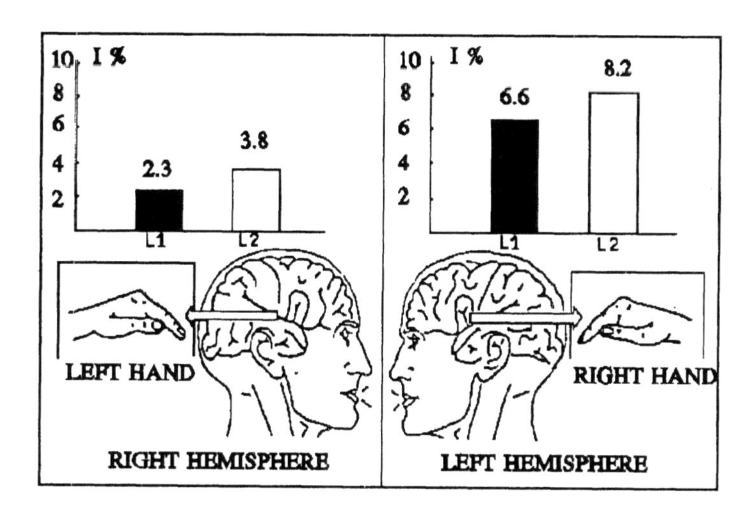

(a) Right-handed students of translation and interpretation

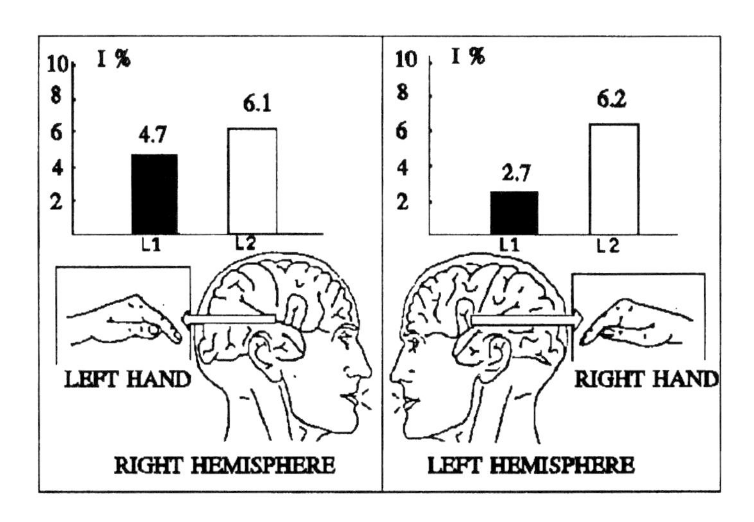

(b) Non-right-handed students of translation and interpretation

Figure 3. *This figure shows the results of an experiment with a verbal-manual interference paradigm in two groups of polyglot (L1: Italian, L2: English, L3: another Indoeuropean language) students attending the School for Interpreters and Translators, subdivided according to hand preference (a) group 1: right handers; (b) group 2: non-right-handed subjects. Only the group of right handers showed the usual greater right-hand (left-hemisphere) disruption for both languages.*

3) The cerebral lateralization of L1 (Italian), L2 (English) and L3 (another Indoeuropean language) was studied in 14 right-handed female student interpreters with a manual-verbal interference paradigm. No significant cerebral asymmetry for either language was found (Fabbro *et al.* 1990b), thus suggesting that simultaneous interpreters in general, and female interpreters in particular, tend to have a less lateralized representation of linguistic functions as opposed to monolingual and polyglot subjects.

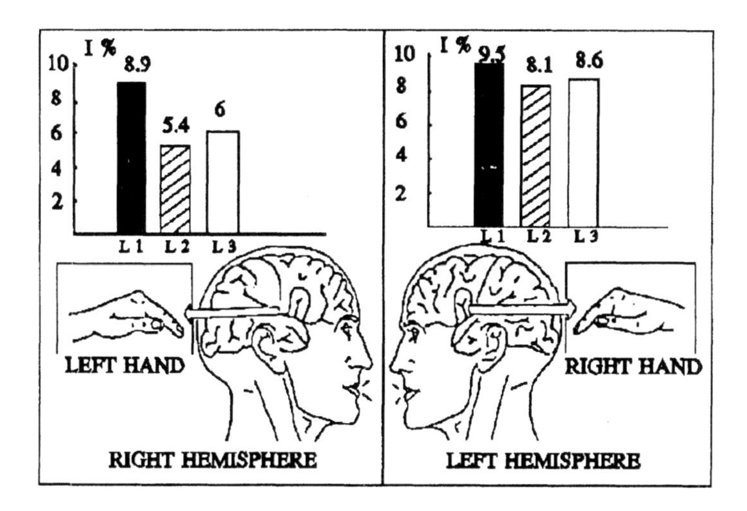

Figure 4. *This figure shows the results of an experiment with a verbal-manual interference paradigm in a group of student interpreters (L1: Italian, L2: English, L3: another Indoeuropean language). A greater right-hand disruption was revealed only for L2 and L3, while no significant difference between hands was found in L1.*

4) Another unpublished experiment on polyglot right-handed female students (L1=Italian; L2=French, learned after age 12) attending the 1st year of the Trieste School for Translators and Interpreters (SSLM) was carried out. The aim was to assess cerebral lateralization for L1 and L2 by means of a verbal-manual interference paradigm with three different concurrent tasks (automatic speech production as well as listening and production of interrogative and affirmative sentences in both languages). A strong left-hemisphere lateralization of linguistic functions for L1 and L2 during all the three tasks was found.

In these experiments with verbal manual-interference paradigms, the experimental procedures as well as the statistical analysis recommended by Sussman and co-workers (1982) were used. It is worth mentioning however that, recently, Sussman (1989) suggested the use of a new type of statistical analysis (ANCOVA), as the one which had been used until then (ANOVA) was found to be unsuitable for verbal-manual interference paradigms.

6. Neurolinguistic Aspects of Simultaneous Interpretation

Simultaneous interpretation consists in listening through earphones to a speech delivered in a source language (SL) while, at the same time, translating it into a target language (TL). The whole process lasts until the original speech in the source language is completed. The term "simultaneous" must therefore be considered in a broad sense, as there is always a short time lag, i.e. a few seconds of *delay*, between the onset of the original speech in the SL and the onset of the interpreter's output in the TL, in order for the interpreter to understand sequential chunks of information before translating them into the TL. According to Barik (1974), during a simultaneously translated speech, the speaker and the interpreter talk at the same time only for 42% of the whole process, for 12% of the time both of them are silent, for 28% of the time only the interpreter speaks, and for the remaining 18% of the time only the speaker talks. Professional interpreters are generally also able to perform *consecutive interpretation*, which consists in translating a 10 to 15-minute speech after it has been delivered by the speaker. For this purpose, interpreters generally aid their memory by means of a particular note-taking technique which helps them reconstruct the whole speech in the TL, without altering its general structure. Consecutive interpretation is mostly used during direct negotiations, or at banquets and similar official events, and whenever booths for simultaneous interpretation are not available. From a neurophysiological point of view, simultaneous interpretation is a very complex cognitive task, requiring a rapid process of language decoding, translation and verbal production in the TL with concurrent auditory control both of the continuous stream of the SL-input and of the TL-output, so as to check if the form, the content and the voice quality of the interpreter's speech are correct and pleasant enough to listen to for long periods of time (Darò 1990b).

A relevant, interesting fact regarding students of simultaneous interpretation, which has been observed at the School for Interpreters and Translators (SSLM) at the University of Trieste where Italian interpreters are trained at an academic level, is that about 92% of them are female. This percentage is even higher among professional interpreters working for International Organizations (European Parliament, Commission of the European Communities, Council of Europe; Gran & Dodds 1989). These data suggest that apparently females have a better aptitude for learning languages at high proficiency levels as well as for performing complex cognitive and motor skills, such as those involved in simultaneous interpreting (Ponton 1987; Hampson & Kimura 1988; Fabbro 1989a, 1992).

In performing simultaneous interpretation, the interpreter may choose between two different approaches: meaning-based translation and word-for-word translation (Paradis 1984; Gran 1989; Fabbro *et al.* 1990b). With the *meaning-based translation* strategy, the interpreter retains sentences or at least brief information chunks by stripping them of their superficial linguistic form, whereas the meaning is recoded in the TL as accurately as possible. There is no need for the interpreter to retain the surface structure of the SL-text in his/her verbal short-term memory, though he/she has to understand the deep structure of it, in order to render its meaning in the TL. Adopting this translating procedure, the interpreter is generally less exposed to syntactic or lexical interferences between his working languages and can therefore choose more appropriate linguistic expressions in the TL. This technique is adopted in most circumstances and is highly recommended during training courses as it produces a real "interpretation" of the original message into the TL. With the *word-for-word translation* strategy, the interpreter translates minimal meaningful units of the SL which have an equivalent in the TL. At a phonetic, phonological, morphological, syntactic and semantic level, the two working languages thus tend to short-circuit, and the overall message is not decoded at a cognitive level. In fact, by using this strategy, the interpreter may not even understand the meaning of the incoming message and nevertheless be able to translate every single word, provided he can store the single elements in his short-term memory for the time needed to find an equivalent translation of the single terms and formulate a syntactically correct sentence in the TL. This interpretation strategy may be chosen even by expert professional interpreters during conferences on highly specialized or technical topics (e.g. mathematics, theoretical physics, etc.), or for parts of a speech including lists of names, numbers, products, countries etc., or it may be adopted in special circumstances, i.e. when the interpreter is confronted with particular difficulties in the process of translation. It may therefore happen that the conference delegates express their complete satisfaction with the interpreters' performance even though the latter have in fact understood only "sequences of words" without thoroughly understanding the meaning underlying those words.

6.1. Aphasic Syndromes and Translation: Some Neurofunctional Considerations

Paradis (1984, 1987, 1989) has repeatedly devoted his attention to the problem of translation abilities in polyglot aphasic patients. In a review of cases of polyglot aphasics reported in the literature prior to his own studies, he summarized different types of syndromes: a) some patients were no longer able to talk in their own mother tongue, though they could translate sentences from L2 into L3 and vice-versa; b) others would resort to their second language to evoke words that they could not find in their first language, thus expressing these words at first in L2 and then translating them immediately into L1; c) other patients spontaneously translated inner verbal thoughts or sentences they had been listening to into another language, without being asked and with no evident reason or necessity to do so; d) others still spontaneously answered in L1 to questions which had been put to them in another language; and e) other patients constantly mixed different languages when talking, without being able to translate from one language into another when explicitly asked to do so; finally f) some patients automatically translated sentences from L2 into L1 correctly without understanding their meaning nor their own output (Paradis 1984).

The cases of alternate antagonism and paradoxical translation phenomena already mentioned (see 1.6. and 1.7. above) which were reported by Paradis and co-workers (Paradis *et al.* 1982) can provide further data for a theory on the cerebral mechanisms subserving translation processes. Generally speaking, translating into one's more fluent, better known language is easier than translating into one's weakest language (Ellis & Hennelly 1980). According to Paradis (1984), paradoxical translation and the ability of aphasic bilinguals to translate sentences in both directions (Veyrac 1931) without understanding their meaning, suggest that during the process of translation, at least four different, reciprocally independent neurofunctional systems are involved: i) the neurofunctional system accounting for the first language (L1) with a component subserving comprehension (CL1) and another subserving expression (EL1); ii) the neurofunctional system accounting for L2 with related comprehension (CL2) and expression (EL2) components; iii) the neurofunctional system accounting for the translation from L1 into L2, and iv) the neurofunctional system accounting for the translation from L2 into L1. According to this hypothesis these four systems are generally related to each other, though they may also sometimes function autonomously. Should one or more than one of them fail, the others may still function.

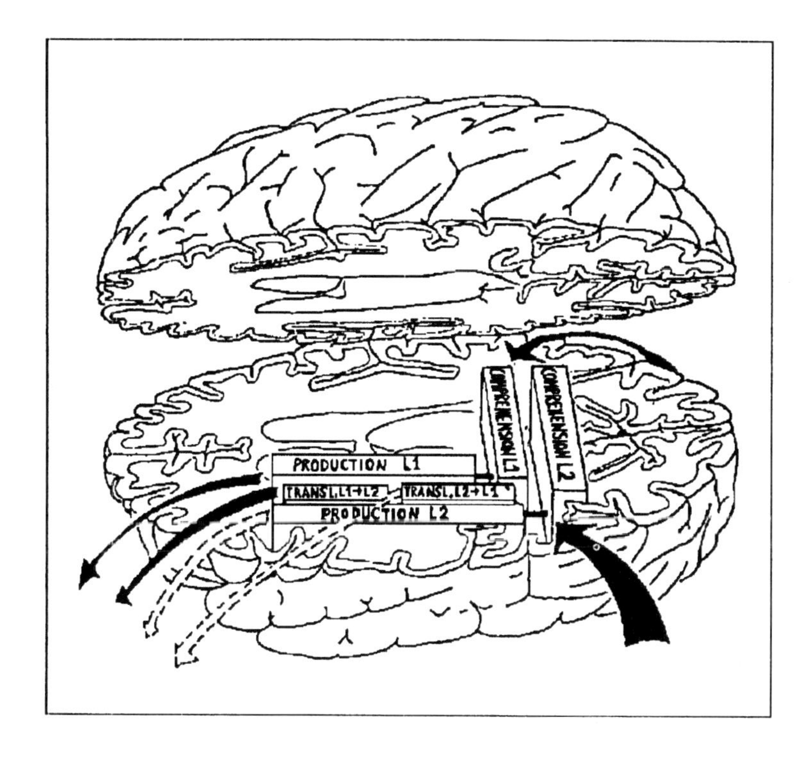

Figure 5. *Schematic representation of the neurofunctional systems implied in the translation process (Paradis 1984). According to this hypothesis, there are four autonomous systems: i) a system accounting for L1; ii) a system accounting for L2; iii) a system accounting for translation from L1 into L2; and iv) a system accounting for translation from L2 into L1. A cerebral lesion may inhibit or impair one or more than one system, without disrupting the others. This figure shows the neurofunctional systems of a bilingual (French/Arabic) aphasic patient described by Paradis et al. (1982), who on a given day had no difficulties when speaking French (solid arrow: expression in L1), but could not speak Arabic (broken arrow: expression in L2); she understood both languages and was able to translate words and sentences from French into Arabic (solid arrow: translation from L1 into L2), but not from Arabic into French (broken arrow: translation from L2 into L1).*

6.2. Hemispheric Specialization and Simultaneous Interpretation

In recent years, several experiments have been carried out for the purpose of inquiring into some of the neurolinguistic and neuropsychological aspects of simultaneous interpretation. A considerable number of these studies have been carried out at the School for Translators and Interpreters (SSLM) of the University of Trieste, Italy.

In an experiment involving translation of words, two groups of student interpreters (beginners in the first interpretation course, and advanced students in the second interpretation course) were studied. The subjects had to listen to and simultaneously translate 60 lists of 50 words each from German (L2) into Italian (L1), 30 of which were sent through earphones to the right ear and the other 30 to the left ear at a rate of 1,5 words per second. The total number of errors made by each subject according to ear of input was assessed and compared. The group of beginners made significantly more errors when listening to the input with their left ear than with their right ear, thus showing a left-hemisphere advantage in this task, whereas there was no such difference between ears in the group of advanced student interpreters (Spiller-Bosatra *et al.* 1989, 1990; Darò 1989). Apparently, longer practice in simultaneous interpretation enhanced the advanced students' ability to carry out a task of translation of words and, at the same time, improved the linguistic competence of their left ear (right hemisphere). In fact, during simultaneous interpretation, interpreters generally tend to listen to the source text only with their left ear so as to control their own output in the target language with their right ear (Sussman 1971)

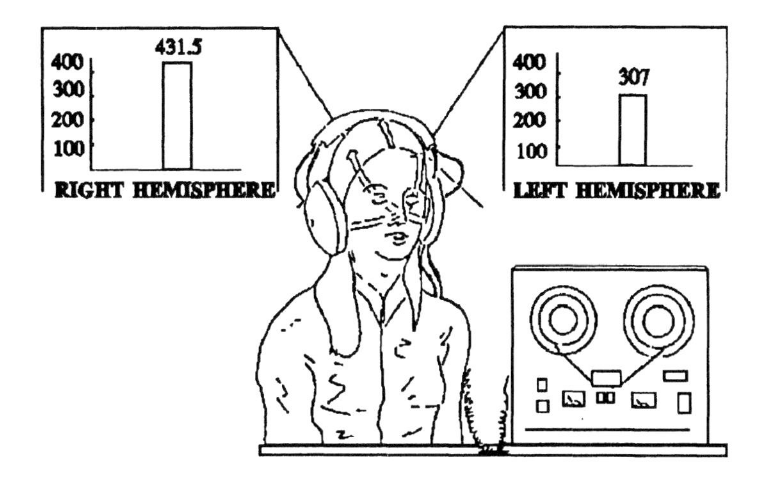

(a) 3rd year student interpreters

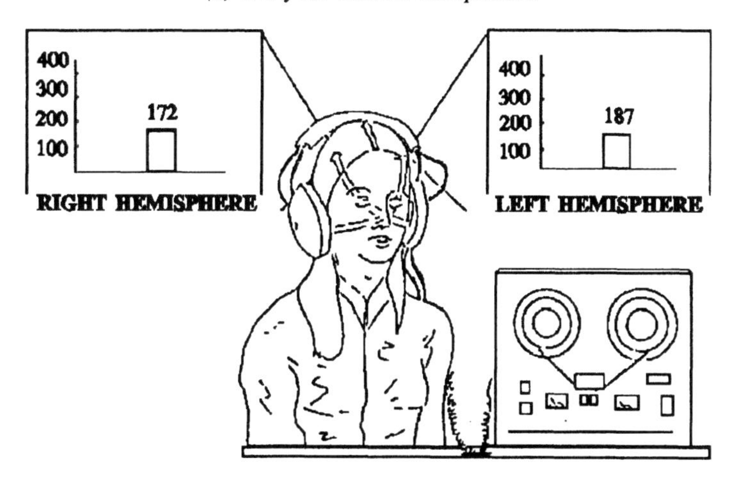

(b) 4th year student interpreters

Figure 6. *This figure shows the results of an experiment of "complex shadowing" (listening to lists of words with concurrent translation) with student interpreters of the 3rd and 4th year. (a) The 3rd-year students made more mistakes when listening to the lists of words with their left ear, thus showing a left-hemispheric superiority. (b) The 4th-year students did not show any significant difference between ears.*

Recently, Sylvie Lambert (1990; 1993) examined ear advantage during simultaneous interpretation from L1 into L2 as well as from L2 into L1 (working languages: French and English) by testing 13 Canadian professional interpreters and 8 student interpreters in three different conditions: i) the subjects listened to the input in the source language (SL) with both ears; ii) the subjects listened to the SL only with their left ear; and iii) the subjects listened to the SL only with their right ear. The results showed that in both directions of translation right-handed subjects made fewer mistakes when listening to the SL with their left ear (right hemisphere).

In another recent experiment (Gran & Fabbro 1989; Fabbro *et al.* 1991) hemispheric specialization for semantic and syntactic language components in L1 and L2 were studied in a group of 24 right-handed female students of interpretation at the SSLM and in a group of 12 right-handed female professional interpreters who had been working at the EEC Commission for at least 10 years. The subjects' mother tongue was Italian (L1), their second language was English (L2), which they had started to learn after age 12. In the first session of a dichotic listening test, the subjects were presented with 60 sentences in Italian (SL), which were sent to one ear only, and at the same time with the English (TL) translation of these sentences, which was sent to the other ear. In the second session, the SL-input and the TL-input, respectively, were inverted so as to reach the contralateral ear. The same procedure was adopted in the third and fourth sessions, where English became the SL and Italian the translated TL. The order of the sessions was random and counterbalanced across subjects. The translation of 20 sentences was correct, whereas 20 translated sentences contained a semantic error and the remaining 20 translated sentences contained a syntactic error. The subjects' task was to determine if there was a mistake in the translated version and whether this was semantic or syntactic. Before listening to each sentence, the subjects were told which was the SL and which was the TL. The amount of correctly recognized pairs of sentences was calculated for each subject. The results showed that both groups generally recognized a significantly higher number of sentences with English (L2) as TL when they listened to it with their left ear than with their right ear (L2 RE=12.20; L2 LE=12.95; $p<0.05$). As regards Italian (L1) as TL, there was no significant difference between ears (L1 RE=12.36; L1 LE=11.98). In recognizing correct sentences (cs) there was no difference between professional interpreters (PI) and student interpreters (SI; SIcs=16.7; PIcs=16.6), whereas the professional interpreters generally recognized more sentences with semantic mistakes (sem) than the students (SIsem=11.52; PIsem=14.3; $p<0.01$). The student interpreters, on the other hand, recognized more sentences with syntactic mistakes (syn) as opposed to the professional interpreters (SIsyn=9.12; PIsyn=6; $p<0.01$). If the two groups were considered separately, the student interpreters did not show any significant difference between ears in recognizing correct sentences, or sentences with semantic or syntactic mistakes in both languages, whereas the professional interpreters were found to recognize significantly more sentences with semantic mistakes in L1 when listening with their right ear (L1 RE=14.50; L1 LE=11.70; $p<0.01$) and in L2 when listening with their left ear (L2 RE=13; L2 LE=18; $p<0.001$). The same group recognized significantly more sentences with syntactic mistakes in L1 when listening with their left ear (L1 RE=5; L1 LE=7.1; $p<0.05$) and in L2 when listening with their right ear (L2 RE=6.9; L2 LE=5; $p<0.05$).

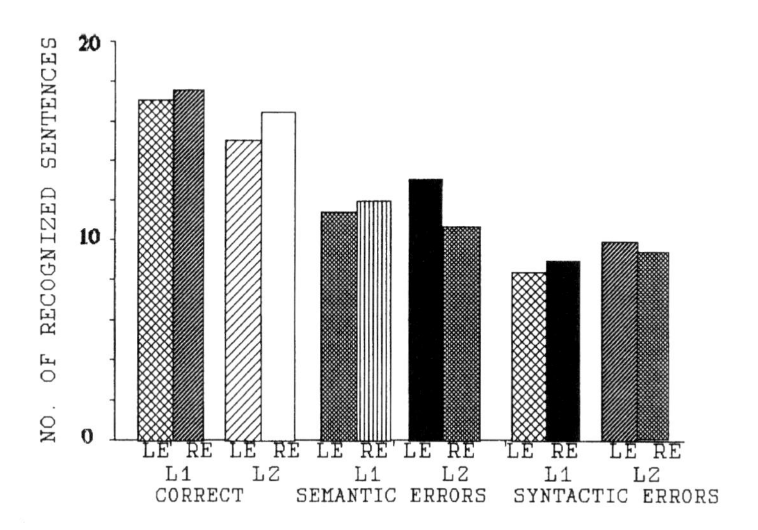

(a) Interpreting students

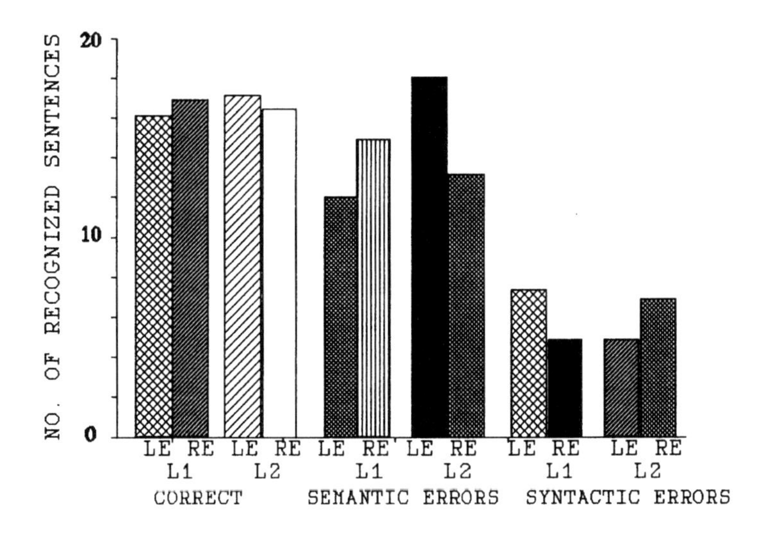

(b) Professional Interpreters

Figure 7. *Schematic representation of the results of an experiment for the assessment of the cerebral organization of syntactic and semantic components of L1 (Italian) and L2 (English) in (a) a group of student interpreters and in (b) a group of professional interpreters, with a dichotic listening paradigm. The subjects listened to sentences sent through earphones to one ear and to their translation sent to the contralateral ear. The translation was either correct, or had semantic or syntactic errors, and the subjects were requested to mention the errors. The student interpreters did not show any significant difference between ears. The professional interpreters showed a right-ear superiority in recognizing semantic errors in L1, and a left-ear superiority in recognizing semantic errors in L2 (* $p<0.01$). As regards syntactic errors, they showed a right-ear superiority in L1 and a left-ear superiority in L2 ($p<0.05$).*

These results show that most probably student interpreters and professional interpreters have a different approach towards simultaneous interpretation. The latter seem to adopt semantic strategies (meaning-based translation), whereas the former apparently divert more of their attention to the syntactic form of the message (word-for-word translation). The fact that the professional interpreters recognized more semantic mistakes in L1 with their right ear (left hemisphere) and in L2 with their left ear (right hemisphere) may be due to their habit and practice of translating only from foreign languages into their mother tongue (as required at the EEC Commission) and of listening to the incoming message in the SL (=L2, L3, etc.) with their left ear only, while controlling their own output in the TL (=L1) with their right ear (Gran 1989). The continuous practice of simultaneous interpretation in this condition as well as the tendency to adopt semantic strategies during translation may perhaps bring about left-hemisphere specialization for semantic components of L1 and right-hemisphere specialization for semantic components of L2 (Darò 1989; Spiller-Bosatra *et al.* 1990; Lambert 1990). In fact, data showing a right-hemisphere advantage for syntactic components in L1 as opposed to a left-hemisphere advantage for syntactic components in L2 are difficult to explain (Fabbro *et al.* 1991). Perhaps a clue may be found in a revision of the role of the various components of attentive functions in simultaneous interpretation (Treisman 1965; McKeever *et al.* 1989).

In another experiment with a verbal-manual interference paradigm, the first attempt to study cerebral lateralization during simultaneous interpretation was made by examining 14 right-handed female student interpreters of 4th year at the SSLM (Gran & Fabbro 1988; Fabbro *et al.* 1990a). The subjects were asked to simultaneously translate proverbs, thus adopting a meaning-based translation strategy, as well as lists of words (word-for-word translation strategy) from L1 (Italian) to L2 (English) and from L2 to L1, while tapping (refer back to section *Experimental Studies with Verbal-manual Interference Paradigms*).

The results did not reveal any significant difference between hands, thus suggesting that probably simultaneous interpretation requires the involvement of both cerebral hemispheres. There was, however, a great difference between the two strategies of interpretation. In fact, during meaning-based interpretation, the percentage of disruption for both hands was higher than during word-for-word interpretation, thus suggesting that the former cognitive task seems to be more difficult than the latter. Recently, these results were corroborated by a similar experiment which was carried out by Green and co-workers (1990a, 1990b), who studied cerebral lateralization during simultaneous interpretation and shadowing in 16 professional interpreters and in 16 bilingual subjects. By means of a verbal-manual interference paradigm, these authors found greater right-hand (left-hemisphere) disruption during shadowing, whereas during simultaneous interpretation, no significant difference between hands was found. In the present state-of-the-art, by using the experimental techniques described in this chapter, it may be concluded that simultaneous interpretation is a particularly complex cognitive task, and requires massive and concurrent activation of *both* cerebral hemispheres, thus apparently engaging more cerebral structures than mere listening and speaking.

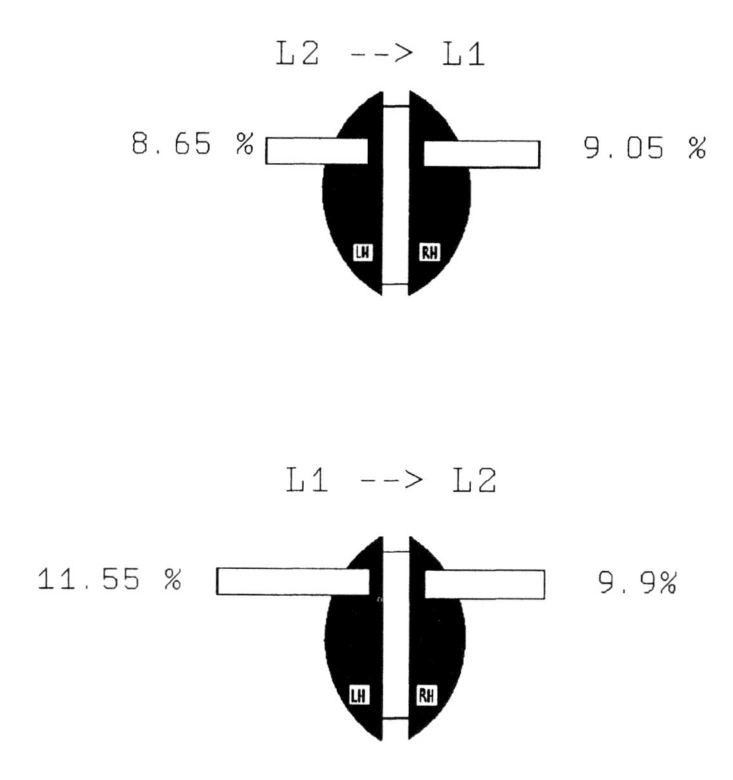

Figure 8. *Schematic representation of the percentage of verbal-manual disruption during simultaneous interpretation from L1 into L2 and from L2 into L1. In both translation directions, no significant difference between hemispheres was found.*

7. Conclusions

While going through this chapter, those readers who do not work in a neurological or neuropsychological domain may probably have the impression of rambling through a host of hands, ears, and cerebral hemispheres, at times being left- and at times right-sided. Moreover, all the presented data deriving from a multitude of similar experiments are always explained in terms of "probably, apparently, perhaps, maybe, etc.", thus only showing hypotheses, suggestions and possible interpretations with no definite statements, which would not be of great comfort to those who are looking for absolute certainties. However, the study of simultaneous and consecutive interpretation with scientific experimental methods, as tedious or speculative as it may sometimes appear, is bound to contribute greatly to general knowledge in this field and ultimately have real practical repercussions. Knowledge achieved through experimental research, as conceived by Galileo, derives from a) experimentation, which requires a continuous contact with the surrounding empirical world based on an exploratory attitude towards it; b) an open, never-ending discussion of methods and results among researchers and scientists; and c) the possibility of questioning and arguing against established authority by means of an experimental method. Authority, embodied by people who are more experienced or simply more numerous, is not necessarily bad *per se*, though it generally ends up in arbitrariness, especially if it makes claims in absolute terms. Even in the field of knowledge, therefore, authority may create myths, one example being the concepts of biblical astronomy supported by the Catholic Church against Galileo's demonstrations.

In our opinion, therefore, being a professional interpreter is not sufficient to explain what interpretation is and how it should be practised and taught. Apart from reports on personal experience and discussions with experimental researchers on the already known aspects of interpretation, inquiries which ought to be carried out to broaden existing knowledge should be started for the benefit of all those who really intend to approach interpretation with a non-arbitrary approach.

References

Albanese, J.F. 1985. "Language Lateralization in English-French Bilinguals". *Brain and Language* 24. 284-296.

Albert, M.L. and Obler L.K. 1978. *The Bilingual Brain. Neuropsychological and Neurolinguistic Aspects of Bilingualism*. New York: Academic Press.
As, A. 1963. "The Recovery of Forgotten Language Knowledge Through Hypnotic Age Regression: A Case Report". *American Journal of Clinical Hypnosis* 5. 24-29.
Barik, H. 1974. "A Look at Simultaneous Translation". *Working Papers in Bilingualism* 4. 20-41.
Basso, A. 1987. "La Riabilitazione del Linguaggio". A. Mazzuchi, ed. *Neuropsicologia riabilitativa*. Bologna: Il Mulino. 57-87.
Bentin, S. 1981. "On the Representation of Second Language in the Cerebral Hemispheres of Right-Handed People". *Neuropsychologia* 19. 599-603.
Bisiacchi, P. 1986. "La Tecnica dell'Ascolto Dicotico e la Specializzazione Emisferica". C. Umilta', ed. *Neuropsicologia Sperimentale*. Milano: Franco Angeli. 311-343.
Bouquet, F., Tuvo, F. and Paci, M. 1981. "Afasia Traumatica in un Bambino Bilingue nel Quinto Anno di Vita". *Neuropsicologia Infantile* 235-236, 159-169.
Braitenberg, V. 1987. *Gescheit Sein und Andere Unwissenschaftliche Essays*. Tübingen: Haffmans Verlag.
Bryden, M.P. 1982. *Laterality: Functional Asymmetry in the Intact Brain*. New York: Academic Press.
Cavalli Sforza L.L., Piazza, A., Menozzi, P. and Mountain J. 1988. "Reconstruction of Human Evolution: Bringing together Genetic, Archaeological, and Linguistic Data". *Proceedings of the National Academy of Science USA* 85. 6002-6006.
Chary P. 1986. "Aphasia in a Multilingual Society: A Preliminary Study". J. Vaid, ed. *Language Processing in Bilinguals*. Hillsdale: Lawrence Erlbaum. 183-198.
Chernigovskaya, T.V., Balonov, L.J., Deglin, V.L. 1983. "Bilingualism and Brain Functional Asymmetry". *Brain and Language* 20. 195-216.
Clark, D.G., Guitar, B., Hoffman, P.R. 1985. "Reliability of Verbal-Manual Interference". *Brain and Cognition* 4. 486-491.
Code, C. 1987. *Language, Aphasia, and the Right Hemisphere*. Chichester: John Wiley and Sons.
Crowder, R.G. 1986. *Psicologia della Lettura*. Bologna: Il Mulino.
Damasio, A.R., Geschwind, N. 1984. "The Neural Basis of Language". *Annual Review of Neuroscience* 7. 127-147.
Darò, V. 1989. "The Role of Memory and Attention in Simultaneous Interpretation: A Neurolinguistic Approach". *The Interpreter's Newsletter* 2. 50-56.
Darò, V. 1990a. "Speaking Speed during Simultaneous Interpretation: A Discussion on its Neuropsychological Aspects and Possible Contributions to Teaching". L. Gran and C. Taylor, eds. *Aspects of Applied and Experimental Research on Conference Interpretation*. Udine: Campanotto. 83-92.

Darò, V. 1990b. "Voice Frequency of Languages during Simultaneous Interpretation". *The Interpreters' Newsletter* 3. 88-92.

De Renzi, E., Faglioni, P. 1975. "L'Esame dei Disturbi Afasici di Comprensione Orale Mediante una Versione Abbreviata del Test dei Gettoni". *Rivista di Patologia Nervosa e Mentale* 96. 252-269.

De Zulueta, F.I.S. 1984. "The Implications of Bilingualism in the Study and Treatment of Psychiatric Disorders: A Review". *Psychological Medicine* 14. 541-557.

Durieu, C. 1969. *La Rééducation des Aphasiques*. Brussels: Dessart.

Ellis, N.C. and Hennelly, R.A. 1980. "A Bilingual Word-Length Effect: Implications for Intelligence Testing and the Relative Ease of Mental Calculation in Welsh and English". *British Journal of Psychology* 71. 43-51.

Endo, M., Shimizu, A. and Hori, T. 1978. "Functional Asymmetry of Visual Fields for Japanese Words in Kana (Syllable-Based), Writing and Japanese Shape-Recognition in Japanese Subjects". *Neuropsychologia* 16. 291-297.

Fabbro, F. 1989a. "Neurobiological Aspects of Bilingualism and Polyglossia". L. Gran and J. Dodds, eds. *The Theoretical and Practical Aspects of Teaching Conference Interpretation*. Udine: Campanotto. 71-82.

Fabbro, F. 1989b. "Cervello, Linguaggio e Stati di Coscienza. Contributi per Uno Studio Sperimentale Sull'Ipnosi". *Rivista Italiana di Ipnosi Clinica e Sperimentale* 9. 21-26.

Fabbro, F. 1990. "The Effects of Hypnosis on Callosal functions: An Experimental Study". *Archivio di Psicolologia, Neurolologia e Psichiatria* 51. 85-93.

Fabbro, F. 1992. "Cerebral Lateralization of Human Languages: Clinical and Experimental Data". J. Wind *et al.*, eds. *Language Origin: A Multidisciplinary Approach*. Dordrecht: Kluwer Academic Publ. 195-224.

Fabbro, F., Clarici, A., Darò, V. and Bava, A. 1990a. "Speech Velocity Affects the Cerebral Lateralization of Motor Functions of Language". *International Journal of Anthropology* 5. 174.

Fabbro, F., and Darò, V. 1990. "Can Human Languages be a Factor of Genetic Diversity?" *International Journal of Anthropology* 5. 175.

Fabbro, F. and Darò, V. 1992. "Linguistic Dichotomies in Two Types of Chilhood Aphasia". [submitted for publication.]

Fabbro, F., Darò, V. and Bava, A. 1988a. "Cerebral Lateralization in Early Learning of a Second Language". *Atti del VI Convegno Nazionale di Primatologia* (Trieste 15-18 giugno). 81-85.

Fabbro, F., Gran, L. and Bava, A. 1988b. "Modifications in Cerebral Lateralization during the Acquisition of a Second Language (English) inAadult Italian-Speaking Females: An Experimental Dichotic Listening Study". A. Tartabini and M.L. Genta, eds. *Perspectives in the Study of Primates*. Cosenza: De Rose. 76-85.

Fabbro F., Gran L., Basso, G. and Bava, A. 1990b. "Cerebral Lateralization in Simultaneous Interpretation". *Brain and Language* 39. 69-89.

Fabbro, F., Gran, B. and Gran, L. 1991. "Hemispheric Specialization for Semantic and Syntactic Components of Languages in Simultaneous Interpreters". *Brain and Language* 41. 1-42.

Fabbro F., Mammano, M., Paci, M. and Trobbei, E. 1987. "Studio-mediante Ascolto Dicotico-delle Lateralizzazioni Linguistiche in Bambini Normali, con 'Learning Disabilities' e con Epilessia a Parossismi Rolandici". *Archivio di Psicologia, Neurologia e Psichiatria* 48. 451-461.

Fabbro F., Petroni, M.G. and Bouquet, F. 1989. "Study of Hemispheric Specializations through Tachistoscopic Discrimination of Physiognomical and Alphabetical Material in Groups of Adults and Children". *Archivio di Psicologia e Psichiatria* 50. 95-107.

Flege, J.E. 1988. "The Production and Perception of Foreign Speech Sounds". H. Wintitz, ed. *Human Communication and Its Disorders*. Norwood N.J.: Ablex Publishing Corporation. 224-401.

Fredman, M. 1975. "The Effect of Therapy Given in Hebrew on the Home Language of the Bilingual or Polyglot Adult Aphasic in Israel". *British Journal of Disorders of Communication* 10. 61-69.

Fromm, E. 1970. "Age Regression with Unexpected Reappearance of a Repressed Childhood Language". *American Journal of Clinical Hypnosis* 18. 79-88.

Galloway, L.M. 1980. "Towards a Neuropsychological Model of Bilingualism and Second Language Performance". *Language Learning* 31. 2.

Galloway, L.M. and Scarcella, R. 1982. "Cerebral Organization in Adult Second Language Acquisition: Is the Right Hemisphere More Involved?" *Brain and Language* 16. 56-60.

Gastaldi, G. 1951. "Osservazioni su un Afasico Bilingue". *Sistema Nervoso* 2. 175-180.

Genesee, F. 1987. "Neuropsychology and Second Language Acquisition". L.M. Beebe, ed. *Issues in Second Language Acquisition*. New York: Harper & Row. 82-112.

Genesee, F., Hamers, J., Lambert, W.E., Mononen, L., Seitz, M. and Starck, R. 1978. "Language Processing in Bilinguals". *Brain and Language* 5. 1-12.

Gordon, H.W. 1980. "Cerebral Organization in Bilinguals". *Brain and Language* 9. 255-268.

Gran, L. 1989. "Interdisciplinary Research on Cerebral Asymmetries: Significance and Prospects for the Teaching of Interpretation". L. Gran and J. Dodds, eds. *The Theoretical and Practical Aspects of Teaching Conference Interpretation*. Udine: Campanotto. 93-100.

Gran, L. 1990. "A Dichotic Listening Study on Error Recognition among Professional Conference Interpreters". *Proceedings of the XII World Congress of FIT* (Belgrade, YU).

Gran, L. and Dodds, J. 1989. *The Theoretical and Practical Aspects of Teaching Conference Interpretation*. Udine: Campanotto Editore.

Gran, L. and Fabbro, F. 1988. "The Role of Neuroscience in the Teaching of Interpretation". *The Interpreter's Newsletter* 1. 23-41.

Gran, L. and Fabbro, F. 1989. "Cerebral Lateralization for Syntactic and Semantic Components in L1 (Italian) and L2 (English) in Interpreting Students: Training Implications for Simultaneous Interpretation". D. Lindberg Hammond, ed. *Coming of Age: American Translators Association Conference 1989*. Medford, N.J.: Learned Information Inc. 133-142.

Green, A. 1986. "A Time Sharing Cross-Sectional Study of Monolinguals and Bilinguals at Different Levels of Second Language Acquisition". *Brain and Cognition* 5. 477-497.

Green, A., Schweda-Nicholson N., Vaid, J., White, N. and Steiner, R. 1990a. "Asymmetry in Tapping Interference during a Shadowing Versus a Paraphrasing Task". *Brain and Language* 39. 103-133.

Green, A., Schweda-Nicholson, N., Vaid, J., White, N. and Steiner R. 1990b. "Hemispheric Involvement in Shadowing vs. Interpretation: A Time-Sharing Study of Simultaneous Interpreters with Matched Bilingual and Monolingual Controls". *Brain and Language* 39. 107-133.

Green, A. and Vaid, J. 1986. "Methodological Issues in the Use of the Concurrent Activities Paradigm". *Brain and Cognition* 5. 465-476.

Green, D.W. 1986. "Control, Activation, and Resource: A Framework and a Model for the Control of Speech in Bilinguals". *Brain and Language* 27. 210-223.

Grosjean, F. 1982. *Life with Two Languages: An Introduction to Bilingualism*. Cambridge, Mass: Harvard University Press.

Grosjean, F. 1989. "Neurolinguists, Beware! The Bilingual is not Two Monolinguals in One Person". *Brain and Language* 36. 3-15.

Hampson, E. and Kimura, D. 1988. "Reciprocal Effects of Hormonal Fluctuation on Human Motor and Perceptual-Spatial Skills". *Behavioral Neurosciences* 102. 456-459.

Hatta, T. 1977. "Recognition of Japanese Kanji in the Left and Right Visual Field". *Neuropsychologia* 15. 685-688.

Hicks, R.E., Provenzano, F.J. and Rybstein, E.D. 1975. "Generalized and Lateralized Effects of Concurrent Verbal Rehearsal upon Performance of Sequential Movements of the Fingers by the Left and the Right Hand". *Acta Psychologica* 29. 119-130.

Hoosain, R. and Shiu, L.P. 1989. "Cerebral Lateralization of Chinese-English Bilingual Functions". *Neuropsychologia* 27. 705-712.

Hynd, G.W. and Scott, S.A. 1980. "Propositional and Appositional Modes of Thought and Differential Speech Lateralization in Navajo Indian and Anglo Children". *Child Development* 5. 909-911.

Jakobson, R. 1964. "General Discussion". A.V.S. De Reuck and M. O'Connor, eds. *Disorders of Language*. London: CIBA Foundation Symposium. 21-47.

Jakobson, R. and Waugh, L.R. 1984. *La Forma Fonica della Lingua*. Milano: Il Saggiatore.

Junqué, C., Vendrell, P., Vendrell Brucet, J.M. and Tobeña, A. 1989. "Differential Recovery in Naming in Bilingual Aphasics". *Brain and Language* 36. 16-22.

Kamhi, A.G. and Masterson, J.J. 1986. "The Reliability of the Time-Sharing Paradigm". *Brain and Language* 29. 324-341.

Kee, D.W., Morris, K., Bathurst, K. and Hellige, J.B. 1986. "Lateralized Interference in Finger Tapping: Comparisons of Rate Variability Measures under Speed and Consistency Tapping Instructions". *Brain and Cognition* 5. 268-279.

Kefee, K. 1985. "Motor and Cognitive Interference Effects on Unimanual Tapping Rates". *Brain and Cognition* 4. 165-170.

Kertesz, A. 1985. "Aphasia". J.A.M. Frederiks, ed. *Handbook of Clinical Neurology, Vol 45: Clinical Neurology*. Amsterdam: North-Holland. 287-330.

Kimura, D. 1961. "Cerebral Dominance and the Perception of Verbal Stimuli". *Canadian Journal of Psychology* 15. 166-171.

Kinsbourne, M. and Cook, J. 1971. "Generalized and Lateralized Effects of Concurrent Verbalization on a Unimanual Skill". *Quarterly Journal of Experimental Psychology* 23. 341-345.

Kinsbourne, M. and McMurray, J. 1975. "The Effect of Cerebral Dominance on Time Sharing between Speaking and Tapping by Preschool Children". *Child Development* 46. 240-242.

Kraetschmer, K. 1982. "Forgotten Cases of Bilingual Aphasics". *Brain and Language* 15. 92-94.

Lambert, S. 1990. "Simultaneous Interpreters: One Ear May be Better than Two". *The Interpreters' Newsletter* 2. 11-16.

Lambert, S. 1993. "The Effect of Ear of Information on the Proficiency of Simultaneous Interpretation". *META* XXXVIII. 198-211.

Lambert, W.E. 1969. "Psychological Studies of the Interdependencies of the Bilinguals' Two Languages". Puhvel, ed. *Substance and Structure of Language*. Berkeley: University of California Press. 99-125.

Lambert, W. and Fillenbaum, S. 1959. "A Pilot Study of Aphasia Among Bilinguals". *Canadian Journal of Psychology* 13. 28-34.

Lamendella, J.T. 1977. "General Principles of Neurofunctional Organization and Their Manifestation in Primary and Nonprimary Language Acquisition". *Language Learning* 27. 155-196.

Lebrun, Y. 1982. "L'Aphasie Chez les Polyglottes". *Linguistique* 18. 129-144.

Lecours, A.R. and Lhermitte, F., eds. 1979. *L'Aphasie*. Paris: Flammarion Médicine-Sciences.

Leischner, A. 1948. "Ueber die Aphasie der Mehrsprachigen". *Archiv für Psychiatrie und Nervenkrankheiten* 180. 118-180, 731-775.

Lenneberg, E. 1967. *Biological Foundations of Language*. New York: Wiley.

Lieberman, P. and Blumstein, S.E. 1988. *Speech Physiology, Speech Perception, and Acoustic Phonetics*. Cambridge: Cambridge University Press.

Lindblom, B. 1989. "Some Remarks on the Origin of the Phonetic Code". C. von Euler, I. Lundberg and G. Lennerstrand, eds. *Brain and Reading*. London: Stockton Press. 27-44.

Lindblom, B. 1990. *Models of Phonetic Variation and Selection*. Personal communication.

Luria, A.R. 1978. *Problemi Fondamentali di Neurolinguistica*. Roma: Armando.

Mägiste, E. 1979. "The Competing Language Systems of the Multilingual: A Developmental Study of Decoding and Encoding Processes". *Journal of Verbal Learning and Verbal Behavior* 18. 79-89.

McFarland, K. and Geffen, G. 1982. "Speech Lateralization Assessed by Concurrent Task Performance". *Neuropsychologia* 20. 383-390.

McGlone, J. 1980. "Sex Differences in Human Brain Organization: A Critical Survey". *The Behavioral and Brain Sciences* 3. 215-227.

McKeever, W.F., Hunt, L.J., Wells, S. and Yazzie, C. 1989. "Language Laterality in Navajo Reservation Children: Dichotic Test Results Depend on Language Context of the Testing". *Brain and Language* 36. 148-158.

Minkowski, M. 1963. "On Aphasia in Polyglots". L. Halpern, ed. *Problems of Dynamic Neurology*. Jerusalem: Hebrew University. 119-161.

Mohr, E. and Costa, L. 1985. "Ear Asymmetries in Dichotic Listening Tasks which Increase in Difficulty". *Brain and Language* 24. 233-245.

Nilipour, R. and Ashayeri, H. 1989. "Alternating Antagonism Between Two Languages With Successive Recovery of a Third in a Trilingual Aphasic Patient". *Brain and Language* 36. 23-48.

Nottebohm, F. 1970. "Ontogeny of Bird Song". *Science* 167. 950-956.

Obler, L.K. and Albert, M.L. 1977. "Influence of Aging on Recovery from Aphasia in Polyglots". *Brain and Language* 4. 460-463.

Obler, L.K., Zatorre, R.J., Galloway L., and Vaid, J. 1982. "Cerebral Lateralization in Bilinguals: Methodological Issues". *Brain and Language* 15. 40-45.

Ojemann, G.A. and Creutzfeldt, O.T. 1987. "Language in Humans and Animals: Contribution of Brain Stimulation and Recording". V.B. Mountcastle *et al.*, eds. *Handbook of Physiology: The Nervous System. Higher Functions of the Brain.* Bethesda: American Physiological Society. 2:V. 675-699.

Ojemann, G.A. and Whitaker, H.A. 1978. "The Bilingual Brain". *Archives oj Neurology* 35. 409-412.

Packard, J.L. 1986. "Tone Production Deficits in Nonfluent Aphasic Chinese Speech". *Brain and Language* 29. 212-223.

Paivio, A. 1986. "Bilingual Cognitive Representation". A. Paivio, ed. *Mental Representations: A Dual Coding Approach.* New York: Oxford University Press. 239-257.

Paradis, M. 1977. "Bilingualism and Aphasia". H. Whitaker and H.A. Whitaker, eds. *Studies in Neurolinguistics, Vol. 3.* New York: Academic Press. 65-121.

Paradis, M. 1984. "Aphasie et Traduction". *META* 29. 57-67.

Paradis, M. 1987. *The Assessment of Bilingual Aphasia.* Hillsdale, N.J.: Lawrence Erlbaum.

Paradis, M. 1989. "Bilingual and Polyglot Aphasia". F. Boller and J. Grafman, eds. *Handbook of Neuropsychology, Vol. 2.* Amsterdam: Elsevier. 117-140.

Paradis, M. and Goldblum, M.C. 1989. "Selective Crossed Aphasia in a Trilingual Aphasic Patient Followed by Reciprocal Antagonism". *Brain and Language* 36. 62-75.

Paradis, M., Goldblum, M.C. and Abidi, R. 1982. "Alternate Antagonism with Paradoxical Translation Behavior in Two Bilingual Aphasic Patients". *Brain and Language* 15. 55-69.

Paradis, M. and Lecours, A.R. 1979. "L'Aphasie Chez les Bilingues et les Polyglottes". A. R. Lecours and F. Lhermitte, eds. *L'Aphasie.* Paris: Flammarion Médicine-Sciences. 605-616.

Penfield, W. and Roberts, L. 1959. *Speech and Brain Mechanisms.* Princeton N.J.: Princeton University Press.

Perecman, E. 1984. "Spontaneous Translation and Language Mixing in a Polyglot Aphasic". *Brain and Language* 23. 43-63.

Piazza Gordon, D. and Zatorre, R.J. 1981. "A Right-Ear Advantage for Dichotic Listening in Bilingual Children". *Brain and Language* 13. 389-396.

Pick, A. 1921. "Zur Erklärung gewisser Ausnahmen von der sogenannten Ribotschen Regel: Abhandlungen aus der Neurologie, Psychiatrie, Psychologie und ihren Grenzgebieten". *Monatsschrift für Psychiatrie und Neurologie* 13. 151-167.

Pitres, A. 1885. "Etudes sur l'Aphasie". *Revue de Médicine* 15. 873-889.

Ponton, C.W. 1987. "Enhanced Articulatory Speed in Ambidexters". *Neuropsychologia* 25. 305-311.

Pötzl, O. 1925. "Über die parietal bedingte Aphasie und ihren Einfluβ auf das Sprechen mehrerer Sprachen". *Zeitschrift für Neurologie* 96. 100-124.

Rapport, R.L., Tan, C.T. and Whitaker, H.A. 1983. "Language Function and Dysfunction among Chinese- and English-Speaking Polyglots: Cortical Stimulation, Wada Testing, and Clinical Studies". *Brain and Language* 18. 342-366.

Ribot, T. 1882. *Diseases of Memory: An Essay in the Positive Psychology*. London: Paul.

Rogers, L., Tenhouten, W., Kaplan, C. and Gardiner, M. 1977. "Hemispheric Specialization of Language: An EEG Study of Bilingual Hopi Children". *International Journal of Neuroscience* 8. 1-6.

Sasanuma, S. 1975. "Kana and Kanji Processing in Japanese Aphasics". *Brain and Language* 2. 369-383.

Sasanuma, S., Itoh, M., Kobayashi, Y. and Mori, K. 1980. "The Nature of the Task-Stimulus Interaction in the Tachistoscopic Recognition of Kana and Kanji Words". *Brain and Language* 9. 298-306.

Schneiderman, E.I. 1986. "Leaning to the Right: Some Thoughts on Hemisphere Involvement in Language Acquisition". J. Vaid, ed. *Language Processing in Bilinguals*. Hillsdale: Lawrence Erlbaum. 233-252.

Scott, S., Hynd, G.W., Hunt, L. and Weed, W. 1979. "Cerebral Speech Lateralization in the Native American Navajo". *Neuropsychologia* 17. 89-92.

Sewell, D.F. and Panou, L. 1982. "Cerebral Organization in Bilingual and Deaf Subjects". D. Rogers and J.A. Sloboda, eds. *The Acquisition of Symbolic Skills*. New York: Plenum Press. 511-518.

Sewell, D.F. and Panou, L. 1983. "Visual Field Asymmetries for Verbal and Dot Localization Tasks in Monolingual and Bilingual Subjects". *Brain and Language* 18. 28-34.

Shanon, B. 1982. "Lateralization Effects in the Perception of Hebrew and English Words". *Brain and Language* 17. 107-123.

Silverberg, R. and Gordon, H.W. 1979. "Differential Aphasia in Two Bilingual Individuals". *Neurology* 29. 51-55.

Simon, T.J. and Sussman, H.M. 1987. "The Dual Task Paradigm: Speech Dominance or Manual Dominance?" *Neuropsychologia* 25. 559-569.

Soares, C. 1982. "Converging Evidence for Left Hemisphere Language Lateralization in Bilinguals". *Neuropsychologia* 20. 653-659.

Soares, C. 1984. "Left-Hemisphere Language Lateralization in Bilinguals: Use of the Concurrent Activities Paradigm". *Brain and Language* 23. 86-96.

Solin, D. 1989. "The Systematic Misrepresentation of Bilingual-Crossed Aphasia Data and its Consequences". *Brain and Language* 36. 92-116.

Spielman, R.S., Migliazza, E.C. and Neel, J.V. 1974. "Regional Linguistic and Genetic Differences among Yanomani Indians". *Science* 184. 637-644.

Spiller Bosatra, E., Darò, V., Fabbro, F. and Bosatra, A. 1989. "Cerebral Lateralization for Languages and Learning of Simultaneous Interpreting". *Suppl. N° 2 European Journal of Neuroscience* 11.31, 30.
Spiller Bosatra, E., Darò, V., Fabbro, F. and Bosatra, A. 1990. "Audio-Phonological and Neuropsychological Aspects of Simultaneous Interpretation: Role of Auditory Shadowing". *Scandinavian Audiology* 19. 81-87.
Streifler, M. and Hofman, S. 1976. "Sinistral Mirror Writing and Reading after Brain Concussion in a Bi-Systemic (Oriento-Occidental) Polyglot". *Cortex* 12. 356-364.
Studdert-Kennedy, M., Shankweiler, D. 1970. "Hemispheric Specialization for Speech Perception". *The Journal of the Acoustical Society of America* 48. 579-595.
Sugishita, M., Iwata, M., Toyokura, Y., Yoshida, M. and Yamada, R. 1978. "Reading of Ideograms and Phonograms in Japanese Patients after Partial Commissurotomy". *Neuropsychologia* 16. 417-426.
Sugishita, M., Toyokura, Y., Yoshioka, M. and Yamada, R. 1980. "Unilateral Agraphia after Section of the Posterior Half of the Truncus of the Corpus Callosum". *Brain and Language* 9. 215-225.
Sussman, H.M. 1971. "The Laterality Effect in Lingual-Auditory Tracking". *The Journal of the Acoustical Society of America* 49. 1874-1880.
Sussman, H.M. 1989. "A Reassessment of the Time-Sharing Paradigm with ANCOVA". *Brain and Language* 37. 514-520.
Sussman, H.M., Franklin, P., Simon, T. 1982. "Bilingual Speech: Bilateral Control?" *Brain and Language* 15. 125-142.
Tassinari, G., Fabbro, F. and Berlucchi, G. 1988. "Effects of Attention Allocation on the Naming of Eccentrically Flashed Digits". *Proceedings of the 4th Conference of the International Organization of Psychophysiology* (Prague, September 12-17), 134.
Taylor-Sarno, M. 1981. *Acquired Aphasia*. New York: Academic Press.
Tenhouten, W.D. 1981. "Lateralized and Generalized EEG Alpha Effects of Sociolinguistically Varied Narratives Heard in Mandarine Chinese and English". *Reports of the 76th Annual Meeting of the American Sociological Association*, Toronto, Canada.
Treisman, A. 1965. "The Effects of Redundancy and Familiarity on Translation and Repeating Back a Foreign and a Native Language". *British Journal of Psychology* 56. 369-379.
Trevarthen, C. 1984. "Hemispheric Specialization". J.M. Brookhart *et al. Handbook of Physiology: The Nervous System. Sensory System, vol. III*, Bethesda: American Physiological Society. 1129-1190.
Tsunoda, T. 1971. "The Difference of the Cerebral Dominance of Vowel Sounds among Different Languages". *J. Auditory Res.* 11. 305-314.

Tsunoda, T. 1975. "Functional Differences between Right and Left Cerebral Hemispheres Detected by the Key-Tapping Method". *Brain and Language* 2. 152-170.

Vaid, J. 1983. "Bilingualism and Brain Lateralization". S. Segalowitz, ed. *Language Functions and Brain Organization*. New York: Academic Press. 315-339.

Vaid, J. 1987. "Visual Field Asymmetries for Rhyme and Syntactic Category Judgments in Monolinguals and Fluent Early and Late Bilinguals". *Brain and Language* 30. 263-277.

Vaid, J. and Corina, D. 1989. "Visual Field Asymmetries in Numerical Size Comparison of Digits, Words and Signs" *Brain and Language* 36. 117-126.

Vaid, J. and Lambert, W.E. 1979. "Differential Cerebral Involvement in the Cognitive Functioning of Bilinguals". *Brain and Language* 8. 92-110.

Veyrac, G.J. 1931. *Etude de l'Aphasie Chez les Sujets Polyglottes*. Thèse pour le Doctorat en Médicine: Paris.

Vignolo, L.A. 1982. "Le Sindromi Afasiche". E. De Renzi and G. Gainotti, eds. *Neuropsicologia Clinica*. Milano: Franco Angeli. 11-42.

Vocate, D.R. 1984. "Differential Cerebral Speech Lateralization in Crow Indian and Anglo Children". *Neuropsychologia* 22. 487-494.

Voinescu, I., Vish, E., Sirian, S. and Maretsis, M. 1977. "Aphasia in Polyglots". *Brain and Language* 4. 165-176.

Walters, J. and Zatorre, R.J. 1978. "Laterality Differences for Word Identification in Bilinguals". *Brain and Language* 6. 158-167.

Waggoner, C. 1987. *Brain Mapping in Second Language Learning*. University of Kansas. [Unpublished Doctoral Dissertation.]

Watamori, T.S. and Sasanuma, S. 1978. "The Recovery Process of Two English-Japanese Bilingual Aphasics". *Brain and Language* 6. 127-140.

Wechsler, A. 1977. "Dissociative Alexia". *Archives of Neurology* 34. 257.

Weinreich, U. 1953. *Languages in Contact*. New York: Linguistic Circle of New York.

Whorf, B.L. 1970. *Linguaggio, Pensiero e Realtà*. Torino: Boringhieri.

Yoshizaki, K. and Hatta, T. 1987. "Shift of Visual Field Advantage by Learning Experience of Foreign Words". *Neuropsychologia* 25. 589-592.

Zatorre, R.J. 1989. "On the Representation of Multiple Languages in the Brain: Old Problems and New Directions". *Brain and Language* 26. 127-147.

Simultaneous Interpreters: One Ear May Be Better Than Two

Sylvie Lambert
University of Ottawa

1. Introduction

Experienced conference interpreters tend to interpret with one headphone placed squarely on one ear and with the other headphone either slightly or completely off the other ear. To explain these proclivities, some claim that the headphone set feels too tight if both ears remain covered; others say that releasing one ear in this fashion enables them to monitor their output for both content and volume while interpreting; others simply state that they "feel better" or "hear better" under such circumstances. Whatever the case may be, only a handful of studies have examined simultaneous interpreters' headphone habits. This paper therefore, purports to review some of the recent laterality studies carried out on conference interpreters when asked to shadow, interpret simultaneously and perform certain finger-tapping exercises when processing information presented to their left ear, their right ear, and both ears.

Lawson (1967) made a brief reference to the use of one ear versus the other when interpreting simultaneously, but the main concern of her paper was selective attention to discourse, in other words, the ability to attend selectively to some aspects of verbal input while rejecting others, rather than the laterality of the more proficient ear.

In a description of the tasks, procedures, and environment of simultaneous interpreters, Parsons (1978) queried her subjects' use of headphones and reported that "... four out of five said they normally kept an earphone off one ear, either completely or a little. Two said it was the right ear, one specified the left ear, one reported alternating, and one did not respond".

More recently, a questionnaire designed for simultaneous interpreters (Lambert & Lambert 1985) asked specific questions as to gender, handedness (based on Oldfield's 1971 Edinburgh Handedness Inventory), mother-tongue, dominant language (L1), second-language (L2), age of acquisition of L2, ear preference when speaking on the telephone, and ear preference when interpreting.

The fact that so little is mentioned about the use of one ear versus the other when examining simultaneous interpretation is somewhat surprising, given that relying on one ear over the other is of considerable importance. The choice, albeit an unconscious one, is directly related to the processing of information via the left or the right hemisphere of the brain (Broadbent 1954; Kimura 1963). Lately, functional asymmetry of the cerebral hemispheres (i.e. processing information via one hemisphere as opposed to the other) has been receiving more and more attention and converging evidence implicates left hemisphere preference in verbal performance and right hemisphere preference for non-verbal performance among male, right-handed unilinguals (for extensive reviews, see Hall & Lambert 1988; Vaid 1983).

Of significant importance to conference interpreters, however, is the fact that a growing body of research now seems to suggest that the brains of individuals who speak more than one language may be functionally different from those of unilinguals (Sussman, Franklin, & Simon 1982; Vaid 1983). Monolingual children, for example, show highly asymmetric lateralization effects in favour of left hemisphere superiority, whereas bilingual children revealed tendencies towards more symmetric hemispheric language laterality because the right hemisphere was more prominently brought into play (for extensive reviews, see Hall & Lambert 1988; Vaid 1983; Vaid & Genesee 1980).

Although the literature on the functional asymmetry of cerebral hemispheres may seem either irrelevant or baffling to the interpretation profession at first glance, interpreter-trainers and cognitive psychologists cannot afford to ignore this informative research that addresses the possibility that distinct lateralization patterns may characterize individuals who speak more than one language and, by extension, both translators and interpreters. This information, therefore, could be of significant importance and interest in the selection and subsequent training of simultaneous interpreters.

2. Earedness and Shadowing

One study carried out at the University of Ottawa (Kraushaar & Lambert 1987) set out to compare trainee-interpreters' shadowing ability in both their first and second languages when shadowing verbal stimuli presented to either one ear or the other. Shadowing is a paced, auditory tracking task which involves the immediate vocalization of auditorily presented stimuli, that is, word-for-word repetition, in the same language, of a message presented to a subject through a set of headphones. The shadowing technique has often been used by cognitive psychologists as a means of studying selective attention in humans: briefly, subjects hear one message in one ear, and a different message in the other ear, and are asked to ignore one message while attending to the other for subsequent recall. But shadowing is also frequently used in various schools of interpretation as part of the training method with beginning interpreters who first need to learn to listen and speak simultaneously in the same language before beginning to interpret from one language into another.

Although most interpreters are familiar with the shadowing technique, it is important to mention at this stage that Norman (1976) distinguishes two types of shadowing, namely phonemic shadowing, where subjects repeat each sound as they hear it, without waiting for the completion of a propositional phrase or "chunk", or even a completed word, so that the shadower remains right "on top of" the speaker. The other form of shadowing is known as phrase shadowing, where subjects repeat the speech at longer latencies, more precisely from 250 milliseconds upwards, and where shadowers wait for a semantic chunk before vocalizing, in the same way that a simultaneous interpreter would lag behind the original speaker. In a study by Chistovitch, Aliakrinskii and Abilian (1960), subjects who shadowed at longer latencies, in other words, with a greater lag, showed superior recall of the shadowed material. It was hypothesized that they used this lag to analyze the semantic content of the material as opposed to those who shadowed without understanding. In the Kraushaar and Lambert experiment, subjects were asked to shadow phonemically so as to minimize the lag as much as possible thus decreasing their chances of analyzing the content of the incoming message, and reducing to a minimum any interfering variables such as deeper forms of semantic processing.

If we are to assume that an interpreter removes one headphone from one ear, for whatever reason, the questions that come to mind are whether or not the same ear is consistently released. Consistent releasing of one ear as opposed to the other could shed light on certain cognitive processes involved during both shadowing and simultaneous interpretation. Other variables such as subjects' handedness, telephone habits (i.e. whether the receiver is consistently placed on the same ear, and whether this ear is the preferred ear during simultaneous interpretation), language dominance and language employed during shadowing (L1 as opposed to L2), were also examined in this study.

Results indicated that each both Francophone and Anglophone shadowers made proportionally more shadowing errors in L2 than in L1. Types of shadowing errors included inversions, contractions, substitutions, hesitations, repetitions, stumbling, mispronunciations, additions and omissions. (Specific examples and the detailed procedure of the experiment are given elsewhere. See Kraushaar & Lambert 1987).

Subjects were also broken down into *early* vs. *late* bilinguals, depending on thc age at which they had acquired their second language. Although the sample sizes were too small to obtain any statistical significance, certain interesting trends did emerge: results suggested that *late* bilinguals made fewer errors in L1, irrespective of ear of input, than *early* bilinguals, who made nearly twice as many errors. However, *late* bilinguals tripled the number of errors in L2, irrespective of ear of input, while *early* bilinguals only doubled theirs.

There was also a tendency for *late* bilinguals to process L1 material more effectively through the right ear (i.e., via the left hemisphere) whereas *early* bilinguals exhibited no such ear preference. Instead, *early* bilinguals scored somewhat better on L2 material when shadowing material presented to their left ear.

In summary, when shadowing in one's L2, subjects are free to process the incoming information through either or both ears. However, there is a suggestion that when shadowing one's mother tongue, L1, subjects process incoming speeches better through the right ear.

The fact that processing incoming information through one ear versus the other may influence performance for a relatively "shallow" task such as shadowing, in the sense that less semantic processing is involved as compared to simultaneous interpretation, raises the question as to what the results would be following deeper and more meaningful tasks such as simultaneous interpretation. In other words, if the performance of a simultaneous interpreter is significantly affected by some interaction of the ear of reception and the language of input (i.e., working *from* or *to* one's L1), then a comprehensive study of such factors might help us not only understand the fascinating process of interpretation but might also entail certain interpreter-training techniques, even possible modifications to headphone design. To this effect, a subsequent experiment was carried out on earedness and simultaneous interpretation.

3. Earedness and Simultaneous Interpretation

3.1. Method

Two twelve-minute long speeches taken from *Hansards* (1984, 1986) were recorded stereophonically at approximately 110 words per minute. One speech was in French, the other in English, and both were welcoming addresses to visiting Heads-of-State, in other words, made no demands on subjects' knowledge of specialized or technical vocabularies.

3.2. Subjects

Twenty-one subjects from the Ottawa area served as subjects and included both beginning interpreters from the two-year Diploma Programme at the University of Ottawa, who had been interpreting for more than six months, as well as professional interpreters working in Ottawa. The breakdown according to sex and language was as follows: 6 female francophones; 6 female anglophones; 2 male francophones; 7 male anglophones.

3.3. Procedure

Although the detailed method and procedure are provided elsewhere (Lambert 1993), one important detail deserves some explanation. Since the experimenter wanted to minimize any bias in the results, it was decided that an incidental learning paradigm would be the best solution: in other words, subjects were not informed of the nature of the experiment beforehand, but were simply told that the experiment involved measuring an interpreter's ability to interpret under different working conditions. It was only after the experiment that subjects were informed of the nature of the experiment and that they were asked to complete the Lambert and Lambert questionnaire (1985) to determine earedness, degree of bilinguality and telephone habits.

To this effect, a special custom-made device (Capello Audio of Ottawa) included a dial which enabled the experimenter to shunt the recorded speeches to one ear or to both ears simultaneously without alerting the subject to this fact. However, in a pilot test, subjects felt that they were unable to hear as well when the message was presented to their non-preferred ear, therefore, an amplifyer was connected to the source speech so that subjects could manipulate the volume at will, to compensate for any loss.

Each twelve-minute long speech was divided into four three-minute segments. The first segment served as a warm-up and was never evaluated. Following the warm-up, and without any interruption in the speech, the experimenter shunted the next three-minute segment to one of three possible directions:

Condition I: both ears simultaneously
Condition II: right ear only
Condition III: left ear only

To facilitate correction of interpreters' output, all subjects' interpretations were transcribed and matched against the original by two independent judges. Interjudge correlation across 21 subjects was .91, both judges blind to subjects' conditions and to the experimental hypotheses. Scoring of interpretation protocols was based on data collected by Henri C. Barik (1975). Briefly put, an interpreter's version may depart from the original in three ways: the interpreter may *omit* some material, *add* some information, or *substitute* material, which, if at considerable variance with the original, may constitute a meaning error. A more detailed description of the procedure followed to arrive at such categorizations can be found elsewhere (Barik 1971).

3.4. Results

Results indicated that *right-handed* subjects (18 subjects of the 21 were right-handed) made significantly *fewer* errors when interpreting a message presented to their *right* hemisphere through their *left* ear ($X = 5.54$; $p < .02$), than to their right ear, or, more arrestingly, to *both ears simultaneously*.

In other words, subjects made significantly *fewer* errors when the message was shunted to *one* ear than to *both* ears simultaneously (Wilcoxon matched-pairs signed ranks test $W=46$, for $n=21$).

If we compare these results with those obtained for shadowing (Kraushaar & Lambert 1987) which suggested that when shadowing in one's L2, the ear of reception does not appear to matter, be it one ear or both ears, but that when shadowing in one's L1, speech may be better processed when directed to the right ear, results for simultaneous interpretation indicate that when interpreting from L2 to L1, right-handed individuals function more efficiently with a left-ear input, and that processing incoming messages through one ear is more effective than through two ears.

The discovery of such a left-ear preference for interpreting verbal information is difficult to reconcile with the dichotic listening literature which clearly suggests that, for right-handed individuals, the right ear (i.e. the left hemisphere) would be chosen over the left ear whenever verbal information is to be processed (Broadbent 1954; Kimura 1963). So how do we explain the fact that interpreters performed significanly better when they interpreted via the left ear, or via both ears simultaneously, but *not* via the right ear?

One possible explanation may lie in the nature of the tasks involved during simultaneous interpretation. Simply put, from a cognitive psychologist's point of view, interpreters are basically involved in two concurrent activities: listening and speaking, or decoding and encoding. Both activities are verbal and hence one would expect a favouring of right-ear-to-left hemisphere route for both tasks, which may be neurologically impossible. But since the results in the interpretation experiment revealed a marked preference for the left-ear-to right-hemisphere route, it could be that interpreters favour the right-ear-to-left-hemisphere route to monitor their own output.

If we are to assume that both decoding and encoding activities cannot be performed simultaneously through the same ear or the same hemisphere, the fact that such a high percentage of interpreters release one headphone may be telling us that interpreters consciously or unconsciously use their left hemisphere (right ear) for what they consider to be the more critical of the two concurrent tasks, namely monitoring his\her own output, and the right hemisphere (left ear) for processing the incoming information.

These results raise an interesting issue, and one that is amenable to further research: what happens when an interpreter works from L1 to L2? Will the same ear preference remain? Will the interpreter release the same ear?

A second explanation may be that bilingual subjects make more use of their right hemisphere than monolingual individuals who serve as subjects in most dichotic listening experiments. Of the many factors found in language acquisition histories, the age of onset of bilingualism has provided the least equivocal results in behavioural studies (Genesee 1977). Bilinguals who acquired their second language at infancy appear to employ a different strategy in processing verbal material than that used by bilinguals who acquired their language later in life. The difference appears to be reflected in the language processing strategy adopted by the two groups: those who became bilingual at infancy or in early childhood appear to use an analytic, semantic approach to verbal material. In contrast, those bilinguals who acquired their second language during adolescence or thereafter, tend to adopt a different approach to verbal material, one that relies more on extralinguistic (e.g. physical) features of the linguistic stimuli.

By extension, therefore, it could be that simultaneous interpreters, as bilinguals, employ different strategies in processing verbal material such as using the right hemisphere to a greater extent, than, say, monolingual individuals.

4. Finger-tapping Experiments

There are various ways to study laterality, earedness and hemispheric specialization in humans, ranging from neurosurgical testing by way of sodium amytal injections into the carotid, electroencephalography, to dichotic listening and the dual-task or time-share paradigm (Kinsbourne & Cook 1971). Obviously, dichotic listening and dual-task testing are more amenable for studying simultaneous interpreters. The most recent experimentation on simultaneous interpretation is being carried out by Gran and Fabbro (1988) in Trieste, Italy, and by Schweda-Nicholson (personal communication) at the University of Delaware.

The dual-task or time-share paradigm was developed by Kinsbourne and Cook in 1971 to study cerebral lateralization for some superior cognitive functions such as speech recognition and production. Briefly, the dual-task procedure requires a subject to tap a key as rapidly as possible while simultaneously speaking. This key is connected to a digital counter which records the exact number of finger taps produced by the subject as well as any disruption while doing so.

During the experiment, subjects are instructed to press the key as quickly as possible, first with their right index finger for example, (the right hand being controlled by the left hemisphere), then with their left index finger (controlled by the right hemisphere). At the same time, subjects are asked to perform a concurrent verbal task, such as reading out loud, reciting a series of words, shadowing, or interpreting simultaneously. As a control, subjects are also asked to finger tap while remaining silent. The number of taps recorded when the verbal task is present is then compared to the number of taps recorded when the subject is silent, as well as the number of taps produced by the left finger vs. the right finger.

Any disruption in the finger tapping rate or any large discrepancy between the number of finger taps by the left finger compared to the right finger indicates that some type of interference occurred and tells the experimenter which hemisphere was involved during the verbal activity. So by analyzing the degree of interference, known as percentage interference, we obtain the following type of information: in monolingual right-handers, a verbal task causes greater interference on right-hand tapping (left hemisphere) than on left-hand tapping (right hemisphere), a finding which is interpreted as a reflection of the demands made on left-hemisphere processing capacities (Kinsbourne and Cook 1971; Hicks 1975).

The same technique has recently been extended to French immersion students (Hall & Lambert 1988) who also used the dual-task procedure and found significantly greater disruption with right-hand tapping, presumably indicating similarly high levels of left hemisphere involvement.

Taking it one step closer to simultaneous interpretation, Albert and Obler (1978) pointed out that studies should be conducted on cerebral asymmetries during simultaneous interpretation. They suggest that cerebral lateralization during simultaneous intepretation from L1 to L2 may be different than interpretation from L2 to L1. To this effect, experiments were conducted by Laura Gran and Franco Fabbro (1987; 1988) at the University of Trieste. Their results indicated that there were no statistically significant differences displayed by the two hands of their subjects which suggests that there is concurrent participation of both cerebral hemispheres in the linguistic functions involved in simultaneous interpretation.

But Gran and Fabbro (1988) did find that fourth-year students, while maintaining left-hemisphere dominance for their mother-tongue (Italian), showed significant right-hemisphere superiority for English as compared to first-year students and monolinguals. Gran adds that if one considers the highly demanding task of simultaneous interpretation, it emerges that a bilateral cerebral representation of languages enhances the efficiency and possibly, the resistance to fatigue among professional interpreters.

Given the unexpected results found in Lambert's (1988) experiment on earedness and simultaneous interpretation, whereby right-handed interpreters performed better when processing information via one ear than via two ears, and that the preferred ear was overwhelmingly the left ear, an extention of the finger-tapping experiment is warranted to confirm the earlier findings.

To this effect, interpreter-subjects will be asked to interpret under the same three conditions, namely via the left ear, then the right ear, followed by both ears, while simultaneously tapping a key as quickly as possible with the left index finger, followed by the right index finger. It is hoped that these results will corroborate the unexpected finding that for simultaneous interpretation, one ear may be better than two.

References

Albert, M.L. and Obler, L.K. 1978. *The Bilingual Brain: Neuropsychological and Neurolinguistic Aspects of Bilingualism.* New York, London: Academic Press.

Barik, H.C. 1971. "A Description of Various Types of Omissions, Additions and Errors of Translation Encountered in Simultaneous Interpretation". *META* XVI. 199.

Barik, H.C. 1975. "Simultaneous Interpretation: Qualitative and Linguistic Data". *Language and Speech* 18. 272-297.

Broadbent, D.E. 1954. "The Role of Auditory Localization in Attention and Memory Span". *Journal of Experimental Psychology* 47. 191-196.

Chistovitch, L.A., Aliakrinskii, A.A., and Abilian, V.A. 1960. "Time Delays in Speech Perception". *Questions of Psychology* 1. 64-70.

Genesee, F. 1977. "Summary and Discussion". P.A. Hornby, ed. *Bilingualism: Psychological, Social and Educational Implications*. New York: Academic Press. 147-164.

Gran, L., and Fabbro, F. 1987. "Cerebral Lateralization in Simultaneous Interpreting". *Proceedings of the Annual American Translators' Association (ATA) Conference*. Albuquerque, New Mexico, October 8-11.

Gran, L., and Fabbro, F. 1988. "The Role of Neuroscience in the Teaching of Interpretation". *The Interpreters' Newsletter* 1. 23-41.

Hall, G., and Lambert, W.E., 1988. "French Immersion and Hemispheric Language Processing: A Dual-Task Study". *Canadian Journal of Behavioural Science* 20. 1-14.

Hansard (1984; 1986) House of Commons Debates; Official Report (Hansard), Vol. 128, No. 204, First Session, 33rd Parliament, Tuesday, May 8, 1984; Monday, January 13, 1986. Speeches welcoming Prime Minister Nakasone of Japan and Mexican President, Miguel de la Madrid Hurtado.

Hicks, R, 1975. "Intra-Hemispheric Response Competition Between Vocal and Unimanual Performance in Normal Adult Human Males". *Journal of Comparative Physiological Psychology* 89, 50-60.
Kimura, D. 1963. "Speech Lateralization in Young Children as Determined by an Auditory Test". *Journal of Comparative Physiological Psychology* 56. 899-902.
Kinsbourne, M., and Cook, J. 1971. "Generalized and Lateralized Effects of Concurrent Verbalization on a Unimanual Skill". *Quarterly Journal of Experimental Psychology* 23, 341-345.
Kraushaar, B., and Lambert, S. 1987. "Shadowing Proficiency According to Ear of Input and Type of Bilinguality". *Bulletin of the Canadian Association of Applied Linguistics* 9:1. 17-31.
Lambert, S. 1993. "The Effect of Ear of Information Reception on the Proficiency of Simultaneous Interpretation". *META* XXXVIII. 198-211.
Lambert S., and Lambert, W.E. 1985. "Physiology: a Questionnaire". *META* XXX, 1. 68-72.
Lawson, E.A. 1967. "Attention and Simultaneous Translation". *Language and Speech*. 10. 29-35.
Norman, D.A. 1976. *Memory and Attention*. New York: Wiley.
Oldfield, R.C. 1971. "The Assessment and Analysis of Handedness: The Edinburgh Inventory". *Neuropsychologia* 9. 97-113.
Parsons, H.M. 1978. "Human Factors Approach to Simultaneous Interpretation". D. Gerver and W.H. Sinaiko, eds. *Language, Interpretation, and Communication*. New York: Plenum Press. 315-322.
Sussman, H., Franklin, P., and Simon, T. 1982. "Bilingual Speech: Bilateral Control?" *Brain and Language* 15. 125-142.
Vaid, J. 1983. "Bilingualism and Brain Lateralization". S.J. Segalowitz, ed. In *Language Functions and Brain Organization*. New York, Academic Press.
Vaid, J., and Genesee, F. 1980. "Neuropsychological Approaches to Bilingualism". *Canadian Journal of Psychology* 34. 417-445.

Lateralization for Shadowing vs. Interpretation: A Comparison of Interpreters with Bilingual and Monolingual Controls

Adele Green
Youngstown State University

Jyotsna Vaid
Texas A & M University

Nancy Schweda-Nicholson
University of Delaware

Nancy White
Youngstown State University

Richard Steiner
University of Akron

1. Introduction

That the left cerebral hemisphere is specialized for language has been known for over a century. Whether cerebral involvement in language processing differs depending on one's language experience (e.g. knowledge of more than one language) has been investigated in brain-intact users only over the past twenty years (see Vaid & Genesee 1980, Mendelsohn 1989, Vaid & Hall 1991 for reviews). Although the meta-analytic review by Vaid and Hall (1991) pointed to some interesting patterns, e.g., that early rather than late onset of bilingualism may be associated with less left lateralization (Vaid & Lambert 1979; Vaid 1984), the literature as a whole is difficult to summarize. This is in part because, unlike monolinguals who are fairly homogenous in when, how and how well they acquire their language, bilinguals differ markedly on all of these parameters, making broad generalizations difficult and even, perhaps, unwarranted. However, even circumscribed generalizations are complicated by the fact that contradictory findings (and, in some cases, predictions) characterize the literature. For example, some studies report no differential laterality effects attributable to bilingualism, while others claim that bilinguals are less lateralized in one language relative to the other, or in either language relative to monolinguals or other bilingual groups. Similarly, some investigators have hypothesized increasing left hemisphere involvement in the second language (L2) with increasing L2 proficiency, whereas others have proposed less left hemisphere involvement (relative to monolinguals) in either language of proficient bilinguals (for further discussion, see Vaid 1983).

To add to the complexity, many of the studies were done without sufficient regard to what we would now consider important methodological concerns (e.g., Obler, Zatorre, Galloway & Vaid 1982; Green & Vaid 1986). Very few studies, for example, have included necessary monolingual or bilingual control groups or used systematic criteria for screening bilingual subjects. The use of ecologically-valid linguistic tasks has been the exception rather than the norm and cognitive processing demands of the tasks used have been ignored in interpreting the outcomes. Findings of no differences between groups or bilateral hemisphere effects have tended to be accepted at face value rather than in terms of possible ceiling or floor effects; indeed, rigorous and thorough statistical analyses have rarely been applied to the data.

2. Present Research

The present research was designed in light of the above limitations characterizing the bilingual laterality literature. The aim of this research was to explore the neuropsychological underpinnings of two linguistic abilities, namely *shadowing* (i.e., rapid repetition of on-line verbal input) and *simultaneous interpretation/paraphrasing*, in a group of professional interpreters, individually paired with closely matched non-interpreter bilingual and monolingual controls. The individual matching process not only makes this a unique laterality study, but also maximizes the confidence one can have in outcomes when groups with different types of experiences are compared. Various outcomes of this project have previously been reported elsewhere (Green, Schweda-Nicholson, Vaid, & White 1989a; Green, Schweda-Nicholson, Vaid & White 1989b; Green, Schweda-Nicholson, Vaid, White & Steiner 1990; Vaid, Green, Schweda-Nicholson & White 1989). The present report synthesizes the previous reports and brings a more complex multivariate statistical analysis to bear on the data.

By including monolinguals, non-interpreter bilinguals and professional interpreters, we are in a position to determine whether cerebral asymmetries for interpretation or shadowing are differentially influenced by a) knowledge of more than one language and/or by b) skill or expertise for the task.

2.1. Professional Interpreters

Professional interpreters are known to be highly practiced in simultaneous interpretation, a task that is not a mere literal translation of input, but onc that involves using linguistic and extralinguistic elements to provide equivalent meaning (Schweda-Nicholson 1987). Simultaneous interpreters have acquired considerable expertise in using various encoding strategies such as chunking and paraphrasing the input, creating imageable keywords of main ideas, and continuously making predictions while concurrently monitoring and reviewing incoming information (Moser 1978). As such, interpreters have been found to simultaneously listen and speak 65% of the time with lag time between input and output ranging from 2 to 8 words, depending on the difficulty of the material (Gerver 1975). Mastery of interpretation skills enable professional interpreters to proficiently decode meaning in one language while reorganizing the input for the concurrent production of speech in another language (Moser 1978).

We wondered whether professional interpreters would be lateralized differently from matched bilingual controls on a task involving interpretation. There is evidence from a PET scan study with monolinguals that task ability as well as task type influence the level and locus of cerebral activation (Haier, Siegel, Nuechterlein, Hazlett, Wu, Paek, Browning & Buchsbaum 1988). Alternatively, it is possible that professional interpreters and non-interpreter bilinguals would be lateralized similarly for interpretation inasmuch as both groups have experience manipulating two languages in daily life. Consistent with this possibility is evidence from a dual-task study that found a bilateral effect for mathematical calculations in both advanced students and experts of abacus, but a left hemisphere effect for beginning students and naive controls (Hatta & Ikeda 1988).

For our study, a time-sharing interference procedure was chosen to assess laterality patterns. We felt that this paradigm was particularly appropriate for use with interpreters given that professional interpreters engage in time sharing in their normal course of work. Moreover, unlike the more frequently used dichotic listening or tachistoscoping viewing methods, laterality studies using a time-sharing methodology, being relatively recent, have been more careful to avoid methodological artifacts.

2.2. Description of Paradigm

The time-sharing paradigm used in the present research was the verbal/manual concurrent activities procedure (see Kinsbourne & Cook 1971). In this procedure, subjects are directed to tap on a telegraph key as rapidly as possible, using their right or left index finger, first alone in a baseline control condition and then again while performing a cognitive task. Lateralization is inferred by comparing the extent to which tapping of each hand is disrupted when the number of taps produced during concurrent activity is subtracted from the number of taps produced during baseline tapping trials. Since the dominant hand generally produces more taps in a given time interval than the nondominant hand in the baseline conditions, it is necessary to use a measure of interference that mathematically neutralizes the dexterity of the dominant hand.

2.3. Interpretive Issues

The method used in the present study is the calculation of a simple difference score, where the variable being analyzed is subtracted directly from the baseline contributing variable. When employed with a time-sharing paradigm, the method allows the direct use of raw scores within the framework of a multivariate general linear models (MGLM) approach to the analysis of left vs. right hand tapping disruption. Moreover, with all relevant combinations of grouping variables compared, no important information is lost and the analysis of outcomes is more refined. With this approach, left hemisphere lateralization is inferred when the tapping of right hand baseline tapping minus right hand concurrent tapping (right intrahand interference) is significantly greater than left intrahand interference.

3. Previous Time-Sharing Studies with Bilinguals

To date, eleven time-sharing laterality studies have used bilinguals (Corina & Vaid 1989; Corina, Vaid & Bellugi 1992; Gran & Fabbro 1990; Green 1986; Furtado & Webster 1991; Hall & Lambert 1988; Hynd, Teeter & Stewart 1980; Sanchez, Manga, Babecki & de Tembleque 1988; Simon & Sussman 1987; Soares 1984; Sussman, Franklin & Simon 1982). Of these, two have studied interpreters. Using a concurrent shadowing and finger tapping procedure with hearing interpreters of American Sign Language (ASL), Corina and Vaid (1989) found greater right than left hand tapping disruption for both languages in both early and late bilinguals. An interpretation task was not included in Corina and Vaid's (1989) study. Gran and Fabbro (1990) who *did* use an interpretation task (with proverbs as the input) in their sample of 14 female Italian-English advanced students of interpretation reported no significant hand differences in tapping disruption. These findings are not incongruous when attentional focus is considered. Steiner, Green and White (1992) and Green, Steiner and White (1993) show that lateralized effects for ideational aspects of cognitive tasks (i.e., representing conscious manipulation of continuous deliberative thought) are different from those produced by nondirected vocalized tasks. In left- and right-handed (monolingual) subjects, nonideational reading aloud and shadowing resulted in lateralized effects reflecting manual dominance, with right-handers being lateralized in the left hemisphere and left-handers right lateralized. Thus, a left lateralized effect for repetition of oral information in bilingual subjects (Corina & Vaid 1989) is consistent with outcomes of studies employing nonideational vocalized tasks.

In addition to the above studies, two studies have examined proficiency in shadowing (Kraushaar & Lambert 1987) and proficiency in interpretation (Lambert, 1993) as a function of whether the input was presented bilaterally or unilaterally, to the left or the right ear [see also Fabbro & Gran 1991]. Kraushaar and Lambert (1987) reported that interpreters tended to make fewer errors while shadowing input in the dominant language presented to the right ear, particularly if they had acquired their second language after the age of 7. Early bilinguals either showed no differences in shadowing accuracy or showed a left ear superiority. In a similar study with interpreters performing a simultaneous interpretation task, Lambert (1993) found fewer errors when the input from L2 to L1 was presented to one ear rather than to both ears and, in particular, for left ear presentation.

Taken together, the existing studies point to a differential pattern of lateralization for shadowing and for interpretation in professional interpreters and/or advanced students of interpretation. Unfortunately, since none of the studies described above considered *both* tasks within the same subject sample or included bilingual or unilingual controls for either task, it is unclear whether the results obtained are subject-specific (i.e., unique to interpreters) or task-specific. Akin to results of studies with interpreters, clinical and experimental research with monolinguals, including studies using a time-sharing procedure, has shown them to be lateralized in the left hemisphere for shadowing tasks (Carnahan, Elliott & Lee 1986; Corina & Vaid 1989; Ikeda 1987; Lackner & Shattuck-Huffnagel 1982: Sabat 1979; Woods, Hillyard & Hansen 1984).

At the same time, shadowing appears to be a rapidly automatized task with minimal attentional demands and, as such, is less affected by concurrent activity than tasks requiring continuous reorganization of input. Studies with bilinguals and interpreters have shown the interpretation task to impose greater cognitive demands and to be more easily disrupted than shadowing (Gerver 1974 a,b; Treisman 1965). Similarly, in monolinguals, interference is much greater when the concurrent task requires ongoing monitoring and simultaneous conversion of input, than with a shadowing task (Waters, Komoda & Arbuckle 1985).

4. Hypotheses

In our own research, we compared the performance of professional interpreters with age, education and gender-matched bilingual and monolingual controls. Subjects were tested on a shadowing task and on an interpretation task (monolinguals were given a paraphrasing task).

The following hypotheses were examined:

1) Tapping interference will be greater for the cognitively more demanding task of paraphrasing/interpreting than for shadowing.

2) The two tasks will be differentially lateralized, with shadowing producing greater right hand tapping disruption (left lateralization) relative to that for paraphrasing or interpretation.

3) To the extent that formal training and acquired expertise in interpretation results in differential processing strategies, the pattern of lateralization for interpretation will differ across the two bilingual groups - the groups should not, however, differ in their shadowing performance. Specifically, interpreters

might be expected to show more right hemisphere involvement for interpreting, relative to bilingual controls.

4) Compared with bilinguals, the monolingual group should be more left lateralized in general.

5. Method

5.1. Subjects

Sixteen childhood bilingual interpreters were closely matched to noninterpreter bilinguals and monolinguals, such that each matched control was of the same sex, had within one year of the same postsecondary schooling, and was within 5 years of age as the interpreter. There were an equal number of males and females per group and all subjects were strongly right-handed, as assessed by a standard questionnaire which examined the extent to which either or both hands are used to perform five common activities, with 25 being the score for those who reported always performing all five activities with the right hand (Bryden 1977). Table 1 presents a summary of the background characteristics for each group.

Table 1. *Summary of Background Characteristics for Groups*

Group	*Age*	*No. of Post High School Education*	*Handedness Scores*
Male Childhd. Bil Interpreters			
Mean	40.1	5.3	25
SD	10.9	1.3	0
Male Childhd. Bil Controls			
Mean	40.1	5.4	25
SD	11.3	1.1	0
Male Monolinguals			
Mean			
SD	41.0	5.5	24.9
	10.4	1.3	0.35
Female Childhd. Bil Interpreters			
Mean			
SD	45.4	4.4	23.9
	4	1.7	2.1
Female Childhd. Bil Controls			
Mean	44	4.25	24.6
SD	4.3	1.8	1.1
Female Monolinguals			
Mean	45.5	4.75	25
SD	4.8	1.7	

All bilinguals had learned Spanish as their first language (L1) and English as their second language (L2), before puberty. In addition, they reported using both languages in their daily lives and rated themselves as equally fluent in their two languages on a detailed language questionnaire.

The simultaneous interpreters were drawn from membership lists of professional interpreter organizations from the United Nations and U.S. Department of State staff, freelance contractors, and rosters of federally certified court interpreters. The matched bilingual and monolingual controls were obtained by solicitation of individuals in the Youngstown-Cleveland area who potentially fit the required profile.

5.2. Apparatus

Finger tapping was measured by an electronically designed device connected to tape recorders and headphones (see Green *et al.* 1990, for a complete description).

5.3. Stimuli and Procedure

Passages used for the shadowing and interpretation/paraphrasing (I/P) tasks were drawn from published speeches in United Nations and U.S. Department of State publications which had both English and Spanish translations. Whereas these speeches are typical of what an interpreter is likely to encounter in his/her work, the particular segments selected contained content with which the lay person would be familiar. These included, for example, the status of tuberculosis in the world, the U.N.'s position on apartheid, the arms race, Reagan's comments on foreign policy, etc.

Passages for the shadowing task were presented at 130 words per minute while those for the I/P tasks were presented at 100 words per minute (see Gerver 1976). In order to ensure sufficient background knowledge among participants, all subjects were given some general information about each passage as well as a brief training period in which the types of strategies used by interpreters (such as chunking and paraphrasing) were explained. This was followed by a demonstration and elaboration of how to use the specified strategies. Bilinguals were asked to restate the ideas in the target language, while monolinguals were to restate them in English. For the shadowing task, all subjects were to repeat what they heard in the input language. Bilingual subjects performed each task once in English and once in Spanish with equivalent stimuli, whereas monolinguals performed each task twice, enabling an equivalent forms reliability assessment. The manual concurrent task required subjects to rapidly press a key using their right or left index finger for 30 seconds.

For each cognitive task, subjects were instructed to focus on the meaning of what they heard as they would be tested on their comprehension of the input. Each passage was followed by three comprehension questions, one pertaining to the specific theme, another to a specific detail, and a third to an inference. Subjects were instructed to tap as quickly as possible while attending to the meaning of the input they were to shadow or interpret/paraphrase.

5.4. Specific Methodological Considerations

In line with suggestions made by Green and Vaid (1986), Hiscock (1986), Hiscock, Kinsbourne and Green (1990), and Kinsbourne and Hiscock (1983), a number of methodological controls were incorporated into the project design. These included the use of tasks varying in difficulty, appropriate counterbalancing of language, tasks and hand used for tapping, and inclusion of baseline trials for tapping and vocalization, preceding and following the concurrent trials.

6. Results

6.1. Order and Description of Analyses

Three sets of analyses were conducted to examine the lateralized effects inferred from disruption in finger tapping during concurrent activity. The first analysis focused on the performance of the monolingual controls, and the second analysis involved a comparison between the early Spanish/English interpreters and matched bilingual controls. The third analysis compared the monolinguals with the two bilingual groups on both tasks in English.

Similar to the analysis of variance method, in the multivariate procedure, both between and within subject factors are examined. Significant main effects are respectively verified and qualified by univariate F tests and, where appropriate, Tukey's HSD procedure in the analysis of between subject factors and by related multivariate contrasts in the analysis of within subject factors. These tests are all part of the general linear model which provides more refined information and relevant insights.

6.2. Analyses of the Monolingual Group

Table 2 presents the means and standard deviation scores of baseline and concurrent tapping sessions. A main effect for Sex was obtained [$F(1,7)$ $16.09, p = .0007$] indicating that men tapped faster than women (161.0 taps vs.

138.2 taps, respectively). The univariate analyses for each baseline and concurrent condition for hand and task verified that this was so in all baseline conditions and during concurrent shadowing ($p < .03$), but not during concurrent paraphrasing.

Table 2. *Means and Standard Deviations for Control and Concurrent Tapping Scores for Monolinguals for Shadowing and Paraphrasing*

	SHADOWING			
	Left Hand		*Right Hand*	
Group	*Control*	*Concurrent*	*Control*	*Concurre nt*
Females				
Mean	137.2	127.5	161.9	134.9
SD	10.6	13.6	19.3	17.8
Males				
Mean	162.7	144.4	186.7	157.4
SD	14.7	14.9	19.9	16.0
	PARAPHRASING			
Females				
Mean	135.4	122.8	160.2	126.2
SD	6.4	18.3	16.3	24.31
Males				
Mean	162.7	139.9	188.4	147.6
SD	13.3	17.4	22.7	15.7

The analysis of within subject factors, showed an asymmetric effect for Hand [$F (2,13)$ 20.92, $p = .0001$], indicating greater right than left hand interference (i.e., a left hemisphere lateralized effect) for shadowing as well as paraphrasing ($p = .0001$). Finally, there was a trend for paraphrasing to produce more disruption in tapping than shadowing ($p = .089$).

6.3. *Reliability*

Reliability of tapping scores was assessed using the Pearson product moment correlational analyses. Reliability coefficients were all above +.85, even when the group had been enlarged to 24 subjects (Green, Schweda-Nicholson, Vaid & White 1989b).

6.4. Comparison of Early Bilingual Interpreters versus Early Bilingual Controls

Unlike the outcomes in the monolingual multivariate and univariate analyses, no main effects of Sex were obtained in the bilingual comparison. In addition, there was no difference between the bilingual groups in lateralized effect or magnitude of interference (i.e., no main effects for Hand or Group). The means and standard deviations for the bilingual scores are presented in Tables 3 and 4.

Nevertheless, there was a significant interaction between Sex and Group [$F(2,27)$ 3.57, $p = .042$], which was replicated in a subsequent univariate F test [$F(1,28) = 7.35$, $p = .011$]. As can be discerned from Tables 3 and 4, the mean difference between right-and left-hand intrahand interference for male interpreters is minuscule (1.95 taps) for Spanish tasks, but substantial (10.8 taps) for English tasks (a left hemisphere effect). In contrast, for male bilingual controls, the mean interference for Spanish tasks (9.4 taps, a left hemisphere effect) is much larger than that for English tasks (1.4 taps, a bilateral effect). For females, the mean differences between languages for each female group is negligible (fewer than 3 taps).

Table 3. *Means and Standard Deviations for Control and Concurrent Tapping for Bilingual Groups for Shadowing in English and Spanish*

Group	*Eng. (L2)*				*Span. (L1)*			
	Lt Hand		*Rt Hand*		*Lt Hand*		*Rt Hand*	
	Contrl	*Cncrt*	*Contrl*	*Cncrt*	*Contrl*	*Cncrt*	*Contrl*	*Cncrt*
Matched Bil Controls								
Females								
Mean	151.4	143.8	177.7	159.2	150.6	129.2	175.1	144.9
SD	21.8	37.2	23.5	31.7	20.8	26.7	25.5	33.9
Males								
Mean	165.7	139.5	192.9	144.8	163.1	133.1	187.4	148.1
SD	18.7	22.5	14.1	26.2	18.3	27.3	17.9	28.6
Interps.								
Females								
Mean	153.1	124.2	175.1	140.5	152.8	133.1	174.1	145.2
SD	16.1	18.5	15.0	17.2	14.3	13.2	17.5	28.4
Males								
Mean	155.1	125.0	182.4	140.0	156.6	127.5	181.1	139.1
SD	9.9	20.0	10.5	29.5	16.5	25.6	15.7	29.5

Table 4. *Means and Standard Deviations for Control and Concurrent Tapping for Bilingual Groups for Interpretation in English and Spanish*

Group	*Eng. (L2)*				*Span. (L1)*			
	Lt Hand		*Rt Hand*		*Lt Hand*		*Rt Hand*	
	Contr	*Cncrn*	*Contr*	*Cncrn*	*Contr*	*Cncrn*	*Contr*	*Cncrn*
Matched Bil Controls								
Females								
Mean	153.8	122.5	178.6	140.6	150.0	123.1	173.1	142.4
SD	21.8	25.1	28.5	29.7	24.0	19.9	18.9	26.9
Males								
Mean	168.6	128.4	182.3	143.4	164.4	125.1	186.4	135.0
SD	19.7	35.1	28.5	26.5	18.8	28.5	19.0	38.7
Interpreters								
Females								
Mean	156.4	116.0	175.9	138.4	148.5	112.9	170.1	124.9
SD	19.3	20.3	17.7	17.0	12.3	31.6	16.4	40.6
Males								
Mean	154.4	110.5	183.3	130.1	155.0	107.5	176.0	137.5
SD	13.0	25.6	13.0	28.5	10.9	32.2	30.8	16.1

The most interesting outcome emerged in the within group analysis. Table 5 presents the means for intrahand interference for each group. Overall, there was more right- than left intrahand interference [$F(4,26) = 5.07$, $p = .004$]. However, the multivariate contrasts for each task in each language reveal that this outcome of a left hemisphere lateralized effect can only be attributed to the shadowing task, in both English ($p = .002$) and Spanish ($p = .02$). There was no hand difference on the interpretation task in either language ($p = .48$ and $p = .30$), suggesting bilateral hemisphere involvement for interpretation. Moreover, interpretation produced more overall mean tapping interference (39.9 taps) than did shadowing (29.8 taps), [$F(1,28) = 18.65$, $p = .0002$].

Table 5. *Mean Intrahand Difference in Tapping for Childhood Bilingual Interpreters and Matched Controls for Shadowing and Interpretation/Paraphrasing*

	SHADOWING			
Group	*English (L2)*		*Spanish (L1)*	
	Lt Hand	*Rt Hand*	*Lt Hand*	*Rt Hand*
Interpreters				
Mean	29.5	38.6	24.4	35.4
SD	19.0	28.5	20.0	33.8
Bil Controls				
Mean	16.9	33.3	25.6	34.8
SD	21.8	27.0	22.8	27.7
Monolinguals				
Mean	14.0	28.2	-----	-----
SD	12.0	12.0	-----	-----
		INTERP./ PARAPH.		
Interpreters				
Mean	42.1	45.4	41.6	41.9
SD	26.6	30.8	28.5	34.4
Bil Controls				
Mean	35.8	38.5	33.1	41.1
SD	24.2	28.1	23.1	29.7
Monolinguals				
Mean	17.7	37.4	-----	-----
SD	14.6	16.8	-----	-----

6.5. *Comparison of Bilinguals and Monolinguals on Tasks in English*

When bilingual groups were compared directly with the monolingual group on their task performance in English, there was a Group effect, [F (8,78) = 206, p = .050]. Subsequent univariate F tests revealed that the group differences were restricted to left hand interference for shadowing (p=.04) and Interpretation/ Paraphrasing--I/P-- (p = .01). Multiple comparisons disclosed what is summarized and can be observed in Table 5, namely, that interpreters were different from monolinguals for left hand intrahand interference in both tasks ($p = .05$), but bilingual controls were not different from monolinguals or interpreters.

Results also revealed only a marginal effect for a difference between groups in lateralized effect ($p = .10$). However, outcomes of exploratory univariate F tests suggested that groups were different in lateralized effects for the I/P task [$F(2,42) = 3.51$, $p = .039$], but not for the shadowing task. Tukey's HSD procedure indicated no significant differences among the group means. However, a single degree of freedom contrast, comparing the monolingual group to the two bilingual groups combined, did reveal a significant difference in hand asymmetry [$F(1,42) = 7.01$, $p = .011$]. This indicated that bilinguals exhibited a bilateral effect for interpretation (mean hand difference of 3 taps), while monolinguals showed a strong left hemisphere effect for paraphrasing (right hand interference 19.7 taps greater than mean left hand interference).

Because the two bilingual groups showed a consistent similarity in lateralized effect, they were collapsed for the within-subject analysis of lateralized effect. The results confirm the earlier between-subject analysis, indicating a significantly smaller asymmetry than the monolingual group for interpretation/paraphrasing. Consequently, there was a left hemisphere effect for the monolingual group for paraphrasing [$F = 33.38$, $p = .0001$]. Both bilingual [$F(1,30)$ 12.11, $p = .002$] and monolingual [$F(1,14)$ 34.44, $p = .0001$] groups showed a left hemisphere effect for shadowing.

A main effect for Task [$F(1,44)$ 10.17, $p = .0026$] indicated that the interpretation task was more disruptive to the concurrent tapping task than was the shadowing task in the bilingual groups ($p = .01$), but not in the monolingual group ($p = .11$).

6.6. Vocalization Disruption and Attentional Tradeoffs

As a check on possible tradeoffs in allocation of attention to the vocal versus the manual tasks, the vocalization data (coded in terms of number of words shadowed or number of propositions translated/paraphrased) were also analyzed in terms of percent-of-change scores (Kinsbourne & Hiscock 1977). The accuracy of vocalized output during right and left hand concurrent activity was compared using dependent t-tests; no significant differences were found for group or task. Consequently, it is inferred that attention did not deviate from the cognitive task more during concurrent tapping with one hand than it did during concurrent tapping with the other hand.

The mean number of comprehension questions following right and left hand concurrent trials was calculated for the groups studied. Comprehension of input was uniformly high and unaffected by the hand used.

6.7. Laterality Profiles

For each subject, a laterality profile was calculated by subtracting the left intrahand interference score (baseline minus concurrent tapping rate) from the right intrahand interference score. Table 6 presents the laterality profiles with the percentage of subjects characterized as being lateralized in the LH or RH, using two criteria (either where the interhand difference is simply greater than zero, or by a more stringent criterion whereby the interhand tapping difference is at least 5 taps; a difference of less than 5 taps would be considered a bilateral effect). The results in Table 6 for the monolingual group indicate that, using the more stringent criterion, 81% showed a left hemisphere for paraphrasing, while 88% showed a LH effect for shadowing. The statistics for the monolingual group in Table 6 are similar even when this group is enlarged to 24 subjects (Green *et al.* 1989b), where 92% in shadowing and 88% in paraphrasing exhibited a right-left difference score greater than zero, and 79% demonstrated a stronger left hemisphere effect with more than a 5 tap greater right than left hand interference.

Table 6. *Laterality Profiles with Percentages of Subjects Categorized By Right Minus Left Intrahand Tapping Difference*

Group	*LH: RT Hand* ▸ 0 Taps	*LH: RT Hand* ▸ 5 Taps	*Bilateral RT-LT* Diff ◂ 5 Taps	*RH: LT Hand* ▸ 5 Taps
		SHADOWING		
Monolinguals	100%	88%	12%	---
Bil Controls				
SPAN (L1)	62%	62%	18%	18%
ENG (L2)	75%	75%	6%	18%
Interpreters				
SPAN (L1)	62%	62%	12%	25%
ENG (L2)	56%	50%	18%	31%

		INTERP./ PARAPH.		
Monolinguals	94%	81%	19%	---
Bil Controls				
SPAN (L1)	75%	56%	25%	18%
ENG (L2)	44%	44%	25%	31%
Interpreters				
SPAN (L1)	44%	38%	18%	44%
ENG (L2)	50%	44%	25%	31%

7. Discussion

Using a dual-task interference procedure, our study sought to establish whether lateralized effects are (1) task-specific within groups, 2) different between groups of bilinguals for an interpretation task, where members of one group have greater expertise, and 3) different across groups where one group has acquired proficiency in two languages. Unlike previous studies in the bilingual or laterality literature, our study of 16 early Spanish/English interpreters (8 male and 8 female) included both monolingual and bilingual controls who were carefully matched in relevant bio-social characteristics. Secondly, in addition to analyzing data in the usual way (i.e., repeated measures analysis of variance on percent-of-change scores), we employed a more refined statistical assessment (a multivariate general linear models procedure) as compared to previous dual-task laterality studies. Results of the present study can also be compared with outcomes from a related study of 24 interpreters (16 early and 8 late Spanish/English interpreters) who were carefully matched to 24 monolingual control subjects (Green *et al.* 1989b; Vaid *et al.* 1989). However, in the latter study, data were analyzed with the procedure traditionally used (percent-of-change scores analyzed with a repeated measures analysis of variance procedure).

The first hypothesis, which proposed that attentional demands are greater (producing more overall mean disruption in tapping) for an Interpretation/Paraphrasing task than for a Shadowing task, was essentially supported. That is, in the monolingual-only analysis there was a marginal Task effect, regardless of the statistical procedure used ($p = .089$ and $p = .098$). However, when the number of monolingual subjects was increased to 24, there was a significant Task effect ($p < .04$), with the paraphrasing task producing more disruption in tapping than the shadowing task (Green *et al.* 1989b). Thus, the marginal Task effect resulting from the analysis of data of 16 monolingual subjects appears to be a function of a lack of statistical power.

Our findings in the bilingual-only analysis revealed that bilingual groups had significantly more interference in their tapping during the interpretation tasks than during the shadowing tasks ($p = .0002$). When all three groups (interpreters, matched bilingual and monolingual controls) were analyzed for their performance in English tasks, the interpreter group had significantly greater left hand interference than the monolingual group for both tasks. In fact, the effect was more pronounced in the related study where 24 interpreters were compared to matched monolingual controls (Vaid *et al.* 1989). Here, a significant Group effect ($p < .02$) showed the interpreters to have greater cognitive involvement than monolinguals (i.e., more disruption in tapping) for processing English language tasks.

The multivariate analysis revealed the rate of tapping was yet another difference between the bilingual and monolingual groups. While monolingual males were found to tap significantly faster than females (in the monolingual-only analysis), there were no differences between bilingual males and females in their baseline tapping rate. The outcome, however, may be unique to Spanish bilingual women, or this sample of subjects. Of the 16 bilingual women, 7 reported proficiency on a professional level with a musical instrument requiring finger agility, while all the monolingual females responded negatively to this question.

The second and third hypotheses respectively proposed differences between groups in lateralized effects as a function of (a) task and (b) expertise. It was predicted that all groups would be left lateralized for shadowing, but bilinguals would show a bilateral effect for the interpretation task. It was further expected that with greater expertise in interpretation, the interpreters might manifest relatively more right hemisphere involvement than their matched bilingual controls for this task. The second hypothesis was supported, but the third hypothesis was rejected.

The outcome of a consistent left hemisphere lateralized effect in the monolingual group for shadowing and paraphrasing tasks is consistent with the findings of Green *et al.* (1993), where there are 64 right-handed monolingual subjects. Consequently, there may be an overall tendency on the part of monolinguals to rely on the left hemisphere in language processing regardless of whether the linguistic task accesses a superficial or a deeper level of processing. The finding corroborates an earlier finding in the literature where the left lateralized effect in monolingual subjects was independent of whether the task involved phonetic judgements or semantic judgements (Vaid 1984, Experiments 2 and 3).

Although we found no differences between the two early bilingual groups in their lateralized effect for either task, they were significantly different from the monolingual control group for the Interpretation/Paraphrasing tasks. That is, whereas all three groups were left lateralized for shadowing, the interpreters and matched bilingual controls exhibited a bilateral effect for the interpretation task.

The different lateralized effects for the two tasks performed by the bilingual groups suggests that shadowing may have been performed on the basis of surface, phonetic characteristics of the input, thereby showing greater left hemisphere interference, while interpretation called for more semantic processing, which is known to be more bilaterally mediated among bilinguals (Vaid & Lambert 1979; Vaid 1984). The lack of a hand asymmetry on tasks where there is demonstrated proficiency is supported by similar findings reported by Gran and Fabbro (1990) with a group of Italian-English advanced students of interpretation on an interpretation task, and by Hatta and Ikeda (1988) with intermediate and advanced students of abacus on a mathematical calculation task.

As noted, all groups in the analyses of data with 16 early Spanish/English interpreters and matched bilingual and monolingual controls were lateralized in the left hemisphere for shadowing. However, in the related study (Vaid *et al.* 1989) twenty-four Spanish/English interpreters (16 early and 8 late bilinguals) were compared with 24 matched monolingual control subjects on the English shadowing and interpretation/paraphrasing tasks. Here, there was a clear difference between the interpreters and monolinguals in their lateralized effect for both English language tasks ($p < .01$), with the interpreters showing a bilateral effect and the monolinguals left lateralized. Alternatively, given that the bilinguals were tested only on interpretation (from one language to another) and not on a paraphrasing task (in the same language), it is possible that the interpreter/monolingual group difference is an artifact of comparing two related but different tasks.

Inquiry into whether language processing in bilinguals is similarly or differentially lateralized in one or both hemispheres has been investigated frequently. The results of our analysis where 16 early Spanish/English interpreters (8 male and 8 female) are compared with matched bilingual noninterpreter controls revealed male interpreters to have an asymmetric lateralized effect for English tasks, but no asymmetry for Spanish tasks. In contrast, the male bilingual controls had the reversed effect. Although all bilinguals rated themselves as approximately equally fluent in both languages on the language and background questionnaire and used both daily, the two male groups responded differently to another question on a forced choice for language fluency, related to the extent of daily language usage. Without exception, all interpreters reported either an inability to make the choice or Spanish as the language used more in daily communication, whereas bilingual controls were either unable to make the choice or designated English as the language used more often. All bilingual controls communicated in English at work. Both groups of male interpreters showed a bilateral effect for the language used more frequently in daily communication.

Thus, our results provide no evidence for overall differences between professional interpreters and matched bilingual controls. While there may well be specific behavioral differences associated with formal training in interpretation, on a dual task laterality procedure, no overall differences were observed in the pattern of lateralization of professional interpreters and that of bilingual controls. Nonetheless, the difference between interpreters and monolinguals in left hand disruption in tapping evidenced in the multivariate analysis (Green *et al.* 1990), and in lateralized effects (Vaid *et al.* 1989) for both English language tasks intimate that disparity between groups in lateralized effects may be more pronounced with corresponding disparity in task related experience, i.e., level of expertise.

In conclusion, the present research differed from previous studies on lateralization in bilinguals and monolinguals in a number of respects - choice of tasks, procedure, subject selection, and statistical evaluation. Our findings indicate that formal mastery of specific cognitive skills may influence level of interference experienced on the tasks used, but does not differentially influence the hemispheric mediation of those tasks.

Acknowledgements

The first author wishes to express appreciation for the interest and support of a life-long mentor, Dr. Carl Auria, at Kent State University. The present research was supported by a grant to Nancy Schweda-Nicholson by the University of Delaware Research Foundation. In addition to the many persons acknowledged in the articles in *Brain and Language*, and *Investigaciones Psicológicas*, the authors wish to express their gratitude to Dr. Frank W. Connolly and the American University Computing Center in Washington, D.C., and Craig Mulder, Assistant Director for Education at the Welch Library at the Johns Hopkins Medical School in Baltimore, Maryland, for technical assistance.

References

Bryden, M.P. 1977. "Measuring Handedness With Questionnaires". *Neuropsychologia* 15. 617-624.

Carnahan, H., Elliott, D., & Lee T.D. 1986. "Dual-Task Interference Between Speaking and Listening and a Unipedal Force Productions Task". *Neuropsychologia* 24:2. 583-586.

Corina, D., & Vaid, J. 1989. "Shadowing Signs Versus Words: A Dual-Task Laterality Study of ASL-English Interpreters". *Investigaciones Psicologicas* 7. 31-42.

Corina, D., Vaid, J., & Bellugi, U. 1992. "The Linguistic Basis for Left Hemisphere Specialization". *Science* 255. 1258-1260.

De Vrees, L.P., Motta, M. & Toschi, A. 1988. "Compulsive and Paradoxical Translation Behavior in a Case of Presenile Dementia of the Alzheimer Type". *Journal of Neurolinguistics* 3:2. 233-260.

Fabbro, F., & Gran, L. 1991. "Hemispheric Specialization for Syntactic Components of Language in Simultaneous Interpreters". *Brain and Language* 41:1. 1-42.

Furtado, J. & Webster, W. 1991. "Concurrent Language and Motor Performance in Bilinguals: A Test of the Age of Acquisition Hypothesis". *Canadian Journal of Psychology* 45:4. 448-461.

Gerver, D. 1974a. "The Effects of Noise on the Performance of Simultaneous Interpreters: Accuracy of Performance". *Acta Psychologica* 38. 159-167.

Gerver, D. 1974b. "Simultaneous Listening and Speaking and Retention of Prose". *The Quarterly Journal of Psychology* 26. 337-341.

Gerver, D. 1975. "A Psychological Approach to Simultaneous Interpretation". *META* XX:2. 119-128.

Gerver, D. 1976. "Empirical Studies of Simultaneous Interpretation: A Review and a Model". R. W. Brislin ed. *Translation, Applications and Research.* New York: Gardner Press. 169-203.

Gran, L., & Fabbro, F. 1990. "Cerebral Lateralization in Simultaneous Interpretation". *Brain and Language* 39:1. 69-89.

Green, A. 1986. "A Time Sharing Cross-Sectional Study of Monolinguals and Bilinguals at different levels of Second Language Acquisition". *Brain and Cognition* 5. 477-497.

Green, A., Schweda-Nicholson, N., Vaid, J., & White, N. 1989a. "Hemispheric Involvement in Shadowing vs. Interpreting: A Time-Sharing Study of Simultaneous Interpreters and Bilingual/Monolingual Controls". Paper presented at the International Neuropsychological Society, Vancouver, Canada.

Green, A., Schweda-Nicholson, N., Vaid, J., & White, N. 1989b. "Why Task Analysis is Important in Dual Task Research". Paper presented at the Annual Conference Reporting Research in Neuropsychology. Niagara Falls, New York.

Green, A., Schweda-Nicholson, N., Vaid, J., White, N., & Steiner, R. 1990. "Hemispheric Involvement in Shadowing vs. Interpretation: A Time-Sharing Study of Simultaneous Interpreters With Matched Bilingual and Monolingual Controls". *Brain and Language* 39. 107-133.

Green, A., & Vaid, J. 1986. "Methodological Issues in the Use of the Concurrent Activities Paradigm". *Brain and Cognition* 5. 465-476.

Green, A., Steiner, R. & White, N. 1993. "A Follow-up Dual-Task Investigation of Lateralized Effects in Right- and Left-Handed Males". [Submitted for publication.]

Haier, R.J., Siegel, B.V. Jr., Nuechterlein, K.H., Hazlett, E., Wu, J.C., Paek, J., Browning, H.L., & Buchsbaum, M.S. 1988. "Cortical Glucose Metabolic Rate Correlates of Abstract Reasoning and Attention Studied with Positron Emission Tomography". *Intelligence* 12. 199-217.

Hall, G. & Lambert, W.E. 1988. "French Immersion and Cerebral Language Processing: A Dual-Task Study". *Canadian Journal of Behavioral Science* 20:1. 1-14.

Hatta, T., & Ikeda, K. 1988. "Hemispheric Specialization of Abacus Experts in Mental Calculation: Evidence From the Results of Time-Sharing Tasks". *Neuropsychologia* 26:6. 877-893.

Hiscock, M. 1986. "Lateral Eye Movements and Dual-Task Performance". H.J. Hannay, ed. *Experimental Techniques in Human Neuropsychology*. New York: Oxford University Press. 264-308.

Hiscock, M., Kinsbourne, M., & Green, A. 1990. "Is Time Sharing a Valid Indicator of Speech Lateralization? Evidence for Left Handers". G.E. Hammond, ed. *Cerebral Control of Speech and Limb Movements*. North Holland: Elsevier Science Publishers B.V. 611-634.

Hynd, G., Teeter, A., & Stewart, J. 1980. "Acculturation and the Lateralization of Speech in the Bilingual Native American". *International Journal of Neuroscience* 11. 1-7.

Ikeda, K. 1987. "Lateralized Interference Effects of Concurrent Verbal Tasks on Sequential Finger Tapping". *Neuropsychologia* 20:1. 43-53.

Kinsbourne, M., & Cook, J. 1971. "Generalized and Lateralized Effects of Concurrent Verbalization on a Unimanual Skill". *Quarterly Journal of Experimental Psychology* 23. 341-345.

Kinsbourne, M., & Hiscock, M. 1977. "Does Cerebral Dominance Develop?" S. Segalowitz & F. Gruber, eds. *Language Development and Neurological Theory*. New York: Academic Press. 171-191.

Kinsbourne, M., & Hiscock, M. 1983. "Asymmetries of Dual-Task Performance". J. Hellige, ed. *Cerebral Hemisphere Asymmetries: Method, Theory and Application*. New York: Praeger. 255-334.

Kraushaar, B. & Lambert, S. 1987. "Shadowing Proficiency According to Ear of Input and Type of Bilinguality". *Bulletin of the Canadian Association of Applied Linguistics* 9:1. 17-31.

Lackner, J. R., & Shattuck-Hufnagel, S. R. 1982. "Alterations in Speech Shadowing Ability After Cerebral Injury in Man". *Neuropsychologia* 20:6. 709-714.

Lambert, S. 1993. "The Effect of Ear of Information Reception on the Proficiency of Simultaneous Interpretation". *META* XXXVIII:3. 198-211.

Mendelsohn, S. 1989. "Lateralization in Bilinguals: Fact and Fantasy". *Journal of Neurolinguistics* 3:2. 261-292.

Moser, B. 1978. "Simultaneous Interpretation: A Hypothetical Model and its Practical Application". D. Gerver and H.W. Sinaiko, eds. *Language, Interpretation and Communication*. New York: Plenum Press. 353-368.

Obler, L., Zatorre, R., Galloway, L., & Vaid, J. 1982. "Cerebral Lateralization in Bilinguals". *Brain and Language* 15:1. 40-54.

Sabat, S.R. 1979. "Selective Attention, Channel Capacity, and the Average Evoked Response in Human Subjects". *Neuropsychologia* 17:1. 103-107.

Sanchez, P., Manga, D., Babecki, P., & de Tembleque, R. 1988. *Language Lateralization in Bilingual Speakers*. Seminario de Bilingüismo, Universidad Complutense, Madrid. [Unpublished Manuscript.]

Schweda-Nicholson, N. 1987. "Linguistic and Extralinguistic Aspects of Simultaneous Interpretation". *Applied Linguistics* 8:2. 194-205.

Simon, T., & Sussman, H. 1987. "The Dual Task Paradigm: Speech Dominance or Manual Dominance?" *Neuropsychologia* 25:3. 559-569.

Soares, C. 1984. "Left Hemisphere Language Lateralization in Bilinguals: Use of the Concurrent Activities Paradigm". *Brain and Language* 23:1. 86-96.

Steiner, R., Green, A., & White, N. 1992. "Clarification of the Dual Task Dilemma: Lateralized Effects for Perfunctory and Purposeful Tasks in Left- and Right-Handed Males". *Brain and Cognition* 19. 148-171.

Sussman, H., Franklin, P., & Simon, T. 1982. "Bilingual Speech: Bilateral Control?" *Brain and Language* 15:1. 125-142.

Treisman, A. 1965. "The Effects of Redundancy and Familiarity on Translation and Repeating Back a Foreign and a Native Language". *British Journal of Psychology* 56. 369-379.

Vaid, J. 1983. "Bilingualism and Brain Lateralization". S. Segalowitz, ed. *Language Functions and Brain organization.* New York: Academic Press. 315-339.

Vaid, J. 1984. "Visual, Phonetic, and Semantic Processing in Early and Late Bilinguals". M. Paradis and Y. Lebrun, eds. *Early Bilingualism and Child Development.* Lisse: Swets and Zeitlinger. 174-191.

Vaid, J. & Genesee, F. 1980. "Neuropsychological Approaches to Bilingualism: A Critical Review". *Canadian Journal of Psychology* 34. 417-445.

Vaid, J., Green, A., Schweda-Nicholson, N., & White, N. 1989. "Are Bilingual Interpreters Differentially Lateralized? A Dual Task Investigation of Spanish-English Interpreters and Unilingual Controls". *Investigaciones Psicológicas* 7. 43-53.

Vaid, J. & Hall, D.G. 1991. "Neuropsychological Perspectives on Bilingualism: Right, Left and Center". A. Reynolds, ed. *Bilingualism, Multiculturalism and Second Language Learning: The McGill Conference in Honor of Wallace E. Lambert.* Hillsdale, NJ: Lawrence Erlbaum.

Vaid, J., & Lambert, W. 1979. "Differential Cerebral Involvement in the Cognitive Functioning of Bilinguals". *Brain and Language* 8. 92-110.

Waters, G.S., Komoda, M.K., & Arbuckle, T.Y. 1985. "The Effects of Concurrent Tasks on Reading: Implications for Phonological Recoding". *Journal of Memory and Language* 24:1. 27-45.

Woods, D. L., Hillyard, S. A., & Hansen, J. C. 1984. "Event-Related Brain Potentials Reveal Similar Attentional Mechanisms During Selective Listening and Shadowing". *Journal of Experimental Psychology: Human Perception and Performance* 10:6. 761-777.

Index of Authors

A

Aaronson, D. 117
Abe, M. 250
Abilian, V.A. 321
Akoi, C. 258
Albanese, J.F. 260, 286
Albert, M.L. 157, 250, 273, 275, 277, 280-282, 286, 327
Alexieva, B. 226-227, 229
Aliakrinksi, A.A. 321
Allen, M.J. 70
Altman, J. 53
Anastasi, A. 70
Anderson, L. 41, 161-162
Anokhin, P.K. 145
Apresyan, Y.D. 140
Arbuckle, G.S. 336
Argyle, M. 104
Arjona, E. 70, 76
Arjona-Tseng, E. 40
As, A. 280
Ashayeri, H. 274
Austin, J.L. 87

B

Babecki, P. 335
Baddeley, A.D. 204
Bakker, D.J. 258
Barik, H.C. 20, 26, 42, 47, 102-103, 139, 156, 204, 214, 226, 296, 324
Barnett, G.A. 117
Basso, G. 278
Battison, R. 238
Bava, A. 206
Bellugi, U. 238, 241, 335
Benedictov, B.A. 151
Bentin, S. 284
Besner, D. 204-205
Blumstein, S.E. 260, 263, 277
Bock, R. 165
Bolinger, D. 231
Borden, G.J. 259
Borden, R.J. 221
Bosatra, A. 206, 251
Bowen, D. 65, 226
Bowen, M. 65, 226
Bracewell, R.J. 162-163
Bransford, D.J. 103
Briggs, G.C. 252
Brislin, R. 213
Broadbent, D.E. 254, 320, 325
Brown, G. 231-232
Browning, H.L. 333
Bryden, M.P. 284, 287, 337
Buchsbaum, M.S. 333
Buehler, H. 47, 91
Bunnell, D.E. 221

C

Carnahan, H. 336
Carpenter, P.A. 112, 156
Carroll, D. 221
Carroll, J.B. 106, 109, 113
Carruthers, M. 222
Cartellieri, C. 226
Chafe, W.L. 141-143
Chary, P. 281-282
Chernigovskaya, T.V. 283
Chernov, Gh.V. 139-140, 142, 144, 149, 151
Cherry, E.C. 112
Chistovitch, L.A. 321
Chomsky, N. 21
Ciarkowska, W. 214
Cirilli, C. 250
Clark, D.G. 289
Clark, H.H. 199
Cochran, W.G. 49
Code, C. 249, 259, 277
Cohen, M. 214
Cokeley, D. 193
Cook, J. 239, 245, 289, 326-327, 334
Corder, S.P. 25-26, 34-35
Corina, D.P. 238-240, 244, 284, 335-336
Costa, L. 286
Creutzfeldt, O.D. 250, 280
Cronbach, L.J. 70, 84
Crowder, R.G. 61, 281

Crystal, D. 226, 229-230, 232-233
Cutler, A. 229, 231-232

D

Damasio, A.R. 278
Daniels, S. 204
Daró, V. 206, 208, 251, 255, 260, 274, 291, 296, 300, 305
Davidson, P. 193, 195
Davies, J. 204
de Tembleque, R. 335
De Renzi, E. 282
Déjean-Le Féal, K. 226
Di Cristo, A. 259, 263
Dillinger, M. 19, 45-46, 49, 155, 158, 165
Dodds, J. 20, 52, 192, 264, 266, 296
Durieu, C. 276

E

Ebel, R.L. 70
Ekman, P. 264
El-Menoufy, A. 225, 229-230
Elliot, D. 336
Ellis, N.C. 298
Enkvist, N. 226
Epstein, W. 222
Ericsson,K. 162
Erikson, M.H. 264
Even-Zohan, J. 213

F

Fabbro, F. 20, 59, 204, 206, 208, 250-251, 254-259, 266, 274, 280, 282, 285-287, 289-292, 294, 297, 326-327, 335, 350
Faglioni, P. 282
Fillmore, C. 163
Finn, J. 165
Flores d'Arcais, G.B. 44
Fourastie, J. 50
Franklin, P. 240, 320, 335
Frederiksen, C. 162, 163, 183
Frederiksen, J. 162
Frey, G. 19
Frisbie, D.A. 70
Fromm, E. 280
Furtado, J. 335

G

Galaburda, A. 254
Galanter, E. 148
Galloway, L.M. 286, 332
Gastaldi, G. 275
Geffen, G. 289
Genesee, F. 283, 286, 320, 325, 331
Gerver, D. 20, 47-48, 61, 63, 69-70, 76, 102-103, 106, 110, 112, 117, 139, 149, 155-156, 158, 185, 192-193, 204, 206, 226, 249, 251, 333, 336, 339
Geschwind, N. 254, 278
Gile, D. 20, 25-27, 43-44, 47, 50, 53, 91, 155, 157-158, 192, 206, 208
Gilewski, W. 213
Gingiani, A. 66
Gliner, J.A. 221
Goldblum, M.C. 274
Goldman-Eisler, F. 19, 102, 110, 193, 195 214, 226
Gordon, H.W. 275, 285-286
Gore, S.M. 53
Gran, B. 204
Gran, L. 20, 40, 51-52, 59, 192, 204, 255-256, 259, 264, 266, 296-297, 302, 305, 326-327, 335, 350
Green, A. 60, 239-240, 246, 250-251, 259, 289-290, 305, 332-333, 335, 339-340, 342, 347-349, 351
Green, D.W. 281, 284
Grosjean, F. 240, 273
Gruber, J. 163

H

Haier, R.J. 333
Hall, G. 238, 240, 320, 327, 331, 335
Halliday, M.A.K. 225, 228-229, 231
Hampson, E. 250, 297
Hansen, M. 49
Hansen, J.C. 336
Harris, B. 156, 183
Harris, K.S. 259
Hatfield, N. 238
Hatta, T. 285, 334, 350
Hazlett, E. 333
Hellawell, J.C. 221
Henderson, A. 226
Hendrickx, P. 151
Hennelly, R.A. 298
Henry, D. 155
Henry, R. 155
Hicks, R.E. 289, 327
Hillyard, S.A. 336
Hiscock, M. 240, 242, 340, 346
Hitch, G. 204
Hoffstaedter, P. 43
Hofman, P.R. 276
Horvath, S.M. 221
Hoosain, R. 291
Hurwitz, W. 49
Hynd, G. 239, 286, 335

I

Ikeda, K. 334, 336, 350
Ilg, G. 91
Isham, W.P. 193-194, 203-204, 206

J

Jackendoff, R. 193
Jakobson, R. 259, 276, 283
Jarvella, R.J. 193-194, 196-197, 203
Johnson, M.K. 103
Jumpelt, R.W. 226

K

Kamhi, A.G. 289
Karten, I. 53
Kee, D.W. 291
Kefee, K. 289
Kent, R.D. 259
Kenyon, D.M. 69
Kertesz, A. 274, 281
Kettrick, C. 238-239
Kimura, D. 245, 250, 285, 297, 320, 325
Kinsbourne, M. 239, 242, 245, 289, 291-292, 326-327, 334, 340, 346
Kirchhoff, H. 90
Klima, E.S. 238
Klonowicz, T. 214-216, 221, 223
Knight, M.L. 221
Koller, W. 213
Komoda, M.K. 336
Kondo, M. 90
Kopczynski, A. 26, 226
Kraetschmer, K. 276
Kraushaar, B. 60, 321-322, 324, 335
Krings, H.P. 41
Kristeva, J. 263
Kuhn, T.S. 18, 21
Kurz, I. 47, 91

L

Lackner, J.R. 336
Ladd, D.R. Jr. 225, 229-232
Lambert, S. 20, 60, 63-64, 69, 254-255, 302, 305, 320-324, 327, 335-336
Lambert, W.E. 117, 240, 285, 320, 323, 327, 332, 335, 350
Lane, H. 193-194, 203-204, 206
Lawson, E.A. 156, 319
Lawson, D. 238-239
Lecours, A.R. 278
Lederer, M. 19, 151, 161
Lee, T.D. 336
Leech, G.N. 144
Leischner, A. 280
Lenneberg, E. 256

Leontyev, A.N. 139
Levy, B.A. 205
Lhermitte, F. 278
Lieberman, P. 259-260, 263, 265, 277
Linden, W. 215
Long, J. 69
Long J.M. 221
Longley, P.E. 69, 156, 183
Lukanina, S.A. 149
Lurçat, L. 104
Luria, A.R. 139, 255, 278, 281
Lynch, J.J. 221
Lyons, J. 142

M

Machiran, N.M. 221
Mackintosh, J. 20, 155
Macnamara, J. 117
MacNeilage, P.F. 254
Madow, W. 49
Magiste, E. 284
Malmberg, B. 259
Manga, D. 335
Manilow, K.L. 221
Mason, I. 34
Massaro, D. 147, 226
Masterson, J.J. 289
McDonald, J. 156
McEachern, H.M. 215
McFarland, K. 289
McKeever, W.F. 286, 305
McKoon, G. 193
McMurray, J. 291
Meak, L. 47
Mehrabian, A. 104
Mendelsohn, S. 331
Messick, S. 84
Meyer, I. 69
Miller, G.A. 140, 148, 255
Minkowski, M. 264, 273
Mohr, E. 286
Morris, C. 87
Morris, R. 90
Moser, B. 20, 64, 155, 333
Moser-Mercer, B. 58, 60, 66, 184
Mossop, B. 226- 227
Mowbray, G.H. 251
Mumolo, E. 260

N

Nanpon, H. 19, 102, 104, 112
Nebes, R.D. 252
Neville, H. 238-239
Newport, E. 239
Nida, E. 156, 185
Nilipour, R. 274
Norman, D.A. 321
Nott, C.R. 117
Nuechterlein, K.H. 333

O

Obler, L. 157, 250, 273, 275, 277, 280-282, 286, 327, 332
Ojemann, G.A. 250, 279-280
Oldfield, R. C. 320
Oléron, P. 19, 102, 104, 112
Osterlind, S.J. 70

P

Packard, J.L. 277
Paek, J. 333
Panou, L. 284
Paradis, M. 264, 266, 273-282, 297-299
Parsons, H.M. 319
Perecman, E. 275-276
Perkins, W.H. 259
Piazza, D. 286
Pike, K.L. 225, 229
Pinter, I. 20, 45
Poizner, H. 238, 241, 244
Ponton, C.W. 297
Potzl, O. 280
Pribram, K.H. 148

R

Rameh, C.A. 229
Rapport, R.L. 279
Ratcliff, R. 193
Reber, A.S. 213
Reiss, K. 88, 90
Rogers, L. 283
Rosenthal, R. 184
Rosnow, R.L. 184

S

Sabat, S.R. 336
Sachs, J.S. 193
Sager, J.C. 34
Sanchez, P. 335
Sanders, A.F. 215, 221
Sandrock, U. 49
Sasanuma, S. 275, 278
Scarcella, R. 286
Scherer, K.R. 259, 264
Schor, S. 53
Schwartz, J. 110, 117
Schweda-Nicholson, N. 246, 326, 333, 342
Scott, M.E. 69
Scott, S. 286
Searle, J.R. 87, 143-144
Seleskovtich, D. 19, 49, 103-104, 110-111
151, 161, 192, 194-195, 207, 226
Sewell, D.F. 284
Shaffer, L.H. 112
Shankweiler, D. 285
Shanon, B. 284
Shattuck-Huffnagel, S.R. 336
Sherwood, B. 156, 183
Shillan, D. 226
Shiryayev, A.F. 139-140, 151
Shiu, L.P. 290
Shlesinger, M. 39
Siegel, B.V. Jr. 333
Siekewitz, P. 258
Silverberg, R. 275
Simon, T.J. 162, 240, 289, 320, 335
Sinaiko, W.H. 249
Snedecor, G.W. 49
Snell-Hornby, M. 90
Snelling, D. 90
Snow, R.E. 70, 84
Soares, C. 240, 284, 289, 335
Solin, D. 282
Spiller, E. 251
Spiller-Bosatra, E. 206, 251, 300, 305
Squire, L.R. 251, 255
Stansfield, C.W. 69
Steiner, R. 33, 246, 333, 335
Stenzl, C. 20, 40, 47
Stewart, J. 239, 335
Streifler, M. 276
Stubbs,J.R. 64
Studdert-Kennedy, M. 285
Supalla, T. 239
Sussman, H.M. 240, 246, 250, 256, 289, 295,
300, 320, 335

T

Tassinari, G. 284
Taylor, C. 40, 51, 206
Taylor, I. 117
Taylor-Sarno, M. 249, 278-279
Teeter, A. 239, 335
Tenhouten, W.D. 283
Thiéry, C. 109
Thomas, S.A. 221
Toury, G. 40, 43, 49, 50, 54, 213
Trabasso, T. 112
Treisman, A. 19, 46, 102-103, 112, 115, 117,
176, 251, 287, 305, 336
Trevarthen, C. 254
Tucker, G.R. 64
Tucker, D.M. 254
Turner, J.R. 221

V

Vaid, J. 238-239, 241, 246, 250, 254, 273, 284-285, 289, 320, 331-336, 340, 342, 348-351
Varantola, K. 226
Vermeer, H.J. 19, 90
Veyrac, G.J. 298
Viezzi, M. 45
Vignolo, L.A. 278
Vocate, D.R. 286
Voinescu, I. 274
Vygodsky, L.S. 139

W

Waggoner, C. 283
Walters, J. 284
Watamori, T.S. 275
Waters, G.S. 336
Waugh, L.R. 259, 283
Webster, W. 335
Wechsler, A. 64, 277
Whitaker, H.A. 279
White, N. 246, 333, 335, 342
Woods, D.L. 336
Wu, J.C. 333

Y

Yoshizaki, K. 285

Z

Zatorre, R.J. 280, 284, 332
Zimnyaya, I. 139

Benjamins Translation Library

A complete list of titles in this series can be found on *www.benjamins.com*

74 **WOLF, Michaela and Alexandra FUKARI (eds.):** Constructing a Sociology of Translation. 2007. vi, 226 pp.

73 **GOUADEC, Daniel:** Translation as a Profession. 2007. xvi, 396 pp.

72 **GAMBIER, Yves, Miriam SHLESINGER and Radegundis STOLZE (eds.):** Doubts and Directions in Translation Studies. Selected contributions from the EST Congress, Lisbon 2004. 2007. xii, 362 pp. **[EST Subseries 4]**

71 **ST-PIERRE, Paul and Prafulla C. KAR (eds.):** In Translation – Reflections, Refractions, Transformations. 2007. xvi, 313 pp.

70 **WADENSJÖ, Cecilia, Birgitta ENGLUND DIMITROVA and Anna-Lena NILSSON (eds.):** The Critical Link 4. Professionalisation of interpreting in the community. Selected papers from the 4th International Conference on Interpreting in Legal, Health and Social Service Settings, Stockholm, Sweden, 20-23 May 2004. 2007. x, 314 pp.

69 **DELABASTITA, Dirk, Lieven D'HULST and Reine MEYLAERTS (eds.):** Functional Approaches to Culture and Translation. Selected papers by José Lambert. 2006. xxviii, 226 pp.

68 **DUARTE, João Ferreira, Alexandra ASSIS ROSA and Teresa SERUYA (eds.):** Translation Studies at the Interface of Disciplines. 2006. vi, 207 pp.

67 **PYM, Anthony, Miriam SHLESINGER and Zuzana JETTMAROVÁ (eds.):** Sociocultural Aspects of Translating and Interpreting. 2006. viii, 255 pp.

66 **SNELL-HORNBY, Mary:** The Turns of Translation Studies. New paradigms or shifting viewpoints? 2006. xi, 205 pp.

65 **DOHERTY, Monika:** Structural Propensities. Translating nominal word groups from English into German. 2006. xxii, 196 pp.

64 **ENGLUND DIMITROVA, Birgitta:** Expertise and Explicitation in the Translation Process. 2005. xx, 295 pp.

63 **JANZEN, Terry (ed.):** Topics in Signed Language Interpreting. Theory and practice. 2005. xii, 362 pp.

62 **POKORN, Nike K.:** Challenging the Traditional Axioms. Translation into a non-mother tongue. 2005. xii, 166 pp. **[EST Subseries 3]**

61 **HUNG, Eva (ed.):** Translation and Cultural Change. Studies in history, norms and image-projection. 2005. xvi, 195 pp.

60 **TENNENT, Martha (ed.):** Training for the New Millennium. Pedagogies for translation and interpreting. 2005. xxvi, 276 pp.

59 **MALMKJÆR, Kirsten (ed.):** Translation in Undergraduate Degree Programmes. 2004. vi, 202 pp.

58 **BRANCHADELL, Albert and Lovell Margaret WEST (eds.):** Less Translated Languages. 2005. viii, 416 pp.

57 **CHERNOV, Ghelly V.:** Inference and Anticipation in Simultaneous Interpreting. A probability-prediction model. Edited with a critical foreword by Robin Setton and Adelina Hild. 2004. xxx, 268 pp. **[EST Subseries 2]**

56 **ORERO, Pilar (ed.):** Topics in Audiovisual Translation. 2004. xiv, 227 pp.

55 **ANGELELLI, Claudia V.:** Revisiting the Interpreter's Role. A study of conference, court, and medical interpreters in Canada, Mexico, and the United States. 2004. xvi, 127 pp.

54 **GONZÁLEZ DAVIES, Maria:** Multiple Voices in the Translation Classroom. Activities, tasks and projects. 2004. x, 262 pp.

53 **DIRIKER, Ebru:** De-/Re-Contextualizing Conference Interpreting. Interpreters in the Ivory Tower? 2004. x, 223 pp.

52 **HALE, Sandra:** The Discourse of Court Interpreting. Discourse practices of the law, the witness and the interpreter. 2004. xviii, 267 pp.

51 **CHAN, Leo Tak-hung:** Twentieth-Century Chinese Translation Theory. Modes, issues and debates. 2004. xvi, 277 pp.

50 **HANSEN, Gyde, Kirsten MALMKJÆR and Daniel GILE (eds.):** Claims, Changes and Challenges in Translation Studies. Selected contributions from the EST Congress, Copenhagen 2001. 2004. xiv, 320 pp. **[EST Subseries 1]**

49 **PYM, Anthony:** The Moving Text. Localization, translation, and distribution. 2004. xviii, 223 pp.

48 **MAURANEN, Anna and Pekka KUJAMÄKI (eds.):** Translation Universals. Do they exist? 2004. vi, 224 pp.

47 **SAWYER, David B.:** Fundamental Aspects of Interpreter Education. Curriculum and Assessment. 2004. xviii, 312 pp.

46 **BRUNETTE, Louise, Georges BASTIN, Isabelle HEMLIN and Heather CLARKE (eds.):** The Critical Link 3. Interpreters in the Community. Selected papers from the Third International Conference on Interpreting in Legal, Health and Social Service Settings, Montréal, Quebec, Canada 22–26 May 2001. 2003. xii, 359 pp.

45 **ALVES, Fabio (ed.):** Triangulating Translation. Perspectives in process oriented research. 2003. x, 165 pp.

44 **SINGERMAN, Robert:** Jewish Translation History. A bibliography of bibliographies and studies. With an introductory essay by Gideon Toury. 2002. xxxvi, 420 pp.

43 **GARZONE, Giuliana and Maurizio VIEZZI (eds.):** Interpreting in the 21st Century. Challenges and opportunities. 2002. x, 337 pp.

42 **HUNG, Eva (ed.):** Teaching Translation and Interpreting 4. Building bridges. 2002. xii, 243 pp.

41 **NIDA, Eugene A.:** Contexts in Translating. 2002. x, 127 pp.

40 **ENGLUND DIMITROVA, Birgitta and Kenneth HYLTENSTAM (eds.):** Language Processing and Simultaneous Interpreting. Interdisciplinary perspectives. 2000. xvi, 164 pp.

39 **CHESTERMAN, Andrew, Natividad GALLARDO SAN SALVADOR and Yves GAMBIER (eds.):** Translation in Context. Selected papers from the EST Congress, Granada 1998. 2000. x, 393 pp.

38 **SCHÄFFNER, Christina and Beverly ADAB (eds.):** Developing Translation Competence. 2000. xvi, 244 pp.

37 **TIRKKONEN-CONDIT, Sonja and Riitta JÄÄSKELÄINEN (eds.):** Tapping and Mapping the Processes of Translation and Interpreting. Outlooks on empirical research. 2000. x, 176 pp.

36 **SCHMID, Monika S.:** Translating the Elusive. Marked word order and subjectivity in English-German translation. 1999. xii, 174 pp.

35 **SOMERS, Harold (ed.):** Computers and Translation. A translator's guide. 2003. xvi, 351 pp.

34 **GAMBIER, Yves and Henrik GOTTLIEB (eds.):** (Multi) Media Translation. Concepts, practices, and research. 2001. xx, 300 pp.

33 **GILE, Daniel, Helle V. DAM, Friedel DUBSLAFF, Bodil MARTINSEN and Anne SCHJOLDAGER (eds.):** Getting Started in Interpreting Research. Methodological reflections, personal accounts and advice for beginners. 2001. xiv, 255 pp.

32 **BEEBY, Allison, Doris ENSINGER and Marisa PRESAS (eds.):** Investigating Translation. Selected papers from the 4th International Congress on Translation, Barcelona, 1998. 2000. xiv, 296 pp.

31 **ROBERTS, Roda P., Silvana E. CARR, Diana ABRAHAM and Aideen DUFOUR (eds.):** The Critical Link 2: Interpreters in the Community. Selected papers from the Second International Conference on Interpreting in legal, health and social service settings, Vancouver, BC, Canada, 19–23 May 1998. 2000. vii, 316 pp.

30 **DOLLERUP, Cay:** Tales and Translation. The Grimm Tales from Pan-Germanic narratives to shared international fairytales. 1999. xiv, 384 pp.

29 **WILSS, Wolfram:** Translation and Interpreting in the 20th Century. Focus on German. 1999. xiii, 256 pp.

28 **SETTON, Robin:** Simultaneous Interpretation. A cognitive-pragmatic analysis. 1999. xvi, 397 pp.

27 **BEYLARD-OZEROFF, Ann, Jana KRÁLOVÁ and Barbara MOSER-MERCER (eds.):** Translators' Strategies and Creativity. Selected Papers from the 9th International Conference on Translation and Interpreting, Prague, September 1995. In honor of Jiří Levý and Anton Popovič. 1998. xiv, 230 pp.

26 **TROSBORG, Anna (ed.):** Text Typology and Translation. 1997. xvi, 342 pp.

25 **POLLARD, David E. (ed.):** Translation and Creation. Readings of Western Literature in Early Modern China, 1840–1918. 1998. vi, 336 pp.

24 **ORERO, Pilar and Juan C. SAGER (eds.):** The Translator's Dialogue. Giovanni Pontiero. 1997. xiv, 252 pp.

23 **GAMBIER, Yves, Daniel GILE and Christopher TAYLOR (eds.):** Conference Interpreting: Current Trends in Research. Proceedings of the International Conference on Interpreting: What do we know and how? 1997. iv, 246 pp.

22 **CHESTERMAN, Andrew:** Memes of Translation. The spread of ideas in translation theory. 1997. vii, 219 pp.

21 **BUSH, Peter and Kirsten MALMKJÆR (eds.):** Rimbaud's Rainbow. Literary translation in higher education. 1998. x, 200 pp.

20 **SNELL-HORNBY, Mary, Zuzana JETTMAROVÁ and Klaus KAINDL (eds.):** Translation as Intercultural Communication. Selected papers from the EST Congress, Prague 1995. 1997. x, 354 pp.

19 **CARR, Silvana E., Roda P. ROBERTS, Aideen DUFOUR and Dini STEYN (eds.):** The Critical Link: Interpreters in the Community. Papers from the 1st international conference on interpreting in legal, health and social service settings, Geneva Park, Canada, 1–4 June 1995. 1997. viii, 322 pp.

18 **SOMERS, Harold (ed.):** Terminology, LSP and Translation. Studies in language engineering in honour of Juan C. Sager. 1996. xii, 250 pp.

17 **POYATOS, Fernando (ed.):** Nonverbal Communication and Translation. New perspectives and challenges in literature, interpretation and the media. 1997. xii, 361 pp.

16 **DOLLERUP, Cay and Vibeke APPEL (eds.):** Teaching Translation and Interpreting 3. New Horizons. Papers from the Third Language International Conference, Elsinore, Denmark, 1995. 1996. viii, 338 pp.

15 **WILSS, Wolfram:** Knowledge and Skills in Translator Behavior. 1996. xiii, 259 pp.

14 **MELBY, Alan K. and Terry WARNER:** The Possibility of Language. A discussion of the nature of language, with implications for human and machine translation. 1995. xxvi, 276 pp.

13 **DELISLE, Jean and Judith WOODSWORTH (eds.):** Translators through History. 1995. xvi, 346 pp.

12 **BERGENHOLTZ, Henning and Sven TARP (eds.):** Manual of Specialised Lexicography. The preparation of specialised dictionaries. 1995. 256 pp.

11 **VINAY, Jean-Paul and Jean DARBELNET:** Comparative Stylistics of French and English. A methodology for translation. Translated and edited by Juan C. Sager, M.-J. Hamel. 1995. xx, 359 pp.

10 **KUSSMAUL, Paul:** Training the Translator. 1995. x, 178 pp.

9 **REY, Alain:** Essays on Terminology. Translated by Juan C. Sager. With an introduction by Bruno de Bessé. 1995. xiv, 223 pp.

8 **GILE, Daniel:** Basic Concepts and Models for Interpreter and Translator Training. 1995. xvi, 278 pp.

7 **BEAUGRANDE, Robert de, Abdullah SHUNNAQ and Mohamed Helmy HELIEL (eds.):** Language, Discourse and Translation in the West and Middle East. 1994. xii, 256 pp.

6 **EDWARDS, Alicia B.:** The Practice of Court Interpreting. 1995. xiii, 192 pp.

5 **DOLLERUP, Cay and Annette LINDEGAARD (eds.):** Teaching Translation and Interpreting 2. Insights, aims and visions. Papers from the Second Language International Conference Elsinore, 1993. 1994. viii, 358 pp.

4 **TOURY, Gideon:** Descriptive Translation Studies – and beyond. 1995. viii, 312 pp.

3 **LAMBERT, Sylvie and Barbara MOSER-MERCER (eds.):** Bridging the Gap. Empirical research in simultaneous interpretation. 1994. 362 pp.

2 **SNELL-HORNBY, Mary, Franz PÖCHHACKER and Klaus KAINDL (eds.):** Translation Studies: An Interdiscipline. Selected papers from the Translation Studies Congress, Vienna, 1992. 1994. xii, 438 pp.

1 **SAGER, Juan C.:** Language Engineering and Translation. Consequences of automation. 1994. xx, 345 pp.